Mona Normand

Markets, States, and Democracy

MARKETS, STATES, AND DEMOCRACY

The Political Economy of Post-Communist Transformation

EDITED BY

Beverly Crawford

University of California–Berkeley

Westview Press

BOULDER • SAN FRANCISCO • OXFORD

Published in 1995 in the United States of America by Westview Press, Inc., 5500 Central Avenue, Boulder, Colorado 80301-2877, and in the United Kingdom by Westview Press, 12 Hid's Copse Road, Cumnor Hill, Oxford OX2 9JJ

Library of Congress Cataloging-in-Publication Data
Markets, states, and democracy : the political economy of post-communist transformation / edited by Beverly Crawford.
p. cm.
Includes bibliographical references and index.
ISBN 0-8133-2384-3. — ISBN 0-8133-2385-1 (pbk.)
1. Europe, Eastern—Politics and government—1989– 2. Europe, Eastern—Economic policy—1989– 3. Post-communism—Europe, Eastern—Forecasting. I. Crawford, Beverly.
JN96.A2M37 1995
320.9171'7'09049—dc20 94-29701
CIP

Printed and bound in the United States of America

The paper used in this publication meets the requirements of the American National Standard for Permanence of Paper for Printed Library Materials Z39.48-1984.

10 9 8 7 6 5 4 3 2 1

Contents

Foreword

DIETER DETTKE

This publication is a critical evaluation of the post-communist economic transformation process in Eastern Europe and of Western aid programs. By focusing on (but not limiting ourselves to) the political economy in Eastern Europe, major difficulties and deficiencies both of reform programs in individual Eastern European countries and of Western aid became apparent.

The changes that were necessary after the revolution of 1989–1990 amounted de facto to the erection of an entirely new economy and at the same time the creation of new democratic institutions, all juxtaposed against the virtual absence of a tradition of functioning institutions of civil society. Therefore, the term "transformation" is almost a euphemism in view of the magnitude of the task that the new post-communist governments had to shoulder.

The term "revolution," too, needs qualification and interpretation, because the events of 1989–1990 were less the result of an overthrow of communist regimes than of a massive implosion of a system that failed miserably to meet the social, political, and economic expectations that it had created. Although there is no lack of victory theories to assert that capitalism—as a result of the triumph of the West in the competition of the two systems—defeated communism, the true story of the demise of communism looks more like a process of self-shackling and finally self-destruction, perhaps best described by Sir Karl Popper:

> The road to serfdom leads to the disappearance of free and rational discussion; or, if you prefer, of the free market of ideas. But this has the most devastating effect on everybody, the so-called leaders included. It leads to a society in which empty verbiage rules the day; verbiage consisting very largely of lies issued by the leaders mainly for no purpose other than self-confirmation and self-glorification. But this marks the end of their ability to think. They themselves become the slaves of their lies, like everybody else. It is also the end of their ability to rule. They disappear, even as despots. (Sir Karl Popper, "Address Before the American Economic Association," New Orleans, January 4, 1992)

Acknowledgments

BEVERLY CRAWFORD

The chapters in this volume are drawn from the work of a project on the political economy of post-Communist transformation convened by the editor on behalf of the Center for German and European Studies of the University of California. Financial support for the research reported here was provided by the Center and by the Friedrich Ebert Foundation. The editor wishes to thank Richard Buxbaum, former director of the Center for German and European Studies; Gerald Feldman, the Center's present director; and Dieter Dettke, director of the Friedrich Ebert Foundation in Washington, D.C.

A number of people have read the various chapters in this volume and made valuable comments. The editor would especially like to thank George Breslauer, Kiren Chaudhry, Heiner Drueke, Barry Eichengreen, Albert Fishlow, Gregory Grossman, Stephan Haggard, Reimut Jochimsen, James Martel, Richard Portes, Keith Savard, and Laura Tyson.

PART ONE

Overview and Historical Legacies

1

Post-Communist Political Economy: A Framework for the Analysis of Reform

BEVERLY CRAWFORD

After the revolutions of 1989 in Eastern Europe and the last gasp of the Communist party's power in Russia, most post-communist regimes embarked on a course of self-proclaimed economic and democratic shock therapy to transform their societies, economies, and political systems. These new regimes' immediate external and internal mandate was the simultaneous introduction of markets and democracy and the dismantling of the discredited socialist state. Under what conditions will they succeed, and why will some fail?

The task faced by the new leaders was unprecedented. Liberalizing reforms were launched in the absence of strong civil societies, a prosperous middle class, and widespread liberal values. New regimes struggled to revive economies that plummeted faster, farther, and longer than anyone anticipated, and these economies entered the international economy with uncompetitive exports in a period of fierce global market competition in which no external power or group of powers appeared to be willing and able to underwrite the costs of liberalization. In other regions of the world and in previous historical periods, new democracies had failed to put down roots under conditions of economic crisis, and successful market reform in the post-war period has most often taken place under authoritarian regimes that sometimes engage in brutal repression to stabilize and develop their economies. The only successful recent *simultaneous* introduction of markets and democracy has occurred when these institutions were "installed" by an external hegemonic power, as in the case of post–World War II Germany and Japan (and experts disagree as to just how "liberal" these countries are).

The current intellectual debate on the "sequencing" of economic and political liberalization suggests that the simultaneous effort to introduce markets and democracy will fail in the post-communist world. Democratic rule has historically not been a necessary condition for establishing a functioning market economy (Comisso, 1991). For "late developers," the chances for economic growth are best under a strong "developmental" state that is insulated from social pressures and is a recipient of generous external support. The conventional wisdom gleaned from the experience of the East Asian Newly Industrializing Countries (NICs), Chile, and China is to hold back democracy until market reforms are consolidated. Simultaneous economic and political liberalization triggers too many demands on resources precisely during the period in which development has been delayed and a rapid accumulation of capital is required. Weak democracies will impede the project of economic liberalization, because society will not accept the painful effects of price reform, a reduction in welfare benefits, and the inevitable massive social dislocation. Liberal democracies find consolidated political support only after successful market reforms have spawned a middle class, a civic culture, and pluralistic societies (Rustow, 1970; Huntington, 1984; and Johnson, 1988).

Theories of collective action suggest that market reforms must precede democratic consolidation if liberalization is to succeed. Assuming that the benefits of economic liberalization are diffuse, aggregate, and long term and that the costs are concentrated, particular, and short term, economic liberalization will create more opponents than supporters. Consider, for example, the privatization process in Poland (Lenway, Mann, and Utter, 1993). The benefits of privatization (in the form of vouchers) were widely distributed throughout the population, but the costs (downsizing and unemployment) fell on the highly organized labor sector. As plants in declining industrial sectors were shut down, those whose livelihoods and political power were threatened agitated against privatization.

Collective action approaches suggest that most organized social groups and the mass electorate are rent-seeking actors who work to inhibit the efficient market allocation of economic resources through the political process. Under democratic regimes, these groups have access to government, and they lobby, bribe, strike, and vote to persuade governments to allocate resources to them. Politicians need resources to distribute in exchange for their support or they will be punished by being ousted in the next election. They have a higher incentive to distribute particular benefits to important supporters *now* than to implement general policies that are likely to lead to overall economic growth in the future (Buchanan and Tollison, 1972; Olson, 1982). Politicians prefer to reward concentrated, well-organized pressure groups such as producers over diffuse and less-organized groups such as consumers (Schattschneider, 1963). Politicians also prefer to reward party activists who mobilize social support for them over external constituencies for whom the rewards may be delayed and whose support is not ensured (Geddes, 1991). Rewards to party activists are especially important in post-communist societies where the social base of political parties is particularly thin, shifting, or altogether nonexistent. Under these conditions, politicians are tempted to hold back markets and perpetuate state intervention in the economy to tap those resources and exchange them for support. It follows that only those regimes that are insulated from these pressures will have the courage to cut state expenditures, sell public enterprises, reduce public employment, and create market allocation of resources to ensure economic growth.

These claims notwithstanding, new democracies, or "polyarchies," can initiate and implement policies of economic liberalization under three conditions: first, if the net benefits of liberalizing reform are not altogether diffuse but accrue to powerful groups that have formed dominant coalitions in the political system to provide support to liberalizing politicians; second, if these politicians are insulated from punishment by those who bear the costs of reform—that is, if the costs fall on groups that are unable to translate their opposition to reform into demands that are represented in the political process; and third, if politicians are able to make side payments to losers, via economywide tax and transfer policies or via discrete channels and linkages between state agencies and various social and economic sectors. Side payments are intended to mitigate some costs *now* in exchange for support and to impose other costs later.

Clearly, the second of these conditions—the insulation of reformers from punishment by those who bear the costs—means the undermining or delay of *liberal* democracy but may be initially possible in post-communist societies where—as discussed by the contributions by Hall (Chapter 4) and Ost (Chapter 8) in this volume—social groups are not well organized politically. The third condition—side payments to losers—can take place in more open political systems but may be difficult under conditions of economic crisis and may discourage or even destroy economic incentives necessary for reform. Certainly there are tradeoffs in economic and political liberalization, but it is not at all certain that markets and democracy cannot be introduced simultaneously. If the above logic holds, simultaneous economic and political liberalization is possible in post-communist regimes. To explore the connection and predict the odds of success, we must first identify the conditions that either support or undermine liberalizers in the political process. That is, we must examine how the costs and benefits of economic liberalization are distributed throughout society. Further, we must identify the particular kinds of institutions that structure political participation in ways that permit either liberalizers or their opponents to achieve dominant or at least influential positions in the policy process. In this volume, we focus primarily on the first set of tasks. In this Introduction, I construct a framework to analyze forces that facilitate support for liberalization and forces that create opposition to such reform. Subsequent chapters explore these forces in specific issue areas.

I begin here with a general discussion of the liberal ideal—its adherents and detractors. I then examine the conditions that bolster and undermine liberalizers at four levels: (1) social legacies, (2) state structures, (3) international aid and trade, and (4) economic policy choice. After establishing this framework, I suggest four hypotheses about how these forces might interact, the political coalitions that each of these hypotheses support, and the potential expected outcomes. These outcomes are expressed in the form of four scenarios: (1) the liberal utopia, (2) the region as a new global "periphery," open to the international economy, where weak democracies persist because their political institutions are required as a condition for international aid and because they provide benefits to rent-seeking domestic groups, (3) the successful state-led transition to economic development and political liberalization, and (4) the failure of liberalization and a return to despotism.

A Framework for Analysis of Post-Communist Transformation

The Liberal Ideal

Economic and political liberalization have at their root the drive for individual freedom. Liberals seek to build institutions that foster and protect the individual's right to enter into contracts, own property, buy and sell, speak and practice religion freely, choose government officials, and be protected in those rights from the state and from others in society who would thwart them (Holmes, 1991). Two institutions are crucial in this quest for freedom: markets and liberal democracy. Economic liberalization means the creation of labor markets, capital markets, and financial markets and the removal of barriers to the creation of those markets in order to efficiently allocate scarce resources in the hope of achieving economic growth. For economic liberals, the creation of markets does not ensure growth, and it does mean that inequalities in income and wealth are likely to characterize social relations. Inequality, however, is tolerated in private economic relations because the growth that should ensue from the efficient allocation of resources will make everyone better off than they would have been in the absence of markets, and economic inequality is offset by equality of citizenship and representation in the political process.

Liberalizing politics in new democracies involves the creation of institutions that ensure representative government and universal citizenship. Under Leninist regimes, political power was vested in a small group of people rather than in a set of impersonal rules. Political liberalization demands that new rules of political contestation be formulated and implemented to remove the *certainty* of power for any one political elite and to permit new contenders for political power to enter the competition. In Chapter 3 in this volume, Stephen Holmes shows how this transformation occurred throughout Eastern Europe and much of the Soviet Union through the process of constitutional reform. He shows how the clause in every Soviet-era constitution stipulating the leading role of the Communist party was deleted and how constitutional amendments represented a legal and "wholly non-Bolshevik" method for "reacting to and promoting social change."

New political institutions would have to be strong enough to resist the intervention of one or another political actor who might wish to reverse the outcomes of the political process (Przeworski, 1991). Old institutions vested power in a single party that prohibited opposition; new institutions would have to be created that encourage a "loyal opposition" and block any incentives on the part of losers to reverse the outcome by force (Hall, 1987). Old institutions concentrated political power; new institutions would have to diffuse it, and they would have to replace regime-coerced political activity with measures that structured the preferences of voters to enhance political participation rather than subvert political institutions. Finally, as Haggard and Kaufman (1992) have noted, party systems would have to be created with the strength to effectively channel the inevitable social struggles over distribution of scarce resources. To ensure the creation of *liberal* democracies, politicians would have to construct and enforce a complex web of legal relationships that affirm equality before the law, protect individual rights and freedoms, guarantee political accountability, and ensure free, fair, and competitive elections.

According to the liberal ideal, these institutions create loyalty to the democratic model and provide a noncoercive form of social mobilization for the state while restricting its control over the population. The success of liberal democracy depends on universal citizenship. If universal citizenship is not ensured, loyalty to the state is undermined and illiberal democracies emerge. Illiberal democracies exhibit many attributes of polyarchy, like fair voting, freedom of speech, freedom of movement, freedom of association, and freedom of religion; however, illiberal democracies are unable or unwilling to protect their citizens from powerful social groups who would thwart those freedoms (Dahl, 1990; O'Donnell, 1992).

Holmes's chapter here outlines the potential contradictions between liberalism and democracy as they are expressed in the amending formulas for liberal constitutions. He argues that a stringent amending formula suggests a bias for liberalism against democracy—that is, the constitution's provisions protecting liberal rights cannot easily be amended at the whim of parliament. On the one hand, if stringent amending formulas are adopted, parliaments faced with large social problems can simply deflect disapproval to the courts and escape democratic accountability. A looser amending formula, on the other hand, suggests the dominance of democratic procedure over the protection of rights. Constitutional amendments can be used as simply another technique for outmaneuvering one's current political enemies.

The Role of the State

The most important theoretical debate in literature on economic and political liberalization concerns the role of the state. There is little debate about the requirement for state strength: Liberals believe that strong states are needed to implement liberalizing reforms and to protect new institutions and individual rights from those who might wish to destroy them (Holmes, 1991; Poznanski, 1992). Liberals therefore caution against confusing state strength with authoritarian rule. The strength of the liberal state comes from its *legitimacy*—that reflects a diffusion of political power within civil society. The strength of the liberalizing state rests not on the concentration of its military or police power but on its constitutional authority and its ability to enforce the law. To protect liberal reforms, the state itself must be a liberal institution, governed by the rule of law. Only those states that have institutionalized a merit-based civil service, a system of "horizontal accountability" through a separation of powers, multilevel governments, and legal impartiality in the policy process can protect and foster liberal rights and principles in the broader society.

Liberals disagree, however, over the *role* that the state should play in both the economy and society. Should the state be a producer? A regulator? To what extent should it provide "safety nets"? For whom? Should it protect citizens from one another or simply restrain its own activity to protect citizens from the emergence of a new totalitarian regime? One group of liberals argues for a "minimal" state: The state must create a legal framework to ensure private property ownership, and it must be strong enough to enforce private contracts and adjudicate disputes. In its most extreme form, economic liberalism argues that markets are a form of "natural" spontaneous social order, requiring few (if any) regulating institutions. Others suggest that states are necessary to provide collective goods not supplied by the market. But even then, the state is clumsy and is less likely to provide collective goods than markets would be (Stigler, 1975). The central assumption of those who argue for a minimal state is that markets, not states, create the conditions for investment and capital accumulation, which, in turn, are the essential conditions for economic growth.

Others argue that the state must foster and protect investment, particularly in the case of "late developers." Alexander Gerschenkron (1962) was the first to make this argument, and it is supported by more recent research on the politics of development and by the previous discussion on rent-seeking behavior of social actors (Fishlow, 1990; Haggard and Kaufman, 1992). Autonomous and reform-oriented states are needed, the argument claims, to stimulate investment, to make markets work, and to support new market institutions. States can intervene by encouraging and promoting selected activities through the provision of low-cost credit to targeted industries, export and interest-rate subsidies, as well as technical assistance to those industries. They are also needed to create the infrastructure to support markets and may be needed to provide technical information not furnished by simple prices. For example, the privatization of public enterprises without infrastructure and information can undermine the market capabilities of new entrepreneurs, leading to the failure of newly privatized industries and thus the failure of the privatization project itself.

According to Alec Nove's argument in Chapter 10 in this volume, the state must play an "entrepreneurial role" if reforms are to be initiated and implemented. Economic crisis provides the credibility in new democracies for the state to play this role; sustained crisis, however, erodes government credibility and undermines political support. Therefore, to successfully push through liberalization policies, reformers in the state apparatus need to be insulated from social pressures by being granted discretion to operate either outside traditional bureaucratic channels (Waterbury, 1992) or by acting within internally cohesive and insulated bureaucracies (Evans, 1992). One way to insulate a reform-minded bureaucracy is to ensure the creation of a liberal state at the outset—that is, rule-based hiring and promotion within the bureaucracy itself—so that political actors are not able to use public employment as a political resource to be exchanged for support.

At the very least, many liberals argue, states play a role in the provision of "safety nets" for those who are dislocated in the transformation process. In centrally planned economies, the state provided health care, employment, and housing. Many liberalizers argue that these benefits must continue in some form as "side payments," particularly if the potential losers in the liberalization process can mobilize political support to oppose further reform. If the losers are diffuse and lack political organization, these safety nets are unlikely to be provided. Women and—as David Ost argues in Chapter 8 in this volume—labor in some sectors in post-communist societies are as yet diffuse and weakly organized. Those losers who are concentrated and politically mobilized—such as some industrialists and labor groups producing for the domestic market—are likely to pressure politicians for safety nets for themselves.

Conditions That Support and Undermine Liberalizers

There are three important conditions created by the fall of communism that support liberalizers in constructing liberal capitalist democracies. First, economic crisis had fully discredited the old regime and its supporters (Hall, 1987; Chirot, 1990; and Janos, 1991) and had destroyed the last ideological universalistic and cosmopolitan alternative to liberal capitalist democracy (Fukuyama, 1989; Jowitt, 1992). Having exhausted their capacity to produce economic growth, command economies were now seen as a fetter on the forces of production; new democratic regimes looked to market prescriptions to remedy their perennial problems of economic "backwardness" in relation to the West.

Paolo Guerrieri and Ivan Berend (in Chapters 5 and 6 of this volume, respectively) trace the legacy of this economic crisis, and their findings support the argument that the collapse of communism can in part be attributed to the fact that isolation from the international technological change "froze" socialist economies in a previous industrial era, triggering a decline in both living standards and in international competitiveness. Global technological change means that national competitiveness no longer rests on heavy industries that depend on relatively simple technology and a large unskilled labor force. Instead, prosperity depends on knowledge-based production, which relies on a cadre of highly trained engineers and a smaller, technologically sophisticated production workforce in all sectors of the economy.

Second, without ideological rivals, a "consensus" among foreign and domestic elites on simultaneous economic and political liberalization in the former communist states emerged, providing ideological legitimacy that could be used as a resource to muster support for reforms. As Berend argues in Chapter 6, elites throughout the region expressed a desire to again be part of "Europe" and knew they could only do so by rushing to adopt both democracy and markets. In Central Europe, particularly, the Left and the Right converged on the need for simultaneous economic and political liberalization. Ideological consensus on liberalization provided an attractive rhetoric for new political parties, especially in areas where the working class—a potential opponent of liberalization—was allergic to class-based political appeals providing alternatives to neoclassical reforms.

Finally, the relatively peaceful character of these revolutions, the communist legacy of civilian control over the military, and the failure of the halfhearted Soviet coup set a precedent against a resort to violence for regime transformation. The military was initially subordinated to civilian control and had little stake in opposing the economic reform policies of new democratic regimes.

These three conditions created initial widespread support for reform, and the benefits of having thrown off the old regime were perceived throughout the mass electorate to be greater than the potential costs of liberalization. Bolstered by these forces and sensitive to both international constraints and domestic public opinion, political elites perceived the need to demonstrate both success in their country's overall economic performance and their distance from Leninism by bringing in a merit-based civil service and institutionalizing procedures for transparency and accountability in government.

Indeed, the degree of initial support for reform contrasted sharply with the situation in many Latin American countries where the Right prefers radical market reform and the maintenance of authoritarian regimes—or the "gradual" introduction of democracy—whereas the Left and the more populist forces prefer the extension of democratic reforms while holding back market forces that could cause initial widespread deprivation in much of the population. In contrast, for most post-communist regimes, the question is not *whether* markets and democracy can be simultaneously introduced; democratic rhetoric—whether liberal or not—remains unchallenged, even if it has yet to be fully realized in practice. Rather, the debates revolve around the sequencing of *economic* reforms.[1] Liberalizers are divided between those who advocate radical and those who advocate gradual economic reform.

Two factors, however, worked in favor of the political opponents of liberalization. First, liberalizers have few resources to distribute in exchange for political support. The features of *liberal* democracy—rule-based behavior, transparency, and accountability—and the requirements for universal citizenship limit opportunities for such exchange. Merit-based hiring and promotion in public employment, competitive contracts, the withdrawal of subsidies, and strict licensing rules limit politicians' ability to reward support with specific benefits. Liberalizers, therefore, have few specific resources to distribute to their constituencies, particularly in a period of economic crisis. Without strong political parties to discipline voters to support reform-minded politicians as the costs of liberalization rise, they are subject to punishment by shifting coalitions of losers seeking to oust them.

Bulgaria's difficulties provide an example: In 1992, Bulgaria experienced one of the sharpest drops in industrial output in Eastern Europe—its traditional markets in Eastern Europe and the Soviet republics had collapsed, and the government had implemented a strict monetary policy mandated by the International Monetary Fund (IMF) and the International Bank for Reconstruction and Development (IBRD, or "World Bank"). The decline in living standards not only resulted in a number of major strikes in 1992, but widespread protests were lodged by company directors and industrial elites whose subsidies were withdrawn. These business groups effectively used the national media to criticize and undermine government policies. In alliance with labor, they were instrumental in mustering widespread social support to vote down Bulgaria's radical reformers (Engelbrekt, 1992). The minimal state and rule-based political behavior will be resisted by rent-seeking social actors and politicians who need to distribute particular resources in exchange for political support. Small fragile firms often ally themselves with large firms that have been dependent on the state in the past to block reforms and provide protection. These actors are joined by legislators who are particularly tempted to resist reforms that reduce the public sector because of their need to distribute resources to particular constituencies.

Second, these incentives to resist liberalization are reinforced by the weak party system and its thin-to-nonexistent ties to a solid social base in most post-communist societies (Geddes, 1991). If these parties are fragmented and disorganized, with shallow roots in society, they intensify the incentive for politicians to exchange favors for support once they are in office. Their short time horizon and weak party platforms do not permit them to impose party discipline; even if they wanted to liberalize political institutions and eschew corruption, politicians would likely be unsuccessful in mobilizing the social or political support needed to keep them in office.

Liberalizers and Their Opponents

These last two factors that work against liberalizers deserve elaboration. In addition to the general conditions in the immediate environment favoring support for liberalizers or support for their opponents, the different roles played by politicians themselves shape their political identity and their policy preferences. Politicians are interested in furthering their careers, and they calculate carefully whether reform policies will advance their own self-interest (Geddes, 1991). Political elites of all types are under pressure to realize the liberal ideal to some degree. They are pressured to dismantle and reform the old socialist state and rapidly construct liberal political and economic institutions. In general, however, some politicians have more incentive to engage in these reforms than others. Presidents are more prone than legislators to support a rapid dismantling of the old system and a new minimal state because they have a relatively long political time horizon and a national constituency for whom symbolic gestures and market-driven, aggregate economic success counts. Presidents negotiate with international creditors and others who pressure them for liberalizing reforms that affect the state's size, role, and strength (Geddes, 1991). Presidents also need infusions of capital to help reduce deficits and target projects that contribute to successful reform.

Former outsiders who have now become part of the political process tend to support both a partial dismantling of the state and merit-based reform of the bureaucracy in order to pull the rug out from under the patronage system that kept the old nomenklatura (i.e., the centrally appointed former elite) in power. They want to eliminate the public sector jobs of their political opponents and build a social base of political support among exporters, finance capital, and labor in export sectors. They therefore may want to "shrink" the state.

But, as noted above, rent-seeking social actors and politicians tend to resist the movement to dismantle the state as their livelihood and future prospects are very much tied in with the nature and degree of state power and patronage. Therefore, despite the triumph of liberal capitalist ideology and new access to the political system for liberalizers, politicians opposing liberal reform can have a weighty influence on the political process. Many of the forces that shape their opposition to liberalization can be traced to the pre-communist history, the legacy of Leninism, and the sudden collapse of the Leninist state. I now turn to focus on the sources of opposition rooted in these legacies.

The Shadows of the Past as Obstacles to Reform

Authors contributing chapters in this volume discuss four legacies that will shape the process of transition from Leninism. The first of these legacies, discussed in Chapters 6 and 7 by Ivan Berend and Andrew Janos, respectively, is the lateness, "backwardness," and peripheral status of the region that post-communist regimes inherited (Chirot, 1989). The peripheral status of the "East" and the conspicuous income disparities between East and West that emerged created social structures, political reactions, movements, and ideologies that now present important obstacles to reform. Peasant societies characterized by a weak middle class were ruled by autocratic, corrupt, and clientalistic elites. In addition, populist anti-Western attitudes, as Berend argues, "strongly penetrated the entire area" and are "deeply rooted in the soil of humiliated peripheral societies." Janos adds that "the symptoms of this backwardness are the emigration of talent, and a deep sense of relative deprivation ..." that manifests itself both in political impatience with economic policy and an increasing sense of collective inferiority that seeks compensation outside the narrowly defined sphere of economic activity. It is to this peripheralization and its effects, he argues, that public policy must adapt.

The second legacy is the interrupted process of nation-building in many post-communist societies. After the Russian Revolution of 1917, communism as a cosmopolitan universalist ideology was supposed to replace particularistic nationalist ideologies as a blueprint for economic modernization; after 1945, this ideology, combined with Soviet domination and cold-war divisions, served to repress national discourse in communist countries. That national discourse—as a tool of social mobilization—has emerged again, particularly with regard to "national self-determination" and the search for state sovereignty in the international system.

This is the subject discussed by Daniel Chirot in Chapter 2. He argues that the imperial legacies and the varieties of nationalism that emerged in Eastern Europe do not have their origins in the more liberal and inclusive "Enlightenment" nationalisms of France and England—where membership in the nation was a function of civic behavior. Nor were these Eastern European nationalisms born in societies that depended on immigrants, a dependence that demanded the acceptance of settlers as equals in the nation-building process. Instead, the nationalisms of post-communist societies had their roots in the Russian and German tradition of "volk," blood, "narod," and race rather than in liberal traditions as the basis for membership in the nation. Collective solidarity within that tradition precluded the development both of a strong sense of individualism and of a strong sense of civic nationalism. The poison of these particular varieties of nationalism in the region was made more potent by the legacies of imperialism. The Ottomans, in particular, mixed up ethnic and religious groups, redrew boundaries that left large numbers of people outside their homelands, and left a bitter administrative legacy that privileged one group over others to maintain social control.

This legacy means that nation-building—the issue of who *is* included in the nation and who is not (Haas, 1986)—is now on the new political agenda in post-communist societies. If that issue has not yet been decided, new democracies are likely to be weak and illiberal in that they will construct institutions that exclude minority groups or weaken their political power. These institutions will thus make minority groups politically vulnerable and fan the flames of ethnic or sectarian resentment and conflict—by forcing minorities to live under political systems that they have not chosen and that do not represent them.

Particularly when liberalizers are trying to gain the upper hand in dismantling the state, when appeals to "class" are no longer credible, and when material resources are increasingly scarce, political entrepreneurs have found that they can offer a "national identity" as a resource in exchange for political support. In multi-ethnic societies, politicians are tempted to privilege—or promise to privilege—the members of one ethnic group over other residents of the state in exchange for votes. Both the historical legacy that Chirot traces in Chapter 2 and this need to exchange resources for support in order to seize and maintain political power leads politicians to define citizenship in exclusive and collective terms and thus to neglect the individual as the basic subject of constitutional law. Individuals are diffuse and their identities are multiple and overlapping. Diffuse groups, as noted previously, provide a weak political support base. Ethnic and sectarian groups are concentrated, and their characteristics can often be easily defined and distinguished from the characteristics of other groups; they are easier targets for mobilization by political entrepreneurs than diffuse individuals. Such groups may harbor historic grudges that can be easily politically manipulated (Laitin, 1985). Moreover, to the extent that national self-determination as a symbol of sovereignty is associated with freedom from oppression for a specific ethnic group, such exclusivity as a resource to mobilize internal support is reinforced.[2]

When the rights of the "nation" are privileged above the rights of the individual, the privileging is usually justified by politically motivated appeals to national "myths" of cultural superiority that glorify one's own ethnic history and character and malign the history and character of others. As Chirot clearly describes, history is reinterpreted in this effort to push back the origins of nationalism to a time when it did not exist. Such appeals garner political support by providing national identity as a political resource in exchange, and they undermine liberal ideology as a basis upon which to build solid nation-states, markets, and democracy. Needless to say, as these politicians gain positions of political power, *illiberal* democracies are likely to emerge if any aspects of polyarchy remain at all.

The creation of illiberal democracies and the institutional features that support them is illustrated by the new Croatian political system (Plestina, 1993). In Croatia, the Croatian Democratic Union (HDZ), espousing exclusive nationalist claims, has gained control of both the legislature and the presidency; the president has broad emergency powers; and there is little separation of powers and horizontal accountability in the government. The judiciary lacks independence; its appointments and dismissals are controlled by the Parliament and there is little freedom of the press. The concentration of political power has given rise to a new elite of party-state functionaries whose decision-making process is not confined to traditional governmental channels.

A third legacy of Leninism that nurtures resistance to liberalization was an industrial structure that left in place a managerial elite positioned to pressure politicians to oppose reform. Indeed, the industrial structure provides the source of power for this particular elite. Command economies were characterized by weak or nonexistent linkages among suppliers, producers, and consumers and by the absence of a "wholesale trading system." The formal distribution—or rationing—of industrial inputs to producers was carried out by the central state, which allocated all industrial inputs and issued supply authorizations for millions of different kinds of goods. Although there was some variance among communist countries, enterprises had little choice of suppliers and clients; relationships between entrepreneurs and their suppliers and clients were difficult to establish because they were mediated by the central authorities (Aslund, 1989).

To overcome the bottlenecks that inevitably resulted from supply centralization, most enterprises had to improvise in order to be certain that critical inputs would be available. Enterprises did this either by finding ways to produce critical inputs themselves—through ad hoc vertical integration—or through informal bartering for inputs. Most enterprises were specifically designed to be as self-sufficient as possible. Indeed, 30 to 40 percent of the value of all Soviet goods was produced on single sites.[3] Vertical integration was not based on cost calculations showing that these enterprises could produce the goods as cheaply or as well as others, but rather on intense uncertainty about supplies (Hewett, 1988). In the former Soviet Union and elsewhere in Central and Eastern Europe, many enterprises thus became "conglomerates" out of necessity: They even raised food and manufactured those consumer goods for their employees that could not be found in retail stores.

These vertically integrated conglomerates came to characterize the industrial structure of Soviet-type economies, placing their managers in strategic economic positions that would give them disproportionate political clout in post-communist political systems. The economic power of these managers was reinforced by the economic bottlenecks caused by central planning that gave rise to a set of privileged informal relationships and unofficial exchange networks that worked as powerful instruments of economic leverage. As a condition for supplying plan-designated industrial inputs, suppliers often demanded other goods as payment. If those goods could not be supplied, the input would not be forthcoming. Soviet tractor manufacturers, for example, could not sign direct contracts with metal suppliers in 1990—even though such contracts were legal—because the metal suppliers demanded meat or sausage or vehicles or building equipment in exchange for metal shipments (ECOTASS, 1990).

Economic reforms, both under communism and in its wake, intensified these relationships in many post-communist societies by simply removing state control without changing the industrial structure. As the state moved away from regulating the supply of industrial inputs, both the vertical integration of industries—the growth of monopolies—and barter were intensified. Economic power thus devolved to monopolistic enterprises. In many cases, these conglomerates used their power to control supplies to more dependent enterprises; as Burawoy and Krotov (1992) describe the situation in Russia, these conglomerates became large trading companies rather than more efficient producers. Their managers had valuable information about supply sources that allowed them to enter new positions of power where they could maintain their economic control. A similar pattern emerged in Central and Eastern Europe (Stark, 1990).

These large conglomerates-turned-trading-companies and webs of personal relationships created a political power base for vested interests to oppose reform in many post-communist societies. As Goldberg, Ickes, and Ryterman argue in

Chapter 11, these large interests—in the case of Russia and much of the former Soviet Union—have been able to block the move toward price liberalization and world market pricing in trade. They continued to benefit from the provision of interfirm credits and credit provided by Russia's central bank as of mid-1993. The lesson is straightforward and perhaps too obvious: Weak states cannot enforce attempted reforms.

Two more insidious effects of this legacy are also evident. First, the socioeconomic division of labor created by this industrial structure, in which the workplace doubled as the marketplace, becoming the only focus of social life, enforced social isolation on the part of the working population that would operate to prevent the creation of civil society (Jowitt, 1992). Secondly, the economic structure worked to prevent the emergence of a "market culture." Although the existence of the "second economy" structured the incentives of the participants to respond to supply and demand signals, its illegal and predatory nature also led to the "exploitation of monopolistic rents," bribery, and exploitation (Poznanski, 1992).

Both of these effects work to undermine the social "trust" that John Hall discusses in Chapter 4 as a necessary condition for the success of market liberalization. He suggests that market institutions must be based on trust; contracts and the overlapping linkages necessary for a successful market economy depend on a kind of cooperation absent in these societies. In particular, it can be argued, the persistence of the culture of the second economy threatens to undermine the emergence of an entrepreneurial market culture that could support liberalization efforts in many regions of the former communist world.

A fourth social legacy of Leninism is that it created an aversion to politics in the wider population, particularly the politics of bargaining, negotiation, and compromise necessary in a democracy. Jowitt (1992) has made this argument most forcefully: With their failed promises, brutal exercise of power, and enforced political participation, Leninist regimes prevented the emergence of a "public realm" and instilled in their societies a deep distrust of government. In the absence of a public realm for debate and discussion, rumor became the vehicle for political discourse, altogether corrupting political debate. Hall's discussion of the necessity of trust also is important regarding this fourth legacy because low voter turnouts throughout the post-communist world indicate that trust in government has not yet been instilled. Furthermore, this legacy reinforces the second one discussed previously: It provides a permissive condition for the rise of political demagoguery based on claims of national exclusiveness and cultural superiority.

Stephen Holmes (Chapter 3) notes another pernicious political effect of this legacy. Under communist regimes, public bargaining over interests was not only absent but was considered immoral. This legacy means that new post-communist parliaments will have to fight the dominant public perception that their very modus operandi is illegitimate. This "culture of communism" combines with the culture of those actually writing the constitutions in these societies—the human rights lawyers. These lawyers are committed to principles of natural law rather than to principles of bargaining and compromise. Their influence permits this legacy to persist.

Weak State Structures as Obstacles to Reform

A fifth legacy and the second set of conditions that undermine liberalizers in our analysis is a weakened state structure. To some, the characterization of these state structures as "weak" is surprising because Leninist regimes were despotic regimes. At one time, they had used centralized power to mobilize resources, displace the peasantry, and create a social and economic infrastructure in the interest of rapid economic growth, distributing resources to labor and managerial elites alike. But these highly centralized regimes could not sustain economic development under conditions of increasing social and economic complexity. Although they possessed the capacity for internal repression, they were ultimately weakened by their own despotism: They could no longer distribute resources in exchange for the support of the population. As their legitimacy dwindled, they became "Wizard of Oz" states—perceived both domestically and internationally as powerful organizations but actually possessing rapidly vanishing power resources.

Command economies were wasteful and inefficient; they reduced wealth and therefore decreased resources that could have been tapped by the state. The state's monopoly of control over the media reduced the flow of information upon which sound policy decisions are based. Moreover, as these states increasingly failed to achieve the goals they proclaimed, they had decreasing authority to mobilize the support of their populations for a collective purpose. They were outwardly despotic but inwardly weak.

Post-communist governments inherited these weakened states. Because of the virtual identity of party and state, the Communist party's fall further undermined the legitimacy and authority of state institutions, leaving in place weak states with illiberal traditions. These weak states undermine the political strength of liberalizers in three ways. First, weak states can be "captured" either by those political entrepreneurs espousing the superiority of particular ethnic and national claims over claims for individual rights or by managerial elites who fight to oppose liberal reform. If these groups capture the state at the outset, they can set it on an illiberal path of reform. Developments in much of the former Yugoslavia illustrate this point: The Croatian constitution, for example, states that only those of Croatian ethnicity can be citizens of Croatia, whether they live there or not. Members of other ethnic groups are not accorded the same rights of citizenship.

Second, as noted above, even if liberal constitutions are drafted and economic reforms are proclaimed, weakened central states cannot enforce reform policies—nor enforce the law that protects citizenship rights. Politicians at the regional and local levels who are most tempted to exchange specific benefits for support can simply ignore the directives of weak central states and continue in the old practices. By ignoring the state in this way, the large enterprises and the partner relations they perpetrated became the economic foundation of nationalism and localism. This is best exemplified by the new states of the former Soviet Union: Markets formerly controlled by the central party apparatus are now controlled by monopoly enterprises within the regions. Politically motivated, irregular enforcement of the law creates what Guillermo O'Donnell (1992) has called "low intensity citizenship," in which a weak legal system fails to protect the rights of *all* citizens. When this happens, unprotected groups ignore existing law, engage in criminal activity, or fall prey to political entrepreneurs espousing chauvinistic ideologies and exclusive ethnic and sectarian claims in an effort to mobilize support against liberalizing governments.

It follows that states weakened by the loss of revenues and discredited by early policy failure do not have the resources either to co-opt or coerce groups who oppose reform in order to gain their compliance. A weakened state becomes a target of opposition for those hurt in the reform process.[4] Frequently, the "losers" (or those who perceive that they will lose) in the distributional struggle that inevitably results from liberalization will turn to the most easily exploitable means to gain a power base from which to extract or negotiate for resources. Conversely, powerful groups (such as the old nomenklatura) may benefit from formal economic reforms and use their positions of influence to cannibalize the state and line their own pockets, thus depleting resources and undermining developmental goals, further enfeebling the state.

These negative legacies, however, have limited power with regard to predicting the success of liberalization. How long is the shadow that the past casts on the present and the future? In the post-war case of West German liberalization, for example, that shadow does not seem long at all: Germany's legacy of authoritarianism and fascism was clearly attenuated by international pressures and the creation of new institutions after World War II. But, in other cases, as noted previously, the shadow of the past can be long if historical memories are manipulated by today's political entrepreneurs. Old industrial structures do indeed create incentives for opposition to reform, but they can be dismantled. As I shall argue in the following sections, international and institutional factors play an essential role in repressing or magnifying past legacies.

International Constraints and Opportunities

While social legacies and weakened states undermine liberalizers and provide support to their opponents, pressures from the international system that might be translated into domestic political agendas have mixed effects. Indeed, as previously discussed, the liberalization of West European—and particularly West German—politics and economics after World War II came about largely because of the pressures and incentives offered by the United States and international organizations (Herz, 1982). At that time, U.S. hegemonic power played an important role in creating and consolidating post-fascist and post-war markets and democracies and setting the terms for global cooperation. The United States not only financed recovery and provided markets for exports but also encouraged economic cooperation among European states and provided military security, relieving liberalizing governments from having to channel precious resources into defense. To pursue the goal of what John Ruggie (1982) called "embedded liberalism," the United States provided aid to West European economies for the purpose of developing their export industries and encouraged the establishment of cooperative institutions, such as the Organization for European Economic Cooperation, the European Coal and Steel Community, and the European Payments Union. In the cold-war shadow of an opposing ideological system and the threat of Soviet military power, Western trade liberalization and economic cooperation was seen as vital to the economic growth of capitalist democracies in their struggle with communism. The United States provided both military security and financial backing in the form of the Marshall Plan, exercised political pressure on European leaders to pursue policies of liberalization, and permitted economic discrimination against its own economy to encourage trade that would lead to economic growth. These measures worked to create a social base that provided political support for liberalizing politicians.

Post-communist Eastern Europe faces a much different milieu than Western European liberalizers faced after World War II, and a number of authors in this volume assess the effects of this new environment on the strength both of liberalizers and their opponents. Today, no external hegemonic power is available to provide aid, credits, and administrative support for reform to strengthen liberalizers in weak states. As Janos argues, post-communist countries are confronted with a "weak international regime." Furthermore, unlike the post-war period of bipolar competition between West and East, aid that flows from West to East is not accompanied by measures to ensure economic cooperation *among* post-communist liberalizers in the region; nor is that aid accompanied by the external provision of security. But, at the same time, the end of the cold war and the cessation of ideological conflict reduced traditional incentives for cooperation. Because it is widely believed that economic power can be quickly translated into military strength, economic threats are perceived by some to be security threats as well. Ironically, the global extinction of Leninism, though a necessary condition for liberalization, poses one of the greatest obstacles to liberalizers in post-communist societies in that it reduces the specter of a threat large enough to mobilize international cooperation in support of those liberalizers.

Capital Flows. Just as in the post-war period of post-fascist liberalization and recovery, the most important international economic determinant of the success of economic reform is the availability of global capital and the level of capital flows into the region. The level and kind of foreign aid and investment will greatly affect the competitiveness and efficiency of industrial enterprises. The availability of foreign capital will influence the exchange rates under which these countries pursue the task of integrating themselves into the world economy; loans, credits, and debt-reduction plans help achieve balance of payments equilibrium and ease the task of achieving currency convertibility.

Capital flows send important signals felt in domestic political struggles. In the absence of domestic resources for recovery, foreign resources can shore up political support on the part of exporters, financiers, and labor in the export sector for reformers—even those saddled with a weak state apparatus. In addition, foreign resources provide liberalizers with the support of the general population if the aid assists in meeting developmental goals and bolsters aggregate economic performance. To achieve these goals and to provide external support for liberalizers who work toward macroeconomic adjustment, international institutions have begun to provide loans, credits, and aid to East European governments. By mid-1992, Western bilateral and multilateral aid to Eastern Europe and the former Soviet Union totaled $52 billion. That sum, however, fell far short of the original commitments and disappointed many East European leaders, discrediting their political promises and undermining their base of support (Wedel, 1992). By early 1993, the region as a whole experienced a net capital outflow.

Foreign aid can, however, have the opposite political effect. Politicians—saddled with weakened states but desperate for resources to maintain political support—threaten to consume aid by distributing it to supporters rather than using it to strengthen national production capabilities for the future. Conditionality requirements could tip the balance; even opponents of reform are tempted to adhere to the conditions that shape policies for liberalization, because financing by international institutions is often provided on terms that are more generous than those offered by private lenders or investors. International agencies, then, can act as an external constituency in support of liberalizers.

Trade Competition. Secondly, Western openness to imports from these transforming economies and their sensitivity to trade competition will bolster support for liberalizers. Protectionist policies in the West support the opponents of liberalizers. Import markets provide both a magnet for the export industries of liberalizing countries and a spur to their growth. Even markets for agricultural goods and manufacturing inputs provide an important source of hard currency that can be directed toward developmental goals, boost aggregate income, and win the support of agricultural interests and exporters in both manufacturing and extractive sectors.

As Guerrieri suggests in his chapter, post-communist Eastern Europe in the early 1990s had a comparative advantage in minerals, fuels, basic manufactured goods, and agricultural products. But it is precisely in these sectors that West European trade barriers were the strongest. And although the European Community (EC) has removed most quantitative restrictions on imports from Eastern Europe, restrictions on steel, agricultural goods, and textiles were still in place at the end of 1992.[5]

Furthermore, despite the 1991 Maastricht Treaty's promise of "widening" the European Community to include post-communist countries, it is unlikely that Eastern Europe as a whole can be integrated into existing EC institutions; without integration, barriers to trade with the West will persist. Exporters, agricultural interests, and some sectors of labor will be harmed, thus undermining a large part of the social base that liberalizers might draw on for support. In his chapter, Nove discusses the particular problems faced by the agricultural sector. He argues that because the terms of trade have turned strongly against agriculture, peasant incomes have fallen sharply while the prices of their necessary "inputs" have risen sharply. Indeed, these groups that are harmed by trade barriers may join right-wing nationalist and populist parties in the hope of maintaining their own market position in the face of import competition or simply as a protest against the West.

In the shift from a bipolar to a multipolar milieu, trade competition among industrial powers is intensified, and there are some indications that former communist countries are rapidly becoming an arena for export competition among the United States, Japan, and Western Europe; their demands create competing political forces within post-communist regimes. Some Western countries, for example, are pressuring East European governments to end the practice of countertrade, a sophisticated form of barter. Indeed, membership in the General Agreement on Tariffs and Trade (GATT), the IMF, and the World Bank is contingent upon halting this practice (Cutts, 1991). Its cessation will weaken the old industrial elite, discussed earlier, who profit from countertrade practices.

Nonetheless, other countries, such as Japan, want to continue countertrade. Countertrade usually involves agreements of long duration and can ensure the Western firms who accept such agreements a share in the Eastern market. In fact, Japan has negotiated new forms of barter and complex countertrade deals, and reformers are tempted to negotiate because they lack hard currency and are pressured by the beneficiaries.

One way to weaken these competitive pressures and expand trade in ways that would provide support to liberalizers would be for East European countries to form their own regional economic institutions to help spur economic development and to provide a forum for political cooperation. Such institutions would be appropriate, because traditional trade patterns are intraregional. Indeed, present regional economic links are deeply rooted in the East, both in trade and in employment and production structures. Transportation networks, including oil and gas pipelines and railways, are oriented toward intraregional trade that moved largely under long-term contracts and that provided a certainty of production runs and employment. For example, the output of machinery and engineering products in Hungary and Czechoslovakia was deeply regionally intertwined, with about 30 percent for use in other Council for Mutual Economic Assistance (CMEA) countries. Intra-CMEA trade represented between 40 and 80 percent of members' overall trade in 1990 (Junz, 1991).

Van Brabant (1991) has suggested the creation of a Central European/Soviet Payments Union, analogous to the European Payments Union of the early postwar period; in his chapter, Nove provides an essential guide to this option. Former CMEA countries face severe liquidity shortages while shifting to hard-currency pricing. Prices have changed dramatically as these countries removed price controls, and this may require changes in the exchange rate in order to protect employment and stimulate production. A regional payments union could facilitate multilateralism by creating currency convertibility and providing credits to stabilize currencies and exchange rates and ease balance-of-payments problems. Chirot goes even farther in his prescription: the creation in the post-communist world of an institution that would function in much the same way as the European Community. "It is neither a new nation nor just a mere alliance or a trade block. … [B]ecause the larger Community has real powers, because it offers considerable economic advantages and protection for its members, and because, most of all, it is dominated by a liberal, non-ethnic, democratic ideology, the new Europe is drastically different than the Europe of the interwar period or of the nineteenth century."

The problem with regional solutions is that they may not be feasible for reasons that have little to do with economic costs and benefits. As noted previously, East European countries and the countries of the former Soviet Union are looking to the West and not to one another for cooperation; as Laszlo Borhi (1993) has written: "[Eastern Europe's] goal is to move from the periphery of a fallen semi-Asiatic traditional empire and to become an integrated part of a dynamic power center—Western Europe and the United States." Clearly, the years of forced interaction under Leninist regimes did not lay a firm foundation for economic cooperation in the East. Those regimes simply repeated the clearing arrangements that began under German domination in the 1930s. Indeed, disputed borders and the presence of substantial ethnic minorities outside their homelands can create widespread suspicion and fear, raising the political costs of economic cooperation. When those costs rise, support for liberalizers diminishes.

Indeed, regional trade *competition* rather than cooperation characterized the first years of post-communist trade liberalization. Former Soviet republics competed with Central and East European countries for Western investment and assistance. For example, subsidized export credits and credit guarantees granted by West European governments for their farmers' agricultural exports to Russia crowded East European farmers out of the Russian market. The smaller countries cannot finance their exports on comparable terms, again providing the incentive for agricultural interests to withdraw support from liberalizers. In short, it will be difficult for these countries to enact meaningful reforms and safeguard economic achievements purchased at high social costs if the international economic climate is unstable and if foreign economic relationships are highly asymmetrical and competitive. Such conditions obviously undermine political support for liberalizers.

In this volume, Goldberg, Ickes, and Ryterman address the issue of cooperation versus competition by examining incentives for the former Soviet republics to stay in or depart from the ruble zone. Goldberg et al. argue that the decision to cooperate or depart is largely influenced by the effects of world market prices in the individual republics. If those republics erect barriers to shield themselves from world market prices, then they are likely to opt for continued cooperation within the ruble zone; the introduction of national currencies would lead to large income losses due to unfavorable terms of trade. (This proposition does *not* hold for the oil-producing states.) "Gradualist" reformers (discussed hereinafter) are likely to opt for staying in the ruble zone. If they needed to placate labor in the course of reform, they would not have to accumulate large cash allocations to pay higher wages; rather, they could keep wages lower because prices would not rise as quickly. If liberalizers open themselves to world market prices and create independent currencies, they are likely to lose political support if their industries are not yet competitive. The income losses that result from unfavorable terms of trade are likely to be blamed on the introduction of a national currency, and the blame is likely to be focused on those governing parties that introduced the national currency.

Nevertheless, by the end of 1992, the ruble zone had largely collapsed—*not* because of perceived economic benefits but because the leadership in the former republics believed they needed to symbolize their national sovereignty with an independent currency. This collapse led to large income losses in the Baltic states (because previous participation in the ruble zone and the staving off of world market pricing in trade with Russia had maintained price stability); in Lithuania, income losses were the result of a premature introduction of a national currency, and reformers were replaced by their opponents. Goldberg et al. argue that if Russia shifts to world market pricing with Belarus and Ukraine, the effects will be equally devastating, undermining support for liberalizers. Nove makes a similar point for the rest of the post-communist world.

In short, Eastern Europe and the former Soviet Union are entering a bleak and unfriendly international political economy. In his chapter in this volume, Janos specifically explores how this environment triggers past legacies to produce different dominant coalitions in the political process. Janos argues that post-communist governments function under a relatively weak international regime that offers economic inducements—prospects and promises rather than direct payoffs—in exchange for conformity with Western standards of national and international behavior. At the same time, the new domestic regimes are far more open than before to public pressures to respond to problems that have emerged as a result of their global marginalization. Three typical responses have begun to take shape: (1) Liberalism—as a broad strategy of economic integration with the West by means of adjusting domestic economies and polities to Western specifications and by subordinating national grievances to economic benefit; (2) Technocratic nationalism—as a rejection of the principles of the market in favor of more autarkic policies. Technocratic nationalists find it convenient to use nationalist symbols while mobilizing populations for policies of austerity; and finally (3) Populism—as a strategy that subordinates economic goals to national and cultural ones. Populists reject the notion of trading national identity for a promised economic advantage and are openly hostile to Western culture. To the degree that economic success is influenced by the international environment, liberal coalitions will dominate; to the extent that these countries are further marginalized by the international environment, past legacies will produce technocratic nationalist or populist pressures.

Alternative Policy and Institutional Choice

The fourth factor affecting the politics of liberalization is policy choice. Many believe that if elites can simply "get the institutions and policies right," stable democracy and stable markets can be simultaneously constructed. This perspective suggests that elites can construct institutions that shut out the influences of the past and mitigate the negative influences of the international system. For these observers, the head of Leninism has been lopped off, leaving space for the development of new institutions to structure social incentives according to the rules of liberal capitalist democracy. The political culture that emerged under communism matters little if institutions can change incentives to conform with democratic and capitalist practices. This is why such observers do not worry that former communists still occupy positions of power in some regions. Their behavior, like the behavior of other powerful social groups, will be shaped by the structure of constraints and incentives that issue from the new institutions.

Some argue, for example, that the lack of a constitutional culture in post-communist societies will doom their attempts to construct democratic constitutions. Holmes, however, suggests that a more important obstacle is the weak legitimacy and internal fragmentation of elected parliaments. In other words, institutions, not legacies, are important determinants of outcomes. The weakness of institutions, therefore, suggests that an incremental or "gradualist" approach be taken toward constitution-building and that the very creation of a constitutional culture in these societies will depend on how constitutional politics and ordinary politics are structured.

Indeed, a "faulty" institutional structure can actually perpetuate those past legacies that undermine liberal reform. Plestina (1992) has shown that in post-communist Croatia, electoral laws favor the dominance of the Croatian majority in the political process. While in the country as a whole, more than half of the seats in the lower house of the legislature are elected by majority vote, proportional representation is the election rule in areas dominated by a majority of the Serbian population; this discrepancy allows Croatian parties from these areas to gain seats in the legislature. Majority rule would have provided Serbs with more representatives. Further, parties present a closed list of candidates in all of Croatia; this further entrenches the dominant nationalist party in power by giving it priority status on the ballot.

As previously noted, an important debate over institutional choice focuses on the *scope*, *speed*, and *sequencing* of economic reform. Two alternative approaches dominate the debate: the "radical" and the "gradualist" perspectives. Each strategy distributes economic resources differently and the distribution of resources affects the distribution of support for politicians who either support or oppose liberalization.

The Radical Blueprint. For the radicals—whose most enthusiastic practitioners have been Czech Prime Minister (and former minister of finance) Klaus, former Russian minister of finance Gaidar, and Poland's former minister of finance Balcerowicz—the key to liberalization is a rapid, widespread, and simultaneous introduction of markets and democratic reforms in the domestic economy and rapid integration into the international economy. The radicals' central hypothesis is that markets and stable democracy will develop simultaneously, because as economic power is diffused, political power will be diffused as well. Therefore, liberal constitutions must be quickly drafted and defended at the outset to ensure both the diffusion of power and universal citizenship. To rapidly construct markets, a large cluster of simultaneous changes is needed because the main elements of a market economy are interrelated. If old institutions that perpetuate the political power of opponents of reform are not quickly swept away, they will block the reform process. Radical reforms will succeed, proponents argue, if they are introduced during the "honeymoon" of the new regime while legitimacy is still high (Remmer, 1990; Przeworski, 1991). As Berend describes in his chapter, the early economic reforms in Poland and Czechoslovakia exemplify this strategy.

Consider price liberalization. As previously noted, under communist regimes, institutions providing access to goods and services were highly politicized. Price controls created scarcities. Informal distribution networks often involving simple barter were created and held together by personal and political ties. Radicals argue that freed prices will abolish these politicized distribution networks and thus eliminate shortages of goods that the networks controlled and create incentives for an entrepreneurial private sector to build new distribution networks and purchase inputs at market prices.

Furthermore, price liberalization across all sectors will leave little room for well-placed former nomenklatura and industrial elites who benefit from the old practices to block the reform process. A more gradual approach, radicals warn, will permit political coalitions to form that obstruct the introduction of market prices in noncompetitive sectors. Some entrenched elites may reap monopoly profits by selling in decontrolled markets and buying in markets still governed by price controls. Therefore, all prices must be decontrolled at once.

For radicals, therefore, the necessary economic reforms must take place rapidly and simultaneously. Price liberalization must be accompanied by spontaneous privatization and by government efforts to restructure industry through the elimination of subsidies, anti-monopoly policies, and the creation of agencies to penalize those who persist in the old practices. Unless these reforms are pursued simultaneously, prices will continue to be distorted by large enterprises that wield monopoly and monopsony power over markets. Given the importance of this legacy, industrial restructuring will undermine the power base of the opponents of reform. Only an industrial structure that includes a significant number of small and mid-sized firms will transmit realistic price signals for production efficiency and increase output diversity (Mann, 1991). The managers of these firms will support liberalizers who create opportunities for them and withdraw subsidies from enterprises that make up the old industrial structure.

According to the radical blueprint, rapid privatization can trigger industrial restructuring; private investors must have the freedom to restructure existing firms that are inefficiently organized; if large conglomerates are inefficient, investors will be guided by price signals to downsize the conglomerates in an optimal way. Furthermore, the extent to which freedom to privatize is granted will, in part, determine the amount and kind of foreign investment that flows into the economies of these countries. In Chapter 9 of this volume, Kazimierz Poznanski argues that the post-1989 stagflation throughout Eastern Europe deprived domestic agents of their savings; foreign actors, therefore, played a dominant role, despite initial efforts to limit their participation. In Hungary, dollar payments by foreigners accounted for three-fourths of the total revenue from privatization in both 1991 and 1992; a similar pattern emerged in Poland.

However, the radical argument continues, price liberalization, privatization, and industrial restructuring must be accompanied by stable macroeconomic policy. Because price liberalization initially creates unstable prices and because privatization will result in a rise in unemployment, the temptation to permit high rates of inflation in order to pay off both labor and business in exchange for continued political support is strong. But such inflationary policies can spiral out of control—and hyperinflation undermines the credibility of liberalizers. Therefore, radical reformers also need to introduce simultaneous measures to bring about macroeconomic stability if liberalization is to succeed.

Macroeconomic stability is ultimately achieved when price levels are *predictable.* Predictability is normally achieved through a monetary policy that controls interest rates and through fiscal policies that balance government budgets. But monetary policy is transmitted to the entire economy through financial markets. These markets, therefore, must be created together with other reforms. The elimination of state subsidies creates opponents of liberalization; market access for startup companies and enterprises that have been transferred to private ownership creates supporters for reform. A banking system that does not simply distribute state funds can provide loans and credit, creating a foundation for properly functioning financial and capital markets, which promotes political support for liberalizers. If a banking system is *not* created, both business and labor will lobby for continued subsidies—blocking radical reform.

Furthermore, as Goldberg et al. argue in their chapter, rather than maintain monetary discipline, governments are tempted to increase the money supply in order to finance fiscal deficits. Therefore, liberalizers must devise fiscal policies that control government budgets. From the radical perspective, the dismantling of the state apparatus, including the elimination of wage and price subsidies and subsidies to enterprises, will help create a sound fiscal policy. All of these measures require rapid implementation before they are blocked by those who will be harmed by them. Such measures therefore require substantial state capacity and bureaucratic insulation to be implemented successfully.

Radicals argue that labor must be disciplined and reformers must be insulated from labor's demands. In particular, labor must be persuaded to accept a flexible labor market and changes in manufacturing technology that require the dismantling of assembly lines and the introduction of "just-in-time" and other modern production techniques. Labor-market rigidities must be destroyed; industrial restructuring will require flexible wage levels and fluctuating levels of employment. In sectors where labor is politically mobilized, there is bound to be political resistance to such changes.

Although Ost's contribution to this volume (discussed in the section that follows) suggests causes for the absence of labor mobilization, Poznanski argues that past legacies have made labor politically powerful. Under communist regimes, the state faced severe wage pressures and had to permit shortages or even price increases to placate labor demands. "It could be that confronting 'new' owners—whose resources are limited and whose 'legitimacy' has yet to be established—may be an easier task for workers threatened with unemployment than dealing with the 'strong' state."

Finally, proponents of radical reform argue that borders must be open to trade, investment, and finance from abroad. The exchange rate must be fixed to a strong foreign currency or a basket of foreign currencies in order to bring about monetary stability. Foreign participation in the economy is necessary to stimulate competition—and rapid privatization is necessary to attract foreign participation. Foreign participants should have the same rights of property ownership as domestic participants; they are essential to ensure an inflow of technology, new management techniques, training, and capital. The radical approach encourages a rapid reorientation of trade toward the West, which demands eliminating quantitative restrictions on imports and resisting the temptation to raise tariffs or to engage in other forms of trade protection. This aspect of the approach benefits competitive exporters and finance capital; it potentially harms producers in the nontraded goods sectors and all uncompetitive producers. *All* economic interests will be potentially harmed by this policy if trade protection in the international economy rises while post-communist regimes are opening their economies.

Gradualist Paths. The "gradualist" approach rejects these radical arguments. It suggests that, particularly under conditions of economic crisis and the Leninist political legacy, markets cannot be created and democracy cannot be stabilized given the minimal role for the state advocated by the radical approach. Radical economic reforms introduced under conditions of economic weakness may at worst mean economic collapse and at best mean severe social dislocation, triggering a backlash against radical policies on the part of powerful and concentrated social groups (Lipton and Sachs, 1990; Gati, 1991). Therefore, gradualists argue that reformers must have enough state resources available to make side payments to those who will bear the costs in exchange for their support of reform.[6] Ost argues in his chapter that labor must be included in this calculation.

Gradualists argue that broad and open access to the political arena must be created to rectify the injustices of totalitarianism but that, in conditions of economic crisis, economic reform must proceed gradually. Gradual reforms will reduce the burden of adjustment for voters who might exert political pressure to halt liberalization. By preserving widespread political access *and* reducing the costs of reform, economic and political liberalization can proceed simultaneously. In Chapter 8 of this volume, Ost represents this "gradualist" position. He argues that since a democratic system is stable only when the majority of the population accepts it, consolidating democracy in Eastern Europe requires the successful integration of labor in order to maintain regime support. Ost also examines how different post-communist economic reform programs, strategies of privatization, approaches to the state sector, and local economic transformation plans affect the development of an independent labor movement and the ongoing support of labor for democratic institutions. Although labor is not yet politically mobilized, Ost argues, if it is *not* integrated into these new democracies as a *class* it will turn to more nationalist and populist alternatives and undermine the project of post-communist democratization.

A comparison between the gradualist and the radical view of price liberalization suggests fundamental differences in approach. For the gradualist, radical reform of food and energy prices imposes high costs on the total population. Voters are then tempted to oust liberalizers in the next election. In contrast, the gradual approach to price decontrol calls for price reform in stages, sometimes with relative price adjustments throughout the economy and often on a sector-by-sector basis as a "side payment" to preserve political support for liberalizers.

Alternatively, consider the issue of privatization. The radical approach assumes that maximum support for liberalizers will be achieved by a swift transfer of property ownership that takes place simultaneously with other liberalization efforts. Proponents of this view argue that the longer the old structures of ownership remain in place, the more opportunity is afforded to existing managers to consume the capital stock and block further liberalization measures. Gradualists—such as Nove in this volume—argue that a radical privatization scheme that simply sells each firm "as is" does not create the weblike industrial structure of large, medium, and small firms necessary both to break the political power of the old elite and to create a new entrepreneurial class that will support reforms.

Gradualists further suggest that "spontaneous" privatization can simply put *more* wealth into the hands of the old elite—who will rapidly consume it. On this issue, Polish sociologist Jadwiga Staniszkis claims that, by the end of 1990, about 20 percent of all productive assets in Poland were converted to the personal property of the former nomenklatura (Szelenyi and Szelenyi, 1993). For these reasons, gradualists call for a larger administrative role for the state in privatization and the transfer of property ownership in stages to guarantee the most appropriate tradeoffs between equity and efficiency and also to ensure more appropriate prices and to limit fraud. Gradualists consider these measures that trade efficiency for equity necessary to ensure widespread political support for liberalizers. Ost's arguments in this volume support this view.

The European Bank for Reconstruction and Development's (EBRD's) activity in its first year of operation supported the gradualist view of privatization, despite its more "radical" mandate. Instead of the 40 percent agreed upon at the outset, 71 percent of its loans went to state-owned enterprises to help with restructuring that would make those firms attractive to private investors. Jacques Attali, the bank's president, argued that administrative guidance was necessary for restructuring and that prior restructuring was necessary to the success of privatization (Okolicsanyi, 1992). The Treuhandanstalt (the German agency charged with privatizing holdings of the former East German state) also took a more gradual approach, requiring buyers to preserve jobs in the face of a 40-percent unemployment rate in East Germany (Akerlof et al., 1991). Privatization could proceed with the "side payment" of assured employment. Both moves shored up labor's support for reform by creating expectations that jobs would be saved.

Gradualists also disagree with radicals on foreign participation in the East European domestic economy (Nove, 1992). Indiscriminate foreign ownership, gradualists argue, will not lead to aggregate growth and may contribute to capital flight, undermining liberalizers in government. Governments should create an investment code that would identify priority sectors for foreign investment—critical sectors in need of restructuring—and restrict foreign ownership in more sensitive sectors. The Czech government, for example, identified certain sectors (e.g., chemicals and auto manufacture) targeted for foreign investment; major companies in those sectors were then sold to Western firms.

Finally, gradualists disagree with radicals on appropriate policies of integration into the international economy. Gradualists argue that fixing the exchange rate to a strong foreign currency or a basket of foreign currencies—the radical liberal approach—can bring about monetary stability but that doing so means dependence on another country's monetary policy and a potential deflationary effect on the domestic economy as a whole. As noted earlier, prices are likely to change dramatically as these countries remove price controls. Gradualists, such as Alec Nove, argue that unstable prices might necessitate market interventions, including but not limited to manipulating exchange rates, in order to protect the economy and society from the adverse effects of inflation. Without these measures, gradualists argue, integration into the international economy can impose costs that drive large sectors of the population—both labor and capital—into the camp of political entrepreneurs espousing xenophobic nationalism as a form of "protection." The odds that radical approaches to economic liberalization will create illiberal politics are especially high if sudden exposure to international competition leads to widespread economic deprivation. Sequential opening, advocated by Guerrieri in this volume—such as a delay in import liberalization until after export opportunities have been created—can create constituencies that favor liberalization. In this case, some costs are eased now so that important social groups will be willing to endure other costs later.

In Chapter 6, Berend describes the original "gradualists," the architects of Hungary's New Economic Mechanism beginning in the late 1960s. Slovakia under Prime Minister Vladimir Meciar may provide a post-communist example. Meciar saw that one way to distance himself from Klaus and the Czech Republic was to argue for slower policies of privatization, continued subsidies, and a mixed economy. In a society marked by an unemployment rate of more than 11 percent, fear of economic dislocation and crisis was high; Meciar's "gradualist" approach provided a political resource to mobilize support. Romania at the end of 1992 pursued a variation on this path. Its third government since the fall of communism consciously distanced itself from the "radical" reformers of Central Europe; that distance proved to be a useful political resource to garner support. Arguing that "spontaneous reform and privatization would only lead to anarchy," Prime Minister Nicolae Vacariou suggested the establishment of a "social market economy" that would take a more gradual approach to reform to minimize social costs. Privatization, for example, now moves at a slow pace in Romania, and Vacariou planned to revive industry through increased investment raised from higher taxes (Marsh, 1992). Protecting jobs in the public sector until opportunities in the private sector have been created can reduce the costs of liberalization and thus undermine support for its opponents.

Three Caveats. As the foregoing discussion has illustrated, economic policies provide part of the rhetoric of political agendas. The intrinsic logic of such policies, therefore, may not be as interesting as their political effects. A declaration of policy "success" from either the radicals or the gradualists is likely to be a function of whether concentrated and powerful interests or voters at large believe that they will benefit from the reform in question, not whether the policy has enhanced aggregate growth or contributed to the growth of liberal societies.

Political expediency as a driving force in the debate over privatization policy is a central argument in Poznanski's chapter. Political parties use alternative positions on different issues to define their identity in opposition to other parties; the debate over privatization is a good example. New parties often adopt a more radical approach in order to distinguish themselves from the more gradualist ex-communists. Holmes, as well, shows how various strategies of constitutional reform have served political purposes.

Secondly, the conscious gradualist approach must be distinguished from the unintended consequences of failed or "slowed-down" policies. This is Poznanski's argument about radicalism. He argues that, with regard to the privatization of state assets, the transfer of ownership is never instantaneous, and the longer it is drawn out, the more chance that the enterprise will be decapitalized. Income losses quickly follow. This, he argues, has been a factor behind the recent recession in the post-communist world.

Often policy failure—of either radicals or gradualists—will result from the political pressure exerted by the opponents of liberalization in their effort to block reform. Two examples from Russia and from trade and currency reform in the former Soviet republics illustrate this point. Through a series of decrees issued by Yeltsin in 1992, "shock therapy" was introduced in Russia: a simultaneous lifting of price controls, introduction of privatization schemes, and elimination of subsidies. Opposition to these measures mounted, however, because they disrupted the process of barter and informal trade between enterprises, thus undermining the economic power base of the industrial elite. It became increasingly clear that Yeltsin had not built the political support necessary to push through the reforms. Furthermore, measures initiated by the central government were often ignored or opposed in regional and city governments; a weak central state—despite authoritarian measures—found it close to impossible to push through market reforms, and the unintended consequence was a slowdown in the reform process. Further, as Goldberg et al. demonstrate in Chapter 11, efforts to engage in price liberalization in inter-republican trade in the former Soviet Union were obstructed both by "the weakness of central institutions"—and their inability to enforce reforms—and the real threat of trade disruption posed by the reforms themselves.

Finally, Janos' argument in Chapter 7 suggests perhaps the most important caveat to gradualism: Those elites that I refer to as economic "gradualists" here may be the technocratic nationalists or the populists that Janos describes. He argues that although the advocacy in these countries of a planned economy, a return to economic subventions and price controls, and the general suspicion of markets contains an element of economic rationality, the leaders and dominant political coalitions in these countries also tend toward authoritarianism. Their economic gradualism is coupled with chauvinism and threats to political liberalization as well. Economic "gradualism" is not necessarily coupled with liberal political democracy.

In looking at the implementation of economic reform in the post-Leninist context, we are examining whether democracies or authoritarian regimes are more appropriate: democracies can implement economic reforms (1) if reformers are insulated in such a way that they cannot be punished by the "losers"; (2) if the reforms themselves undermine the political power of those losers who would oppose reform; or (3) if the costs of reform are accompanied by side payments that make those costs tolerable to groups whose support is necessary for continued reform and regime stability.

Radical reformers focus on the first two of these conditions; gradualist liberalizers focus on the third. In many post-communist societies, reformers are relatively insulated from political pressure exercised by the popular sectors, because those groups are not politically mobilized and have little access to politicians to pressure them to alter the course of reform. However, the mass electorate can oust reformers in the next election and are tempted by nationalist and xenophobic political appeals that offer more than long-term aggregate economic growth rates, particularly in societies where "nation-building" is incomplete. Second, radical reforms promise to remove the conditions that perpetuate continued demands for protection and subsidies, thus undermining the political power of the managerial elite still operating within the old industrial structure. Nonetheless, the gradualist approach—with its promise of side payments—seems both to promise more political access and to offer more incentives to support reformers than the radical blueprint.

What of the future? Democracies—whether more or less democratic—can initiate policies of economic liberalization, but will they eventually become *liberal democracies?* Moreover, under what conditions will the reforms succeed in bringing about *both* growth and development? In the following section, I hypothesize four outcomes in the form of scenarios for the future; each scenario weighs the factors differently to produce alternative hypotheses about the political base of support for liberalizers or their opponents.

The Consequences of Transition for Development, Democracy, and the State: Four Scenarios

The "Radical" Liberal Utopia

The radical's central hypothesis is the following: A favorable international environment, construction of institutions that shrink the state's role in the market, and the appropriate radical policies will quickly undermine the political base of the opponents of liberalization and thus provide insulation for liberalizers from the demands of the most powerful social groups. Rapid liberalization abolishes the power of entrenched managerial elites; markets and democracy undermine social legacies that shore up the power of the opponents of liberalization. The dismantling of the swollen, despotic state and its replacement with minimal, rule-based state institutions will weaken the patronage system of the old nomenklatura.

Rapid marketization and integration into the global economy will lead to export growth in manufactured goods, debt reduction, and economic growth. A weak entrepreneurial class throughout the region means that, initially, Western aid and direct foreign investment will be the central agents of successful economic transformation and the key support base for liberalizers; foreign firms will bring in the latest technology; markets will diffuse it throughout the domestic economy; capital will flow to competitive, export-oriented, high-technology industries, increasing the political clout of exporters who support radical liberalizers. Because foreign capital will flow into post-communist economies, currencies need not be undervalued, and therefore managers' incentives to compete in export markets in goods produced with cheap labor will be reduced. Foreign investors will locate their manufacturing and service facilities in Eastern Europe because of market and customer considerations rather than proximity to needed raw materials or low labor rates. These investors will use their clout in the political process to support liberalizers and radical policy choices.

As late developers, East European countries and the regions of the former Soviet Union will be able to leapfrog old industrial practices and import the latest manufacturing techniques and infrastructure technologies. If the "advantages of backwardness" permit the most efficient production methods to take root in competitive industries, these countries can begin to produce for export more quickly. Because skill and education levels are high and can be enhanced by the inflow of foreign capital and technology, countries that adopt the "radical" approach will develop a comparative advantage in high value-added goods.

The prosperity created by the rapid introduction of markets will create the conditions under which polyarchies can be transformed into stable democracies; social groups can be mobilized by stable political parties; "illiberal" politics, once nurtured by past legacies, can be undermined, and citizenship rights can be extended. An increase in aggregate growth rates will create widespread political support for liberalizers. With stable democracies and growing economies, these countries are viable candidates for membership in the EC.

The Gradualist Critique: The Region as Europe's "Periphery"

The gradualist approach puts forth an alternative hypothesis about the effects of radical reform. It argues that an unfavorable international environment will combine with the weakened state to overwhelm the radical's fragile institutions (even if they are the "right" ones) and that economic crises will shore up the political power of opponents of reform to create unstable democracies and weak economies. This "dark" side of the radical scenario assumes the role of the state as being the agent of foreign interests, and as such it is denied both autonomy and legitimacy. Without strong states directing the project of *economic* liberalization, the gradualist argues, former communist regimes will not be able to attract the capital needed for development; and without an infusion of capital, these countries will become low-wage "Third World" raw materials suppliers and export platforms for the European Community's industrial machine. In order to participate in the international economy, weak regimes will undervalue national currencies, leading to a comparative advantage in low-skill, labor-intensive goods. To the extent that foreign direct investment flows into the region, it will be attracted by low-cost labor and will concentrate in labor-intensive production methods across the industrial spectrum. In modern sectors, plants in these countries might be simply "screwdriver factories"—assembling final products, importing key components, and using few local suppliers. Other foreign investments might be in "services"—sales, marketing, and distribution outlets for imports produced in the West. Alternatively, as Berend points out, investments will flow to low-technology extractive sectors, such as oil and mining. Indeed, this is the dominant form of investment in Russia today (Crawford, 1993). All innovative activity would be concentrated in the West, and competition with the less-developed countries of the EC would impede rapid acceptance of these countries into the Community. Under this scenario, prospects for rapid economic development are bleak. Growth will continue to decline, thus undermining support for liberalizers. Because weak democracies create their own systems of patronage, state funds are squandered.

With massive debt problems brought on by unfavorable terms of trade, high income inequality, and halting or even stalled development, the fate of Central and Eastern Europe could be that of many Third World countries—the periphery or semiperiphery—weak states with weak economies providing commodities and light manufactured goods to the EC and the rest of the world. The income gap between East and West will contribute to a condition of chronic political instability, weakening democratic regimes because populations experience a sense of relative deprivation that further undermines the legitimacy of their democratically elected governments. Highly visible social and income inequalities lead to intermittent political crises and mass migration to the West.

In this scenario, then, international constraints weaken post-communist economies, which, in turn, weakens liberalizing politicians. These two factors mitigate the effects of reform intended to wipe out the social legacies of the past. Although partial reforms are implemented and aspects of polyarchy exist, instability and poverty characterize the region, meaning that liberalization succeeds in some areas and fails in others; in the absence of strong states and a favorable international environment, liberalization is weakened and cannot lead to strong democracy and market-led development.

The Gradualist Hope: State-Led Development and Consolidated Democracy

The gradualist hypothesis is that a combination of strong state guidance and gradual reforms will weaken past legacies and direct international forces in such a way that stable democracy and economic development will be the outcome. Assuming that "peripheralization" will result from both the radical approach to liberalization and the pressures imposed by the international environment, the gradualist hypothesis asserts that "late developers" require real state capacity and a large role for the state to mobilize and educate their societies as well as to protect them from the worst consequences of the market. If "unfettered" market forces direct investment, they will squelch the ability of nations-in-transition to compete and do so at great social cost. Thus, interventionist states must provide side payments to those who shoulder the costs of economic liberalization; side payments create social support for an interventionist state.

In the successful gradualist scenario, open, liberal, but still "strong" states direct development and provide a social infrastructure to ensure mobilized political support for economic success. This is the scenario that one associates with modern post-war democracies in Western Europe. It is the model of the extensive welfare state with corporatist interest representation—that is, peak-level negotiations between capital, labor, and the state; the hoped-for result in this model is economic growth that leaves room for profits and redistribution and ensures harmonious labor relations. Growth with a just resource distribution is assured, and liberal democracy is strengthened. Berend argues in his contribution to this volume that variations on this scenario were the hope of "reformers and uncompromising opposition leaders who gathered around the cradle of the newly born system" after the revolutions of 1989." These political elites dreamed of worker self-management, Scandinavian Socialism, and "Sozialpartnerschaft," or a mix of the Austrian and South Korean systems.

Failure to Liberalize and the Return to Despotism

This scenario presents the "dark" side of gradualism. Its central hypothesis is that weak states and an unfavorable international environment will permit past legacies to sustain the opponents of liberalization, leading reform governments to fall. Structures of patronage will be kept intact, blocking incentives to divest the state of its assets. Failure will result in a return to despotic and predatory rule with the support of rent-seeking industrial elites and even labor, who exchange their support for state subsidies, contracts, licenses, and public employment. Fragile democracies will be destroyed and prospects for economic growth will decline even further. This scenario, therefore, assumes the failure of both the radical and the gradualist alternatives because weak states can be cannibalized by rent-seeking groups, undermining support for liberalizers who are then unable either to pull these countries out of economic crisis or to destroy the old political culture.

Thus, the scenario predicts the collapse of the project of liberalizing former communist regimes. Predatory despotism emerges from the failure of *liberal* democracy, and authoritarian rulers seize power and direct the project of economic change. Political loyalty rather than technical expertise becomes the basis for employment in the state bureaucracy; thus, there is little chance for a developmental state to emerge. Political elites preserve as much of the original social structure as possible, and the old political culture remains undisturbed. These elites refuse to liberalize the economy, because the redistribution of wealth undermines their ability to exchange favors for support. The rulers also are tempted to sever their domestic economies from the international economic system, because successful participation in the international economy demands technical skills rather than political loyalty, and the freedom of movement and information. Despotic rulers suppress technical elites in favor of maintaining their own political power base. All Western capital is withdrawn, and development is further impeded.

This final scenario differs from the peripheralization outcome—the second scenario—in that all pretense of democratic institutions is abandoned. In the second scenario, a "democratic"—not a liberal democratic—legislature persists with a weak president, and legislators plunder the state treasury to maintain the support of powerful social groups. The institutions of polyarchy must be preserved to maintain links to international lending institutions and meet their political conditionality requirements. In this final scenario, however, democratic institutions are completely abandoned. What O'Donnell (1992) refers to as "delegative democracy" emerges. Under this system, the winner of a presidential election governs as he sees fit, ignoring the constitution and abolishing other democratic institutions. Because the party system is weak and undeveloped, his political base is a mass social "movement" rather than a political party.

Conclusions and Prospects

Which of these scenarios is most likely to correspond to the emerging reality of post-communist transformation? Of course, each represents an ideal type, and reality is always messier than the neat predictions of social scientists. Post-communist regions must be differentiated: some regions will successfully liberalize and others will not. Further, what I have presented in this chapter is a conceptual framework rather than a theory of change. Therefore, the reader will find no mechanism in these pages that would help predict one outcome over others. Nonetheless, my argument in this chapter has been that the interaction of trends in four arenas—the strength or weakness of social legacies, the strength and role of the state, the constraints and incentives of the international environment, and alternative policy choices—will shape future outcomes.

Anecdotal evidence suggests that the first scenario—the radical utopia—is unlikely to emerge in most of the post-communist world for two reasons: the emergence of an unfavorable global environment and the weakness of the state in the region. When these two conditions hold, reform governments are neither able to buffer themselves from opposition nor, because of insufficient resources, to offer side payments for cooperation with reformers. For those countries that *are* able to attract aid and investment and in which international institutions augment and support the state in strengthening liberal reforms, success is possible. For those regions partially integrated into the international economy but unable to compete and unable to shore up state capacity, the second scenario—the emergence of a post-communist global "periphery"—is the likely outcome.

The conditionality requirements of international lending institutions are likely to perpetuate the circumstances that lead to this peripheralization but that prevent the conditions that would lead to the fourth scenario—a return to despotism. The Commission of the European Communities was given the authority to direct and oversee bilateral assistance to Eastern Europe from EC members. In order to receive that assistance, recipients were required "to have pluralistic political systems with no institutionally favored party, to make rapid movement toward free-market economies, to have free labor unions, and to demonstrate respect for human rights" (United States Government Accounting Office, 1990). Similarly, the EBRD requires that recipient countries apply the principles of multiparty democracy. Liberalizers in power who wish to maintain their links to these institutions might prevent their countries from falling into despotism, but their nations may nevertheless remain on the periphery.

The third gradualist scenario—the emergence of "infrastructurally powerful" welfare states modeled on those of Western Europe—is unlikely for two reasons: First, it is coming less and less to characterize the political economy of *Western* Europe, as low rates of growth and increasing international competition have undermined corporatist interest representation. Because knowledge-based production demands freer labor markets, West European governments have begun to dismantle union power and to support corporations in their efforts to reorganize the workplace in order to create firm-level loyalties that undermine union commitments (Ross, 1991). Corporatist decisionmaking has given way to reliance on technical elites.

Secondly, this scenario describes already functioning market economies in a period of rapid economic growth but is inappropriate for former communist regimes in transition under conditions of economic crisis. This scenario is based on the assumption of a strong state and a growing economy. Those East European liberalizers whose strategies succeed in the liberalization process may evolve in this direction; that is, they may be able to buffer themselves from opposition *and* offer side payments. But that process will probably be far down the road.

Recent problems faced by Bulgaria underscore this point. The post-communist Bulgarian government had established a Tripartite Commission with the participation of business, labor, and the state to discuss major economic and social issues emerging in the reform process. Although dependent on a coalition of parties for support, the ruling Union of Democratic Forces (UDF) was ideologically opposed to this "corporatist" practice and disbanded the commission. The result was a series of major strikes, crippling the economy, and a deterioration of relations between business groups and the government. Not only was a corporatist solution not viable under the liberal orthodoxy, but the breakdown of corporatist practice weakened the state (Engelbrekt, 1992).

The final scenario—a return to despotism—is most likely in regions where economic crises deepen, where few links to international institutions exist, and where anti-Western political forces dominate. Here, in the absence of international constraints such as political conditionality requirements and the drive on the part of political elites to build liberal institutions, legacies of the past are most likely to persist—and these social legacies will be used by opponents of liberalization to shape the political and economic future.

Finally, what do post-communist transformations tell us about the sequencing and simultaneity of economic and political liberalization? First, some fragile democracies may be taken over by authoritarian rulers who attempt to push through economic reform (Ukraine may be an example). But most regimes that maintain democratic institutions will be able to initiate economic reforms if the regimes insulate reformers from social pressures, if the reforms themselves remove the economic and social power base of the opponents of liberalization, and if the reformers are able to make side payments to the losers. The most important initial danger to economic and political liberalization arises from the incomplete process of nation-building where incentives are created for ethnic and sectarian conflict. This conflict defeats the liberalization project.

As Janos emphasizes in his chapter, the long-term prospects for stable economic and political liberalization, of course, depend on the conditions that foster or undermine economic growth. For Janos, a necessary condition for growth is a favorable international environment—meaning a more assertive Western hegemony. A second condition might be the guidance of a strong state. In the absence of these conditions, post-communist societies will have difficulty moving in the direction of the liberal ideal. As Janos argues, the failure of market reforms or the rise of restorationist challenges to the West will favor various forms of national radicalism. These conditions might even favor the rise of a post-Leninist international entity that justifies its existence as an alliance of nations victimized by Western cultural and economic aggression.

Notes

1. Ellen Comisso made this point in remarks at the Southern California Workshop on Political and Economic Liberalization held at the University of Southern California Center for International Affairs, Los Angeles, California, November 23, 1992. Nonetheless, a snapshot of the Ukraine at the end of 1992 might illustrate the publicly stated exception. Leonid Kuchma, the Ukrainian prime minister, expressed few reservations about using state intervention to secure his economic goals so as to avert potential economic collapse. His program included efforts to balance the budget, the lifting of price controls, tight control over credit and money supply, and a program of "forced" privatization. To implement his economic program—considered "radical" by previous Ukrainian standards—he hinted at limiting the right to strike and the freedom of political parties. See Chrystia Freeland, "A Very Ukrainian Reformist," the *Financial Times,* November 17, 1992, p. 2; Edward Balls and Chrystia Freeland, "Ukraine on Radical Road," *Financial Times,* December 2, 1992, p. 8.

2. Note the following quote from a member of Ukraine's Party of Democratic Birth, now part of an opposition coalition called New Ukraine: "What is at issue is the difference be-

tween the emphasis on the individual and his rights on the one hand, and on the nation and national independence as the highest goal on the other." Quoted in Abraham Brumberg, "Not So Free at Last," the *New York Review of Books*, October 22, 1992, p. 61.

3. For example, 45 percent of all metalworking equipment in the Soviet Union was produced in non-machine-building enterprises, and 84 percent of machine-building enterprises produced their own forgings; 65 percent produced their own metal hardware; and 76 percent produced their own stock. See "The Best of All Monopoly Profits" in the *Economist*, August 11, 1990, p. 67.

4. This is particularly the case when markets are underdeveloped. In market economies, opposition is more likely to be directed against the employer than against the state.

5. Although the EC agreed in 1991 to a gradual process of trade liberalization vis-à-vis Poland, Hungary, the Czech Republic, and Slovakia, to be completed within a five-year period, sensitive sectors like agriculture were omitted from the agreement. In November 1992, for example, the EC imposed antidumping duties on steel imported from Croatia, Poland, Czechoslovakia, and Hungary. See "Dumping Duties Anger Eastern Europe," the *Financial Times*, November 20, 1992. See also Richard W. Stevenson, "East Europe Says Barriers to Trade Hurt Its Economies," the *New York Times*, January 25, 1993, pp. A1 and C8.

6. An alternative version of gradualism is that discussed at the beginning of this chapter: the sequencing of economic and political liberalization so that markets are created under authoritarian regimes and democracy is gradually introduced later. As noted at the outset, this version of gradualism is not generally politically feasible in most post-communist societies and not considered legitimate in most scholarly discourse on post-communist transformation. Nonetheless, as the above example of Ukraine and as trends in other post-Soviet regions illustrate, authoritarian regimes may indeed emerge to push through market reforms.

References

Akerlof, George; Andrew Rose; Janet Yellen; and Helga Hessenius. 1991. "East Germany in from the Cold: The Economic Aftermath of Currency Union." *Brookings Papers on Economic Activity* 1: 67.

Aslund, Anders. 1989. *Gorbachev's Struggle for Economic Reform*. Ithaca: Cornell University Press.

Borhi, Laszlo. 1993. "East European Security in the Post-Bipolar System." In *European Dilemmas After Maastricht*, Beverly Crawford and Peter W. Schulze, eds., 263–272. Berkeley: International and Area Studies.

Buchanan, James M., and Robert D. Tollison, eds. 1972. *Theory of Public Choice: Political Application of Economics*. Ann Arbor: University of Michigan Press.

Burawoy, Michael, and Pavel Krotov. 1992. "The Soviet Transition from Socialism to Capitalism: Worker Control and Economic Bargaining in the Wood Industry." *American Sociological Review* 57 (February): 16–38.

Chirot, Daniel, ed. 1989. *The Origins of Backwardness in Eastern Europe: Economics and Politics from the Middle Ages Until the Early Twentieth Century*. Berkeley: University of California Press.

______. 1990. "What Happened in Eastern Europe in 1989?" In *The Crisis of Leninism and the Decline of the Left: The Revolutions of 1989,* edited by Daniel Chirot, 3–32. Seattle: University of Washington Press.

Comisso, Ellen. 1991. "Property Rights, Liberalism, and the Transition from 'Actually Existing' Socialism." *East European Politics and Society* 5 (Winter): 162–163.

Crawford, Beverly. 1993. *Economic Vulnerability in International Relations: East-West Trade, Investment and Finance.* New York: Columbia University Press.

Cutts, Robert L. 1991. "Eastern Europe's Troubles Open Door for Japanese Expansion." *California Management Review* 33, no. 3 (Spring): 58–72.

Dahl, Robert. 1990. *Democracy and Its Critics.* New Haven: Yale University Press.

ECOTASS. 1990. April 9: 20.

Engelbrekt, Kjell. 1992. "The Fall of Bulgaria's First Noncommunist Government." *Radio Free Europe/Radio Liberty Research Report* no. 45, November.

Evans, Peter. 1992. "The State as Problem and Solution: Predation, Embedded Autonomy, and Structural Change." In *The Politics of Economic Adjustment,* Stephan Haggard and Robert Kaufman, eds., 139–181. Princeton: Princeton University Press.

Fishlow, Albert. 1990. "The Latin American State." *Journal of Economic Perspectives* 4, no. 3: 61–74.

Fukuyama, Francis. 1989. "The End of History." *The National Interest* 16 (Summer): 3–18.

Gati, Charles. 1991. "East-Central Europe: The Morning After," *Foreign Affairs* (Winter): 129–145.

Geddes, Barbara. 1991. "Political Institutions and Economic Policy or How Politicians Decide Who Bears the Costs of Structural Adjustment." Paper presented at the American Political Science Association meetings, Washington, D.C., September.

Gerschenkron, Alexander. 1962. *Economic Backwardness in Historical Perspective.* Cambridge: Belknap Press of Harvard University.

Haas, Ernst B. 1986. "What Is Nationalism and Why Should We Study It?" *International Organization* 40, no. 3: 709.

Haggard, Stephan, and Robert Kaufman. 1992. "Economic Adjustment and the Prospects for Democracy." In *The Politics of Economic Adjustment,* Stephan Haggard and Robert Kaufman, eds., 319–350. Princeton: Princeton University Press.

Hall, John A. 1987. "Classical Liberalism and the Modern State." *Daedalus* 116, no. 3: 95–118.

Herz, John. 1982. *From Dictatorship to Democracy.* Westport, Conn.: Greenwood Press.

Hewett, E. A. 1988. *Reforming the Soviet Economy.* Washington, D.C.: The Brookings Institution.

Holmes, Stephen. 1991. "The Liberal Idea." *The American Prospect* (Fall): 84.

Huntington, Samuel P. 1984. "Will More Countries Become Democratic?" *Political Science Quarterly* 99, no. 2: 193–218.

Janos, Andrew C. 1991. "Social Science, Communism, and the Dynamics of Political Change." *World Politics* 44, no. 1: 81–112.

Johnson, Chalmers. 1988. "The Democratization of South Korea: What Role Does Economic Development Play?" Paper presented at the Second Ilhae-Carnegie Conference on Democracy and Political Institutions, The Ilhae Institute, Seoul, Korea, July 8–9.

Jowitt, Ken. 1992. *New World Disorder: The Leninist Extinction.* Berkeley: University of California Press.

Junz, Helen B. 1991. "Integration of Eastern Europe into the World Trading System." *American Economic Association Papers and Proceedings* 81, no. 2 (May): 176–180.
Laitin, David D. 1985. "Hegemony and Religious Conflict: British Imperial Control and Political Cleavages in Yorubaland." In *Bringing the State Back In,* Peter B. Evans, Dietrich Rueschemeyer, and Theda Skocpol, eds., 285–317. New York: Cambridge University Press.
Lenway, Stephanie; Catherine Mann; and Derek Utter. 1993. "Political and Economic Consequences of Alternative Privatization Schemes." University of California Center for German and European Studies (Working Paper no. 5.14), June.
Lipton, David, and Jeffrey Sachs. 1990. "Creating a Market Economy in Eastern Europe: The Case of Poland." *Brookings Papers on Economic Activity* 1: 87.
Mann, Catherine. 1991. "Industry Restructuring in East-Central Europe: The Challenge and Role for Foreign Investment." *American Economic Association Papers and Proceedings.* May: 181–184.
Marsh, Virginia. 1992. "Bucharest Steps Back from a Market Economy." *Financial Times* (December 8): 8.
Nove, Alec. 1992. "Economics of the Transition Period." *The Harriman Institute Forum* 5, (July-August): 10.
O'Donnell, Guillermo. 1992. "On the State, Various Crises, and Problematic Democratizations." Paper presented at the Social Science Research Council Conference on Economic Liberalization and Democratic Consolidation, University of Bologna, Forli, April 2–4.
Okolicsanyi, Karoly. 1992. "The EBRD's First Year." *Radio Free Europe/Radio Liberty Research Report* No. 23, June 5.
Olson, Mancur. 1982. *The Rise and Decline of Nations.* New Haven: Yale University Press.
Plestina, Dijana. 1992. *Regional Development in Communist Yugoslavia: Success, Failure, and Consequences.* Boulder: Westview Press.
Poznanski, Kazimierz. 1992. "Market Alternative to State Activism in Restoring the Capitalist Economy." *Economics of Planning* 25: 55–77.
Przeworski, Adam. 1991. *Democracy and the Market: Political and Economic Reforms in Eastern Europe and Latin America.* Cambridge: Cambridge University Press.
Remmer, Karen. 1990. "Democracy and Economic Crises: The Latin American Experience." *World Politics* 42, no. 3: 321.
Ross, George. 1991. "Turning Technocratic: Euro-Socialists and 1992." In *Socialist Review* 21, no. 2: 133–157.
Ruggie, John G. 1982. "International Regimes, Transactions, and Change: Embedded Liberalism in the Postwar Economic Order." *International Organization* 36 (Spring): 379–416.
Rustow, Dankwart. 1970. "Transitions to Democracy." *Comparative Politics* 2, no. 3: 337–363.
Schattschneider, E. E. 1963. *Politics, Pressures, and the Tariff: A Study of Free Private Enterprise in Pressure Politics as Shown in the 1929–1930 Revision of the Tariff.* Hamden, Conn.: Archon Books.
Stark, David. 1990. "Privatization in Hungary: From Plan to Market or From Plan to Clan?" *East European Politics and Society* 4, no. 3, 351–392.
Stigler, George. 1975. *The Citizen and the State: Essays on Regulation.* Chicago: University of Chicago Press.

Szelenyi, Ivan, and Szonja Szelenyi. 1993. "Changes in Social Structure in Eastern Europe in the Transition to Post-Communism." Paper presented at the Social Science Research Council Conference on Reconfiguring State and Society: Social and Political Consequences of Liberalization in Comparative Perspective, University of California at Berkeley, April 22–24.

United States Government Accounting Office. 1990. *Eastern Europe: Donor Assistance and Reform Efforts*. Washington, D.C.: U.S. Government Printing Office: 21.

Van Brabant, Jozef M. 1991. "A Central European Payments Union: Technical Aspects." *Public Policy Paper 3*. New York: Institute for East-West Security Studies.

Waterbury, John. 1992. "The Heart of the Matter? Public Enterprise and the Adjustment Process." In *The Politics of Economic Adjustment*, Stephan Haggard and Robert Kaufman, eds., 182–217. Princeton: Princeton University Press.

Wedel, Janin R. 1992. "The Unintended Consequences of Western Aid to Post-Communist Europe." *Telos* 92 (Summer): 131–138.

2

National Liberations and Nationalist Nightmares: The Consequences of the End of Empires in the Twentieth Century

DANIEL CHIROT

Political and economic changes in post-communist societies cannot be analyzed without first looking at the legacies left by the past. In this chapter, I argue that those who claim that the end of the Soviet Empire will produce liberal societies make too many assumptions about the shared cultural legacies between Eastern and Western Europe. Nationalism, which has been a force of liberalization in the West will not necessarily be such a force in the East. A careful look at the comparative historical development of nationalism between Eastern and Western Europe reveals that in an illiberal context, nationalism, like many other apparantly familiar institutions, actually does nothing to advance the cause of liberalization.

Most—by some definitions, all—of the great empires that dominated the majority of the world in the early twentieth century have now broken apart. Some of those were obviously marked for decay at the start of the twentieth century. The Ottoman and Habsburg Austro-Hungarian Empires were thought to be fragile entities in 1900, and indeed they were. But others were vigorous and in many cases still growing. After the Japanese Empire defeated Russia in 1905, it seemed destined for greater glories. The British Empire was secure and had greatly expanded its size in the last two decades of the nineteenth century. The lesser European empires, most notably the French but also the Belgian, Dutch, Portuguese, and Spanish, were rounding out their territories in Africa and Asia. Germany was expanding overseas. Russia, despite its weaknesses, also was still growing and it commanded immense resources and territories. The United States was creating a Central American, Caribbean, and Pacific Empire.

What a surprise the twentieth century has been! After World War I, the expected happened: The weakest of the great empires fell apart. But after World War II, it was the turn of the victorious European empires to be dissolved, and with a few exceptions, this took place in a mere two decades, though the Portuguese held out for three. By 1975, the only remaining old-fashioned European empire, ruling vast domains inhabited by peoples of different languages and cultures, was the Russian one.

In part, this was because its imperial ideology had been rejuvenated by communism. The fact that the foreign people who fell under Russian rule were next door to the Russians helped. Also, by not being open to the pressures of democracy, the Russians could simply pay the growing cost of keeping unwilling people subjugated without having to face the consequences. Finally, by not having a market economy that properly priced costs and weighed benefits, the managers of the Soviet Union had little way of telling whether their empire actually brought them more benefits than costs.[1] Within the USSR, Russia was increasingly subsidizing inefficiency and corruption to maintain control. This is one reason why despite the naïve hopes of many former Soviet dependencies, both within and outside the old USSR, the road to economic recovery is tougher than anticipated. The Russian subsidies are gone, but the grossly wasteful structures and the crooked officials remain, masquerading as born-again nationalists.[2]

Whatever the benefits of imperialism may have been in the more distant past, the great empires accumulated in the last imperialist scramble in the late-nineteenth century were not paying propositions. Some individuals and companies, to be sure, made money; but for imperial countries as a whole, the balance was almost certainly negative. Eric Hobsbawm, perhaps the most balanced and careful of the eminent Marxist historians of the second half of the twentieth century, elegantly sidestepped the issue of why it was that imperialism was all the rage from the 1870s to the 1910s if it actually yielded such small benefits. In his recent history of *The Age of Empire*, he recognizes that it is impossible to prove that there were net economic gains, but after all, if there were not, why were so many sure that there were? In other words, though he cannot prove that imperialism was economically rational, he does not want to abandon this central postulate of Marxist theory entirely.[3] The problem with that approach, which tries to salvage what was once the accepted Marxist dogma but now looks increasingly fragile, is that it obscures the real cause of the frenetic imperialism of that time—the intellectual climate that was driving European politics.

In the second half of the nineteenth century, European nationalism combined with a growing sense that human history was really a Darwinian struggle between strong and weak societies. By the 1890s, almost all the significant European powers were in a desperate race for empire because they believed that strong biological entities expanded while weak ones shrank.[4] The weak were to be conquered; the strong would survive because they were the fittest. Petty calculations about costs and benefits were irrelevant. The German view on this was expressed this way:

> Every virile people has established colonial power. ... All real nations in the fulness of their strength have desired to set their mark upon barbarian lands and those who fail to participate in this great rivalry will play a pitiable role in time to come. The colonizing impulse has become a vital question for every great nation.[5]

Later, Marxists, who could never quite bring themselves to believe that ideas can be so powerful, spent a century trying to find economic rationales for what was really an important ideological rather than an economic shift. But to be fair to Hobsbawm, he recognizes the power of the ideology, too, though he insists that it was only a "metaphor."[6]

The capitalist democracies discovered in about the middle of the twentieth century that once the natives learned enough about European arms and organizing techniques to fight back, imperialism was far too costly a proposition to sustain. By then, also, after the two world wars and Nazism, Darwinian theories of human history were considerably less popular. As far as economic benefits went, what valuable raw materials the colonies had could always be purchased; and the markets offered by the wretchedly poor colonies of Africa and Asia were meager compared to what could be purchased by the ever more prosperous rich parts of the world. So the colonies were abandoned, more or less, to their own fates. Aid and military intervention has continued in some cases until now, but at a diminishing rate. The United States will no longer subsidize Philippine corruption in order to maintain bases, and even the French are less eager to prop up client regimes in Africa than they were until recently.

Now, too, the Russians have joined the rest of Europe in abandoning their empire. The profits were never very great, and it was only their dogged adherence to outdated nineteenth-century models that made them so slow to notice.[7] It seems that societies are made strong by their scientific and technological skills, by efficient infrastructures, and by plunging into the world market to buy and sell according to rational market criteria rather than political ones. If so, then that late-nineteenth-century vision of empires as being the essential bedrock on which every dynamic society must rest can be tossed out.

So, now that the end of the age of imperialism is upon us, can we expect a more rational, more peaceful, more benign, and a much freer world? This was not just George Bush's vision of a "new world order," but a much older vision of Herbert Spencer's. Though he failed to see that his prediction would be sidetracked by the Darwinism he himself so admired, now that our misdirected century of imperialism is over, perhaps Spencer's theory can be proved right. As he put it:

> With the absence of need for that corporate action by which the efforts of the whole society may be utilized for war, there goes the absence of need for a despotic controlling agency. Not only is such an agency unnecessary, but it cannot exist. For since, as we see, it is an essential requirement of the industrial type, that the individuality of each man shall have the fullest play compatible with the like play of other men's individualities, despotic control, showing itself as it must by otherwise restricting men's individualities, is necessarily excluded. Indeed, by his mere presence an autocratic ruler is an aggressor on citizens.[8]

The end of the age of imperialism, then, will also put an end to war, and that, in turn, can finally bring to fruition the promises of democratic capitalism.

This may indeed be how future historians will look at the revolutions in the communist world from 1989 to 1991, as the last part of a long learning process that taught the world the folly of aggressive imperialism. First, these historians might conclude, the European capitalist powers had to learn how fruitless it was to wage imperialist wars of conquest. The hard lessons of 1914–1918 and 1939–1945, especially for Germany, were followed by the pitiful European rearguard actions against decolonization in Asia and Africa. These taught the West Europeans once and for all that in this respect they had all been making a mistake. The Americans learned this, too, in Vietnam, and the Russians in Afghanistan and Eastern Europe. The Japanese had learned it earlier from their long struggle to conquer China and Southeast Asia, which ended with the disaster of 1945. With the end of imperialism, everyone can concentrate on trade and manufacturing, governments can begin to disarm, and liberty can prevail.

Perhaps so. But there are some disturbing elements to all this, and they were made clear from the very start of the wave of imperial dissolutions after World War I. In some measure, the negative consequences of the liberation of so many societies formerly bound into great multi-ethnic, multicultural empires have themselves contributed to the failure of social life to move into the peaceful, democratic, liberal paths that Spencer thought so natural. It is not just because it took so long for old imperial structures to collapse that the twentieth century has been such a nightmare, or that so many Europeans were oddly enamored of a Darwinian vision of human history, but that the very liberation struggles against empires have been infected by the same ideas that created modern imperialism to begin with. Thus, as old empires have disintegrated, they have spread their poison to the new political entities that have succeeded them. If the old centers of imperialism, Western Europe, the United States, and Japan have learned their lesson, it is not evident that the rest of the world has absorbed the same lessons. It may be that the great, revolutionary liberations of the twentieth century—from the creation of newly independent states in Central Europe after 1918 to the enormous proliferation of new states in Africa and Asia from the 1940s to the 1970s and the equally impressive creation of yet more new states since 1991 in the former communist world—all point to something quite different than the hoped-for order of Spencerian harmony and peace.

The Collapse of Empires in the Twentieth Century

Until the late-nineteenth-century, fallen empires were not replaced by entities that claimed to be nations. Conflicts were always a part of imperial collapses; however, more recently, dying empires have left behind something new—very angry legacies of competing nationalisms.

This is quite obvious with the Ottoman Empire. Taking a quick look at the borderlands of that empire can only cause wonderment about the role it may have played in leaving behind such bitterness. Along the old northeastern boundary of the empire are the Caucasus Mountains, now the home of several ethnic wars, largely between various Christian and Muslim populations. Of course, as John Armstrong has pointed out, the great, long, jagged faultline—where Muslims and Christians have met, fought, and intermixed—has been a source of unending conflict for centuries.[9] But the severity of ethnic conflict increased sharply with the first massacres of Armenians in 1895–96 and again during World War I, when it became clear that the physical annihilation of a whole people had become a possible outcome of such rivalries. Now the Armenian-Azeri conflict in the Caucasus is one of the most destructive and bitter in the former Soviet Union.[10]

Not far from the Armenian situation, there is Kurdistan, involved in multiple and overlapping conflicts with Turks, Arabs, and Persians since the end of World War I. Though the Kurds were themselves major actors in perpetrating the Armenian massacres, they have become the victims since then. Further to the southeast, the disputes between Sunnis and Shi'ites in Iraq, the terrible border war between Iraq and Iran in the 1980s, and the recent contest over the status of Kuwait might be interpreted as something other than purely ethnic disputes, but they certainly represent wars between conflicting nationalisms that are far from being resolved and that have only intensified since the collapse of Ottoman power in 1918. Then, further west, there is the Israeli-Palestinian conflict. There are also Lebanon and Syria, both of them the scene of long, bloody contests between various groups of Christians, Muslims, Druzes, and Alawites. These antagonisms were present by late Ottoman times but have only grown worse with time.[11]

In the former western Ottoman borderlands are the Balkans. Aside from the fighting between Serbs, Croats, Bosnians, and Albanians and the unresolved Macedonian situation in the former Yugoslavia, there remains the looming possibility of a Turkish-Greek war, which was only narrowly avoided in 1974 over the Cyprus issue. Nor is Bulgaria, with its own splits between Muslims and Christians and its late-nineteenth-century claims to adjoining territories, immune from trouble.[12]

Is all this trouble due to something the Ottomans did, mixing together different religious and linguistic communities and setting them against each other? In former Yugoslavia, the tendency is to blame Tito and the communists or ancient historical conflicts rather than the Ottomans. And who can blame the Ottoman Empire for the Israeli-Arab conflict or for the many nationalist rivalries within the Arab world itself? But if the Ottoman legacy were unique, or even unusual, it would still be useful to consider that this empire had a particularly baleful effect. There is no evidence of this at all.

In the twentieth century, Transylvania has been the scene of one of the Balkans' most intractable ethnic-nationalist rivalries between Magyars and Romanians, and this area was part of the Habsburg Empire from 1699 to 1918. As we know perfectly well, the collapse of the Austro-Hungarian monarchy left behind Slovak-Czech, Italian–South Slav, Sudeten German–Czech, and many other ethnic-religious conflicts, not the least of which were anti-Semitisms of various strengths and widespread anti-Gypsy sentiments. These conflicts all began before the fall of the Habsburgs, though they intensified and in many cases became serious only in the second half of the nineteenth century. Many of these conflicts are not necessarily "age-old," as they have been portrayed by some nationalist historians from these regions or by the contemporary press. Croat-Serb hostility, for example, is actually neither ancient nor of Ottoman origin but began in late Austria-Hungary. As Ivo Banac has demonstrated, it really became full blown only with the fall of the Habsburg Empire in 1918 and the creation of Yugoslavia.[13] Moreover, it became genocidal only during World War II under German prompting.

It is easy to show that the pattern extends much further than the Ottoman and Habsburg cases. The great Indian Empire abandoned by the British in 1947 contains as long a list of conflicts as any part of the world. Many of these conflicts are not only bitter but are getting worse as the twentieth century draws to a close. From Burma to Kashmir, from the Afghan borderlands to the Tamils in the south, the old British Indian Empire is a bloody mess. The extraordinarily vicious episode of the Pakistani-Bengali conflict that led to Bangladeshi independence may have cost up to three million lives in the early 1970s.[14] There have been several Indian-Pakistani wars, and there may be more. Both sides now have nuclear weapons. And in Sri Lanka at the southernmost end of the old British domain, there is one of the bloodiest and most intractable civil wars in the world between Tamils and Sinhalese.[15]

The situation is not so different in what were the French, British, Belgian, and Portuguese empires in Africa. Nigeria experienced a civil war in the late 1960s in which over one million people died, and it is still a fragile entity. Sudan, another former British colony, has had more than two million (probably more than three million) deaths because of ethnic and religious civil war since independence. And this conflict seems to be intensifying and spreading. The emergence of a radically fundamentalist Islamic regime in Sudan accentuates the divide between the Christian and animist, black southerners and the Muslim Arab majority in the north.[16] The former Belgium Congo, now Zaire, has had more than its share of troubles, and these are again threatening to tear apart the feeble state. Furthermore, the former Belgian colonies of Rwanda and Burundi have had some of the most savage ethnically inspired massacres in modern times, though these places are so small that they rarely attract the world's attention.[17] Mozambique and Angola, partly because of South African interference (and South Africa itself, that quintessential cauldron of ethnic conflict, is a product of the former British African Empire) and partly for internal reasons, have been in almost permanent civil wars since independence, and much of the problem is due to ethnic conflict. Even the tiny Spanish African Empire, rarely noticed because it was so insignificant, left the bloody Fang-Bubi divide, which, under the rule of the late, self-styled "indefatigable and unique miracle of Equatorial Guinea, president for life Macias Nguema," killed from 5 percent to 10 percent of the population and drove 25 percent more into exile in the 1970s.[18] Then, in the other part of the former Spanish Empire, there is the continuing war between Morocco and the Sarawis over control of the former Spanish Sahara. Finally, in Africa, the collapse of the only African non-European twentieth-century empire, that of Ethiopia, familiar to most of us, has left at least another three million dead in its wake. Nor has the conflict there ended.[19]

In the East Indies, the departure of the Dutch left ethnic conflicts that still simmer in Indonesia, as the Javanese continue to have to fight to impose their will on centers of resistance in Aceh in far western Sumatra, former Portuguese Timor, and the highlands of New Guinea in the Far East.[20]

And now, as if to confirm the rule that modern empires do not collapse gracefully, we are seeing a whole new set of tragedies being prepared in the Soviet-Russian Empire as adjoining and often intermixed nationalities, ethnicities, and religious communities struggle with each other over the spoils of the last of the great modern empires to die. Aside from the Caucasus region, there are a host of potential wars in Central Asia, conflicts between Romanians and Slavs in what used to be called Bessarabia, and the great, looming potential of an eventual war between Russians, Ukrainians, and White Russians over borders that make no intrinsic ethnic, economic, or geographic sense. These conflicts will most certainly continue well into the next century, and at least some of them will grow to be much worse than anything we have witnessed so far in the former Soviet Union.

Having briefly looked at the disorders left by other collapsed empires, let's return to the Ottomans and Habsburgs. Are they to blame for the chaotic situations that arose following the dissolutions of their empires? Most assuredly, whatever the Ottomans and Habsburgs did was not unique; the British, French, Belgians, Portuguese, Russians, and Ethiopians all did it, too. In general, the prevalence of such conflict in collapsing empires suggests that its causes lie beyond the policies and behavior of any single imperial entity. We are faced by a widespread phenomenon that needs to be explained—otherwise, we have no way of understanding why current, similar post-imperial conflicts in the former communist countries are taking place.

Are There Successful Nation-States?

Before I examine the answer to this question, it would be useful to begin by posing a slightly different one: Are there any parts of the world where the "nation-state" really operates without continual war between competing nationalist claims, either those within a state trying to establish their own, new state, or between neighboring states with irredentist claims? To some extent, though the pattern is hardly perfect, there are substantial parts of Western Europe and of the Americas where there are such things as nation-states that are not being torn apart by antagonistic religious, linguistic, or ethnic competition and that do not have irredentist claims against them. Further, the East Asian states are real nation-states with only minor separatist claims. China, which is about 93 percent Han Chinese, suffers from competing nationalisms only along its old imperial borderlands, chiefly in Tibet and Xinjiang, but not in its heartland. Vietnam, the two Koreas (whose conflict is not in any way ethnic—both Koreas agree there should be only one Korean state), and Japan are quite obviously functioning nation-states. Even Taiwan, politically separate from mainland China, identifies itself as solidly Han Chinese and is well on its way to becoming a true nation-state despite a modern history of considerable tensions between its "old" Chinese immigrants (whose ancestors arrived from the seventeenth to late-nineteenth centuries) and its "new" ones, who came after 1945.

Today, the United States forms a fairly solid nation-state. It was not always so, as a major civil war had to be fought to establish the unity of the nation. Furthermore, given the direction in which it is heading, it may not always be so unified a nation; however, for well over a century the United States has been a success in that respect. A number of Latin American states have also turned into true nation-states, though it took them quite a long time to create unified national cultures after they achieved independence. These states also were fortunate that the Spanish Empire broke up and that Brazil separated from Portugal before the age of modern nationalism. They were allowed to build their own nationalist identities slowly, without having to face existing separatists unwilling to be assimilated. So, it has been possible for some of the new states gradually to absorb and integrate culturally diverse populations and to create a more or less unified sense of nationalism—for example, in Mexico, Brazil, Argentina, and many other countries, even though it would be hard to claim that such a sense existed much before the late-nineteenth century, or in a case like Mexico's, before the revolutionary civil wars of the 1910s.[21] However, in the Andean states of Bolivia and Peru (and probably in Guatemala as well), national consciousness has not unified European and Amerindian populations, certainly not to the degree that this has happened in Mexico.

In contrast to these successes, we know that the attempt to create a unified Canadian nationalism has probably failed, even if, in the end, Quebec remains in the union for pragmatic reasons. It may be that the effort was begun too late because the English in Canada remained too tied to Imperial Britain until well into the second half of the twentieth century.[22]

In Western Europe, Spain, Belgium, and Northern Ireland have serious competing nationalisms within their borders, and even Great Britain, politically unified at least since the late-sixteenth century, still contains Scottish and Welsh nationalist sentiments. In Italy, too, there is a fairly serious and popular secessionist movement in the north, the Lombard Leagues.

Yet in Western Europe, internal nationalist disputes are the exception, not the rule: Only in Northern Ireland and over the Spanish Basque issue is there much violence. Most states are also genuinely unified nations except for very minor peripheral provinces. Aside from the possible exception of Corsica, France is a true nation-state. Neither attempts by a few French intellectuals to re-create Occitanian nationalism nor the limited revival of Breton interest in their Celtic culture has produced major results.[23] In France, as in Germany and most of the other states of the area (including the only truly multilingual working nation in the world, Switzerland), the prevailing type of political entity is the nation-state.

It was, in fact, the West European model—first of all the British, then the French, and later the German and Italian examples—that impressed the rest of the world in the late-nineteenth and early twentieth centuries and provided guidelines of how states ought to be organized.

So, most of Western Europe, some of the Americas (to which I will add the oceanic English settler colonies of Australia and New Zealand, which, without any separatist elements—such as Quebec in Canada—have also become real nation-states), and a small number of East Asian states more or less fit the definition of successful nation-states—that is, governments in relatively secure boundaries ruling populations that agree that they form a nation. Nonetheless, to say this is to highlight one of the great contradictions of the twentieth century. The majority of the world's people have never lived in proper nation-states and still do not, even though that has been the internationally accepted model of what constitutes a legitimate political unit for well over one hundred years. Aside from Western Europe and some of its settler colonies, almost the only other examples of solid nations-states are a few (albeit some very important and large) East Asian nation-states that long ago came to be ruled by culturally unified elites. It was the power of a common Confucian bureaucratic and literary culture that created this sense of unity at the top, if not yet at the grass roots, long before the arrival of European power to East Asia. This elite culture was invented by the Chinese; nevertheless, first in Japan and later in Korea and Vietnam, quasi-national identities developed. Upon these, it proved relatively easy to build united, modern nationalisms after contact with the Europeans.

Everywhere else in the world, solid nation-states are rare. But then, everywhere else—or almost everywhere else—was part of some larger imperial structure at the beginning of the twentieth century.

There is one notable exception, Thailand, which also seems to have succeeded in nation-building and to have unified fairly disparate groups of potentially rival ethnicities, though most of them speak related languages and are Buddhist. This is obviously connected to Thailand's ability to avoid being absorbed by European empires in the nineteenth century, to the Thai elite's success in imitating European state forms, but also to the fact that the French and English took away about half of the Thai monarchy's borderlands, precisely those areas with the largest concentrations of non-Thai peoples. If the British had taken away all of the Malay-Muslim parts of Thailand, instead of just the southernmost part, that country would now be rid of its single major ethnic-religious problem.[24]

On the one hand, perhaps if empires had left behind smaller and more homogeneous independent entities, the empires would not have bequeathed such serious problems. On the other hand, comparing Thailand to Burma, where there is a similar historical legacy and religion but a much more mixed ethnic and religious situation; or looking at many African states or at most of the Balkans, it is obvious that in many cases it would have been almost impossible to disentangle culturally different populations from each other. Moreover, because most of the countries that emerged in these areas were imperial domains ruled by outsiders until the moment of independence, few had even as much time as Thailand to prepare and unite national elites. Furthermore, few national elites had the good sense to restrain their territorial ambitions.

Ethiopia is an interesting example. After World War II, Ethiopia was given former Italian Eritrea, and this was the beginning of Ethiopia's undoing as a potentially solid nation-state. It would have done much better to give up territory instead and remain restricted to its largely Christian highlands.[25]

The Origin of Nationalism and Its Spread

In an excellent book on the origins of European nationalism, Liah Greenfeld has shown that modern European nationalism was invented by the English, with a major contribution from the French. The concept as it is now understood means that all the people, not just a small political elite, in the society ruled by their state form a community that has a right to demand from its members their highest allegiance. In return the state, acting on behalf of the nation, protects the people. The concept is therefore democratic in the sense of being inclusive. Greenfeld explains how the English in early Tudor times were looking for a new definition of who they were at a time when they had a new royal dynasty, an almost entirely new aristocracy, and a new religion. In finding their new identity, they invented nationalism. Greenfeld then traces the expansion of the concept to include all of the English, and its spread to France, where it was at first the possession of the aristocracy and the monarchy. But in France in the late-eighteenth century, and especially with the Revolution of 1789, nationalism was extended to the whole population, too.[26]

Confucian elites in East Asia created the institutional and cultural unity that established the only other really favorable setting outside of Europe or the European settler colonies for the creation of modern nations. So, it is safe to conclude that the idea of the nation is something that was actually invented in one place—Western Europe—or perhaps (in somewhat different forms) in two specific places—the other being Confucian East Asia. The old Fairbank-Reischauer distinction between "culturalism" in East Asia and "nationalism" in Europe is valid enough, because nationalism was meant to apply to masses as well as elites, and culturalism was meant for elites only; yet, the similarities and power of the two sets of ideas are sufficiently alike to be startling. Further, in both cases, elites thought up the idea, though the Confucian intellectuals never included their masses as did the English and French.[27]

Societies in direct contact with and sharing cultural attributes of these two loci of original nationalism could adopt the idea fairly quickly. Its appeal was obvious because it seemed to be the basis of the great powers' strength. Furthermore, what the English and French did came to be viewed in the nineteenth century as the normal way of organizing the state. Yet, for societies not closely resembling the original European model or not prepared for modern nationalism by centuries of cultural integration among elites, practicing nationalism as the English and French did was much harder than just adopting the idea. Even in Europe itself, as the concept spread it retained the inclusive definition of the nation as "all the people," but those adopting the concept were much slower to conclude from this definition that the nation as a whole, rather than just the self-appointed elite, had the right to determine its political future.

That is the heart of the problem. Elites everywhere want to create strong states in which their nations can reside. Elites also are willing to lead their people into battle in order to achieve this end. But when these leaders try to impose their definition of what the nation-state's boundaries should be, fierce competitors who are as determined as those in power are to create their own, quite different nation-states emerge in opposition. Without a long period of preparation, at least at the level of elites, and without a preexisting sense of unity, attempts to impose cultural uniformity quickly by one group only frighten and alienate other groups. And since the idea of nationalism as the birthright of every people has become widespread, resistance to nationalism imposed by others is much fiercer today than when the idea was less prevalent.

Nationalism is not just a matter of jobs in the civil service, of discrimination against those who are not part of the "true nation," or of competition over scarce economic resources, though all these factor in. It is a problem of basic identity. Once seized by the idea, nationalist elites come to believe that they have a historical right to establish their nation as a sovereign entity. This they can do by proving through pseudo histories that theirs is a nation that was and is destined to be great. It may be submerged for the time being, but the nation will regain its rightful place. That is the basis of what Benedict Anderson meant by "imagined communities," though his version is rather more benign than the reality in most cases.[28]

Without trying to speculate why it is that the cultural preconditions of nationalism developed first in two widely separated parts of the globe, and without trying to trace all the developments associated with the birth of nationalism in these two loci, one more striking fact needs to be emphasized. Whatever the causal connections (and logic would suggest that there must be some very complex ones), it is precisely in that part of the world that invented nationalism that the Industrial Revolution occurred. The modern nation-states of England and France, then other Western European powers and the United States experienced the most rapid economic development and became the great, imitated powers of the globe. Further, of the non-European parts of the world, it was the East Asian Confucian states, with long traditions of highly developed literacy, unified bureaucratic cultures, and relatively efficient government that have adapted best to the exigencies of modern economic and political change in the twentieth century. Ezra Vogel's new book about the "four little dragons" explains why those Confucian societies that managed to escape communism have all been outstanding economic successes in the latter part of the twentieth century; and his book about Guangdong shows that those parts of communist China that have been allowed to develop private agriculture and industry are undergoing a similar economic boom. No doubt these successes have further persuaded elites around the world that establishing the nation-state is the prerequisite to economic success as well.[29]

It is no wonder that elites everywhere have wanted to adopt the political model of the nation-state, just as they have wanted economic development for their people. The world's most successful and powerful societies have given them the example. But we have found out that it is not so easy to copy economic success: We should realize that the political transformation involved in creating united nation-states may be no easier, and may, in fact, be harder. What was present in the successful cases—time—has been conspicuously missing in the many competing "nations" that have sprung from the dissolved empires of the twentieth century.

Imperial Legacies and the Nationalisms of Blood: Eastern Europe as a Typical Example

Newly liberated former imperial possessions trying to form united nation-states were faced first with the divisive policies of imperial rulers who had generally favored one or another group over others because that made it easier to maintain control. Secondly, these newly independent regions were confronted by the relative tolerance of imperial structures that freely mixed various ethnicities and religions. However much peoples may have been mixed before, being ruled by empires, they tended to be more mixed afterward. Finally, the newly independent regions inherited borders that generally paid little attention to cultural differences. In some cases, as in the Middle East, cultures that were quite similar and could have developed united elites were separated from each other by the French and English after 1918. In other cases, dissimilar peoples who would have taken centuries to build any sense of unity, even at elite levels, were intermixed. Few former imperial possessions were as fortunate as Thailand to be forced to give up dangerous border areas.

Large empires tended to be multilingual and multireligious and to favor certain groups over others for certain functional requirements. Any variation in local cultures—different levels of literacy, different degrees of skill in dealing with markets, different propensities to produce fighting men, or sometimes simply differential spatial location (nearness to the capital city, or location on particularly tense borderlands where quasi-permanent mobilization was necessary, for example)—produced various degrees of privilege. These differences, acceptable to imperial overlords, were no longer acceptable when it came to forming new nation-states. This was especially true if formerly unprivileged but more numerous groups gained majority status and used it to turn against those who had held more favored positions in the imperial realm. This is what lies at the heart of the Sinhalese-Tamil conflict in Sri Lanka, the Magyar-Romanian hostility in Transylvania, and the dislike of the Malays, Vietnamese, Khmer, Indonesians, and Burmans for the Chinese. In prenationalist situations, these differences were tolerable, and in fact, individuals could augment their chances for social mobility by changing ethnicity. Romanians or Magyars in Transylvania moving into German-speaking towns could, with time, become Germans, as long as the influx was slow and ethnicity was defined by behavior rather than by assumed ties of blood.

Greenfeld's work emphasizes the difference between the original, English type of nationalism that defined membership in the nation as a matter of civic behavior, and the German and Russian type that came to define the national community as a matter of race or blood. The liberal, democratic notions that derive from the English and French Enlightenment made it possible for nationalism to accept those who were willing to learn the national culture. This is a tradition that never spread deeply into most of Central or Eastern Europe, nor into Russia, Asia, or Africa.

Settler nations dependent on attracting immigrants were also obliged to define nationalism more broadly than other nations. The United States, which combined both the liberal Enlightenment tradition and the need to accept settlers as equals, has had an unusually civic type of nationalism able to absorb wave after wave of different peoples. Though the process has been far from easy or perfect, it stands at one end of the typology, "civic vs. blood" nationalism, whereas German and Russian nationalism, which were defined by blood—that is, fictitious kinship—rather than by civic behavior, stand at the other end.[30] Nationalisms that have neither a liberal tradition nor any perceived need to absorb outsiders are particularly unlikely to foster tolerance toward minorities.

Most of the nationalisms in Africa and Asia (including the secure ones in East Asia) have been much more like German and Russian nationalism than like English, American, or French nationalism. This is partly because an appeal to blood kinship is easier to understand than a broad appeal to civic virtues. The notion that one's kin are somehow more trustworthy than others seems to be one of the fundamental attributes of human beings. The introduction of racial theories that defined "nations" as biologically related "volk" in mid-nineteenth century Europe inherently appealed to nationalists all over the world because it combined an almost instinctive confirmation in people's affinity for kin with a seal of modern "scientific" validity. Thus, the combination of racial exclusiveness and social Darwinism that were all the rage in Europe in the late-nineteenth and early twentieth centuries, at the very time that modern forms of nationalism were spreading, left a deep mark on subsequent forms of nationalism around the world.[31]

Furthermore, few if any societies outside of the very small number deeply influenced by the Enlightenment have developed a strong sense of individualism. Rather, collectivistic solidarity remains far more common, and this makes the idea that an individual might transcend the community into which he or she was born seem quite strange.

But to make matters worse, virtually all forms of nationalism that have developed since the eighteenth-century English, American, and French versions have been based largely on a desire to imitate the successful European nation-states, combined with fear and resentment of the West. Therefore, these nations have tended to share, with the Germans and Russians, a resentment and bitterness about being behind the dominant English and French (or later the Americans).[32]

This bitter resentment, which makes up such a large portion of the sense of nationalism in most of the world, has been turned against any minority ethnicities who can be blamed for the continuing inferiority of the nation. Whether reasonable or not, those who seem to have been more easily Westernized, and who, on top of that, are of a different "blood," get accused of collaborating with the admired but hated West. To seem more adaptable to Western ways and more at home in the new market structures also brought by Western influence was to invite the rage of the new nationalists: The antagonisms toward the Jews in Europe, particularly in Central Europe (including Germany), Eastern Europe, and Russia; toward the Chinese in Southeast Asia; toward the Greeks, Armenians, and Jews in the Near East; and toward Indians in East and Southern Africa are the best-known cases of this. But there are many other, more localized examples. As we know that similar tendencies constantly resurface in even the most liberal nations and are only overcome when Enlightenment-inspired toleration survives as the dominant political ideology, it should come as no surprise that in nations without strong liberalism, ethnic persecution and warfare have become the rule rather than the exception.[33] That leaves out minorities, who then have little choice but to suffer in silence or to develop their own counternationalisms.

It may well be, as Hobsbawm suggests in his recent, influential book on nationalism, that it is all an irrational, unlucky coincidence that this is the way things have turned out.[34] But it does not make the sentiments of conflicting national groups any less real to point out that such feelings are neither terribly old nor inevitable. Once present and accepted by intellectuals, the mythologized histories that ascribe conflicts to ancient events and propensities rooted in blood (and, therefore, as something unalterable) might as well be true. Taught in schools that train vast numbers of children, made a part of officially sanctioned histories, and ingrained in the basic political ideology of each nation, these myths become the "truth." Such self-evident "truths" make it all the more important for minorities within new nations to fight back, because otherwise they become truly disadvantaged. So they make up their own "truths," their intellectuals find reasons for legitimating new national causes, and the vicious circle begins. It is virtually impossible to find any cases in the twentieth century in which such a sequence, once begun, has been stopped in a harmonious way. Reconciliations cannot occur until boundaries are changed, populations are exchanged or exterminated, and the myths of the past have been turned into brand new geographic and political realities.

All of this can be seen in the new countries of East-Central Europe created in the late-nineteenth century and after World War I. There are no cases in which the issues of competing nationalisms were ever peacefully resolved, except Finland, which is not normally considered a part of "East-Central" Europe. No doubt the Finns' fear of Russia made them very careful not to persecute their substantial and prosperous Swedish minority. Sweden was Finland's only other neighbor aside from Russia.

The Hungarians spent the interwar years teaching their school children that "no, no, never!" would they accept the boundaries imposed by the Treaty of Trianon. Far from being pleased by the near absence of vocal minorities within little Hungary, the Hungarian political elite made every effort to recapture unwilling South Slavs, Slovaks, and Romanians—and even printed Hungary's currency in those languages as well as Magyar. This led to their alliance with Hitler in the late 1930s.

It is easy to forget, now that Poland has been moved westward and largely purged of its Belorussian, Ukrainian, Jewish, and German minorities, that during the late 1930s it was drifting further right toward extreme anti-Semitism and the persecution of minorities.

Even democratic Czechoslovakia was, if anything, further away from resolving the tension between its German minority and the Czechs or between the Czechs and Slovaks in the late 1930s than it was in the 1920s. This issue went unresolved until on January 1, 1993, freed from external constraints, the Czechs and Slovaks finally broke apart.[35]

A similar, even more distressing pattern can be seen in the modern history of the Balkans. In the very early nineteenth century, there were no nationalist conflicts in this exceedingly mixed linguistic and religious area. Gale Stokes has shown that even the Serbian uprising of 1804 was hardly the product of nationalist fervor but simply one more of the dozens of uprisings and attempts by local elites to seize power from the center. Only later, with the creation of school systems and with the importation of better-educated Serbs from the Habsburg Empire, did nationalism come to play a role. Similarly, the early Greek revolt, motivated by Greeks living outside Greece proper who were trying to re-create a Byzantine Empire, was taken over by local elites in Greece who were not interested in any national ideal. But in both Greece and Serbia, local notables who took power quickly found that to gain and keep the support of the big powers, namely the English and French, they had to present themselves as "nations"—so they did.[36]

Many similar examples can be found elsewhere in the Balkans. In some cases, knowing the real histories of "nationalist" uprisings in the early nineteenth century can make an outsider laugh. The legendary hero Tudor Vladimirescu, supposedly the leader of a Romanian national uprising in 1821, was indeed a Romanian. However, his adventure was set in motion by Greek paymasters trying to start a Christian revolt in the Balkans to re-create a Byzantine Empire. These Greeks, as it turns out, were working for the Russians, who wanted only to weaken the Ottomans. Most of Vladimirescu's soldiers were Albanian mercenaries. Only latter-day historians could have turned this into a nationalist undertaking, but after several generations of assiduous, polemical historical work, that is precisely what Vladimirescu's ill-fated adventure has become. Later, the Romanian nation was unified under a German royal dynasty, that now wants to return to Romania as a symbol of national unity![37]

When combined with notions of racial purity, the importance of blood, and ludicrous claims based on truly ancient history, these nationalist mythologies are prescriptions for endless warfare. The Serbian claim to its medieval homeland of Kosovo, which is 90 percent Albanian, or the Greek claim, which recently brought out hundreds of thousands of demonstrators in Greek cities, that it alone has the right to the name of Macedonia, will bring more violence. Not only blood but a deep resentment against the outside world, particularly the Western European powers (because they have failed to recognize the unique claim to superiority of this or that people in the conflict), further embitters Balkan nationalism.

The basis of the Serbian claim to Kosovo is actually a wonderful example of how important intellectual delusions are in creating such problems. The reason Kosovo ought to belong to Serbia is that the area now occupied by Kosovo was at the heart of the medieval Serbian Empire and that an epic battle was fought there between the Serbs and the Ottomans six hundred years ago. I have no doubt that this was so, but why that should make the slightest bit of difference six centuries later can only be explained in reference to intellectuals whose concept of their identities is wrapped up in literary, thoroughly modernized, and distorted reconstructions of history.[38]

An even more astonishing piece of historical legend was thought up by Croatian nationalists trying to define themselves as better than their linguistically almost identical Serbian neighbors. These nationalists came up with the notion that Croatians were somehow descended from the ancient Persians and that they were therefore "Aryan." This piece of nonsense was supposed to justify their alliance to Nazi Germany and to justify the brutal mass murders the Croatian fascists carried out during World War II against Serbs. But a recent Croatian publication sanctioned by the newly independent government of President Tudjman claims that the first known reference to Croatians dates from Persian sources in about

500 B.C. This reference, which would be an obscure and silly piece of legend if it had not been for the atrocities of World War II, is hardly reassuring to those who know the history of the fable.[39]

More than anything else, it is the carefully nurtured memory of Croatian Ustasha killings of Serbs, and the role played by the Croats' Muslim mercenaries, that is used by the current Serbian government to justify its bloody war against Croatia. Nor has the Croatian government of Franjo Tudjman responded well to accusations that it would re-create an Ustasha regime. That is not to say that there is any indication that this is what the Croation government really wants to do, much less that Tudjman ever had any association with the Croatian fascists. But out of nationalist defensiveness, the Croats over the past couple of years have tended to be excessively protective of Croatia's wartime record, sometimes claiming, for example, that the massacres of that time were entirely conducted by Serbs against Croatians, or otherwise seriously downplaying the extent of Ustasha crimes.[40]

As for Bosnia, Serbian intellectuals have claimed to see a (totally invented) rise of Islamic fundamentalism that threatens Serbs and Christians. In fact throughout the 1980s, Serbian intellectuals were beating the war drums for a return to the great ethnically pure Serbian state of the mythical past.[41] Yet, as Misha Glenny has shown, the insensitivity of the Croatians and, later, of the Bosnian Muslims to Serbian fears made a catastrophe almost inevitable once independence was declared.[42]

One can only speculate about the potentially disastrous effects of similar insensitivities and the cultivation of noxious historical legends in other East European countries and in the many new states of the former Soviet Union. Rather than rejecting such past stories, many East European nationalists are busy trying to rehabilitate the worst of their past and to shore up the mythologies of blood and pseudo history that legitimized the excesses in the first place.

We know from what happened in Eastern Europe after 1918 that simply redrawing borders and giving in to maximalist demands of nationalists is no solution. In Poland and Romania, two of the great winners of the post-1918 settlement, there was immense frustration because the new states overproduced intellectuals and did not have enough official positions for them. Many business and professional positions were taken by minorities—Germans, Jews, Hungarians, or others, depending on the particular country. In Romania, this is what was behind the rise of the Iron Guard, perhaps the most successful and vicious fascist movement in Eastern Europe. In Yugoslavia, another great winner in 1918, the years that followed saw the competition between Serbs and Croats become immeasurably more bitter. Meanwhile in Hungary, Austria, and Germany, the anger of the losers—of those who had once controlled greater imperial territories—and their eagerness to blame all of this on the "corrupt" and undeserving bourgeois democracies of the West and on their internal Jewish agents, led to the rise of fascism and the massacres of World War II.[43]

The attempt to exploit memories of World War II excesses is not unique to Yugoslavia. In Romania, there has been a powerful move to rehabilitate Marshall Ion Antonescu on the grounds that he was a loyal nationalist defending Romanian territorial integrity against Russian communism. Indeed he was, but Romanian intellectuals do not appreciate that there are few less-reassuring symbols for the outside world or for the Hungarians in Romania than this close ally of Hitler.[44] In Slovakia, there is every reason to fear that the inevitable decline of the economy will lead to a similar attempt to rally the nation around a call to arms. The purging of Gypsies and Hungarians would then be only a matter of time.

Eastern Europe is not unique. On the contrary, it is typical of former imperial areas. Many such stories could be told about Africa, the Near East, or South Asia. In many cases, for example in the old Indian Empire, the problems simply get worse as time goes by. Moreover, in Africa, despite one major—though still far from secure—success at creating greater harmony in Nigeria, most of the ethnic conflicts that existed in the 1960s are no closer to solution today. Meanwhile, a whole new set of false histories and conflicting claims to peoples, cultures, and territories are being created right now in Central Asia, as entirely fictitious new nations originally carved out by the Soviets to facilitate their rule now lay claim to imagined ancient glories and boundaries.[45]

The point is that the intellectual and political elites in modern states have no better way to define themselves and measure their success than on nationalist grounds. In ethnically mixed states where nationalism developed too late to create culturally and emotionally united elites, there is practically no way of solving the resulting conflicts. One group's gain is another's loss, in jobs, self-esteem, and international recognition.

Without elite enthusiasm, both on the part of intellectuals who legitimate and perpetually renew nationalist images and on the part of leading politicians, who define their success in nationalist terms, competing nationalisms would rarely be able to start wars against one another. Most ordinary people stand to lose much by war; they are unlikely to feel as rewarded by the abstract triumphs of securing "historical boundaries" as are their better-educated compatriots. Yet, once wars such as the one between Serbs, Croats, and Bosnians have begun, that is exactly the position in which people are placed—their survival truly becomes endangered. It only takes a "little" massacre to persuade Armenians, Kurds, Jews, Karens, Croatians, Dinkas, or any other group subjected to such outrages that the situation has become desperate and that only by securing their own nation-state can they be protected.

Must We Preserve Artificial Nation-States?

It should be clear that the dream of liberty following necessarily from anti-imperial revolutions and the establishment of new nation-states has turned out to be illusory. This is only one of the intellectual errors of the twentieth century based on false analogies drawn from Western European history. Another such error has been that economic progress necessarily follows, and rather quickly, from the establishment of independent states. This is based on the notion that "our nation," whatever it may be, possesses a superior culture or at least one equal to that of established, powerful nations of the West. Therefore, the only reason for "our poverty" is the fact of foreign—that is, usually, Western—domination. Once independent, "our nation" can accomplish what any other nation has accomplished.

But this is not so, at least not in the short term. It took many centuries for Western Europe to lay the cultural foundations of what eventually became nations and took many more to prepare the groundwork for the Industrial Revolution. Evidently, in some East Asian cases, a strong base was laid for both national unity and eventual economic development, too. But elsewhere?

Much of the bitterness and rage of modern nationalism is a function of the realization that catching up to the English, to the French, and, eventually, to the Americans, is not so easy. Leninism became an appealing model to intellectuals in many of the poorer parts of the world because it promised a quick fix and then revenge on that much-admired, much-resented "West." Earlier, in the 1930s, Italian, German, and Japanese fascism offered a similarly attractive model. The collapse of alternative models of economic development seems to leave the Anglo-American model of liberal capitalism supreme. But the failure of these other alternatives has done little to alleviate either the resentment felt toward the West or the problems of creating economically strong, nationally unified states. All the old problems remain.[46]

But if this is so, how can the bitter ethnic jealousies and wars that could lead to the reimposition of tyranny be avoided? One thing we might do is reconsider the concept of the nation and ask whether analogies drawn from Europe's past ought to be perpetuated.

Take, for example, the egregious case of Iraq, run since its creation by its Sunni Arab minority that includes only some 20 percent of the population. The British included the largely Kurdish part of the country, the province of Mosul, so that Iraq and its king, their old Hashemite ally driven out of Mecca by the Saudis and out of Damascus by the French, would have a viable kingdom. In addition, the Shi'ite province of Basra was thrown in so Iraq would have an outlet to the sea. One may suppose that when the British set all of this up in the early 1920s, they did not foresee the awful massacres that would occur 60 years later. But after the massacres, when the United States had a chance to undo the damage done by the British in setting up such an artificial "nation," after winning the Gulf War, the Americans stopped short of overthrowing the Ba'thist regime in Baghdad in order to preserve the state of Iraq![47]

Why does anyone think that such artificial entities as Sudan, or Chad, or Lebanon or Afghanistan need to be preserved because they are defined as states in the process of "nation-building"? Why is it that after almost two decades of peace on Cyprus, it is still the official policy of the United States to put that island back together as a single, entirely artificial state? How much suffering is required to please those infatuated by large, rounded borders and outdated geopolitical concepts? How many more massacres and persecutions are necessary before the world as a whole recognizes that the model of the united nation-state that has worked well in some Western European and East Asian states may not be applicable elsewhere and was, in any case, only a transitional stage rather than the ultimate step in humanity's political evolution?

Democracy Would Help, and So Would a New Model

Though violent nationalist passions often seem to feed on mob hysteria, democracy is more likely to make life bearable in situations of conflict. Thus, Czech democrats have been more willing to let Slovakia go than Serbian communists and military leaders have been to give up Croatia, Bosnia, and Kosovo. Democratic Belgium and Canada, even if they break up, will do it more peacefully than authoritarian Yugoslavia or Pakistan, though the example of democratic India's repeated attempts to keep its rebellious provinces under control is not particularly reassuring.

This is where elite ideology counts, just as it does in determining both whether nationalism will be more a matter of "blood" or of "civic" behavior and whether the mood of the nation-state will be angry and resentful or relatively more peaceful. Ideology counts, and the mythologies invented to justify various forms of nationalism have greatly influenced actual behavior.

Because the ideas that come from the most successful, richest nations in the world have a powerful influence on how ideologies evolve elsewhere, there may be more hope for the future than my gloomy assessment has suggested so far. Furthermore, using recent developments, it might even be possible to suggest some forms of action that we, as intellectuals, might take to improve the chances of creating a more benign future. This is particularly relevant for post-communist Europe.

However, it is not enough at this point merely to direct attention to the fact that collapsed imperial structures in an age of nationalism are almost certain to leave terrible linguistic, religious, and ethnic conflicts. The notion that once the imperial powers were removed, various groups would naturally come together in a friendly way and create new, harmonious nations must rank as one of the two or three most bizarre social and political theories of the modern age, along with Marxism and neo-Darwinian theories of race. Removing imperial powers did nothing of the sort, any more than removing capitalists could rid societies of exploitation, poverty, and social conflict, or any more than removing Jews could have solved any of Nazi Germany's problems.

It no longer suffices to blame Ottoman, Habsburg, British, or Russian imperialism for the problems left behind in their former empires, though earlier imperialism may have been the starting point for many contemporary problems. Rather, it is better to think of what alternative definitions of political organization we might suggest in order to defuse hatreds and wars.

There is a possible solution, and we can see its outlines. Western Europe has begun to enter what might be a postnationalist age. The European Community is slowly—perhaps too unevenly and certainly very hesitantly, but still noticeably—moving toward a new kind of political association. There is little likelihood that the European Community will, at any time soon, abandon local nationalisms. Yet, because the larger Community has real powers, because it offers considerable economic advantages and protection for its members, and because, most of all, it is dominated by a liberal, non-ethnic, democratic ideology, the new Europe is drastically different than the Europe of the interwar period or of the nineteenth century.

The European Community will be able to ensure for its members security against outsiders and against overly ambitious insiders. It will guarantee military security and unity in negotiating international trade matters. It will, in short, provide all of the benefits that made state unification useful for the promotion of economic development in the past and that made it important for nation-states to be *big* or at least *as big as possible* within defensible borders. It will make access to the nation-state's raw materials and markets largely irrelevant because Europe as a whole will be able to guarantee these. But it will not insist on making any individual national culture superior. Quite the opposite should result, because the emergence of the new Europe will allow various provinces and cultural minorities to reclaim greater independence.

Now that Italy no longer needs to be a big nation-state in order to defend its interests against other predatory Europeans, what does it really matter if it splits into three parts, as the Lombard Leagues suggest? The Belgians can break apart if they decide that they want to, or they can remain together in a state that admits it is not a nation.

Little Switzerland, which is so full of quaint anachronisms at the same time that it possesses one of the world's most advanced and richest economies, may in fact be the appropriate model of the future.[48] Not only do its cantons and communes still retain a surprising degree of autonomy (though not nearly as much as in the past), but when there was a French-German ethnic dispute within its biggest canton, Berne, in the 1960s, it simply decided to split up that canton and create a new one, Jura. It will come as a surprise to most Swiss who recently rejected unity with Europe that when that integration comes, as it inevitably must, the cantons and communes in Switzerland will actually gain, not lose, strength with respect to their central government.This, clearly, would have been the only possible solution for former Yugoslavia. It is too late to save much of anything there, but the insistence by Slovene, Croat, Serb, and Bosnian Muslim leaders that they all had the right to build unitary nation-states made disaster inevitable. "Cantonization" was proposed and rejected.

Abandoning the notion that the security of a people depends on their commanding as large a state of their own as possible is the first requirement for finding a solution to the many other ethnic, linguistic, and religious differences in the post-communist regions of Europe. But for that to happen, there must be supranational, suprastate institutions, such as the European Community, to reassure people. Ultimately, the refusal of the West Europeans to spread some sort of security and economic guarantees to the former communist states of Eastern Europe will be deemed responsible for the Yugoslav tragedy. If Europe fails to act, other such situations will develop.

The Yugoslav problem is hardly unique. Veteran party apparatchik Slobodan Milosevic, looking for a way to hold on to power in Serbia, jumped on the nationalist bandwagon in 1987 and took it over.[49] Obviously this was a solution for many lesser officials as well. The same thing is going on in many parts of the former Soviet Union, including most of Central Asia, and to some extent in Romania and Slovakia. Discredited party elites cling to power by being more nationalist than the nationalists.[50]

Given the immense problems of conversion to modern capitalist economies and the potential for destructive ethnic and religious wars in post-communist Europe, there is nothing more important than providing the security that a strong Europe could give to these states. The extremist nationalists would not change their minds, but the fear they are able to generate among their populations and the resentment on which they thrive would be dissipated. In a real sense, this would be an even bigger help than, say, Europe providing capital and expertise for economic reconstruction.

The Marshall Plan and the North Atlantic Treaty Organization gave this security to Western Europe after World War II, and it was the sense of security as well as the presence of a benign arbitrator in European affairs that made the extraordinary reconciliation between France and Germany possible within half a generation.

We can predict that the European Community is unlikely to extend its protective mantle very far into Eastern Europe. At most, Poland, Hungary, and the Czech Republic may be accepted as associate members. The Balkan countries and those of the former Soviet Union, with the possible exception of the Baltic states, are not wanted. That is a great pity, and it makes the peaceful resolution of political problems and nationalist conflicts in this part of the world unlikely.

Nevertheless, it is possible to use the example of Western Europe to start to promote a new model that may eventually persuade political thinkers in other parts of the world that they ought to abandon their admiration for the older, nationalistic images of proper nationhood they also learned from Europe.

That Western Europe, which invented modern nationalism and almost destroyed itself by so doing, should have reformed and regained much of its economic and political power must give all of us hope. Nationalism proved to be a poor solution for the fragments of empires that tried to reconstitute themselves as nation-states in the twentieth century. Even if Western Europe is not meeting its larger political responsibilities, at least it is now offering something more suitable as a form of political organization than what it gave the world in the nineteenth century.

What is this new idea and how does it differ from what European, particularly German, nationalism gave the world in the nineteenth century? The new model, as opposed to the old one, recognizes that there are no sacred people specially chosen by divine will to carry out the mission of either saving or dominating the world. It admits that there are no "natural" boundaries of nation-states. The European Community has given up the idea that justice demands revenge for events that took place centuries or, for that matter, even decades ago. Even in Germany and throughout most of Western Europe, it is now accepted that neither "blood" nor "race" have much to do with culture or its transmission. Western Europe discovered that such concepts are worse than silly; they are criminal. Even if Europe gives too little actual aid or political protection to the post-communist world, it can at least use the prestige of its accomplishments to teach these lessons. All European political intellectuals, as well as their associates in America, have an obligation to participate in this effort.

Notes

1. The issue of subsidies and the relative advantages or costs of maintaining the Soviet Empire in Eastern Europe was elegantly discussed by Valerie Bunce in "The Empire Strikes Back: The Evolution of the Eastern Bloc from a Soviet Asset to a Soviet Liability," *International Organizations* 39 (1985), pp. 1–46. A debate among economists was carried out on this subject in the journal *Soviet Studies* during the 1980s.

2. David Remnick, "Dons of the Don," *New York Review of Books,* July 16, 1992, pp. 45–50.

3. Eric J. Hobsbawm, *The Age of Empire 1875–1914* (London: Weindenfeld and Nicolson, 1987).

4. Alfred Kelly, *The Descent of Darwin: The Popularization of Darwinism in Germany, 1860–1914* (Chapel Hill: University of North Carolina Press, 1981), makes a good case for showing that this was even more the case in Germany than in other European countries.

5. From 1879, cited by D. K. Fieldhouse, "Imperialism: An Historiographic Revision," in Kenneth E. Boulding and Tapan Mukerjee, *Economic Imperialism* (Ann Arbor: University of Michigan Press, 1972), p. 120.

6. Eric J. Hobsbawm, *The Age of Capital, 1848–1875* (New York: Meridian, 1984 {1975}), p. 126.

7. One finds the same fascination with late-nineteenth-century models in the Soviet industrial structure, probably because the founding fathers of Bolshevism who set up the whole structure were young men at that time. Unfortunately, by the late-twentieth century, the massive "smokestack" industries that made Western Europe and the United States so strong in 1900 were no longer appropriate. See Daniel Chirot, "What Happened in Eastern

Europe in 1989," in Chirot, ed., *The Crisis of Leninism and the Decline of the Left: The Revolutions of 1989* (Seattle: University of Washington Press, 1991), pp. 3–32.

8. Herbert Spencer, *The Principles of Sociology,* Part V, #565, Vol. II-2 (New York: D. Appleton, 1897), p. 608.

9. John A. Armstrong, "Toward a Framework for Considering Nationalism in East Europe," *Eastern European Politics and Societies* 2, no. 2 (1988), pp. 280–305.

10. A good bibliography on the Armenian massacres in the late-nineteenth and early twentieth centuries is found in Frank Chalk and Kurt Jonassohn, *The History and Sociology of Genocide* (New Haven: Yale University, 1990), pp. 433–434, and in Richard Hovannisian's essay in the same book, "The Armenians in Turkey."

11. Some sense of the ethnic and religious complexities of this area in the nineteenth and twentieth centuries can be found in such major works as Philip S. Khoury, *Syria and the French Mandate: The Politics of Arab Nationalism, 1920–1945* (Princeton: Princeton University Press, 1987), and Hanna Batatu, *The Old Social Classes and the Revolutionary Movements of Iraq* (Princeton: Princeton University Press, 1978).

12. It is important to emphasize that though these ethnic groups existed in the Balkans long before the nineteenth and twentieth centuries, there were no issues of conflicting nationalism before the late-nineteenth century. See Daniel Chirot and Karen Barkey, "States in Search of Legitimacy: Was There Nationalism in the Balkans of the Early Nineteenth Century?" *International Journal of Comparative Sociology,* 24, nos. 1–2 (1983), pp. 30–46.

13. Ivo Banac, *The National Question in Yugoslavia: Origin, History, Politics* (Ithaca: Cornell University Press, 1984). On the rise of ethnic tensions in the late Habsburg Empire in general, see Alan Sked, *The Decline and Fall of the Habsburg Empire, 1815–1918* (London: Longman, 1989), pp. 202–238.

14. Leo Kuper in his work *Genocide* (New Haven: Yale University Press, 1981) covers some of the aspects of what happened in Bangladesh.

15. S. J. Tambiah, *Sri Lanka: Ethnic Fratricide and the Dismantling of Democracy* (Chicago: University of Chicago Press, 1986).

16. For anyone doubting the grim outlook in the Sudan, it is useful to read the recent story by Raymond Bonner, "Letter from Sudan," *The New Yorker,* July 13, 1992, pp. 70–83.

17. Kuper's *Genocide* gives many of the details.

18. Max Liniger-Goumaz, *Small Is Not Always Beautiful: The Story of Equatorial Guinea* (London: C. Hurst, 1988). The massacres in Equatorial Guinea in the 1970s, part of which were ethnic, were among the most brutal and the least well reported in Africa.

19. Robert H. Jackson and Carl G. Rosberg cover many of the African cases in *Personal Rule in Black Africa: Prince, Autocrat, Prophet, and Tyrant* (Berkeley and Los Angeles: University of California Press, 1982).

20. The background is provided by Harold Crouch, *The Army and Politics in Indonesia* (Ithaca: Cornell University Press, 1978).

21. An interesting example is how Argentina "invented" itself. Nicolas Shumway, *The Invention of Argentina* (Berkeley and Los Angeles: University of California Press, 1991).

22. Katherine O'Sullivan, *First World Nationalisms: Class and Ethnic Politics in Northern Ireland and Quebec* (Chicago: University of Chicago Press, 1986).

23. Jean Sagnes, *Le Midi Rouge, Mythe et Réalité: Études d'Histoire Occitane* (Paris: Éditions Anthropos, 1982).

24. Charles Keyes, *Thailand: Buddhist Kingdom as Modern Nation-State* (Boulder: Westview Press, 1987).

25. Edmond J. Keller, *Revolutionary Ethiopia: From Empire to People's Republic* (Bloomington: Indiana University Press, 1988), pp. 149–163.

26. Liah Greenfeld, *Nationalism: The Origins of Modern Reality* (Cambridge: Harvard University Press, 1992).

27. Edwin O. Reischauer and John K. Fairbank, *East Asia: The Great Tradition* (Boston: Houghton Mifflin, 1960).

28. Benedict R. O. Anderson, *Imagined Communities: Reflections on the Origin and Spread of Nationalism* (London: Verso, 1983) has a much more benign view of "anti-imperialist" forms of nationalism than I do—or than Greenfeld's emphasis on *ressentiment* as a main aspect of modern nationalism would suggest.

29. Ezra F. Vogel, *One Step Ahead in China: Guandong Under Reform* (Cambridge: Harvard University Press, 1989) and Vogel, *The Four Little Dragons: The Spread of Industrialization in East Asia* (Cambridge: Harvard University Press, 1991).

30. Rogers Brubaker has published an excellent book on the differences between French and German attitudes toward naturalizing foreigners—the former based more on behavior and acculturation, the latter still largely, though no longer entirely based on "blood"—that is, physical ancestry. See *Citizenship and Nationhood in France and Germany* (Cambridge: Harvard University Press, 1992).

31. Daniel Chirot, *Modern Tyrants: The Power and Prevalence of Evil in Our Age* (New York: Free Press, 1994), chapter II.

32. Greenfeld, *Nationalism.*

33. Donald Horowitz, *Ethnic Groups in Conflict* (Berkeley and Los Angeles: University of California Press, 1985).

34. Eric J. Hobsbawm, *Nations and Nationalism* (Cambridge: Cambridge University Press, 1990).

35. The best review of the political history of the area during the interwar years remains Joseph Rothschild's *East Central Europe Between the Two World Wars* (Seattle: University of Washington Press, 1974).

36. Gale Stokes, "The Absence of Nationalism in Serbian Politics Before 1840," *Canadian Review of Studies of Nationalism* 4, no. 1 (1975), pp. 77–90.

37. Chirot and Barkey, "States in Search of Legitimacy."

38. In former Yugoslavia, there is a current joke: Slovenia was the warmup, Croatia the quarter-finals, Bosnia the semi-finals, and Kosovo will be the finals. For some recent detail, see *Soviet/East European Report,* Radio Free Europe/Radio Liberty Research Institute, Washington, D.C., Vol. IX, no. 3 (October 20, 1991), and the letter by Ivo Banac et al., *New York Review of Books,* July 16, 1992, p. 53.

39. *Historical Maps of Croatia* (Zagreb: Croatian Information Centre, 1992), chronology, p. 32.

40. Robert D. Kaplan, "Croatianism," *The New Republic,* November 25, 1991, pp. 16–18. The book *Historical Maps of Croatia* says only this about the atrocities during World War II: "Serbian terrorists and Chetniks ... carry out horrible massacres in eastern and southern parts of the Croatian state" (p. 34). There is absolutely no mention of the massacres carried out by the Croats.

41. Veljko Gubernia, "Serbian Nationalism," from *Politika,* January 20, 1989, p. 15, translated by Gale Stokes for his edited volume, *From Stalinism to Pluralism* (New York: Oxford University Press, 1991), pp. 226–228.

42. Misha Glenny, *The Fall of Yugoslavia: The Third Balkan War* (New York: Penguin, 1992).

43. Rothschild, *East Central Europe Between the Two World Wars,* has many of the details. Particularly good accounts of the frustrations that led to the rise of fascism are Andrew Janos, *The Politics of Backwardness in Hungary, 1825–1945* (Princeton: Princeton University Press, 1982), and Eugen Weber, "Romania," in Hans Rogger and Eugen Weber, eds., *The European Right* (Berkeley and Los Angeles: University of California Press, 1966).

44. On the fascination Romanian intellectuals have with their fascist intellectual tradition, see Norman Manea, "Mircea Eliade, Fascism, and the Unhappy Fate of Romania: Happy Guilt," the *New Republic,* August 5, 1991, pp. 27–36.

45. On the artificiality of the boundaries carved out within the Soviet Union and on the newness of any "nationalism," see Edward Allworth, ed., *The Nationality Question in Soviet Central Asia* (New York: Praeger, 1973), especially chapters 10–14.

46. Ken Jowitt, *The Leninist Response To National Dependency* (Berkeley: Institute for International Studies, 1978); and Jowitt's recent essays warning about the consequences of the void left by the collapse of the Leninist model in the poorer parts of the world, in *New World Disorder: The Leninist Extinction* (Berkeley and Los Angeles: University of California Press, 1992).

47. Batatu, *The Old Social Classes and the Revolutionary Movements of Iraq;* and on the nature of Ba'thist nationalism in Iraq, see Samir al-Khalil, *Republic of Fear: The Politics of Modern Iraq* (Berkeley and Los Angeles: University of California Press, 1989).

48. Benjamin R. Barber's history of communal independence in one of the important Swiss cantons, the Graubünden, explains how the communes survived for so long. Barber laments the loss of their former virtually total independence, but by modern European standards, Switzerland remains extraordinarily decentralized, and this, no doubt, is one of the reasons for its success as a multilingual nation. See *The Death of Communal Liberty: A History of Freedom in a Swiss Mountain Canton* (Princeton: Princeton University Press, 1974).

49. Glenny, *The Fall of Yugoslavia,* pp. 32–33.

50. Abraham Brumberg, "The Road to Minsk," *New York Review of Books,* January 30, 1992, pp. 21–26.

PART TWO

The Liberal Ideal

3

Conceptions of Democracy in the Draft Constitutions of Post-Communist Countries

STEPHEN HOLMES

The process of democratization in Eastern Europe is made more difficult by the painful legacies of the past, including, in random order, ethnic tensions, personal habits of dependency, low tolerance for economic inequality, the absence of a middle class, lack of experience with the rule of law and electoral politics, poorly trained judicial personnel, a willingness to accept rumor as a basis for political discourse, and a tendency to defeatism born of a regional inferiority complex vis-à-vis the West. These cultural and structural residua of communist and pre-communist periods, however, are not the only obstacles to reform. The weight of the past is matched by the weight of the present. For instance, the huge economic shock resulting from the overnight collapse of existing trade relations has produced the East European equivalent of the Great Depression. This is a new problem, not an old one. Although economic underdevelopment is partly a result of cultural and structural legacies of Leninism, the present economic catastrophe is the product of *sudden decolonization*—a regional breakup with which former members of the now-disbanded Soviet Empire were wholly unprepared to cope.

Similarly, the past alone cannot be blamed for tensions resulting from the historically unprecedented combination of political and economic transitions. As Beverly Crawford points out in Chapter 1, there is an inherent paradox in using democratic means to create a government that will reform the economy, since democracy gives ultimate authority to an electoral majority that, in turn, will be most harmed in the short term by the pain and dislocation of economic reform. China suffers from most of the cultural and structural legacies that beset Eastern Europe but does not face the same economic problems confronting Eastern Europe because China has not attempted a *simultaneous* reform of both the polity and the economy.

But the obstacle to reform that is perhaps most obviously *not* a legacy of the past is current-day Western advice. It may seem odd to describe the importation of political and economic models, patented in the West, as an obstacle to reform. We are certainly more accustomed to hearing complaints, perfectly justified I believe, about the absence of timely Western aid. For a sincere desire to become part of the West is admittedly one of the most promising features of post-communist societies, and one that may help these societies to overcome their tragic sense that endowment is fate—that the legacies of the past doom them to enduring penury and a never-ending seesaw between chaos and autocracy. Yet it remains reasonable to ask, in the field of constitutional law, which Western models are likely to be helpful and which are not, given the actual conditions in Eastern Europe today. Technology transfer is promising; however, it must be *selective*. Of the Western experiments with institutional design, which ones are most relevant for post-communist societies? What lessons can be carefully extrapolated from what cases and then usefully applied?

The Limits of Liberalism

A preliminary point is somewhat speculative and concerns the inherent limits of liberalism or the philosophical foundations of Western constitutionalism. For instance, the liberalism that developed from the seventeenth through the nineteenth centuries in Holland, England, France, and the United States is both individualistic and cosmopolitan. It is, therefore, not a wholly satisfying doctrine for helping East Europeans deal with permanent ethnic minorities. Yet hostility toward such minorities promises to cause serious political strains in the coming decades throughout the region. And consider the great liberal-democratic principles of equality before the law and majority rule. These principles can take effect only after territorial borders are fixed and after an answer has been given to the question: Who is a member of the community? The fundamental norms of liberal democracy, in other words, depend on decisions being made that cannot themselves be justified by liberal-democratic norms. Societies that have to make such decisions—as the societies of Eastern Europe must do—and that try to do so solely on the basis of liberal-democratic norms will inevitably fail.

Another inherent limit to liberalism concerns private property. Liberal theory asserts that economic inequality is tolerable if, by accepting it, we can wipe out poverty and dependency. A system of private ownership will certainly produce wide disparities of income and wealth; and these disparities are morally justified only if the property system that produces them also results in an improvement of living standards and an increase in personal autonomy for society's worst-off members. So liberal norms can, in principle, justify a system of private property.

What they cannot justify is *the assignment of first property rights.* Why should one man own a newspaper while another sleeps under a newspaper? In all Western societies, this question has been "answered" by the mists of time, by just and voluntary transfers ostensibly stretching back in a long chain of inheritance and exchange. But much private property, such as all land now owned in the territorial United States, was originally seized by force. In such cases, the legitimacy of current patterns of ownership depends wholly on an act of social forgetting. However, this is a luxury not available to the countries of Eastern Europe, whose citizens must stand by and witness nomenklatura privatization—that is, the skillful accumulation of first property rights by individuals who, by hook or by crook, were well placed under the old regime. Thus, the inhabitants of post-communist societies have to deal with a problem never encountered by their Western counterparts. The distribution of social wealth is going to be a burning issue throughout the region for the next decade at least; and *no outcome can be justified* by the basic norms of liberal democracy imported from the West.

Now what conclusion should we draw from this incapacity of Western liberal norms to help solve the basic political problems facing the fledgling democracies of Eastern Europe? Consider first the general *unbehagen* (discontent) with the constitution-making process in Eastern Europe, blamed from many quarters for failing to live up to the high standards set in the West. The principal complaints are the following. The process has been highly politicized, critics say, so that the constitutions in effect, whether permanent or temporary, are all tainted with the political interests of the drafters. The constitutions result from bargains between groups and therefore resemble bundles of compromises rather than acts of legal professionalism. Conversely, the political process takes the form of an ongoing constitutional crisis. No firm distinction has been established between the tools of action and the framework of action. The constitutional provisions in force are, in fact, treated cavalierly and almost never revered. Sometimes they are flatly ignored. The constitution should be treated as a strategic weapon, but it is treated instead as a tactical weapon. It is used as an instrument for outmaneuvering political enemies of the moment. Legislators should not negotiate the rules of the game while they are playing the game, but, since ordinary parliaments are everywhere doubling as constituent assemblies, this is exactly what East European politicians are doing.

Why have the new would-be democracies of Eastern Europe been unable to "sacralize" their constitutions in the Western manner? Some observers attribute this failure to a deplorable lack of *constitutional culture.* But I prefer a different explanation. It is very difficult to get anyone to revere the will of the framers when circumstances continue to change so rapidly. It is hard to respect a bargain made yesterday when one's bargaining partner has now completely disappeared from the scene. Why should Lech Walesa or Arpad Goncz rest satisfied with hamstrung presidencies designed for Wojciech Jaruzelski and Imre Pozsgay? Myopic political bargains made under turbulent circumstances are unlikely to be treated as beyond the reach of political recasting.

Under such conditions, and in countries where the great issues of political membership and the allocation of social wealth are still unresolved, it is a great mistake to cry out against the politicization of constitution-making. More specifically, it is a mistake to import German perspectives on constitutional law, particularly a fondness for unamendable provisions and an overly prestigious Constitutional Court, empowered, for example, to overturn procedurally correct constitutional amendments passed by the political branches on the ground of incompatibility with the constitution. The Kantianism of the *Grundgesetz,* which elevates the Constitutional Court above the Parliament, has been associated with the creation of the first liberal-democratic state in Central Europe. But the German model, with the exception of its technical details such as the constructive vote of no-confidence, is not appropriate for struggling post-communist societies that do not have the luxury of an inherited property system or of indisputable answers to the questions of membership and territorial borders imposed by a victorious army and accepted by a twice-defeated and chastened people. The German polity did not have to solve certain large political questions after 1945 and could, therefore, afford to elevate the constitution quickly above the reach of political struggles. After 1989, the polities of Eastern Europe are in a very different situation.

In addition to the size and nature of the problems faced by Eastern Europe, which cannot be solved by invoking liberal legality, and to the speed and all-pervasiveness of the ongoing transformations, which quickly render many power-sharing arrangements obsolete, there also is the all-important fact of the *heteronomy* of the revolutions of 1989. The Great Transformation of 1989 was accompanied by public euphoria, but it was not truly instigated by mass mobilization, not even in Poland. The die were cast by Moscow, as in the post-war communist takeovers of 1948, and in the ensuing power vacuum, governments were established and eventually elected. But it is hard to say that the populations involved actually chose the new political orders or that the populations were psychologically prepared for the radicalness of the change. The consequence, again, is that constitution-making (including the choice of the basic structure of the new regime) cannot be depoliticized, nor taken out of the hands of politicians and assigned first to legal experts and then to constitutional courts. For only through a political process, dominated by actors who know how to speak to ordinary citizens (as judges and experts seldom do), can a revolution imposed from abroad gain the kind of public acceptance it needs if it is to endure.

Recommendations to Reformers

What are the policy implications of this analysis? My first suggestion is that actors and observers all develop a high tolerance for stopgap constitutions and for the suffusion of ordinary politics with an atmosphere of constitutional crisis. Hungary's constitution begins with a "declaration of temporariness," and Poland is currently governed under the rules of an "interim constitution." If successful constitutionalism could be gauged by the speed at which a country hammered a "definitive" constitution into shape, then Bulgaria and Romania would be the most legally advanced countries in Eastern Europe. Some observers have argued that Hungary and Poland missed a "window of opportunity" in which to establish a definitive constitution. The opposite seems to me to be the case. The rush to establish unchangeable institutional arrangements in the immediate aftermath of communism's collapse, *la rage de vouloir conclure* (in Albert Hirschman's phrase), was only successful in those countries where former communists retained sufficient power to impose voting discipline on the assembly. Moreover, there are good reasons to think that a drawn-out process of constitution-making, with false starts and half steps, and in which constitutional committees proceed by trial and error, and go periodically back to the drawing board, has some tremendous advantages under present conditions.

In the first years after Sovietism's collapse, there is no great harm in *failing* to achieve deep entrenchment of the rules of the game by adopting stringent amending formulas and unamendable provisions. We in the West tend to associate rigidity with predictability, but as Juan Linz has explained, rigid institutional arrangements can produce more unpredictability and uncertainty than flexible ones under conditions of rapid social change.[1] One of the main priorities in Eastern Europe today is to preserve the government's capacity to re-adjust to changing circumstances. Politicians must therefore be able to renegotiate the rules while they are playing the game, or to repair the bus and install replacement parts while the bus is hurtling down the hill. To prevent such re-adjustments in the name of constitutionalism is to court political disaster.

An additional argument in favor of stopgap constitutionalism is that constitution-makers in Eastern Europe are undergoing a process of political learning. Constitution-making in Poland today, for example, is much more sophisticated than it was in 1989; and the new constitution, which may perhaps be drafted in the summer of 1994, if it is eventually ratified, will be an improvement over the models discussed in 1990. It is my impression that constitution-making throughout the region, in its first stages, was dominated by human-rights lawyers who tended to assume that the main (and perhaps sole) function of a constitution was to establish a bill of rights, limit the government, and outlaw abuses of power. They advocated what can be called *negative constitutionalism*—the notion that constitutions have a primarily negative purpose of preventing tyranny. The core of the constitution, from this one-sided perspective, is the bill of rights and the provisions concerning judicial review. The separation of powers and other provisions establishing the structure of government are secondary and can perhaps be viewed as mere techniques whereby the crooks divide the spoils.

Creating Parliament-Centered Democratic Authority

During the first phases of constitution-making, the culture of human-rights lawyers may have been so powerful not only because of their personal association with resistance to tyranny but also because their contempt for interest-group politics resonates well with the legacy of Leninism. One of the most important principles of communism was that public bargaining about private interests was immoral. Human-rights lawyers, too, believe in principles about which no bargaining should be permitted and the validity of which should never be made dependent on the outcome of elections. These individuals are intelligent, courageous, and well meaning, but their point of view, especially their Tocquevillean warning about a tyranny of the majority, is not necessarily helpful for the process of democratization. *The most difficult problem facing the countries of Eastern Europe today is the creation of a government that can pursue effective reforms while maintaining public confidence and remaining democratically accountable.* The core institution of the fledgling democracies, therefore, is the Parliament. What is the effect on public opinion, we might ask, of publicists who imply that the only institution that truly represents the deepest interests of citizens is the Constitutional Court? To overlegitimate the court and to raise it high above the deputies is to diminish the assembly in the public's eyes and to help discredit the entire concept (which has barely been learned) of representation through periodic elections. Might not the overlegitimation of constitutional courts in Eastern Europe, so often praised by legalistic observers, result from the fact that these bodies of unelected men (who deliberate in secret and who refuse to bargain publicly about differing interests) resemble the old Politburos?

What message is conveyed to the citizenry, similarly, if popular referenda are given a central role in the amending and legislative processes? Such a provision registers a belief that *the voice of the people is not adequately expressed through the representative process.* In other words, referenda implicitly erode the legitimacy of democratically elected assemblies. They express the seemingly reasonable belief that the most important choices should not be left up to politicians. But this principle is less democratic than it first sounds. Since the parliaments in question have little enough legitimacy as it is, reliance on referenda may be the straw that breaks the camel's back. A parliament that does not deal directly with the major choices facing society but, instead, leaves these problems to be resolved by referenda cannot pretend to a position of leadership in the nation. In its first stages, at least, democracy should be parliament centered. Any system that preempts the right of parliament to make the most vital decisions will ultimately damage the prospects of both democracy and limited government. (The Czech-Slovak divorce is not a persuasive counterexample to this argument, I believe, even though a national referendum might have saved the union for a time. No state can be governed by referenda, of course, and if the federal parliament was not able to wrest powers from the republic parliaments, as it showed no signs of being able to do in this case, then the federation was doomed, referendum or no referendum.)

The main political task in Eastern Europe today is the creation of democratic authority. The main political danger, conversely, is *the spirit of antiparliamentarianism.* Antiparliamentary feelings are already growing in the populations of the region—and for good reasons. The deputies are amateurs and opportunists. They are ceaselessly feuding for petty personal reasons. Unseemly scandals are constantly coming to light. Absenteeism is rife and the empty rows can be witnessed with dismay by the entire nation on television. The "forum" parties continue to splinter in haphazard ways. The Left-Right scheme, which greatly helped the post-fascist systems of Western Europe to organize parliamentary rivalry and cooperation, has completely lost its potency with the end of the East-West conflict. (This, too, incidentally, is a *new* problem, not a legacy of the past.) Last but not least, the parliamentary governments across the region have a very slight capacity to "deliver the goods"—to produce economic prosperity while alleviating economic insecurity, as well as to promote capitalist wages and socialist benefits.

All these factors tend to diminish the status of Parliament in the eyes of the public. This is an immensely dangerous development, however, and one that constitution-makers should keep in mind. If Parliament is viewed with general contempt, then what will prevent a Fujimori-like figure from simply disbanding the deputies with troops while the population stands passively by? The Constitutional Court may call itself the "guardian of the constitution," but it would be completely helpless in such a military intervention. Democratization will succeed in Eastern Europe only if the parliaments of the region manage to combine legitimacy with effectiveness and public acceptance with successful strategies of economic reform. The source of legitimacy in a democratic system is success in competitive elections. But an electoral victory does not necessarily bring deep public confidence in countries with a tradition of compulsory voting in fake elections. Therefore, the challenge in Eastern Europe today is to prevent *extraparliamentary* leaders from building public support on the basis of nondemocratic and nonelectoral forms of legitimacy, such as appeals to national pride, ethnic superiority, Christian values, personal charisma, and so forth. Democratic legitimacy, because it is largely procedural, is inherently disadvantaged in comparison to these other more substantive sources of public support. This comparative political disadvantage is why democratization must be reinforced by successful economic reform. And this is also why constitution-makers should avoid any arrangements, such as an overly prestigious Constitutional Court or easy recourse to popular referenda, that add to the denigration of Parliament in the public's mind.

Limited but Effective Government

Negative constitutionalism is the political equivalent of libertarianism in economics. Libertarians believe that freedom will come when the state is prevented from interfering in civil society, when government simply leaves people alone. Negative constitutionalists believe that freedom will be secured when the constitution erects safeguards against abuses of power. These attitudes are well meaning but ultimately simplistic. In countries suffering from an unprecedented disintegration of political institutions, such a negative approach is not always helpful. A liberal constitution must be enabling as well as disabling. A useful warning is provided by Somalia, a country where the state can no longer "intervene" into society. When limited government is taken to an extreme, it appears that brutal anarchy, not freedom, is the result. Individual rights are enforced by the state. Stateless peoples (such as migrating Kurds or Vietnamese and Caribbean boat-people) have no rights. Therefore, it is absurd to associate the establishment of rights with the radical weakening of the state.

This lesson, ignored at first, is gradually being learned across Eastern Europe. Constitution-makers and economic reformers alike have come to see their main task with new eyes. Building strong institutions amid the general rubble now appears to be just as important as placing limits on power. The problem that post-communist constitution-makers face, as *they* now see it, is to liberalize and strengthen the state simultaneously. The enthusiastic exponents of "civil society," who at first thought that Western-style freedom could be built from the bottom up, have found themselves confronting, in the nonpolitical sphere, varieties of mafia and tribal bands. Private initiatives—of the most brutal sort—are spreading like wildfire in the private brushwood beyond the reach of the state. As "civil society" has been progressively colonized by organized crime, however, the original proponents of limited government have slowly discovered the positive uses of state power. In the same vein, the rise of ordinary street crime, too, has been educational. One thing has now become perfectly clear: If policemen whose behavior is limited by law cannot control violent crime, then the public will happily acquiesce in the removal of all limits on the police. If liberalization is perceived as impeding effectiveness in this area, liberalization will be dropped without a tear.

Further, this lesson is being learned by friends of liberalization in the area of constitutional law as well. Limited government, if it is to last, cannot be purchased at the cost of paralyzed or ineffective government. Constitution-makers must aim to create a government that is simultaneously limited and effective. If they concentrate exclusively on creating a limited government, the result will be disgust among the electorate and frustration among public officials. The predictable next step would be a move to solve the most pressing problems outside of the framework established by the constitution. Phrased differently, *negative constitutionalism* is quite likely to produce a new autocracy in the not-so-long run.

So here is another reason to accept a go-slow approach to constitution-making in Eastern Europe. The first months following the collapse of communism presented a false window of opportunity. For these new regimes to have made a constitution immediately on exiting from tyranny would have been a great mistake, for such constitutions likely would have been biased in a negative direction, aimed primarily at the prevention of abuses of power. With the passage of time and with accumulated experience of the problems of ungovernability, constitution-makers are going to take a more balanced approach. They are trying to liberalize and strengthen government simultaneously. They are becoming more concerned with constructing institutions, and they now understand that individual rights can be guaranteed only so long as Parliament maintains legitimacy in the public eye.

A good example of constitutional learning, which is also the premier case of "technology transfer," is the gradual acceptance among experts across the region of the postwar German innovation of a constructive vote of no-confidence (or the French equivalent whereby the government can stake its confidence on a specific bill). The constructive vote of no-confidence, of course, is a method for strengthening the government, not for limiting it. Moreover, it is a perfect example of *positive constitutionalism,* which considers the building and reinforcement of electorally accountable institutions to be just as important as the protection of individual rights through the courts.

Another example of creative technology transfer concerns the separation of powers. A constitutional bargain has a chance of becoming the basis for political life over the long-term if the constitutional bargainers "get it right." That is, a durable bargain is one that manages to balance the interests of the important forces in society, not merely the interests of the particular bargain-makers sitting, for fortuitous reasons, around the table. To understand what this implies for Eastern Europe, we must first ascertain what the main forces in society are that must be balanced against one another. According to J. F. Brown, "the real political struggle in Eastern Europe today [is] between 'moderates' and 'radicals' in the anticommunist camp, between Girondists and Jacobins, those seeking conciliation and those seeking confrontation."[2] This is not a complete analysis of the important lines of division within post-communist societies; however, the raging debate about decommunization, lustration, and screening laws does reveal an important social cleavage that constitutionalism must take into account. (The legitimacy of the roundtable negotiations also is at stake here, for the radical decommunizers tend to view the results of these negotiations as bargains with the devil.) For some purposes, at least, these societies seem divided into anticommunists and anti-anticommunists, lustrators and antilustrators, fundamentalists and pragmatists. What are the implications of this division for democratization?

The most successful constitutions in Eastern Europe will be those that take this division into account. This may occur intentionally or, as an unexpected by-product, unintentionally. The most striking example of the latter alternative concerns the subtle transformation of the Western system of "separation of powers" when transplanted to Eastern Europe. No one intended it to work out this way, but the separation of powers in post-communist systems has, in several cases, been transformed into a form of "mixed regime," whereby two different social interests and value perspectives—those of Brown's "moderates" and "radicals"—are balanced with one another. In general, the radical anticommunist forces tend to dominate in the parliaments. To some extent, this is useful, for virulent anticommunism, channeled to and through Parliament, tends to lend an aura of legitimacy to the government as a whole. Unfortunately or fortunately, these countries cannot be governed without some degree of cooperation with ex-communists. As a result, there is an urgent need for some branches of government to balance the (increasingly) rabid anticommunism of the parliaments with the interests and perspectives of the former members of the party *apparat.* The presidency and the Constitutional Court have jumped in to fulfill this role. They are vehicles for bringing the ex-communists back in. Presidents Walesa (Poland), Havel (Czech Republic), Goncz (Hungary), Zhelev (Bulgaria), and others, have all opposed lustration and fought to keep decommunization within narrow limits. One can call this a form of power sharing. Alternatively, one can say that this system combines legitimacy with effectiveness, and parliamentary anticommunism with strategies for compromise developed by the other branches.

Conclusion

I began by asking what lessons can be learned from what Western experiences with constitution-making. Some of the advantages of postponement, I believe, can be learned by comparing the American and French experiences at the end of the eighteenth century. The endurance of the Constitution written at Philadelphia in 1787 was not foreordained. The members of the Constituent Assembly in Paris in 1791, whose ideals were not radically discrepant from those of the American Founders, produced a respectable, if not perfect, liberal constitution that guttered to a swift and miserable end. Why did the Americans succeed and the French fail? There are many reasons, of course, stemming from the vastly different political, religious, economic, demographic, and military situations of the two countries. (While France was saddled with Louis XVI, moreover, the United States was favored with George Washington.)

However, one additional reason for the success of the Americans deserves to be pointed out. Unlike their French contemporaries, the American Founders devised their Constitution *after a period of frustration with the weakness of the central government.* They aimed, therefore, not only to prevent tyranny but also to create an energetic government with the capacity to govern, to rule effectively, and to "promote the general welfare" (Preamble to U.S. Constitution). This devotion to governmental effectiveness, this passion for state-building, was virtually absent at the Paris Constituent Assembly. Framed in response to the unpredictable arbitrariness of monarchical rule, the French Constitution of 1791 proved so constricting that, when the first crisis struck, authorities were driven to slough it off and govern extraconstitutionally. By contrast, the desire simultaneously to limit and reinforce the state resulted, in the American case, in a stable constitutional regime that was neither tyrannical nor weak.

The American case again suggests that there is nothing healthy about *la rage de vouloir conclure.* The longer the countries of Eastern Europe wait to create a "definitive" constitution, the more likely they are to supplement negative with positive constitutionalism. If they rush to cement a constitution in place, they are likely to overestimate the problem of tyranny and underestimate the problem of anarchy. The optimal moment to draft and ratify a constitution, therefore, is the period when the memory of autocracy is balanced by the experience of chaos. In such a situation, the framers will be more likely to create a set of institutions that have a chance to endure. Whatever the virtues of a "big bang" in the economic domain, therefore, a gradual process of trial and error, which allows drafters to return to the drawing board after a process of constitutional learning, seems the most suited to the creation of a liberal democratic constitution. In Crawford's typology then, I am in the gradualist camp.

Those who believed that free societies could be built from the bottom up have not found their expectations fulfilled since 1989. Where are the spontaneously emerging institutions on which a democratic society can be built? (Where is the Solidarity trade union today?) Institutional disintegration and social chaos puts a great burden on the political system. There is no choice in Eastern Europe but to start the reconstruction of society politically, by forming democratically accountable assemblies that can unite legitimacy and effectiveness. This amounts to constructing the building of liberal democracy from the top floor down. If such an operation sounds architecturally unprecedented and highly risky, it is.

Notes

1. Juan Linz and Arturo Valenzuela, *The Failures of Presidential Democracy* (Baltimore: Johns Hopkins University Press, 1994).

2. J. F. Brown, "Eastern Europe: The Revolutions So Far," *RFE/RL Research Report* 2, number 1 (January 1, 1993).

4

After the Vacuum: Post-Communism in the Light of Tocqueville

JOHN A. HALL

Socialist society in its last two decades (the 1970s and 1980s) did not seem to me to be frozen. On the one hand, a significant degree of liberalization had typically already been achieved: The era of high totalitarianism had ended, no matter how repulsive were the remaining mechanisms of social control. On the other hand, possibilities of further liberalization—that is, of the replacement of a power system by a more limited one, of ideocracy by technocracy—seemed good, particularly given the presence both of splits within the party and of blocked middle-class social mobility more generally. If these were facts, the extent to which I endorsed them reflected hope as well as analysis.[1] It might be possible for slow decompression to lead to something more. If the ruling elite within authoritarian socialism learned to replace control with coordination of and cooperation with different interest groups, as well as to tolerate difference in order to make opposition loyal, then a later evolutionary transition to democracy might well succeed, somewhat along the lines suggested by the burgeoning literature on transitions in Southern Europe and Latin America.[2] This position entailed support for Gorbachev, even at the expense of the Baltic states—whose actions at times seemed to endanger the whole process, and recklessly so, given the implicit offer of the benefits of Finlandization.

Any reversion of major parts of the former Soviet Union to authoritarianism may restore appreciation of the virtues of gradualness. Nonetheless, the starting point for this chapter is that this scenario of gradual liberalization was *not* realized; concentration must accordingly be refocused on an altogether different reality. There are in fact good reasons—classically given by Alexis de Tocqueville and now powerfully reinforced by Adam Przeworski—insisting that all liberalization is inherently unstable.[3] Certainly there proved to be no resting place between communism and democratization, and an application of the transitions-to-democracy literature to the determining case of the Soviet Union powerfully suggests that this lack of a resting place resulted from the uniqueness of socialist society. State socialism's attack on non-official, lateral self-organization—that is, on civil society—meant that no lasting pact akin to that made in Spain in the 1970s could be made by the elite with society—thereby limiting and controlling social forces—because no organized body existed that was capable, so to speak, of disciplining its troops.[4]

But democratization within post-communist regions is of a particular kind. It results from the staggeringly complete collapse of a whole social world. The situation resembles nothing so much as a vacuum, and our initial task must be to characterize this extraordinary social emptiness (see Holmes's discussion in Chapter 3). This chaper, then, may perhaps part company with others in this volume in terms of its focus. Rather than looking at the effects of various institutions and legacies to determine how they led to various outcomes, I examine the profound impact that a sudden and complete loss of legitimacy has had in Eastern Europe and the former Soviet Union.

An element of such a characterization is necessarily banal. Democratization in post-communist societies—with the important exception of Solidarity, without which the collapse of socialism is inconceivable[5]—came by accident, without much popular involvement. Once the Russian card was withdrawn, regimes which had always had minimal legitimacy simply crumbled. The fact that there was little pressure from below makes for a contrast with most other democratizations. Still more different was the position of those at the top. It seemed for some time—and perhaps was—wise to treat the socialist elite as if it was equivalent to elites in Southern Europe or Latin America. But the analogy seems less and less plausible. The marked absence of a military tradition within socialism and the fact that the land-owning upper class has been destroyed is one factor of relevance here. More important and less banal is the almost total loss of belief in the socialist project. In society as a whole, the extent to which any attachment to socialist concepts has been punished electorally is as striking as it was unexpected. But perhaps there is not great novelty here: The extent to which most parties in Central Europe were hated by their societies was apparent for many years. What is more striking is the loss of belief among the elite itself. It seems as if few any longer have sufficient conviction to rule by means of socialism. It is not altogether easy to explain why this loss of conviction has been so total. Ernest Gellner may well be right to suggest that the idiosyncratic nature of this secular religion—the fact that it promised salvation in this world, here and now—meant that it had no escape clauses that allowed it to deal with the shoddy years of the Brezhnev stagnation.[6] Equally important, historical sociology makes us aware that communist moral ideals are extremely rare and, accordingly, difficult to sustain.[7] Whatever the case, the fact that the loss of conviction has been total cannot be doubted. Former believers are the living dead: confused, uncertain, and deprived of faith. A world historical project has come to an end.

But the character of the vacuum needs further explication. It is often remarked that Tocqueville best furnishes the mind of those seeking to understand the situation of post-communist societies.[8] I agree with this sentiment but wish to move beyond asserting it to a demonstration of the usefulness of Tocqueville's concepts. Perhaps the greatest use of Tocqueville's concepts is in understanding the vacuum of the post-communist world.

Tocqueville's early writings show him to have been very much a member of a generation that, particularly in the light of the Revolution, had come to distrust the people.[9] More particularly, Tocqueville believed that the reign of the masses might well be such as to undermine the chances of liberty—that is, of the condition to which he was at all times devoted.[10] Generalized dislike was shown to the individualism of bourgeois society, together with premonitions as to the political consequences of the isolation that its social form encouraged. Tocqueville insisted that individualism was a modern concept, "unknown to our ancestors, for the good reason that in their days every individual necessarily belonged to a group and no one could regard himself as an isolated unit."[11] Such individualism began by encouraging a retreat into private life, only then to create an egoism opposed to all public spirit.[12] But Tocqueville's visceral dread of a tyranny of the majority was based on something more: The people would be prone to envy—that is, to the desire to equalize social disparities, even—or perhaps especially—if such equality could only be realized under a common dictatorship.[13] This bias in Tocqueville can be seen in the surprise he showed when discovering that the Americans were able to combine liberty with equal social conditions. He confided to his travel journal his contempt for the middle classes, noting, almost reluctantly, that "in spite of their petty passions, their incomplete education and their vulgar manners, they clearly can provide practical intelligence."[14]

Tocqueville's loathing of this syndrome—privatization in combination with envy, resulting in despotism—remained constant. Nonetheless, he very distinctively changed his mind as to the causes that lay behind this syndrome. If awareness of that change will prove helpful later, there is an immediate gain in noting what is involved: It is Tocqueville's final position that allows proper characterization of post-communism.

The happy conclusions to the study of America were in fact of limited use to Tocqueville. The United States had effectively been born free and could thereby cast little light on those societies which had to make a transition, with or without liberty, from the aristocratic era to that characterized by equal social conditions. Moreover, the second volume of *Democracy in America* sees Tocqueville beginning to doubt this argument.[15] It was only in the second part of his masterpiece, *The Old Regime and the French Revolution*, that he arrived at a settled line of argument. The analysis of centralization forcefully highlights the state's distrust of its own people:

> Any independent group, however small, which seemed desirous of taking action otherwise than under the aegis of the administration filled it with alarm, and the tiniest free association of citizens, however harmless its aims, was regarded as a nuisance. The only corporate bodies tolerated were those whose members had been handpicked by the administration and which were under its control. Even big industrial concerns were frowned upon. In a word, our administration resented the idea of private citizens' having any say in the control of their own enterprises, and preferred sterility to competition.[16]

This was a type of negative political rule in which security was felt to reside in depoliticization. We have already seen that the destruction of civil society that this involved undermined the very possibility of controlled liberalization. But much more important is the analysis contained in chapters eight to ten. The first of these three chapters explains "how France had become the country in which men were most like each other." What was involved here was the convergence of income levels and styles of life of the aristocracy and the bourgeoisie. The second stage of the argument is a nice example of Tocqueville's love of paradox: In chapter nine, he considers "how, though in many respects so similar, the French were split up more than ever before into small, isolated, self-regarding groups." This section begins with an analysis of local politics before the advent of absolutism. Records showed that classes had once been able to trust each other and to cooperate with each other in defending regional interests. This spirit of class cooperation was destroyed most of all by the granting of tax and legal immunities to the French aristocracy: This destroyed all community of interest and naturally made it senseless to serve as leaders against the encroachments of the state. The final stage in the argument, chapter ten, bluntly considers "the barriers set up between classes." It is important to emphasize what is being claimed here since it represents a fundamental reversal of Tocqueville's initial set of preconceptions. Liberty is undermined less by passions released by the age of social conditions and much more by the strategy of the dominant elite. Kings rather than the people are to be blamed for France's inability to embrace liberty in modernity:

> Almost all the vices, miscalculations and disastrous prejudices that I have been describing owed their origin, their continuance, and their proliferation to a line of conduct practised by so many of our Kings, that of dividing men so as the better to rule them.[17]

The exercise of political liberty, according to Tocqueville, depends upon trust between different social classes, while it in turn breeds responsibility; differently put, participation is the only effective means of training citizens suited to liberty. At best, the old regime had enforced a type of social atomism that led to extreme privatization. At worst, the old regime had taught people how to hate each other. This legacy was not without consequence:

> It was no easy task bringing together fellow citizens who had lived for many centuries aloof from, or even hostile to, each other and teaching them to co-operate in their own affairs. It had been far easier to estrange them than it now was to reunite them, and in so doing France gave the world a memorable example. Yet, when sixty years ago the various classes which under the old order had been isolated units in the social system came once again in touch, it was on their sore spots that they made contact and their first gesture was to fly at each other's throats. Indeed, even today, though class distinctions are no more, the jealousies and antipathies they caused have not died out.[18]

This is a stunning passage, and it rather exactly characterizes the nature of the vacuum in Eastern Europe. The extent of privatization is seen in the very low turnout at recent elections in both Poland and Hungary, and also in the generalized uncertainty as to what one's interests are and how to best represent them.[19] More generally, the absence of trust may well make it difficult to install market relations: All the overlapping linkages necessary for flexible late-industrial society may be undermined by this lack of cooperation.[20] Most obvious of all is the tendency of some groups to "fly at each other's throats"—a topic so vital that it must be taken first. I will then focus on the relations between capitalism and democracy and between state and society in the post-communist world. I will conclude this chapter with some hunches about possible strategies and likely scenarios.

Nationalism

The fundamental property of a vacuum is that it is unstable. Forces rush in to fill a void. What this involves in personal terms has been graphically portrayed by existentialism. Living without fixed identity is painful and confusing. The point about Mathieu, the hero of Sartre's *Roads to Freedom* sequence of novels, is that freedom is a burden: Everything has to be thought through, and nobody can be trusted. It is scarcely surprising to discover that human beings flee this condition. Bluntly, social life per se depends on the ability to trust—to so regularize encounters that fear and uncertainty are contained.[21]

The most obvious way in which this has already taken place in Eastern and Central Europe is by means of nationalism. It is very probable that the emergence of nationalism was inevitable. In retrospect, it has become obvious that the Bolsheviks carried on the legacy of the Russian Empire, with Stalin adding to it in the years immediately after 1945.[22] Differently put, the end of World War I saw the destruction of the Ottoman and Habsburg Empires but the remarkable restoration of Russian power by military means. States such as Georgia and Ukraine quickly lost the independence that they had gained because of revolutionary turmoil, and they were thereafter reintegrated into the empire. That this was supposedly a union of socialist republics misled many, with some of the analyses declaring the impossibility of nationalism under socialism being published astonishingly late.[23] The Soviet state did, of course, seek to control nationalism by traditional means—that is, by the stick of brutality (including a licentious use of deportations) and the carrot of metropolitan subsidies.[24] However, it remained the case that the empire was run for and by Russians.[25] It is vital to stress this since perhaps the key variable involved in the classical pattern of nationalism is that of the blocked social mobility of the local elite.[26] This most certainly applied within the direct Soviet sphere. When this was added to a model of industrialization that caused almost unbelievable ecological catastrophes for a Baltic republic such as Estonia, the provenance of nationalism becomes unproblematic. Indeed, it is not strictly accurate to talk about nationalism filling the gap left by the fall of communism: Cooperation by ethnic means was far more than an idea limited to intellectuals well before communism's collapse.

The slight hesitation in the above paragraph deserves to be explained. Not every potential nationalism comes to fruition—that is, nationalism often is but an idea, limited to a group of intellectuals. What matters for an ethnic group is the ability to gain the good things in life, but it is not inevitable that this will occasion raising the nationalist flag. In one notable exception to this rule, the Scots were proud to be—as Smith and Hume had it—North Britons. The point to be emphasized about North Britons is that they had amazing mobility within the British Empire.[27] But it would be a mistake to characterize the situation in purely material terms.[28] What made it possible for the Scots to realize interest was regime. The fundamental way in which nationalism can be controlled is by granting political rights. Voice undermines exit.[29] It is worth noting in this connection that historians of Austro-Hungary now debate the extent to which the empire was doomed by nationalism.[30] There is a revisionist camp among historians that insists that the granting of autonomy would have drawn the teeth of the nationalist movements, not least among these being the Slavs, who were extremely aware of the way the empire protected them against Russia and Prussia. In this same vein, it is worth noting that few separatist movements within established democracies have succeeded. Quebec has great difficulties in this regard: Its nationalists, interestingly, gained power precisely when their internal voice was restricted. This principle returns us to the vacuum created by the fall of communism.

In a striking article, Linz and Stepan have demonstrated that the Spanish liberalizers were able to defuse the demands of the nationalities by first holding national rather than provincial elections.[31] This move immediately undermined support for separatist parties: The public demonstration that the system was open and that benefits could be gained within the regime without the costs of separation confirmed that the axis of political life would continue to be that of the traditional Spanish state. Linz and Stepan further note that such a democratic opening was not turned to advantage by the regimes in Yugoslavia and the Soviet Union. This certainly mattered: Slovenes might have been prepared to stay in a democratic Yugoslavia but chose to exit from what seemed to be a Serb autocracy.[32] In this context, it is well worth noting that nationalism is by no means out of control in post-communist societies: Both Ukraine and Russia have, at the time of this writing in mid-1993, pulled the teeth of a mass of nationalist movements because they have remained loyal to democracy.[33] A consideration of Czechoslovakia—where federal and regional elections were held simultaneously—also becomes relevant at this point: It is extremely unlikely that Slovak independence would have been supported by a majority of Slovaks in a referendum, albeit the Czechs might have chosen to divest themselves of a demanding region looking set to block Czech reforms. Nonetheless, no referendum was held there. For Soviet or Yugoslav leaders to have chosen this option would have required nothing less than a metamorphosis in the character of the elite. Democratic centralism did not encourage this sort of mentality. Very much to the contrary, those members of the old nomenklatura who had no capacity or opportunity to retain privilege by means of capitalism found in the "nationalist card" the perfect vehicle to avoid downward social mobility.

The pessimism engendered by this last point can in part be mitigated. Strong nationalism, especially within unitary societies, can help development in the long run.[34] The energies of the Baltic states cannot be exaggerated: The extent to which they are prepared to undergo sacrifice is already being tested but may well remain a considerable resource. More obviously, some of the states that are being created are effectively mono-ethnic: This may well ensure the Czech Republic and Slovenia a future at once affluent and democratic. Poland and Hungary were, of course, turned into unitary societies through the ethnic cleansings of Hitler and Stalin. This is not to deny that these countries still have the capacity for symbolic politics. Hungarian minorities in Slovakia and Transylvania ensure that a nationalist card can still be played in those regions, as does the possibility of large amounts of German investment in western Poland. Nonetheless, the role of symbolic politics has declined sufficiently throughout Eastern Europe to make it necessary to return to the original focus of our attention. Where symbols do not dominate, the vacuum remains. What are the chances for the double transition to democracy and to capitalism under these circumstances?

Democracy and Capitalism

The absence of nationalist politics would naturally seem to encourage optimism. However, work done on the politics of transition, East and West, by scholars influenced by rational choice theory tends toward pessimism: Economic reform cannot proceed without democracy, but democracy has no chance without prior economic change.[35] This analysis needs both to be appreciated and to be treated with a measure of skepticism.

The necessity of democracy for economic reform is clear enough. The people will not accept any reforms that cause a devastating decrease in their standard of living while a few are enriched; this rejection is likely to be especially visceral if members of the old nomenklatura are seen to be doing well as a result of the new order. The immediate consequence of democracy is accordingly likely to be the rejection of economic reform. If this becomes full blooded, disaster will surely follow. For the legitimacy of the new regime can only be secured by some measure of economic success, and this will never occur unless the principle of the market is embraced. Descriptively, this leads Przeworski to argue (from a global perspective) that the East is becoming like the South: A cyclical process is likely to be repeated in which authoritarian rule will be followed by episodes of popular control—whose economic mismanagement will then ensure the breakdown of democratic regime.[36] Prescriptively, this line of argument leads Przeworski to favor gradual change over the various versions of shock therapy: The costs of change must not so hurt the people that they abandon democracy.[37]

This suggests an alternate view that democracy depends on a prior introduction of economic reforms by authoritarian means. The logic of this position is much reinforced by banal considerations of the political benefits of economic growth. On the one hand, money-making may serve as an avenue of advancement sufficient to distract former power-holders; on the other hand, adjustments will be made by larger sections of the populace through bribery, that is, social peace will be purchased by the provision of *Danegeld*. The early liberalization of British and American politics was certainly much aided by the surrounding presence of prosperous capitalist relations.[38] The logic of this point suggests that it may be easier to achieve democracy in China than it is in East and Central Europe: Perestroika (restructuring) before glasnost (openness) may be the best nostrum. The strategy that most obviously follows from this position is one prepared to contemplate curtailing popular politics so as to sustain economic reforms. Poland's Minister of Finance Leszek Balcerowicz put this case with unequalled force: What matters in his view is creating capitalists by any means, not least among his reasons being that successful capitalism will inevitably lead to democracy.

These authors powerfully describe a vicious trap. But there are good reasons not to accept uncritically the whole case that they present. Most obviously, society is still in a vacuum: Differently put, amazingly little resistance from below has come to those reforms that have been instituted. One element causing that vacuum—the destruction of belief in the socialist project—can usefully be accentuated. The claim that, globally speaking, the East may share the same fate as the South is outdated. The remarkable extent to which the South has changed can be seen in the endorsement of market principles by leaders as different as President Carlos Menem (Argentina) and President Carlos Salinas de Gortari (Mexico). Differently put, there is now remarkable elite unity in many countries as to the costs of exiting from the international economy.

Despite four different governments and a president potentially of populist character, there has not been any clear reversal of Polish economic reforms; equally, Czech President Havel's instinctive distrust of the market has not led him to criticize Klaus's (his minister of finance's) reforms. More generally, skepticism should be directed at the economism of the position outlined—which is not to deny that economic growth often helps social peace and may finally be necessary to it. It would be wise for post-communist societies to continue to be aware of the fact that political can be worse than mere social inequality. Some do remember the humiliation involved in being subservient to the powerful, and welcome a monied society with relief; but memory is generally rather short, and to that extent the logic of "democracy by way of authoritarian economic means" makes sense. Nonetheless, consideration needs to be given to an entirely different principle which runs counter to economism.

The collapse of communist regimes should highlight the essential stability of liberal capitalist regimes. In principle, an order based on social inequality and political democracy might well seem a prescription for chaos. It is scarcely surprising that many have therefore insisted that social peace has resulted from economic growth. But this may not be altogether correct. Britain survived the mass unemployment of the Thatcherite experiment without any real threat to social peace. This may well be because those disadvantaged by radical economic policies had limited capacity to mobilize: The unemployed were not unionized, while the young—but not the old—were given special handouts. In general, greater political instability was evident in Britain when the state involved itself in industrial relations by seeking to enforce corporatist arrangements than when it ignored the unions, blaming everything on the market.[39]

Historical sociology goes a little further to suggest that a generalizable pattern is at work here. This pattern can be highlighted by noting that the political militancy of nineteenth-century working classes varied by nation. At times, Russian workers were genuinely revolutionary and, therefore, to the left of the rather respectable socialism of the German Social Democrats. At the opposite end of the spectrum, there was famously no socialism in the United States, with Britain only slightly more radical in having a Labour rather than a Socialist party. What seems to best explain the different degree of militancy is the attitude of the state. The presence of a liberal regime meant that class conflict took on an industrial rather than a political character—with Britain gaining a *Labour* party because of the occasional interference of the state. In contrast, the political exclusion of autocracy and authoritarianism concentrated attention on the state for the most obvious of reasons: The state became the enemy because of its arbitrariness and its refusal to allow unions to organize.[40] Early realization of this point lay behind Max Weber's call for limits to Wilhelmine authoritarianism. Neither capitalists nor the state had anything to fear from liberal measures toward the working class; to the contrary, the more that class felt itself to be part of society, the less likely it was to embrace radicalism.[41]

One way in which the point can be highlighted is by endorsing the ethic of eighteenth- rather than of nineteenth-century social theorists: Political arbitrariness creates much more anger than does social inequality. People prefer reform to revolution, and the possibility of peaceful change to the dangers of the barricades. Liberalism diffuses conflict through society whereas authoritarianism concentrates it. Had Havel, for example, been able to act as a reformer—that is, as a member of a loyal opposition within socialist society—it is probably unlikely that he would have been forced to fight the state. A further implication can be derived by recalling the way, already noted, in which Tocqueville changed his mind, thereby replacing a social with a political explanation for habits of the heart incapable of embracing liberty. Social movements gain their character from the state with which they interact. We have seen this to be true of nationalism. Equally, there was no essence to the working classes of the late-nineteenth century: Their political behavior varied, according to the circumstances in which they had to exist.

The immediate relevance of this analysis for post-communist societies has been neatly captured by Ellen Comisso. There may be less to fear from movements from below than had been expected:

> It also follows that it is entirely possible to have pluralism and a wide variety of small groups competing for influence without ever pulling large numbers of people into political life. ... If states remain strictly liberal and do not grant organizational advantages to large groups, it may well be possible to maintain pluralism without extensive mass movements. If, for example, workers are free not to join unions, many will simply not join.[42]

Liberalism before democracy may be best, especially if it is part of a package that includes a successful economy; but liberalism by itself may depoliticize—and so continue that vacuum of post-communism that leaves the state sufficient autonomy to press through economic reforms. There is some evidence that this is beginning to happen. One recent strike in the Fiat works in southern Poland was not broken by the state but by workers prepared to accept the company's offer; and there is evidence that varied negotiations are beginning to take place between capitalists and workers, without benefit of state involvement. Such depoliticization is secure when the sociological principle involved is understood. No evidence is available to me as to the *extent* of such understanding within post-communist societies, but it is worth noting that calls—both from within those societies and from outsiders such as Przeworski—for the state to continue to claim responsibility for industrial relations is likely to increase social conflict. Gradualism has dangers of its own. As it is, the current depoliticization brought by liberalism presents a window of opportunity that allows economic reforms to continue. Furthermore, one crucial factor may currently be increasing such depoliticization. The basic fact that capitalism is being created by the state in post-communist societies is, according to the logic of the preceding principle, likely to lead to social mobilization. But the move away from political capitalism toward voucher schemes of various sorts has so muddied the waters that perception of state responsibility for basic accumulation is declining.[43]

The argument being made can usefully be underlined by returning to the confessional note that I offered at the start of this chapter. My hopes for liberalization probably reflected British experience in a particularly provincial manner. The national experience of that country was, in comparative terms, hugely helped by favorable preconditions. Liberalism was distinctively aided both by the presence of a robust economy that created elite unity by making politics less than everything and by the fact that threats from below were removed by a curtailment of democratic rights—albeit the continuing liberalism of the state explains the moderation of movements from below, a factor that in turn meant that the middle classes did not resist extensions of the franchise. This was a package deal in which economics supported politics and politics economics.[44] The argument here has essentially been that variables can be abstracted from this package. Thus, elite unity about the need for economic reforms is broad in scope, and liberalism may ensure depoliticization by itself. The task for reformers would be easier if every precondition were favorable: that some conditions are favorable may allow sufficient space for enough reforms to allow for the beginnings of economic transformation. Such beginnings are clearly present in the Czech Republic and not wholly absent in Poland and Hungary; this suggests that the skepticism regarding the pessimistic case of the rational choice theorists may well increase.

The State and Civil Society

If a measure of state autonomy represents a window of opportunity, that in itself is no guarantee, pace Balcerowicz, of successful outcomes. If we are to understand the situation in post-communist societies, it is necessary to analyze—mostly in the abstract and in terms of the type of relations that are needed—the nature of the relations between state and society. Let us begin by considering the belief apparently held by Adam Smith to the effect that "little else is requisite to carry a state to the highest degree of opulence from the lowest barbarism, but peace, easy taxes, and a tolerable administration of justice; all the rest being brought about by the natural course of things."[45]

No sociologist with any sort of indebtedness to Max Weber can easily accept Smith's sentiment. For Weber's point was that the work ethic was by no means universal and, indeed, that it was born from the "irrational," antimaterialistic desire to fulfill divine purpose. It would most certainly not make sense either to limit economic success to the presence or absence of the work ethic or to insist that this ethic always has religious sources. It may be that socialist engineering has increased chances for national economic success by changing the occupational structure and by improving both the position of women and standards of education. These Eastern European societies are less "dual" than they were historically; in this sense, at least, they have outpaced Latin America.[46] To be set against this, however, is the existence of differential microeconomic capacities resulting from the societies' varying lengths of time under socialism. It is often claimed that the work ethic can survive forty-five but not seventy-five years; this looks set to favor the Czech Republic and Hungary, and to disadvantage Russia.[47]

However, the principal rationale for citing Smith's views is to stress that he most certainly had a positive conception of the state. *The Wealth of Nations* was itself meant to be "a handbook for the legislator." Its theme was that capitalists were dangerous because they could so easily conspire against the public: Only the enlightened—that is, the political aristocracy who bought Smith's works—were capable of defending the market principle against those whose immediate interest might make them destroy it.[48] In addition, the state had to counteract the effect of mental mutilation by means of education, to provide defense, to improve transportation and public facilities, and above all to protect property. The tasks of "a tolerable administration of justice" are extensive. The reason that I am stressing this point is, of course, to question the wisdom of neoliberal reformers in post-communist societies, whose attack on the state is at times unremitting. If the abuses of state power in the past make this entirely comprehensible, it should nonetheless be stressed that what is actually needed is both the destruction of dangerous state power *and* the creation of much needed state capacities.

One can gain further practical understanding of the matter by thinking in abstract terms about what causes states to have strength. Michael Mann has usefully suggested that states have both infrastructural and despotic powers.[49] It is certainly useful to realize that despotically powerful states may in fact be very weak and unable to penetrate and organize their societies; and it is also true that modern conditions—railroads, bureaucracy, improved means of communication—lend all industrial states considerable power. Nonetheless, Mann's notion of infrastructure is severely limited, and his conception far too static. The capacity to penetrate society depends on the state's capacity to cooperate with society. Tocqueville realized this particularly clearly. A lessening of despotism and retention of local liberties increased total taxation in Languedoc, to whose political economy he devoted an important appendix in *The Old Regime and the French Revolution.* The aristocracy contributed to a government that it could control; by virtue of this and of the greater knowledge created by an environment of trust, the level of social infrastructure and general prosperity was strikingly higher in Languedoc than in the rest of France. Constitutionalism breeds trust, and trust empowers. Additionally, this was true more generally of England as compared to France: For Tocqueville, what matters about England is that its state is far more powerful than that of France, despite—or, rather, *because of*—its lack of absolutist powers.[50] Differently put, a civil society is not one simply marked by the presence of powerful groups organized apart from the state, but also one in which the capacity for cooperation channels different sources of power to point in the same direction. Perhaps the best phrase to sum this up is that applied by Richard Samuels to the Japanese state. His revisionist account shows MITI to be anything but all powerful: It is listened to partly because it listens in the manner of a curious "politics of reciprocal consent."[51] Recent accounts of the developmental states of

East Asia have shown that their tremendous skill in protecting infant industries by differential pricing, so as then to escort them into the market, does depend in part on their despotic powers; nevertheless, cooperation is surely helped by the fact that businessmen actually know that it is, so to speak, *their* developmental state.[52]

The pattern of historical development has given Eastern and Central Europe a tradition of unwieldy, despotic, and infrastructurally weak states.[53] Such states had been colonized by land-owning elites opposed to commerce; late industrialization added to this by making state service an avenue of social mobility for new middle-class segments. In principle, social revolution was supposed to have changed all this, but in fact severe limits to basic legitimacy meant that socialist states remained cumbersome and essentially weak—as was so dramatically proved by the manner of their demise.

Not much has yet changed. At present, states have few interlocutors:

> There is no new class of big farmers, with more than, say, 100 hectares. And although some specialization has occurred in farming, there are not yet any strong producers' organizations—a meat-producers' association, for example, or a flower growers' association. There is no organization of middle class self-employed professionals, to protect and promote their interests. Small tradesmen have not been very keen to organise themselves, while the few big capitalists have been more interested in setting up social clubs than business associations.[54]

It is important to note that these words come from a Pole analyzing the current situation in his country. Solidarity was a great crusade, based on an extraordinary national tradition of romanticism, nationalism, and Christian salvationism, representing a move of society against the state. But organization against the state is not the same thing as the self-organization of society—and of cooperation with a constitutional polity. Civil society has not yet been born. The state may have some autonomy, but this scarcely makes up in power terms for the limited capacities resulting from its lack of linkages with society. In the long run, a democratic deficit is a problem, not a solution.[55] The absence of settled structures, especially those of stable political parties, means that there is a continuing risk that the present vacuum in Central and Eastern Europe may yet be filled by symbolic politics that are superficially attractive but in fact societally regressive. The candidacy of Tyminski in the last presidential campaign in Poland is a clear example of this sort of politics, and it is all too easy to imagine alternate sources of symbolic outpouring.[56] The analytic point here is that social groups and political parties lead to regularity and predictability because they control their members. But this is only one way of looking at the matter, and it is not perhaps the most important. The ultimate justification for democracy lies in its capacity to produce better political rule than that provided by other systems. Wise men can no more be relied on to produce economic success than to promote social harmony; only democracy has the capacity to correct mistakes that arise and to provide the input of information necessary for rational policymaking.

It is hard to take a venal and weak state and turn it into a body capable of coordinating and cooperating with society. This transition has often been accompanied by foreign intervention. Even Britain managed the last stages of its endogenous transition only due to the intense pressure of war with France in the eighteenth century.[57] The situation in post-communist societies in comparative terms is especially difficult. Most obviously, the victors of the cold war are tending to shun the defeated rather than to reconstruct them. But perhaps the key problem can be highlighted by noting that it is a mistake to say that the old nomenklatura has the choice either of becoming nationalists or of entering into the market. There is a third option: Such actors can benefit from privatization while retaining linkages with the state. This situation—of privatization without marketization, of a class dependent upon the state—is extremely dangerous.[58] Such political capitalists may not be efficient, although their skimming-off of profitable sectors will subject the state to an intolerable fiscal crisis if greater subsidies are required to support remaining industry; both processes may well give capitalism a bad name and, thereby, encourage cynicism and apathy—*and* rage.[59] All in all, it is easy to envisage the emergence of just the sort of state against which Adam Smith inveighed.[60] One factor that may well determine different paths within the post-communist world is the extent to which the state was freed, in largest part because of different patterns of collapse, from the Communist party.[61] It already looks as if the greater the break, then the greater the chances of economic success.

Insofar as democracy stands against this sort of political capitalism, it is profoundly to be welcomed. To put it in another way, my thesis is that more rather than less democracy is needed. For democracy is on the side of economic efficiency, protesting against too great a continuity between old and new—thereby signaling willingness to accept thorough economic reform. Differently put, Balcerowicz is wrong to presume that every capitalist is good: To the contrary, some have the capacity, through extant linkages to the state, to conspire against the public. Two theoretical points should be kept in mind when contemplating active democratic conflict. First, a democratic transition requires that struggle ("a hot family feud," as Rustow has it) follow pacts—a sequence, however, that is probably now less suited to Russia than it is to East Central Europe.[62] The second point is closely related to this. Tocqueville was essentially a pessimist about liberalization: Nations that had liberty in aristocratic conditions have the right habits to sustain liberty in modernity; however, those nations that had once lost their liberty find it thereafter almost impossible to regain—whatever the social conditions. Nonetheless, if there is an activist hope in Tocqueville, it is simple: The exercise of liberty can and will re-create trust, thereby making liberty secure. The learning capacity of the Poles, seen in their ability to put an end to the initial plethora of small parties, allows us a measure of optimism in this regard.

Conclusion

It is likely, to begin with, that post-communist societies will see the emergence of a variety of regimes. At worst, Tocqueville may prove to be prescient:

> The segregation of classes, which was the crime of the late monarchy, became at a late stage a justification for it, since when the wealthy and enlightened classes were no longer able to act in concert and to take part in the government, the country became, to all intents and purposes, incapable of administering itself and it was needful that a master should step in.[63]

Any such reversion to authoritarianism is likely to be married to nationalism, whose future role can scarcely be exaggerated. Further, it is likely that different forms of corporatism—"societal" ones including workers, "statist" ones closest to new capitalists—will emerge in the region, given that this form has the capacity to manage crisis.[64] Only a few states are likely to make a full transition to recognizably Western politics. The Vysehrad countries (Poland, the Czech Republic, Slovakia, and Hungary) are obviously best favored: They have some memory of oppositional politics from Austro-Hungary, suffer least from symbolic politics, broke clearly with communism, are beginning to gain stable political parties, are likely to draw most investment, and may gain access to the European Community. Success is of course not guaranteed: Nationalist sentiments may still cost Hungary dearly, albeit they have probably ensured Czech success—at the cost of Slovak backwardness; the European Union may seek to deepen rather than to broaden; and reversion to the interwar situation of a set of geopolitically nonviable states threatened on both sides is a real possibility. Slovenia may draw close to Austria, and the Baltic states to Scandinavia, thereby ensuring a successful transition. It is hard not to be more and more pessimistic, in contrast, the further toward the East that one looks. It is hard to see the role of the state diminishing in Bulgaria and Romania, and the situation in Russia always suggested a pessimism, now justified by the electoral success of the radical nationalist Vladimir Zhirinovsky.

A second conclusion concerns the speed with which reforms should be enacted. It is very important to stress that speed is often confused with thoroughness: The Polish "Big Bang," for example, was not followed by further reforms, very much to the disappointment of many Polish commentators. One reason for that was the neoliberal belief that all good things would automatically follow the introduction of markets. That was naive, most importantly because it ignored the need to address the democratic deficit. Further, generalization about speed is made difficult given differential capacities to adjust. This should not be taken necessarily to imply that speed was suitable for, say, Czechoslovakia but not for Russia: Perhaps, to the contrary, the Czechs could afford to go slowly; however, the window of opportunity for reform in Russia was always so small that it had to be seized immediately. Notwithstanding these reservations, generally speaking, speed is to be recommended. The economic radicals had the capacity to act, whereas the gradualists were immobilized by their distrust of capitalism; the mistakes of the radicals can be repaired, but those of the gradualists may well be ruinous.

Notes

1. J. A. Hall, *Powers and Liberties,* Blackwell, Oxford, 1985, chapter 7.

2. G. O'Donnell, P. Schmitter, and L. Whitehead, eds., *Transitions from Authoritarian Rule,* Johns Hopkins University Press, Baltimore, 1986.

3. I am thinking, of course, of the sociology surrounding Tocqueville's maxim that a regime is at maximal danger at the moment it seeks to reform itself: See A. de Tocqueville, *The Old Regime and the French Revolution,* trans. S. Gilbert, Anchor Books, New York, 1955, part three, chapters 4–7. A. Przeworski's fullest analysis is in "The Games of Transition," in S. Mainwaring, G. O'Donnell, and J. S. Valenzuela, eds., *Issues in Democratic Consolidation: The New South American Democracies in Comparative Perspective,* University of Notre Dame Press, Notre Dame, 1992; but see also Przeworski's *Democracy and the Market: Political and Economic Reforms in Eastern Europe and Latin America,* Cambridge University Press, Cambridge, 1991.

4. R. Bova, "Political Dynamics of the Post-Communist Transition: A Comparative Perspective," *World Politics,* vol. 44, 1991, especially pp. 131–132.

5. L. Kolakowski, "Amidst Moving Ruins," *Daedalus,* vol. 121, 1992.

6. E. Gellner, *Civil Society and Its Enemies,* forthcoming.

7. J. A. Hall, *Coercion and Consent,* Polity Press, Cambridge, 1994, chapter 3.

8. For a recent example, see K. Jowitt, "The Leninist Legacy," in I. Banac, ed., *Eastern Europe in Revolution,* Cornell University Press, Ithaca, 1992, p. 213.

9. R. Boesche, *The Strange Liberalism of Alexis de Tocqueville,* Cornell University Press, Ithaca, 1987, part one.

10. A. de Tocqueville, *Selected Letters on Politics and Society,* ed. R. Boesche, trans. J. Toupin and R. Boesche, University of California Press, Berkeley, 1985, p. 115.

11. Tocqueville, *The Old Regime and the French Revolution,* p. 96.

12. A. de Tocqueville, *Democracy in America,* trans. G. Lawrence, Anchor Books, New York, 1969, pp. 539–541. See also J. C. Lamberti, *Tocqueville et les deux democraties,* Presses Universitaires de France, Paris, 1970.

13. It is important to realize that Tocqueville understood the difference between envy and jealousy. On that distinction, see H. Schoeck's remarkable *Envy: A Theory of Social Behavior,* trans. M. Glenny and B. Ross, Harcourt, Brace and World, New York, 1969.

14. A. de Tocqueville, *Journey to America,* trans. G. Lawrence, ed. J. P. Mayer, rev. ed. in collaboration with A. P. Kerr, Doubleday, New York, 1971, p. 259; cited by Boesche, *The Strange Liberalism of Alexis de Tocqueville,* p. 89.

15. Tocqueville, *Democracy in America,* pp. 505–506.

16. Tocqueville, *The Old Regime and the French Revolution,* p. 64.

17. Ibid., 136.

18. Ibid., 107.

19. I learned a great deal about this from discussions with Andrzej Rychard. Some of his views are available in "Participation and Interests: Dilemmas of the Emerging Social and

Political Structure in Poland," in W. Connor and P. Ploszajski, eds., *Escape from Socialism: The Polish Route*, Instytut Filozofii i Socjologii Publishers, Warsaw, 1992.

20. I. Gabor, "On the Immediate Prospects for Private Entrepreneurship and Re-embourgeoisement in Hungary: A Pessimistic Meditation in the Wake of Ivan Szelenyi's Prognosis of Continuity and Janos Kornai's Program of Discontinuity," Cornell Project on Comparative Institutional Analysis, cited in D. Stark, "Privatisation in Hungary: From Plan to Market or from Plan to Clan?," *East European Politics and Society*, vol. 4, 1990, pp. 390–392.

21. The analyses of Erving Goffman on this point—especially *Relations in Public*, Penguin, London, 1971—remain unsurpassed.

22. E. Gellner, "Nationalism and Politics in Eastern Europe," *New Left Review*, no. 189, 1991.

23. A. Motyl, *Will the Non-Russians Rebel? State, Ethnicity, and Society in the USSR*, Cornell University Press, Ithaca, 1987.

24. A. Khazanov, *Soviet Nationality Policy during Perestroika*, Delphic Associates, Falls Church, Virginia, 1991.

25. A. Khazanov, "The Collapse of the Soviet Union: Nationalism During Perestroika and Afterwards," *Nationalities Papers*, forthcoming.

26. I have in mind here the influential thought of Ernest Gellner. I find the emphasis on blocked mobility in *Thought and Change* (Weidenfeld and Nicolson, London, 1964, chapter 7) more convincing than the "industrial society" functionalism that has come to the fore in E. Gellner, *Nations and Nationalism*, Blackwell, Oxford, 1983.

27. L. Colley, *Britons*, Yale University Press, New Haven, 1992, chapter 3, especially pp. 117–132.

28. For a full defense of this position, see J. A. Hall, "Nationalisms: Classified and Explained," *Daedalus*, vol. 122, 1993.

29. A. Hirschman, *Exit, Voice and Loyalty*, Harvard University Press, Cambridge, 1972.

30. M. Mann, *The Rise of Classes and Nation-States, 1760–1914*, vol. 2 of *Sources of Social Power*, Cambridge University Press, Cambridge, 1993.

31. J. Linz and A. Stepan, "Political Identities and Electoral Sequences: Spain, the Soviet Union and Yugoslavia," *Daedalus*, vol. 121, 1992.

32. I. Banac, "The Fearful Asymmetry of War: The Causes and Consequences of Yugoslavia's Demise," *Daedalus*, vol. 121, 1992.

33. B. Krawchenko, "Ukraine: The Politics of Independence," in I. Bremmer and R. Taras, eds., *Nations and Politics in the Soviet Successor States*, Cambridge University Press, Cambridge, 1993.

34. R. Szporluk, *Communism and Nationalism: Karl Marx versus Friedrich List*, Oxford University Press, Oxford, 1988; Ding-xin Zhao and J. A. Hall, "State Power and Patterns of Late Development," *Sociology*, vol. 28, 1994.

35. The most sustained analysis is that of Przeworski, *Democracy and the Market*, but see too J. Elster, "When Communism Dissolves," *London Review of Books*, January 24, 1990, and C. Offe, "Capitalism by Democratic Design? Democratic Theory Facing the Triple Transition in East Central Europe," *Social Research*, vol. 58, 1991. These three authors do not, it should be made clear, agree on every detailed point; however, they do share a common style of analysis.

36. Przeworski, *Democracy and the Market*, conclusions.

37. A. Przeworski, "The Neo-Liberal Fallacy," *Journal of Democracy*, vol. 3, 1992.

38. J. H. Plumb, *The Growth of Political Stability in England, 1675–1725*, Penguin, London, 1969; R. Hofstader, *The Idea of a Party System: The Rise of Legitimate Opposition in the United States, 1780–1840*, University of California Press, Berkeley, 1969.

39. A. Gelb and K. Bradley, "The Radical Potential of Cash Nexus Breaks," *British Journal of Sociology*, vol. 31, 1980.

40. There is a large and high-powered literature on this point. See, among other works, D. Geary, *European Labour Protest, 1848–1945*, Methuen, London, 1984; M. Mann, "Ruling Class Strategies and Citizenship," *Sociology*, vol. 21, 1987; I. Katznelson and A. Zolberg, eds., *Working Class Formation*, Princeton University Press, Princeton, 1986; T. McDaniel, *Capitalism, Autocracy and Revolution in Russia*, University of California Press, Berkeley, 1987; and R. McKibbin, *The Ideologies of Class*, Oxford University Press, Oxford, 1990.

41. Weber made his views especially clear in his wartime reflections on the historical sociology of Wilhelmine Germany. These writings are available as "Parliament and Government in a Reconstructed Germany," in his *Economy and Society*, trans. G. Roth and C. Wittich, University of California Press, Berkeley, 1978, especially p. 1391. For the context of these writings and a comprehensive account of Weber's views, see W. Mommsen, *Max Weber and German Politics, 1890–1920*, University of Chicago Press, Chicago, 1984, chapter 5.

42. E. Comisso, "Property Rights, Liberalism, and the Transition from Actually Existing Socialism," *East European Politics and Society*, vol. 5, 1991.

43. D. Stark, "Path Dependency and Privatisation in East Central Europe" and L. Bruszt, "Transformative Politics: Social Costs and Social Peace in East Central Europe," both in *East European Politics and Society*, vol. 6, 1992.

44. J. A. Hall, "Consolidations of Democracy," in D. Held, ed., *Prospects for Democracy: North, South, East, West*, Polity Press, Cambridge, 1993.

45. D. Stewart, "Account of the Life and Writing of Adam Smith, Ll.D.," in vol. 3 of *The Glasgow Edition of the Works and Correspondence of Adam Smith*, that is, *Essays on Philosophical Subjects*, Oxford University Press, Oxford, 1980, p. 322.

46. A. Janos, "The Politics of Economic Backwardness in Continental Europe, 1848–1945," *World Politics*, vol. 41, 1989.

47. I. Szelenyi, *Socialist Entrepreneurs*, University of Wisconsin Press, Madison, 1988.

48. N. Philippson, "Adam Smith as Civic Moralist," in I. Hont and M. Ignatieff, eds., *Wealth and Virtue*, Cambridge University Press, Cambridge, 1986. Comisso makes similar points about the state needing to stand apart from capitalists in "Property Rights, Liberalism and the Transition from 'Actually Existing' Socialism."

49. M. Mann, "The Autonomous Power of the State," *European Journal of Sociology*, vol. 25, 1984.

50. Tocqueville's view is strikingly shown to be true by J. Brewer, *The Sinews of Power*, Knopf, New York, 1989.

51. R. Samuels, *The Business of the Japanese State*, Cornell University Press, Ithaca, 1987.

52. F. C. Deyo, ed., *The Political Economy of the New Asian Industrialism*, Cornell University Press, Ithaca, 1987; A. Amsden, *Asia's Next Giant*, Oxford University Press, Oxford, 1989; R. Wade, *Governing the Market*, Princeton University Press, Princeton, 1990.

53. Janos, "The Politics of Economic Backwardness"; G. Schopflin, "The Political Traditions of Eastern Europe," *Daedalus*, vol. 119, 1990.

54. W. Wesolowski, "Associative, Communal and Communitarian Ties in the Transition from Communism to Democracy," paper given at the first European Conference of Sociology, August 1992, p. 17.

55. B. Misztal, "Must Eastern Europe Follow the Latin American Way?" *European Journal of Sociology,* vol. 33, 1992, especially pp. 167–177.

56. A. Seligman, *The Idea of Civil Society,* Free Press, New York, 1992, chapter 4.

57. W. D. Rubinstein, "The End of 'Old Corruption' in Britain, 1760–1860," *Past and Present,* no. 101, 1983; Mann, *Sources of Social Power.* (vol. 2), chapter 4.

58. J. Staniszkis, *The Dynamics of the Breakthrough in Eastern Europe,* University of California Press, Berkeley, 1991, part one.

59. See F. Hagopian, "Democracy by Undemocratic Means—Elites, Political Pacts, and Regime Transition in Brazil," *Comparative Political Studies,* vol. 23, 1990.

60. G. Schopflin, "Obstacles to Liberalism in Post-Communist Politics," *East European Politics and Society,* vol. 5, 1991.

61. This is the view of Anatoly Khazanov, to whose conversation I am much indebted.

62. D. Rustow, "Transitions to Democracy," *Comparative Politics,* vol. 2, 1970, p. 355.

63. Tocqueville, *The Old Regime and the French Revolution,* p. 107.

64. J. Staniszkis, "Contribution to the Analysis of the Corporative State Emerging in Poland," *Politicus,* 1992. See also C. Maier, *Recasting Bourgeois Europe,* Princeton University Press, Princeton, 1990.

PART THREE

The International Context

5

Trade Integration of Eastern Europe and the Former Soviet Union into the World Economy: A Structuralist Approach

PAOLO GUERRIERI

There is no doubt that trade liberalization and greater export orientation are a necessity in the transformation process of Eastern Europe and the former Soviet Union, regions that have long relied on a highly protected pattern of industrial development. There is, however, considerable controversy on how to attain these two objectives. The core of the controversy is whether sustained outward-oriented growth together with the needed industrial restructuring is best achieved through rapid, across-the-board import liberalization and passive government policies or whether it requires selective trade and industrial policies to encourage a sustained increase in exports of manufactures and to diversify the export structures. Two contrasting approaches dominate the debate. In the first view—the "neoliberal" or "radical" perspective—only wholesale trade liberalization and currency convertibility can provide a rational set of market incentives, since they are considered catalysts for strong growth rates of output and exports. The alternative approach—a "structuralist" or "gradualist" perspective—stresses the importance of incentive selectivity, dynamic technical efficiency, and government guidance, pointing out that they are more likely to determine industrial restructuring and sustained outward-oriented growth than an allocation of resources driven entirely by the market.

In the following, we will address this controversial issue that is becoming more and more important for the East European economies and the former Soviet Union. Their growing integration into the European and the international economy are imposing costs that are going to affect social support for economic reforms. This chapter is divided into three parts. The first deals with the theoretical backgrounds of the two alternative approaches drawing on recent literature on innovation and growth theory. In the second, an analysis of the trade pattern and international competitiveness of Eastern Europe and the former Soviet Union over the past two decades is carried out. By employing an original data base for trade flows, the analysis focuses on structural changes and export diversification of the former socialist countries. These findings are used in the third part of the chapter to assess the perspectives of the integration of Eastern Europe and the former Soviet Union into the international economy. In particular, it aims at examining the constraint and incentives stemming from the international and European environments to the trade liberalization process that is taking place in the former communist area.

Trade Liberalization and Industrial Growth

The successful outcome of the transition to new market-type economies in East-Central Europe and in the former Soviet Union largely depends on their ability to restore the growth potential of their economic systems. Above all, this requires a fundamental restructuring and modernization of the industrial sector. Until quite recently, patterns of production were dominated by state investment decisions. The problem is, therefore, how to shift these patterns in such a way as to generate endogenous sources of investment, innovation, and, therefore, economic growth.

Compared with stabilization and liberalization, restructuring needs have received less attention. In any case, following what could be called a radical or neoliberal approach, a broad agreement has been reached concerning the key elements of an effective program of restructuring. Wholesale trade liberalization and currency convertibility are seen as central elements in a strategy for radical modifications of production structures, by allowing for importing competitive conditions and an efficient (world) price structure. In effect, in the neoclassical perspective, the fact of "getting prices right"—in the sense of the relative prices established in freely operating domestic and international markets—is considered a requirement for short-run optimal resource allocation and thus for maximizing the rate of these countries' long-term growth. And the move to an open economy may be regarded as constituting the most powerful mechanism for "rationalizing" domestic relative prices. In this perspective, a standard adjustment package for industry includes measures to fully liberalize import protection, reduce government intervention in domestic industry, privatize firms, correct factor prices, and let the market decide the pattern of comparative advantage.

In recent years, the economic success of the industrial strategies of the Newly Industrializing Countries (NICs), particularly those "export-led" strategies formulated in East Asia, often has been quoted to confirm the effectiveness of these policy prescriptions (Hughes, 1988). Actually, the neoclassical view merely equates Asian NIC strategies with "noninterventionist" and free-trade policies, which would have made it possible for these countries to take advantage of the expanding world trade. Thus, East Asian strategies are contrasted with the distortions and failures inevitably connected with government interventions of all kinds. Therefore, relatively homogeneous adjustment policies are formulated for industry in developing countries: These policies combine measures to remove all obstacles to the proper functioning of the markets with macroeconomic stabilization measures to achieve a targeted level of savings. In these outward-looking, market-oriented strategies, governments should not adopt policies that interfere with the free working of the markets; rather, they should provide only those "public goods" (i.e., law enforcement, infrastructures, macroeconomic stability, general education) that are difficult to obtain through private agents.

This policy package should be considered even more important for the East European economies and the former Soviet Union, beause liberalization measures and reforms should lead to increased integration of the former state-trading countries into international free trade. If they were to liberalize their trade and establish convertibility, the effect may be not only the restructuring of the industries in the former Council for Mutual Economic Assistance (CMEA) area but also the reinforcement of the process of domestic economic reforms. In this respect, the advantages for Eastern Europe of being quickly and fully included in the international division of labor may even be greater than the usual advantages.

The objections that can be made to the neoliberal policy prescriptions are basically of two orders: (1) The significance of the "outward-looking" strategies of the East Asian NICs is much more complex and ambiguous than the neoclassical view suggests. Governments in the economies of all the East Asian countries have been actively engaged in managing domestic industrial and trade structures (Haggard, 1990; Wade, 1990). The experience of the Asian NICs, therefore, shows that a proper structure of market incentives, such as those created by "outward-oriented" policies, can at the most be considered a necessary condition for the success of an industrialization process; (2) Restructuring, in the sense of structural change, is treated implicitly in the neoclassical approach as a smooth and continuous process that follows automatically from a correct incentive structure (right prices), once the latter is set in place in the economy as a whole. In an open economy, in particular, restructuring (structural change) is simply considered an automatic consequence of an efficient sectoral allocation of resources driven entirely by the market according to each country's comparative advantage.

As will be shown later in this chapter, the major reason for this view stems from the peculiar role attributed to "technology" in the neoclassical analysis of economic growth. Much of the outward-oriented literature, referred to earlier, considers technology to be an easy, costless, and instantaneous activity. Indeed, technology as a factor affecting industrial competitiveness and economic growth of developing countries is hardly mentioned in these studies.

To analyze the relationship between restructuring needs and international trade in Eastern Europe and the former Soviet Union, I include in this chapter an alternative approach to economic growth—a structuralist perspective—that draws on recent theoretical and empirical works on the role of technology in international competitiveness.[1] This view stresses the central role of technological change and dynamic efficiency to explain countries' relative industrial performance. Technological capability is considered a key factor driving international trade performance and the competitiveness of individual countries; this capability is a combination of knowledge, organization, and skills (Krugman, 1979, 1987; Soete, 1987; Dosi, Pavitt, and Soete, 1990). Technology, therefore, cannot be equated to "information" that is generally applicable and easily reproducible, as the neoclassical view suggests. In effect, innovative activity is a cumulative process that is both country- and firm-specific, since it is differentiated in its technical characteristics and its market application (Amendola et al., 1992; Pavitt, 1988; Cantwell, 1989). Furthermore, processes of technological change tend to assume varying sectoral features, in terms of differences in technological opportunities, sources, and appropriability conditions (Pavitt, 1984; Dosi et al., 1990; Guerrieri, 1992).

Although a rational structure of incentives (rational price structures) is significant for industrial development, the ability to respond to those incentives depends on the skill and knowledge of the countries concerned—that is, on their technological capability. This national ability to cope with industrial technology depends on the rate of generation-diffusion of technology and on the structural changes that such progress requires (Ernst and O'Connor, 1989; Lall, 1990). The industrial development may thus be seen as a sequence of structural change within the manufacturing sector, contributing to the emergence of new sectors (Justman and Teubal, 1991). In this regard, structural change is a cause of growth and should not be considered an automatic result of outward-oriented growth and efficient market forces (Nelson and Winter, 1982). Also, the linkages between different industrial sectors assume great importance (Schmookler, 1966; Rosenberg, 1976, 1982; Pavitt, 1988), in the form of innovative user-producer relationships (Scherer, 1982; Lundvall, 1988). In this perspective, the generation of comparative advantages is also a complex process in which the accumulation of physical capital interacts with the development of skill and technological endowments (Chesnais, 1986; Dosi et al., 1990). The structuralist approach —as we shall see repeatedly in this chapter—may be particularly fruitful for analyzing the current transition phase of Eastern Europe and the former Soviet Union.

Trade and Industrial Patterns of Former CMEA Countries

The structuralist approach will be used here to analyze the general trade pattern of Eastern Europe[2] and the former Soviet Union in order to discern the future direction along which these economies need to restructure their production sys-

TABLE 5.1 Shares in World Exports of the Former Soviet Union*

Category	*1970*	*1976*	*1979*	*1982*	*1985*	*1987*	*1989*
Total trade	1.02	1.35	1.38	1.71	1.33	1.03	1.00
Total manufactures	0.74	0.96	1.02	1.07	0.92	0.66	0.63
Agricultural products	1.71	1.93	1.44	1.26	0.99	1.21	1.34
Fuels	3.10	2.91	3.22	4.73	4.17	5.27	5.64
Other raw materials	2.16	2.33	0.72	0.88	0.73	0.63	0.78
Food industries	0.66	0.32	0.21	0.16	0.19	0.16	0.19
Traditional products	0.81	1.09	0.62	0.52	0.44	0.46	0.42
Resource-intensive products	2.52	4.26	4.84	5.97	5.10	4.09	3.76
Scale-intensive products	0.48	0.40	0.48	0.47	0.45	0.40	0.43
Specialized-supplier products	0.23	0.34	0.20	0.20	0.18	0.16	0.13
Science-based products	0.17	0.38	0.72	0.26	0.17	0.17	0.10

*Ratio of Soviet Union export to world export in each product group; percentage shares in values.
SOURCE: SIE–World Trade Data Base.

tems. It is certainly true that trade among the Eastern European countries and with the former Soviet Union has been conducted on the basis of centrally planned principles leading to peculiarly distorted production structures; yet, it is also true that the trade with the rest of the world (Western countries) was conducted, for the most part, on the basis of market conditions and may be used to individuate, at least in its broad outlines, the *revealed* comparative (absolute) advantage that Eastern Europe and the former Soviet Union could follow in their process of economic restructuring. The aim is also to provide empirical evidence for the evolution of technological and innovative capabilities of former CMEA countries (Guerrieri, 1993). To this end all traded industrial products are classified into six different types of industries according to a combination of sources, user requirements, and means of appropriation of technology: science-based, scale-intensive, specialized-supplier, primary resource-intensive, supplier-dominated or traditional, and food industries. All other nonindustrial products are grouped into three broad economic categories (agricultural products, fuels, and other raw materials), for a total of nine product groups. (See the Appendix for sectors within each group.)

The sectoral taxonomy adopted is consistent with the recent theoretical works on technological change and economic growth mentioned in the first part of the chapter. The analysis uses a variety of indicators and relies on an original trade data base (Servizi Informativi Estero: SIE-World Trade) comprising United Nations (U.N.) and Organization for Economic Cooperation and Development (OECD) statistical sources (400 product classes, 98 sectors, and 25 commodity groups) from more than 80 countries (OECDs, NICs, ex-CMEA, and LDCs).[3] Tables 5.1 through 5.4 show the trade performances of the former Soviet Union and Eastern Europe. The former Soviet Union substantially increased its world export share during the 1970s and the first half of the 1980s, but since then it experienced a sharp decline. These wide fluctuations should be attributed mainly to the oil

TABLE 5.2 Trade Balance of the Former Soviet Union*

Category	1970	1976	1979	1982	1985	1987	1989
Total trade	−0.170	−0.469	−0.091	−0.052	−0.180	−0.043	−0.148
Agricultural products	−0.386	−3.000	−2.579	−4.073	−4.476	−1.211	−2.099
Fuels	3.043	2.904	3.218	4.727	4.163	5.273	5.642
Other raw materials	1.960	1.736	−0.326	−0.095	0.182	0.049	−0.115
Food industries	0.094	−0.664	−1.094	−2.830	−1.469	−0.938	−0.792
Traditional products	−0.511	−0.304	−0.240	−1.073	−0.857	−0.302	−0.259
Resource-intensive products	1.758	3.504	4.107	5.059	4.422	3.457	3.156
Scale-intensive products	−0.718	−1.813	−1.388	−1.632	−1.375	−0.888	−0.901
Specialized-supplier products	−2.122	−3.802	−2.968	−2.903	−2.296	−1.920	−2.184
Science-based products	−0.705	−0.733	−0.349	−0.592	−0.546	−0.460	−0.487

*Standardized trade balance expressed as percentage of total trade in single product groups.
SOURCE: SIE–World Trade Data Base.

TABLE 5.3 Shares in World Exports of Eastern Europe*

Category	1970	1976	1979	1982	1985	1987	1989
Total trade	1.51	1.38	1.29	1.06	1.09	1.03	0.93
Total manufactures	1.49	1.50	1.44	1.20	1.18	1.03	0.96
Agricultural products	2.22	1.52	1.18	1.03	1.12	1.23	1.19
Fuels	1.28	0.89	0.62	0.40	0.54	0.62	0.54
Other raw materials	0.97	1.15	1.30	1.73	2.01	1.68	1.37
Food industries	2.78	2.25	1.80	1.21	1.47	1.54	1.61
Traditional products	2.00	2.17	1.95	1.70	1.57	1.55	1.34
Resource-intensive products	1.36	2.06	2.30	2.05	2.37	2.06	1.76
Scale-intensive products	1.41	1.30	1.31	1.15	1.08	0.94	0.92
Specialized-supplier products	1.08	1.05	1.08	0.92	0.79	0.69	0.65
Science-based products	0.60	0.61	0.53	0.39	0.31	0.31	0.26

*Ratio of Eastern Europe export to world export in each product group; percentage shares in values.
SOURCE: SIE–World Trade Data Base.

events throughout the last two decades. The share of oil and petroleum refinery products in the former Soviet Union's exports was very high in 1970 (32.3 percent) and has been strongly increasing ever since, reaching 60 percent in the late 1980s. Thus, the former Soviet Union increased its world export share thanks to the oil price increase in 1973–74 and 1979–80; however, the sharp decrease in oil price by 1986 severely penalized Soviet exports.

TABLE 5.4 Trade Balance of Eastern Europe*

Category	*1970*	*1976*	*1979*	*1982*	*1985*	*1987*	*1989*
Total trade	−0.089	−0.405	−0.200	0.062	0.146	0.119	0.090
Agricultural products	−0.065	−1.489	−1.743	−0.896	−0.485	−0.039	−0.118
Fuels	1.122	0.849	0.578	0.340	0.296	0.452	0.431
Other raw materials	−0.333	−1.589	−1.002	−0.357	−0.031	0.082	0.281
Food industries	1.209	0.741	0.270	−0.194	0.440	0.456	0.824
Traditional products	0.694	0.607	0.800	0.727	0.633	0.776	0.596
Resource-intensive products	−0.028	0.630	1.090	1.196	1.530	1.256	1.098
Scale-intensive products	−0.101	−0.636	−0.374	0.103	0.150	0.117	0.118
Specialized-supplier products	−1.684	−2.561	−2.010	−0.991	−1.105	−1.369	−1.188
Science-based products	−0.911	−1.072	−0.616	−0.344	−0.348	−0.323	−0.373

*Standardized trade balance expressed as percentage of total trade in single product groups.
SOURCE: SIE–World Trade Data Base.

Apart from energy sectors and primary resource-intensive products connected with raw materials exploitation, in which the Soviet share in world exports increased, competitiveness of the Soviet exports, already low at the beginning of the 1970s, experienced a sharp decline in food items and all other manufactures in the entire period considered here—and especially in the 1980s. The evolution of trade balances (standardized)[4] in the food items and all other manufactures sectors display similar negative trends. The decrease in Soviet market share has been particularly drastic in the more technologically sophisticated manufactured products included in specialized-supplier and science-based product groups.

Further evidence of the trade performances of the former Soviet Union is provided by its specialization patterns in the period just considered. To evaluate the patterns of specialization of the former Soviet Union we will now use both the well-known index of revealed comparative advantage[5] and the indicator measuring the relative contribution to the trade balance of the various product groups in consideration.[6] Note that a positive value of the latter indicates a comparative advantage in a given product group, whereas a negative value represents a comparative disadvantage. Both indices have been calculated with respect to the nine broad trade categories previously discussed.

A first overall view reveals clearly defined comparative advantage patterns for the former Soviet Union (Figure 5.1; Table 5.5). During the last two decades, this group of countries has consolidated its sound revealed comparative (absolute) advantages in fuels and in primary resource-intensive sectors (those connected with coal and oil), such as petroleum refineries and products. In all other manufactured product groups, particularly in mechanical engineering (specialized-supplier products) and food items, the former Soviet Union had and continues to

FIGURE 5.1 Patterns of Trade Specialization of the Former Soviet Union*

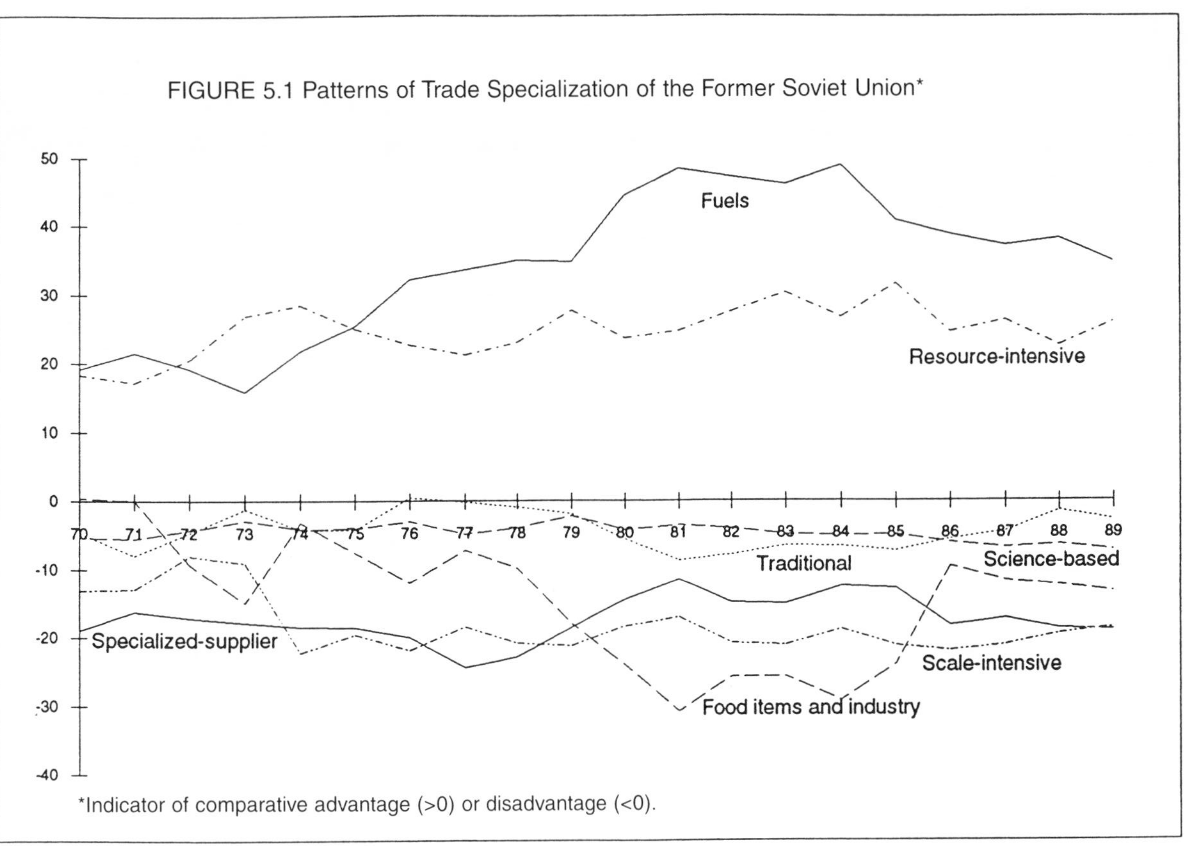

*Indicator of comparative advantage (>0) or disadvantage (<0).

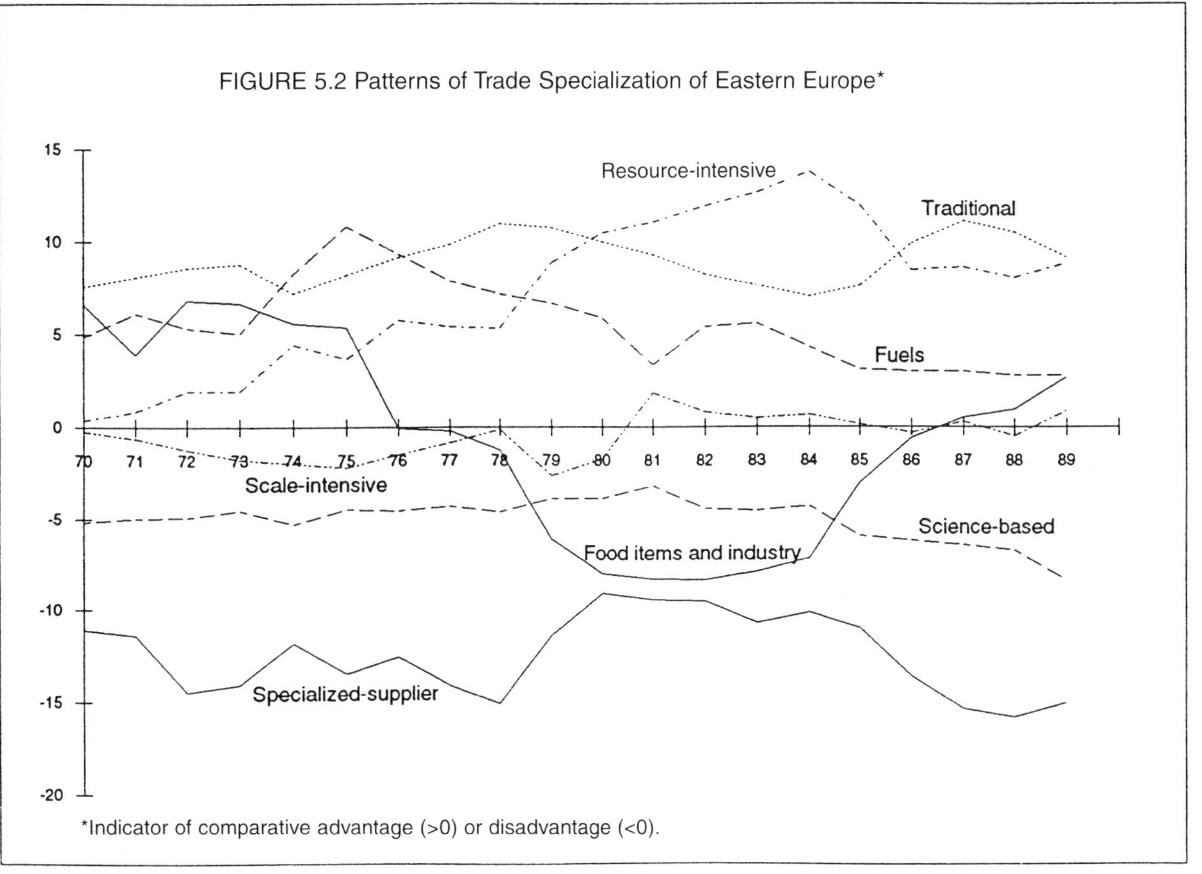

FIGURE 5.2 Patterns of Trade Specialization of Eastern Europe*

*Indicator of comparative advantage (>0) or disadvantage (<0).

have strong comparative disadvantages. Despite short-term fluctuations, this overall trade pattern was relatively stable over the entire 1970–1989 period.

As to Eastern Europe, the data in Tables 5.3 and 5.4 also provide clear evidence of a substantial loss of international competitiveness. In manufactured products, the most negative results have been those in mechanical engineerings (specialized-supplier) and science-based sectors, such as fine chemicals, electronics, and telecommunications, for which Eastern Europe's shares dropped by 50 percent during the 1980s. Trade balances (standardized) of Eastern Europe both in specialized-supplier and science-based sectors display less negative results. These, however, should be attributed to the fact that since the late 1970s, debt crisis has forced the East European countries to abandon ambitious growth plans. Consequently, imports, particularly those of investment goods, were reduced to improve trade balances. The trade balances actually improved, but at the cost of a further deterioration in the competitive position and trade performance of Eastern Europe. With regard to labor-intensive products (traditional products, such as textiles, apparel, footwear, metal products, etc.), Eastern Europe experienced a decline in its share of world exports but achieved substantial positive trade balances throughout the period considered here. There is, however, a sharp contrast with the performance of the South European and Asian countries, which are net exporters of traditional goods (Table 5.7). Furthermore, it should be noted that Eastern Europe's exports have also been falling behind those of the Asian NICs in all other manufactures groups, with the exception of the primary resource-intensive category (Tables 5.3 through 5.7). The widest gap between export performances of the East Europeans and Asian NICs was in specialized-supplier and, particularly, in research and development (R&D)-intensive (science-based) sectors, which are the two manufacturing groups with the highest technological content.

The specialization pattern of the East European countries closely reflects the evolution of their competitiveness in world markets (Figure 5.2; Table 5.6). By the end of the 1980s, Eastern Europe appeared to hold a sound comparative advantage in (1) traditional goods—such as textiles, apparel, footwear, and paper products; (2) fuels; and (3) natural resource-intensive sectors, such as basic metals and petroleum products. In the resource-intensive sector, the specialization of Eastern Europe increased sharply all through the 1980s, and its share in world exports of primary resource-intensive products also substantially increased over the 1970–1989 period. It should be recalled that during the first half of the 1980s, the lower price of oil imported from the former Soviet Union favored Eastern Europe's exports of petroleum products to OECD countries. Furthermore, since the early 1980s the exports of petroleum products strongly supported the volume of Eastern Europe's exports towards OECD countries. In the agricultural products group, the comparative advantage of Eastern Europe experienced sharp fluctuations throughout the 1970–1989 period, increasing to reach positive values in the late 1980s after having declined in previous years.

TABLE 5.5 The Former Soviet Union Trade: Product Composition and Specialization

	*Product Composition**						*Index of Revealed Comparative Advantages (I)*		
	Exports			*Imports*					
Category	*1970–73*	*1979–82*	*1986–89*	*1970–73*	*1979–82*	*1986–89*	*1970–73*	*1979–82*	*1986–89*
Agricultural products	16.9	6.7	7.6	23.1	22.3	15.5	172	89	129
Fuels	19.3	43.7	37.2	0.2	0.1	0.0	257	256	577
Other raw materials	5.1	0.9	0.8	0.4	1.0	0.7	212	51	69
Food industries	4.0	0.7	1.0	3.8	9.8	4.9	51	12	18
Traditional products	11.0	5.1	7.4	15.6	11.1	11.0	69	37	45
Resource-intensive products	26.1	30.6	29.2	5.2	4.8	4.4	306	325	374
Scale-intensive products	11.6	7.0	10.7	22.5	26.4	31.1	46	31	42
Specialized-supplier products	3.2	1.2	1.6	20.9	16.1	20.0	30	13	14
Science-based products	1.8	3.2	2.5	6.3	6.7	9.2	19	27	15
Residuals	1.1	0.9	2.0	1.8	1.8	3.2	34	40	72

*Percentage values.

(I) The index is the ratio of the share of the former Soviet Union in world exports of a given product group to the share of the former Soviet Union in total world exports (percentages).

SOURCE: SIE–World Trade Data Base.

TABLE 5.6 Eastern Europe Trade: Product Composition and Specialization

	Product Composition*						Index of Revealed Comparative Advantages (I)		
	Exports			Imports					
Category	*1970–73*	*1979–82*	*1986–89*	*1970–73*	*1979–82*	*1986–89*	*1970–73*	*1979–82*	*1986–89*
Agricultural products	13.8	6.9	7.2	13.7	16.0	9.1	14 0	94	119
Fuels	6.0	6.1	4.2	0.6	0.7	1.3	81	35	61
Other raw materials	1.6	2.2	1.9	2.0	3.2	1.9	66	121	161
Food industries	13.3	7.6	8.7	7.4	8.1	5.9	179	126	159
Traditional products	21.5	21.3	24.6	13.2	11.7	14.4	139	158	149
Resource-intensive products	8.5	18.5	15.3	7.2	7.8	6.7	96	197	192
Scale-intensive products	22.6	23.9	24.8	23.6	24.3	24.4	90	107	96
Specialized-supplier products	7.7	7.8	6.8	20.5	17.2	21.8	71	87	68
Science-based products	3.7	4.4	5.0	8.7	8.3	12.0	39	40	30
Residuals	1.4	1.4	1.5	3.2	2.6	2.5	43	60	45

*Percentage values.

(I) The index is the ratio of the share of Eastern Europe in world exports of a given product group to the share of Eastern Europe in total world exports (percentages).

SOURCE: SIE–World Trade Data Base.

TABLE 5.7 Shares in World Exports of Selected Groups of Countries (percentages, U.S. dollars, current prices)

	Greece, Portugal, Spain			*Asian NICs*[a]			*Asian NECs*[b]		
	1970	*1979*	*1989*	*1970*	*1979*	*1989*	*1970*	*1979*	*1989*
Total trade	1.39	1.68	2.25	2.07	3.72	6.51	1.57	2.41	2.52
Total manufactures	1.40	1.96	2.33	2.25	4.60	7.51	0.67	1.24	2.21
Agricultural products	2.38	2.34	3.47	2.58	3.29	3.05	7.23	7.77	7.17
Fuels	0.06	0.01	0.03	0.03	0.02	0.03	1.96	5.05	6.39
Other raw materials	1.34	1.55	2.78	0.71	0.82	0.73	4.84	3.90	3.68
Food industries	3.46	2.96	3.22	1.78	2.31	3.13	2.82	4.86	4.24
Traditional products	2.48	3.25	3.48	6.13	10.64	13.55	0.54	1.52	3.92
Resource-intensive products	1.15	1.45	2.99	1.51	2.99	4.77	1.93	2.16	1.70
Scale-intensive products	1.00	2.01	2.53	0.95	2.95	5.39	0.08	0.18	0.81
Specialized-supplier products	0.68	1.37	1.53	0.80	1.64	3.86	0.05	0.13	0.54
Science-based products	0.40	0.73	1.13	1.00	4.64	9.28	0.04	0.84	1.96

[a] Asian NICs: Hong Kong, Singapore, South Korea, and Taiwan.

[b] Asian NECs: Philippines, Indonesia, Malaysia, and Thailand.

SOURCE: SIE–World Trade Data Base.

To sum up, it seems clear that all through the 1980s the increase of Eastern European exports to world markets took place together with a deterioration of its trade patterns. The strong points of Eastern Europe's specialization continued to be and/or shifted toward those sectors that have been at the core of the delocalization processes of advanced countries toward the NICs: on one hand, energy-intensive intermediate industries (primary resource-intensive) and, on the other, labor-intensive products in traditional industries.[7]

Comparative disadvantages of Eastern Europe lie in most of the manufactures product groups aside from traditional and primary resource-intensive ones. In particular, in the mechanical engineerings (specialized-suppliers) group, Eastern Europe has continued to be strongly dependent on foreign suppliers.[8] The Asian NICs have surpassed Eastern Europe in many industries, not only in traditional and natural resource-intensive product groups but also in other more technologically sophisticated sectors. Additional insights into the trade specialization of Eastern Europe may be gained from a more disaggregated analysis of individual Eastern European countries. Tables 5.8, 5.9, and 5.10 show the evolution over the past two decades (1970–89) of trade patterns of three major East European countries—the former Czechoslovakia, Hungary, and Poland. These data highlight both the country-specific nature of trade specialization and some common sectoral features. By the late 1980s, the comparative advantages of the former Czechoslovakia were mostly concentrated in manufacturing—traditional goods being the strongest area of specialization. There was also a significant increase in the values of the indicator of contributions to trade balance for both the primary resource-intensive groups and agricultural products all through the 1980s. In scale-intensive industries (especially chemicals and iron-steel), of the three Eastern European countries, only Czechoslovakia maintained a positive specialization.

Hungary shows a rather different specialization pattern, distinguished by strength in agricultural products and food industries. As in all East European industries, there has been an increasing comparative advantage of Hungarian industry in natural resource-intensive sectors throughout the 1980s.

The specialization pattern of Poland lies somewhere between Czechoslovakia's and Hungary's. By the late 1980s, there were high comparative advantages in raw materials, especially in fuels, as well as significant positive values for the specialization measure in various industrial product groups. In food items, after a disappointing period of decreasing competitiveness, Poland improved its trade performance, particularly since the mid-1980s. In addition to this country-specific nature of specialization, the trade patterns of the three major Eastern European economies display common sectoral features: increasingly high comparative disadvantages in specialized-supplier and science-based sectors, especially throughout the 1980s. As previously discussed, this stems from the sharp deterioration of the technological capability of Eastern Europe during the past decade.

TABLE 5.8 Czechoslovakia Trade: Product Composition and Specialization

	*Product Composition**						*Index of Revealed Comparative Advantages (I)*		
	Exports			*Imports*					
Category	*1970–73*	*1979–82*	*1986–89*	*1970–73*	*1979–82*	*1986–89*	*1970–73*	*1979–82*	*1986–89*
Agricultural products	7.02	6.30	3.28	15.24	17.03	9.61	67	79	61
Fuels	2.30	4.46	2.39	0.27	0.25	0.01	41	29	41
Other raw materials	2.15	1.52	1.68	2.79	2.79	1.36	75	86	134
Food industries	6.25	4.63	7.19	7.29	4.73	3.90	86	71	109
Traditional products	25.17	26.79	28.33	11.86	9.71	10.77	169	197	175
Resource-intensive products	7.92	9.41	12.09	5.38	8.20	7.60	89	111	141
Scale-intensive products	30.00	27.53	28.04	18.97	23.22	21.52	117	120	107
Specialized-supplier products	14.07	11.87	8.86	23.12	21.87	28.74	120	123	96
Science-based products	3.63	5.96	6.43	10.69	9.55	14.48	40	52	38
Residuals	1.49	1.53	1.71	4.39	2.65	2.01	48	61	55

*Percentage values.

(I) The index is the ratio of the share of Czechoslovakia in world exports of a given product group to the share of Czechoslovakia in total world exports (percentages).

SOURCE: SIE–World Trade Data Base.

TABLE 5.9 Hungary Trade: Product Composition and Specialization

	*Product Composition**						*Index of Revealed Comparative Advantages (I)*		
	Exports			*Imports*					
Category	*1970–73*	*1979–82*	*1986–89*	*1970–73*	*1979–82*	*1986–89*	*1970–73*	*1979–82*	*1986–89*
Agricultural products	25.83	11.43	11.44	9.46	6.22	3.16	265	153	182
Fuels	0.06	0.77	0.25	0.05	0.1	0.09	1	5	7
Other raw materials	1.04	1.36	0.99	0.91	0.72	0.69	35	98	80
Food industries	15.54	16.34	18.48	11.14	4.79	2.71	226	279	301
Traditional products	19.59	24.66	22.48	17.72	18.32	19.18	140	175	141
Resource-intensive products	7.66	9.15	11.05	9.77	8.61	6.06	75	97	144
Scale-intensive products	19.91	23.11	21.05	23.02	26.42	30.52	74	104	82
Specialized-supplier products	4.28	6.42	7.16	12.36	21.39	21.57	42	78	69
Science-based products	3.28	5.07	5.71	10.83	10.86	14.28	36	41	34
Residuals	2.81	1.69	1.39	4.74	2.57	1.74	55	77	47

*Percentage values.

(I) The index is the ratio of the share of Hungary in world exports of a given product group to the share of Hungary in total world exports (percentages).

SOURCE: SIE–World Trade Data Base.

TABLE 5.10 Poland Trade: Product Composition and Specialization

	*Product Composition**						*Index of Revealed Comparative Advantages (I)*		
	Exports			*Imports*					
Category	*1970–73*	*1979–82*	*1986–89*	*1970–73*	*1979–82*	*1986–89*	*1970–73*	*1979–82*	*1986–89*
Agricultural products	12.69	7.75	11.59	17.8	20.53	10.77	126	105	182
Fuels	17.17	20.62	11.2	0.01	0.01	0.2	239	106	203
Other raw materials	2.97	2.84	3.46	4.15	3.81	1.19	109	265	366
Food industries	20.04	10.36	11.92	8.38	8.2	7.9	238	157	205
Traditional products	15.23	16.88	20.2	10.08	10.18	14.22	102	124	122
Resource-intensive products	7.32	12.05	10.68	9.98	5.5	4.63	83	136	123
Scale-intensive products	17.45	18.6	19.88	23.93	25.12	25	73	86	71
Specialized-supplier products	4.07	6.38	6.03	15.36	17.19	20.08	41	70	55
Science-based products	1.92	3.43	3.42	7.06	6.34	12.88	22	31	19
Residuals	1.14	1.09	1.62	3.25	3.12	3.13	35	52	60

*Percentage values.

(I) The index is the ratio of the share of Poland in world exports of a given product group to the share of Poland in total world exports (percentages).

SOURCE: SIE–World Trade Data Base.

Policy Implications

The specialization pattern clearly indicates the backwardness of the former CMEA countries' trade structure. Many factors may be used to explain this poor trade performance. Among those, a key role was played by the "technology factor," which negatively affected the competitive position of all CMEA countries throughout the last two decades (Poznanski, 1987; Hanson and Pavitt, 1987). Eastern Europe's long-standing technological lag behind not only the major OECD countries but also the group of NICs has expanded. This poor technological capability also reflects Eastern Europe's failure to adopt advanced technologies imported from the West, due to a highly inefficient system of intra- and inter-sector technological diffusion. This may be explained by the nature of centrally planned economies in the period considered.[9]

The poor competitive conditions of industrial systems in the former CMEA area confirm the need for real restructuring—that is, for structural changes in patterns of domestic production (Hamilton and Winters, 1992). The problem is how to shift these patterns in such a way as to generate endogenous sources of innovation and accumulation. In that regard, wholesale liberalization, currency convertibility, and a minimal state approach—as suggested by neoliberal doctrine—would not seem able to generate the best environment in which such an adjustment process can take place. Given their relatively poor technological capability when compared with other industrial nations, the former CMEA countries are at best only able to participate in world trade at a level similar to that of the NICs. This situation is likely to prevail for the foreseeable future. That is confirmed by the evidence previously examined in Tables 5.8 through 5.10 concerning the revealed comparative advantage of former CMEA countries.

The former Soviet Union is likely to export fuels and raw materials, exploiting its abundance of natural resources, while importing a wide range of manufactured products, especially those included in the specialized-supplier and science-based groups. Furthermore, the likely adoption of Western technologies could substantially improve the future performance of the currently inefficient energy sector of the former Soviet Union, so that its net export of energy could increase significantly as well as its import of manufactures from Western countries.

The analysis of the commodity composition of Eastern Europe's trade has shown that its comparative advantages in manufacturing lie in resource-intensive and labor-intensive traditional products. As a consequence, these countries are likely to expand their manufactures exports in sectors such as textiles, clothing, footwear, and other product groups in which labor-cost rather than technology plays an important role.[10] The future competitiveness of Eastern Europe's heavy industry is less clear-cut, because the adoption of market criteria and Western environmental standards in Eastern Europe could penalize the region's supply capacity and exports. In regard to fuels and related products, however, the comparative advantage of many Eastern European countries was based on cheap imports of petroleum from the USRR and may entirely disappear as a consequence of the new market price of oil from the former Soviet Union. In addition, net exports of agricultural products from Eastern Europe are likely to increase—as its supply is going to become more efficient and expand (Guerrieri, 1993). On the import side, capital goods and technological inputs, both deriving from specialized-supplier and science-based groups, will constitute the bulk of Eastern Europe purchases from foreign markets.

Trade flows of Eastern Europe and the former Soviet Union with Western countries in 1990 and 1991 have provided, both in terms of geographical and sectoral changes, the first significative confirmations of the trade specialization pattern discussed above (ECE, 1992, pp. 63 and 67).

Under these conditions, a neoliberal strategy of following across-the-board liberalization, convertibility, and removal of capital control does not seem able to promote the needed industrial restructuring and technological upgrading of former CMEA economies. The problem is that there are no examples of countries that have achieved strong growth rates of exports and output following wholesale liberalization policies. As a number of theoretical and empirical investigations have indicated, export orientation *per se* could provide benefits; however, together with premature across-the-board import liberalization, it may knock out industries that have not set up the needed technological capability (Ernst and O'Connor, 1989). Even in countries with a large, well-educated, and low-paid labor force—as in many Eastern European countries —it could lead to static specialization and a poorly diversified industrial base at the low end of the technological scale (Lall, 1990).

In contrast, as the cases of the two leading East Asian NICs (Taiwan and South Korea) show, the success of an export-oriented strategy greatly depends on how it combines a rational structure of incentives (relative prices) with: (1) an adequate supply of trained people; (2) an environment that encourages technological effort; (3) protection for selected activities involving difficult "learning"; (4) industrial/technological policies that strengthen local capabilities and overcome many market failures (Wade, 1990). It is evident that this requires the implementation of highly selective trade and structural policies to encourage the necessary restructuring. Of course, in the new market-directed environment, the former CMEA countries can no longer rely on active government control as in the former command economy. The success of the NICs suggests, however, that government interventions still have a key role to play in the current transition period of former CMEA countries. In this regard, one should be reminded that, although major discussions and efforts of policymakers, international institutions, and economists have been devoted to macroeconomic stabilization and liberalization policies, the designing and implementation of structural policies, such as those previously mentioned, have largely been neglected so far (Nove, 1992).

The need for alternative strategies and policy instruments to a neoliberal radical path are even greater in light of the hostile international environment that all former CMEA countries face. In particular, the integration of the European market could negatively affect the prospects for access by CMEA exports. In this respect, it is certain that Western countries, in general, and the European Community (EC), in particular, can provide major help in addition to financial and technical assistance, in moving toward a free-trade relationship with former CMEA countries. Guaranteeing the products of Eastern European countries free access to the Community markets is the most effective way to reduce their balance-of-payments constraints and to stimulate the restructuring of their systems of production while promoting direct investments of Western firms to the former CMEA countries. In order to fully liberalize its imports, however, the EC has some hard decisions to make that are connected with the effects within and outside the EC of the future integration of Eastern Europe into the world economy.

Although increased trade will provide economic gains to both Eastern and Western Europe in the long run, there seems to be a real possibility that, in the short to medium term, the pattern of specialization of the former CMEA countries will cause problems for intra-European trade, although the trade flows of the former CMEA area constitute a small fraction of the EC market as a whole. The imports and exports of Eastern Europe could have asymmetrical effects, in terms of costs and benefits associated with trade flows, on EC member countries. On the import front, the rich, northern members of the EC—Germany in particular—that hold strong comparative advantages in specialized-supplier and science-based sectors, are likely to be major beneficiaries of the new markets in Eastern Europe (see Table 5.11). In contrast, the growth of exports of manufactures labor-intensive goods (traditional products) and, to a lesser extent, agricultural products of former CMEA members are going to penalize the southern, poorer members of the EC most—Spain, Portugal, and Greece—that are firmly specialized in traditional sectors and in food items (see Table 5.11). Eastern Europe-EC exchanges will take the form of interindustry trade and will thus be akin to the existing North-South trade pattern within the EC and that between the EC and regions south of it. This would imply that Eastern Europe-EC trade could produce serious income-distribution effects and, consequently, significant adjustment problems within the Community area.

As is well known, in the actual politics of trade policy, income distribution is of crucial importance. It is desirable that the EC absorb these effects without shifting the major impact onto poor southern EC members, exacerbating their adjustment costs connected with the completion of the Single European Market and, thus, widening the economic disparities that already exist within the EC.

Steps should therefore be taken by the EC to implement structural policies and a redistributive program to favor trade adjustment within the Community (Jacquemin and Sapir, 1991). However, many have acknowledged that this will not be very easy in today's dreary economic climate. Important steps have already been taken by the EC in the elimination of barriers to EC trade with Eastern Europe, but even more important work remains to be done in a variety of sectors

TABLE 5.11 Index of Revealed Comparative Advantages of the EC Countries (1987–89)

	*Exports**						
Category	*EEC (12)*	*Germany*	*France*	*United Kingdom*	*Italy*	*Greece, Portugal, Spain*	*Other EEC Countries*
Agricultural products	66	19	120	44	38	152	102
Fuels	22	6	3	103	1	3	24
Other raw materials	42	25	37	47	30	106	54
Food industries	138	76	176	98	80	144	250
Traditional products	107	87	86	78	208	165	95
Resource-intensive products	84	66	67	81	69	133	119
Scale-intensive products	117	140	124	102	87	106	109
Specialized-supplier products	126	174	95	118	176	65	75
Science-based products	96	105	112	134	70	47	76

	*Imports***						
	EEC (12)	*Germany*	*France*	*United Kingdom*	*Italy*	*Greece, Portugal, Spain*	*Other EEC Countries*
Agricultural products	104	109	84	79	137	137	100
Fuels	98	83	107	59	139	159	91
Other raw materials	98	115	73	94	93	94	104
Food industries	126	112	125	131	149	111	133
Traditional products	104	114	108	110	75	71	117
Resource-intensive products	108	123	107	100	116	77	104
Scale-intensive products	97	89	98	99	99	106	99
Specialized-supplier products	88	79	99	90	77	114	84
Science-based products	96	100	100	112	89	88	83

*Ratio of the share of each individual country in world exports of a given product group to the share of the same country in total world exports (percentages).

**Ratio of the share of each individual country in world imports of a given product group to the share of the same country in total world imports (percentages).

SOURCE: SIE–World Trade Data Base.

(e.g., textiles, the iron and steel industry, and agriculture) that hold the greatest export potential, as previously shown, for most Eastern European countries. It is, therefore, a growing risk that divergent national interests within the Community could hinder the further liberalization of EC markets. The outcomes could be extremely negative, because Community openness, together with adequate financial and technical assistance, constitutes a necessary condition for recovery in Eastern Europe.

Conclusion

This chapter has considered the debate surrounding the role of the international environment and trade liberalization policies in the transition to new market-type economies in East-Central Europe and in the former Soviet Union. In this regard, we surveyed in some detail the two alternative approaches—the neoliberal and the structuralist perspectives—and examined the statistical evidence surrounding the long-run trade performance of the former CMEA countries.

The statistical evidence confirms that trade liberalization and greater export orientation are a "must" in the transformation process of Eastern Europe and the former Soviet Union. In order to attain it, market forces may play an important role; however, an equally decisive role in the creation and exploitation of market potential rests with efficient, selective government policies. In fact, a system of incentives such as those created by wholesale import liberalization, suggested by the neoliberal approach, does not seem to be able to produce the results its adherents expect in terms of resource reallocation and industrial growth in an emerging economy. As the experience of Asian NICs strongly confirms, highly selective trade and industrial policies play a dominant role in the setup and consolidation phase of an outward-oriented industrialization, also underlining the crucial role of government in a transforming economy.

Therefore, a more realistic view of the process of industrialization requires a more pragmatic, gradualist approach to economic reforms in the former CMEA countries. The need for reform is evident. While some elements of the current reform package may well remain, others need to be modified, extended, or changed. Most important, the long-term nature of the structural changes to be induced clearly must be recognized. Thus, new and more efficient prescriptions for industrial development need to be found; a highly complex and eclectic approach must be adopted rather than generalizations that may be attractive but are of little practical use—especially because the international and European economic environment is far from being favorable.

One final note: The new selective trade and industrial policies suggested by this analysis are certainly not meant to replace traditional macroeconomic stabilization policy but rather to complement it. In this regard, it should be recalled that the growth in trade volume of countries in the former CMEA area will heavily depend on the future evolution of overall macroeconomic conditions. Slow growth in the EC region increases the likelihood that adjustment policies in the transition phase will turn defensive and protectionistic; whereas sustained EC growth increases the likelihood that trade integration will enhance the openness and efficient industrial specialization of European countries and, therefore, reinforce future economic growth. In this respect, the EC macroeconomic policy also is going to play a very important role—one that, whatever its structure, is inextricably linked to the fate of the transformation process itself.

Appendix: SIE–World Trade Data Base

The foreign trade statistics used in this paper stem from the SIE–World Trade data base, which provides detailed information on the exports and imports of 83 countries with respect to 400 product groups, 98 sectors, 25 broad commodity groups, and 5 main product categories. The data base includes trade statistics with respect to the 24 OECD countries, the newly industrializing countries (NICs), the other developing countries, and the former CMEA countries and makes it possible to examine and analyze the entire world trade matrix. The source for the basic trade statistics of the SIE–World Trade data base is the publications of the OECD and the United Nations, which are provided on magnetic tapes.

The SIE data base is organized in different product group classifications at various levels of disaggregation (400 product groups, 98 sectors, 25 categories, 5 main branches), according to the three Standard International Trade Classifications (SITC)—*Revised, Revision 2,* and *Revision 3,*—defined by the Statistical Office of the United Nations (1961, 1975, and 1985, which correspond to the periods 1961–75, 1978–87, and 1988–present).

The broad product group classifications used in this chapter are based on the 400 product groups of the SIE–World Trade data base. A summary of the product groups included in each broad product group is as follows:

1. *Food items and Agricultural raw materials* (41 product groups): Food; live animals; animal oil and fats; natural rubber; vegetable and animal textile fibers; cork and wood; skins; and so forth.
2. *Fuels* (4 product groups): Coal; petroleum; oil; and gas.
3. *Other raw materials* (17 product groups): Iron ore; ores of base metals; and other crude minerals.
4. *Food industry* (36 product groups): Meat and meat preparations; dairy products; vegetables and fruit preparations; cereal preparations; sugar preparations; and other such edible products.
5. *Science-based group* (59 product groups): Synthetic organic dyestuffs; radioactive and associated materials; polymerization and copolymerization products; antibiotics and other pharmaceuticals; nuclear reactors; automatic data-processing machines and units; telecommunications equipment; semiconductor devices; electronic microcircuits; electronic measuring instruments; electric power machinery and associated apparatuses; internal-combustion piston engines; aircraft and associated equipment; medical instruments; optical instruments; photographic equipment and associated apparatuses; and so forth.
6. *Scale-intensive group* (88 product groups): Organic chemicals; inorganic chemicals; other chemical materials and products; medicinal and pharmaceutical products; rubber manufactures; iron and steel; television, radio, and other image-sound recorders and reproducers; household-type electrical equipment; ships and boats; railway vehicles and equipment; road vehicles; and so on.
7. *Specialized-supplier group* (43 product groups): Agricultural machinery; machine tools for working metals; metal-working machinery; other machine tools for specialized industries; construction and mining machinery; textile and leather machinery; paper and paperboard machinery; other machinery for specialized indus-

tries; other general industrial machinery and equipment; electrical equipment and components; measuring, checking, and analyzing instruments; optical goods; and other miscellaneous products.

8. *Resource-intensive group* (18 product groups): Paper and paperboard; petroleum products; nonmetallic mineral manufactures; nonferrous metal products, and the like.
9. *Traditionals or Supplier-dominated group* (76 product groups): Textile products; articles of apparel and clothing accessories; leather manufactures; footwear; wood manufactures; furniture; paper and printed products; ceramic materials products; glass products; miscellaneous manufactures of metal (structures, tools, cutlery, and other articles); jewelry, goldsmiths; imitation jewelry; musical instruments; sporting goods; toys and games; and other miscellaneous products.
10. *Residuals* (18 product groups): Other product groups not elsewhere specified.

Notes

1. Surveys of the recent literature on innovation and technological change are in Freeman (1982), Rosenberg (1982), Scherer (1986), and Dosi et al. (1988).

2. Reference to Eastern Europe in this chapter includes the following countries: Bulgaria, the Czech Republic, Slovakia, Hungary, Poland, Romania, and the former East Germany.

3. For further information on the SIE–World Trade data base, see Guerrieri-Milana (1990) and Guerrieri (1992). It should be noted that the exports and imports of Eastern Europe in the present analysis do not include intra-CMEA trade flows.

4. The standardized trade balance or the indicator of relative competitive position (IRCP) highlights the international distribution over time of trade surpluses and deficits among countries in each group of products. Trade surpluses and deficits are standardized by total world trade in the same group of products (CEPII 1983; CEPII 1989). The evolution of trade balance distribution reveals competitiveness patterns of various countries in a certain group of products. For each country (j) the indicator is given by:

$$\text{IRCP} = \frac{\text{Xi - Mi}}{\text{WTi}}$$

5. This is the ratio of the share of individual countries in world exports (imports) of a given product group to the share of the same country in total world exports (imports).

6. The indicator of the contribution to trade balance (ICTB) of a country (j) with respect to a given group of products (i) is the following:

$$\text{ICTBi} = [\ \frac{(\text{Xi - Mi})}{(\text{X + M})/2} - \frac{(\text{X - M})}{(\text{X + M})/2} \text{ x } \frac{(\text{Xi + Mi})}{(\text{x + M})}\ ] \text{ x } 100$$

The sum of the indicators with respect to the various product groups (i) in which the total trade of a country is disaggregated equals zero (see CEPII, 1983).

7. Given the high share of Eastern Europe-European Community (EC) trade in total trade of Eastern Europe, the specialization of Eastern Europe toward the Community displays a pattern as similar as the overall one just discussed; however, it should be pointed out that the values of indicators of Eastern Europe's comparative advantage in traditional goods and food items are substantially higher in Eastern Europe-EC trade than in Eastern Europe's trade with the world.

8. It should be noted that most of these sectors constitute the strong point of specialization of Eastern Europe in intra-CMEA trade and especially in trade with the Soviet Union (Drabek, 1989). This essentially dual trade specialization structure provides further evidence of the poor competitiveness of Eastern Europe in technologically complex sectors.

9. A classical analysis of the major shortcomings of a planned economy is in Kornai (1982 and 1985).

10. For similar results on the impact of Eastern Europe, see Collins and Rodrik (1991); Landesman and Szekely (1991). In contrast, a Centre for Economic Policy Research (CEPR) report (1990) and Hamilton and Winters (1992) both suggest that the East European comparative advantage will be in high-technology goods (intra-industry) rather than in labor-intensive ones.

References

Amendola, G., Guerrieri, P., and Padoan, P. C. 1992. "International Patterns of Technological Accumulation and Trade." *Journal of International Comparative Economics,* No. 2.

Cantwell, J. A. 1989. *Technological Innovations and Multinational Corporations.* Oxford: Basil Blackwell.

CEPII. 1983. *Economie mondiale: la montee des tensions.* Paris: Economica.

CEPII. 1989. *Commerce internationale: la fin des avantages acquis.* Paris: Economica.

CEPR, 1990. *Monitoring Eastern Europe: The Impact of Eastern Europe.* London: Centre for Economic Policy Research Annual Report.

Chesnais, F. 1986. "Science, Technology and Competitiveness." *OECD STI Review,* No. 1.

Collins, S. M., and Rodrik, D., 1991. *Eastern Europe and the Soviet Union in the World Economy.* Washington, D.C.: Institute for International Economics.

Dosi, G., Pavitt, K., and Soete, L. 1990. *The Economics of Technical Change and International Trade.* Brighton: Wheatsheaf.

Dosi, G., et al. 1988. *Technical Change and Economic Theory.* London: Frances Pinter.

Drabek, Z., 1989. "CMEA: The Primitive Socialist Integration and Its Prospects." In *Economic Aspects of Regional Trading Arrangements,* edited by D. Greenaway et al. New York: New York University Press.

ECE (Economic Commission for Europe). 1992. *Economic Bulletin for Europe,* vol. 44, United Nations.

Ernst, D., and O'Connor, D. 1989. *Technology and Global Competition: The Challenge from Newly Industrialising Economies,* Paris: Organization for Economic Cooperation and Development.

Freeman, C. 1982. *The Economics of Industrial Innovation.* London: Frances Pinter.

Guerrieri, P. 1992. "Technological and Trade Competition: The Case of the United States, Japan and Germany." In *Linking Trade and Technology Policies,* edited by M. Harris and G. E. Moore. Washington, D.C.: National Academy of Engineering.

Guerrieri, P. 1993. "Trade Patterns of Eastern Europe and European Economic Integration." In *Mixed Economies in Europe: East and West,* edited by Wolfgang Blaas and John Foster. Cheltenham: Elgar.

Guerrieri, P. and Milana, C. 1990. *L'Italia e il commercio mondiale,* Bologna: Il Mulino.

Haggard, S. 1990. *Pathways from the Periphery: The Politics of Growth in the Newly Industrializing Countries,* Ithaca, Cornell University Press.

Hamilton, C., and Winters, A. 1992. "Opening Up International Trade with Eastern Europe," *Economic Policy,* No. 14.

Hanson, P., and Pavitt, K. 1987. *The Comparative Economics of Research, Development and Innovation in East and West: A Survey.* London and New York: Harwood Academic Publishers.

Hughes, H., ed. 1988. *Achieving Industrialization in East Asia.* Cambridge: Cambridge University Press.

Jacquemin, A., and Sapir, A. 1991. "The Internal and External Opening-Up of the Single Community Market: Efficiency Gains, Adjustment Costs and New Community Instruments," *The International Spectator* XXVI, No. 3, July–September.

Justman, M., and Teubal, M. 1991. "A Structuralist Perspective on the Role of Technology in Economic Growth and Development." *World Development* 19, No. 9.

Kornai, J. 1982. *The Economics of Shortage.* Amsterdam: North Holland.

Kornai, J. 1985. *Contradictions and Dilemmas.* New York: Corvina.

Krugman, P. 1979. "A Model of Innovation, Technology Transfer, and the World Distribution of Income." *Journal of Political Economy* 82, 253–266.

Krugman, P. 1987. "The Narrow Moving Band, the Dutch Disease, and the Competitive Consequences of Mrs. Thatcher: Notes on Trade in the Presence of Dynamic Scale Economies." *Journal of Development Economics* 27.

Lall, S. 1990. *Building Industrial Competitiveness in Developing Countries.* Paris: Organization for Economic Cooperation and Development.

Landesman, M., and Szekely, I. 1991. "Industrial Restructuring and the Reorientation of Trade in Czechoslovakia, Hungary and Poland." *CEPR Discussion Paper,* No. 546, April.

Linz, Juan J., and Valenzuela, Arturo, eds. 1994. *The Failure of Presidential Democracy.* Baltimore: Johns Hopkins University Press.

Lundvall, B. A. 1988. "Innovation as an Interactive Process: From User-Producer Interaction to the National System of Innovation." In *Technical Change and Economic Theory,* edited by G. Dosi et al. London: Frances Pinter.

Nelson, R. R., and Winter, S. G. 1982. *An Evolutionary Theory of Economic Change.* Cambridge: Harvard University Press.

Nove, A. 1992. "Economics of the Transition Period." *The Harriman Institute Forum* 5, Nos. 11–12.

Pavitt, K. 1984. "Sectoral Patterns of Technical Change: Towards a Taxonomy and a Theory." *Research Policy,* 13, 343–373.

Pavitt, K. 1988. "International Patterns of Technological Accumulation." In *Strategies in Global Competition,* edited by N. Hood and J. E. Vahlne. London: Croom Helm.

Poznanski, K., 1987. *Technology, Competition, and the Soviet Bloc.* Berkeley: University of California, Institute of International Studies.

Rosenberg, N. 1976. *Perspectives on Technology.* Cambridge: Cambridge University Press.

Rosenberg, N. 1982. *Inside the Black Box.* Cambridge: Cambridge University Press.

Scherer, F. M. 1986. *Innovation and Growth: Schumpeterian Perspectives.* Cambridge: Massachusetts Institute of Technology Press.

Scherer, F. M. 1982. "Inter-industry Technology Flows in the United States." *Research Policy* 11, 227–245.

Schmookler, J. 1966. *Invention and Economic Growth.* Cambridge: Harvard University Press.

Soete, L. 1987. "The Impact of Technological Innovation on International Trade Patterns: The Evidence Reconsidered." *Research Policy* 16, 101–130.

Wade, R. 1990. *Governing the Market: Economic Theory and the Role of Government in East Asian Industrialization.* Princeton: Princeton University Press.

6

Alternatives of Transformation: Choices and Determinants— East-Central Europe in the 1990s

IVAN T. BEREND

At the beginning of the fifth year of transition in the post-communist countries, it pays to recall the major conceptual changes that characterized the initial phase of transformation.

The transition began with rather uncertain and foggy concepts on the future. Radical reformers and uncompromising opposition leaders who gathered around the cradle of the newly born system were decisive in developing it as a proper democracy, a "Rechtsstaat" and an efficient (equated with market-oriented) economic regime, able to react and adjust to a transforming world economy. However, the political-ideological leaders of the transition expressed rather more unclarified views: Their ideals were a kind of mixture of efficient laissez-faire capitalism; worker self-managerial participation in a "Sozialpartnerschaft," Scandinavian Socialism; a mixed economy and ownership; and an East European populist "Third Road" between capitalism and socialism.

At the first stage, dissident intellectuals, writers, philosophers, and sociologists described their dreams of an ideal society. They had no hope of realizing their ideas, and they expressed their views at "flying university" lectures and in *Samizdat* publications. Several of them dreamed of a society that was not compromised by consumerism. Analyzing and criticizing "post-totalitarian" socialism in his "Power of the Powerless," President Vaclav Havel of the Czech Republic expressed his rather negative conviction about consumer societies and maintained that state socialism was only one version of it.[1] The strong and militant Polish Solidarity, as well as Yugoslav reformers, sympathized with worker self-management, a system of "real" democracy where firms and society are directly managed by workers and the people. Ante Marković, the Croat reform economist and Yugoslav prime minister, sought to combine worker self-management with a proper market environment in his radical program of January 1989. The Hungarian Democratic Forum (HDF), a mixture of Christian democratic-conservative-populist trends and the triumphant opposition winner of the first free elections in Hungary, declared a "Third Road" program in its first and second congresses in March and October 1989, maintaining that "a strict market-based economy would only enrich a narrow group and impoverish the majority." Radio Free Europe reported on the HDF's second congress that "the Forum did not endorse total privatization ... and by privatization it did not mean ownership by individuals but groups."[2]

Because the former Communist party had transformed itself into the Romanian National Salvation Front, there is small wonder that the leading ideologue of the Front, Silviu Brucan, advocated to mix the South Korean and Austrian systems (Sozialpartnerschaft), "if [Romania] wants to avoid becoming an exhausted half-colony of the West." This strategy, he argued, offers both "a great opening to Western investors ... while maintaining a strong state sector and thus efficient control over development."[3]

Both the idea to choose and create an "ideal-typical" society, as well as the more pragmatic reformist concept that shunned a 180-degree turn (which, historically speaking, is hardly possible) and advocated building the foundations of the new system on East-Central European reality, soon evaporated.

At the second stage, the former reformers and opposition leaders, now in power, had to face reality. Several uncompromising and idealistic former dissidents were pushed aside as hard-nosed pragmatists attempted to adjust to the extremely demanding situation.

Dreams conceptualized without practical applications for those in government responsible for administering reform soon disappeared, and the newly emerged political elite shifted toward a more uniform free-market concept.

The requirement of changing the system, and the logic of opposing and destroying a failed state socialism, led those in power in an opposite direction: toward the antithesis of a state-owned, planned economy. The new program encouraged, according to the Zeitgeist, a triumphant free-market ideology that prevailed without rivals and embodied the success and prosperity of the 1980s—the unparalleled victory of Reaganomics and Thatcherism.

Additionally, the only hope for successful reform was rapid integration into an enlarged European Community. The watchword of those years was "Europe," or "back to Europe." Idealist intellectuals and steadfast opposition leaders, who by now had become politicians, strongly believed in this principle. Lech Walesa and many others often expressed their hope that their services in destroying the Soviet Bloc and state socialism would be honored and rewarded with massive Western assistance in rebuilding East-Central Europe. In other words, these leaders were saying "We did our job that you urged us to do for so long, and now it is your turn (and moral obligation) to pay the bill!" This kind of philosophy, although unrealistic, was quite natural. The memorandum of Lech Walesa and Jacek Merkel on "International Assistance Program for Poland" of July 6, 1989, asked for $10 billion—arguing that "changes in Poland may serve as an example for other countries. If successful ... [they] will alter the existing situation within the socialist bloc. ..."[4]

These expectations were accompanied by a strong attempt by Poland to adjust both to Europe and to the United States, the leading Western powers and future patrons and partners. Adapting to a painful transformation based on the Western laissez-faire model was considered Poland's price for Western acceptance and assistance. Tadeusz Kowalik quoted two leading Polish politicians who explicitly expressed this broadly shared view: "I understood the difficulties that we faced because of shock therapy," maintained Bronislaw Geremek, "but at the same time I knew that this was the only way that we could secure for Poland the chance of getting a place in the European economic order." In other words, without renunciation and self-denials, Poland had "no chance to overcome the distance separating us from the threshold allowing us to start the process of integration." Andrzej Olechovski added: "Even unilateral opening of the economy to the world is advantageous to a country which undertakes it. Liberalization may be harmful ... nevertheless, the overall prosperity will increase."[5]

Competent Western politicians and institutions such as the World Bank and the International Monetary Fund often frankly expressed that the condition of assistance was a rapid and radical transformation, the introduction of a multiparty system in politics and a liberal market economy based on private ownership. In such a situation, it was quite rational that a sort of competition began: Whoever is faster and most radical would presumably gain a greater part of sympathy, recognition, and last but not least, Western help and acceptance of the European Community.

Poland, Hungary, and Czechoslovakia took the leading role. The Czech elite were convinced that they could do it easier and faster without Slovakia and were ready even to sacrifice the federation. Slovenia and Croatia hoped for an earlier and easier acceptance without Serbia. The Balkans, with its slower-moving peasant majority and political inertia, followed behind.

After the initial uncertainty, a firm belief in "de-statization," free markets, and private ownership became dominant. "Let there be light and there was light." The darkness disappeared and an almost religious free-market ideology victoriously conquered the entire region.

The speed of transition in introducing the model acquired a special value in itself. If this was the single best solution, it had to be realized in the shortest time possible. "Big Bangers," such as Leszek Balcerowicz, Vaclav Klaus, Egor Gaidar, and their Western advisers, such as Jeffrey Sachs and Anders Aslund, were all convinced that they should pay any price to ensure the new system's fastest possible introduction.

Three Early Strategies of Transition: Gradualism, Shock Therapy, and the "Third Road"

In the early 1990s, it appeared that it was a question of free choice by the countries and governments to decide which reform path to follow. In spite of existing national solutions, at a certain stage of abstraction one may generalize three major types of strategies of transition applied in the region in 1990–91. Two of them did not differ in goals and were based on the same concept of a free-market economy and private ownership but diverged on the question of the pace of implementation. The third, however, represented a somewhat dissimilar concept.

Chronologically, the *first model* of transition, which emerged in Hungary, was later often called the *gradualist* approach. This model, deliberately chosen by the first freely elected coalition government of Prime Minister József Antall in the spring of 1990, developed, so to speak, spontaneously from the Hungarian market-oriented reform process begun in the 1960s. The first stage of the reform, in the mid- to late sixties, was the introduction of the well-known "New Economic Mechanism," with its partial market prices and profit motivation, as well as an abolition of compulsory plan directives and their replacement with so-called regulators. This development represented the most radical half-measures of market orientation that were determined by historical circumstances (considering both the ideological self-limitations and naivete of the reformers and the strict Soviet domination and control).

The second stage of the reform, which began in the late 1970s, went much further, partly because of the deepening economic crisis and gradually diminishing Soviet pressure. Major institutional changes in strengthening a firm's independence, a continuation of price reforms and marketization, as well as the introduction of a market-oriented, two-level banking system and value-added taxes sowed the seeds of a real market economy. During the 1980s, the legalization of a private "second economy" led to impressive initial results in the grassroots privatization of services. The market of goods and services, however, was not accompanied by a market of labor and capital; therefore, a real breakthrough did not occur, and the Hungarian model still remained essentially unable to adjust the country's economy to the world-market requirements.

As previous reforms already paved the way toward marketization, and a partial privatization began before the multiparty elections, a third stage of reform emerged as a part of the "refolution" (using Timothy Garton Ash's term), which exploded in May 1988 with the dismissal of János Kádár and his old guard and with the gradual takeover by a "sozialdemocratized" reform-wing. In the summer of 1988, a huge network of six expert, government-appointed committees, headed by Rezsö Nyers, the rehabilitated "father" of the reform of the 1960s and minister of state in the first post-Kádár government, began to work out a detailed, long-term strategy. Working Committee No. 1 was responsible for presenting a complex short-term program of transition in early 1989. Its introduction already stressed that it sought to break with "partial, weakened by compromises ... [and] over-gradualist [approaches] ... [and wanted to] radically transform the basis of the economic system." It was a plan to turn a "half-market economy" into a complete one, and it suggested "an immediate start of a widespread privatization of property and a long-term leasing of state property ... [and the] attraction of foreign capital," the foundation of the stock exchange, and a whole set of deregulating measures, including a three-year plan of import liberalization (of about 80 percent of total imports).[6]

The last reformist government of Miklós Németh adopted and began to implement this transition plan; thus, the freely elected Antall government inherited not only a plan but a process of radical transformation.

When the new government took office in the spring of 1990, the marketization of the economy was almost accomplished; liberalization of imports had reached almost 60 percent of total imports, and privatization had already begun. Since market prices were gradually introduced, there was no longer an unbearable inflationary pressure on the economy, and the rate of inflation in the first two years did not surpass the annual level of 25 to 35 percent. Besides, in spite of the high indebtedness, Hungary, unlike Poland and Yugoslavia, was not insolvent.

The situation thus automatically offered a means of continuation, since it was absolutely clear that in three to four years the greatest part of the transition would be realized and about half of the state-owned sector would be privatized. The "Joint Hungarian-International Blue Ribbon Commission" was founded in the summer of 1989 with the participation of outstanding Western experts and with the deliberate goal of setting policy for the newly elected government. Characteristically enough, it also suggested a three- to four-year speeding up and radicalization in several fields but accepted the "gradualist" approach as the only rational and realistic one for the Hungarian circumstances. There was no one among the Hungarian economists or government officials who, after the change of regime, would have suggested any kind of shock therapy.

The *second model* of transition emerged from the *Polish* historical situation. The first Solidarity government of Tadeusz Mazowiecki and his minister of finance, Leszek Balcerowicz, had to face the tragic legacy of Polish state socialism. The country's economy was bankrupt: A hyperinflation of 740 percent was coupled with severe shortages and empty shelves in the shops. The country could not repay its foreign debt of $40 billion and became insolvent. The belated market reforms of the Jaruzelski regime, which were introduced behind the shield of martial law, failed because of the complete lack of legitimacy of the government. The Solidarity government was convinced that it had no other choice but to attempt to achieve a *tabula rasa.* The government seized the advantage of its popularity and strongly based legitimacy and was courageous enough to implement harsh and painful proposals. The "Balcerowicz plan" was a combined macroeconomic stabilization and marketization program. Subsidies of basic food, housing, and energy were drastically cut (from 30 percent of budgetary expenditures to 15 percent from 1989 to 1990). A strict wage control policy allowed a wage increase of only 20 to 60 percent of the inflation rate (of the previous month) while prices were totally liberalized.

The austerity policy was combined with monetary stabilization policy. The Polish zloty was tied to a basket of convertible currencies, and the exchange rate was kept relatively stable. The currency became partially convertible, and the "black market" exchange rate disappeared. Inflation was curbed and dropped to 70 percent in 1991, and the shops, after decades of shortage, were filled. The privatization of small-scale business and retail networks gained a great impetus, though the shock strategy was not employed in privatizing big, state-owned industry at that time.

The shock treatment was thus a set of mandatory measures. As Andrzej Kozminski remarked, Balcerowicz "wanted Polish society to swallow such bitter medicine as quickly as possible before the massive popular support for the new government evaporated and the foreign help was diverted toward other [countries]."[7] The pioneers of the so-called shock therapy, advertised as the introduction of market capitalism overnight, attempted first of all a macroeconomic stabilization and a level of marketization and privatization that was already achieved in Hungary during its "gradualist" period.

Although the shock therapy was linked with the Polish road of transition, the Czechoslovak government followed an even more consistent strategy of a "Big Bang," especially in its privatization drive. After a year of preparation, Vaclav Klaus, the minister of finance, introduced a radical marketization program in January 1991. Prices and imports were liberalized, causing immediate price increases of 50 percent in January and again in February, and resulting in a decline of consumption by 37 percent, though both processes then slowed down radically. Klaus also initiated a shock privatization; the Federal Assembly passed a law on restitution in October 1990. This unique step in the region guaranteed to return to their former owners those private properties that were confiscated between 1955 and 1961. By January 1991, the program of so-called small privatization (100,000 state-owned stores, hotels, and restaurants were auctioned to private bidders) began.

According to the law of large-scale privatization, passed in November 1990, about 3,000 big state-owned companies were reorganized and transformed into joint-stock companies. Their privatization was initiated by distributing their shares among adult Czechoslovak citizens. According to the law, each adult citizen was offered investment vouchers worth 1,000 points each for a nominal fee equal to $80, which authorized the citizens to buy 30 shares of the stock exchange, opened in 1991. "Almost overnight," reported the World Bank's Bulletin, "Czechoslovakia will boast the biggest private sector in Eastern Europe—and one of the highest rates of individual shareholding in the world."[8] In fact, 5.7 million people decided to sell their voucher-booklets to different private, partly foreign-owned investment funds, which resulted in the accumulation of two-thirds of the total voucher points in the hands of 420 private investment funds. Thus, a secondary market of shares was instantly created.

Although the burden of shock treatment was heavy, especially in the Slovak part of the Republic, Czechoslovakia, previously one of the most rigid semi-Stalinist, nonreforming countries in the region, made a spectacular advance in its transition process. Its impact, especially the idea of voucher privatization, influenced some other countries as well. Poland, for example, followed the new pattern, adopting a Mass Privatization Program in June 1991. Accordingly, 60 percent of shares of selected state-owned companies would be allocated to a National Investment Fund, and via the Fund, to the public. A further 10 percent would be given to the employees of the firms on the basis of citizen rights.

Moreover, after an overcautious beginning, connected with the victory of the former opposition in a second parliamentary election, Bulgaria also followed this pattern: A restitution law guaranteed the return to previous owners of residential, industrial, commercial, and landed properties that were nationalized or confiscated after 1947. This uniquely radical step became the most important element of the Bulgarian privatization. The Law of April 1992 also adopted a version of voucher privatization: The option was given to the employees of big state-owned companies to buy 20 to 30 percent of the shares of their firms.

The Bulgarian example is already connected with the *third model* of transition in East-Central Europe, which characterized the *Balkan countries* at least at the beginning of their transformation.

Compared to Hungarian "gradualism" and Polish-Czechoslovak "shock strategy," the Balkans' pattern represented not only a more gradual gradualism, but a somewhat different set of goals: It aimed to follow a "Third Road" approach and to create a mixed economy. This was the situation in the Balkan countries partly because of their later start and partly due to a different political environment, especially in the first period of the transformation. With the exception of Bosnia-Herzegovina and Macedonia, the reformed former communist parties won an absolute majority in the first free, multiparty elections throughout the Balkans. These parties followed the road of marketization but decided to liberalize prices gradually. They also initiated privatization but preferred only a small-scale program and sought to preserve a strong state-owned sector together with state interventionism. To illustrate this road, one of the best examples of the strategy's most consistent implementation is the Romanian case.

The Government Commission for the Transition to a Market Economy, set up in January 1990, presented its report in the following spring with the suggestion of a gradual, three-stage price reform. In the summer of 1991, the government decided on the partial privatization of both agriculture and nonagricultural sectors. They sought to privatize 53 percent of state assets, about 6,000 so-called commercial companies, while the strategic sectors, such as mining, transportation, armament, and communication, making up 47 percent of the state's capital, would remain in the framework of reorganized, autonomous state-owned companies. The "commercial" companies were to be privatized in seven years by distributing 30 percent of the assets in a version of voucher privatization, and 70 percent of the shares was to be sold on the market.

Even with grassroots privatization, the foundation of private firms was strictly regulated and restricted: It was only allowed in trade, services, and tourism, and the number of their employees was not to exceed 20.

On the whole, the various countries and governments of East-Central Europe turned toward the adoption of Western market systems, with each deciding its own strategy for transition, which were rather different in speed and even in goals.

Consequently, the years of transition were accompanied by sharp confrontations and debates. In several countries, opposition parties and politicians, as well as workers and their unions criticized and denounced the adopted strategies and often defeated government parties at newly held elections. These elections, such as September 1993 in Poland, May 1994 in Hungary, previous ones in Bulgaria and Albania in 1992, and all second or third free parliamentary elections, radically changed former political settings. Outside experts debated the different roads and their effectiveness, and attempted to evaluate their economic and political impact on the future.

There are, however, harsh internal and external realities, inherited and created by the new processes themselves, that produced austere conditions and determinations. After three to four years of transition, the possibility of free choice seems partly to be an illusion. The region is shifted by stringent determinants.

Major Determinants of Transition

Beyond the mirage of free choice, it is, first of all, the *legacy of the past* that creates limitations.

East-Central Europe, integrated into the modern world system as its periphery, could not change its position during and after the age of the Industrial Revolution. The countries of the region remained agricultural and rural, and roughly 75 percent of their exports was mostly unprocessed agricultural products and food in the beginning of the twentieth century. Poland and Hungary, not to mention the Balkans, with a per-capita gross national product (GNP) of one-half to two-thirds of the European average, were characterized by low-level capital accumulation even on the eve of World War II. Capital accumulation in the interwar decades did not surpass 6 to 8 percent of GNP. Thus, a traditionally low level of accumulation characterized the stormy history of East-Central European modernization.

This economic sluggishness had a dual consequence of a central role of foreign investments and crediting, and a distinctive role of direct state interventionism. During the half-century of a semisuccessful modernization in the region before World War I, modern railroads, banks, mining, and some industry were mostly financed by foreign capital. Between 1867 and 1914, 40 percent of Hungarian investments came from external sources. At the end of the nineteenth century, 92 percent of the weak Romanian industry, including oil extraction, was in foreign hands. Serbia and Bulgaria became insolvent at that time, having been unable to repay foreign loans.

As Alexander Gerschenkron, the Harvard doyen of post-war economic historians, suggested, the state played a kind of substituting role by introducing guaranteed interest payments for railroad investors throughout the region, subsidizing industry in Hungary and Bulgaria, and so forth. In the interwar period, especially in the 1930s, state intervention culminated in having established state-owned firms and some kind of planning, such as the so-called Industrial Triangle project in Poland and the Hungarian five-year plan of the "Györ Program" in 1938.

Lateness, backwardness, and peripheral status were not only economic issues but generated special social structures, political reactions, movements, and ideologies as well. One of the consequences was the well-known populist, anti-Westernization attitude that strongly penetrated the entire area. The Pan-Slav populists in Russia in the last third of the nineteenth century refused either to follow the West or to adopt its values. Instead, they praised the superiority of the Slavic nation, which had the only "just" society based on the system of the egalitarian village-commune as well as the only true religion, in contrast with a decadent, chaotic Western liberal capitalism that was to be avoided at all costs.

The conservative Hungarian historian, Gyula Szekfü, in his *Három Nemzedék* ("Three generations"),[9] created an ideological foundation for the Horthy regime, blaming liberalism and communism equally, indeed actually equating the two and claiming that both led Hungary to a mistaken dead-end road. Real, true "Hungarianness," and the basis to rebuild the country, were to be found in the "historical classes" (nobility) and the "pure" peasantry. Both capitalism and communism were alien, "Jewish import" ideologies that were smuggled into the country.

The populist writer, Péter Veres, proudly declared in the 1930s: "We Hungarians have not a capitalistic character. ... We should not seek to adjust to the West." The populist-fascist Romanian Zelea-Codreanu, with his infamous "Legion" (together with other populist-nationalist-fascists of the region), dreamed of an undivided national community, cleansed from Jewish-capitalist ideas.

Although East European communism struggled against these trends, and though Bolshevism had emerged by fighting against "Narodnik" populism, its Stalinist form not only defeated but also absorbed several elements of these ideas. The "melting-form" of Bolshevism (as it was often analytically called) was made up of at least as much of Russian traditionalism as of genuine Marxism.

After the collapse of Marxist communism, there was an easy return to populist-nationalist ways. Not only coat-turning former communist politicians sought to survive by riding on nationalist sentiments (as it is sometimes interpreted regarding, for example, the case of a Slobodan Milosević), but time-honored traditions are filling the vacuum that remained after the demise of a failed ideology. "A left deprived of Marxist underpinnings," formulated Giovanni Sartori, "easily drifts into sheer populism, into sheer demagogic rhetoric."[10]

All in all, there was a rather limited pre-history of self-financing, self-regulating market capitalism and liberal market ideology in East-Central Europe. It is, of course, not only a question of legacy (a sort of historical memory and burden) but much more than that: The automatism of a well-functioning market economy hardly ever worked in this peripheral area. Anti-Western populism is deeply rooted in the soil of humiliated peripheral societies. It is quite naive to suggest that it is only a question of political will to follow the Western path from "primitive accumulation" to post-industrial capitalism.

That was the reason of another determinant in the transformation of East-Central Europe: The region was *unable to respond* to the *challenges* of the three major *structural crises* of the last 120 years. The Schumpeterian "creative destruction" of the structural crisis—that is, the whole set of technological changes that made the old leading sectors obsolete and led to their decline, while generating the introduction of new technology and the emergence of modern, new leading industries in the advanced core—appeared only partially in the peripheries. The "destruction" was strong, but the "creation" was mostly lacking.

The structural crisis of the 1870s undermined East-Central Europe's modernization attempt based on traditional agricultural exports, and the old structures were frozen up to the middle of the twentieth century. The most frightening illustration of the peripheral answer to a structural crisis, however, was witnessed in the 1930s. The Great Depression, which with all its pains and troubles strongly contributed to a technological-structural renewal in the West, pushed East-Central Europe to a suicidal defensive: In the Nazi-German "Grossraumwirtschaft" (Great economic sphere), they welcomed the guaranteed market for their unsalable old export goods (still unprocessed agricultural products). Moreover, they were even grateful for the somewhat-higher-than-world-market prices paid by Hitler and hoped to escape from the crisis through a special regional agreement system (based on a set of bilateral trade agreements with Germany in 1934 and 1935), which isolated the region from the world market. They ceased using convertible currency and introduced the clearing system (barter trade).

By escaping the world market and improving their trade balance and employment situation, East-Central Europe thus failed to adjust to a technologically and structurally transforming international economic regime.

The area's inability to adjust was repeated a third time in the period of the emergence of the "post-industrial" societies, also known as the "communication and service revolution," which generated the structural crisis of the 1970s to 1980s. East-Central Europe, like many other peripheral regions, could not adequately react. According to Angus Maddison's calculations, previously rapid growth (3.9 percent and 2.5 percent in East-Central Europe and Latin America, respectively, between 1950 and 1973) dramatically slowed down (to 1.9 percent and 0.8 percent in the two regions, respectively, between 1973 and 1987).[11] Both regions walked into the same indebtedness trap. Living standards began to decline, budget deficits and inflation skyrocketed, and the regions' economies collapsed. The trap buried both East-Central European state socialism and the dictatorships of Latin American peripheral capitalism.

As has been extensively analyzed in recent decades, the rigidity of the Soviet-type planned economy, the misleading ideological commitments, and the lack of market incentives and interests due to a lack of private ownership and initiative all contributed to the economic malfunctioning of East-Central Europe. A long-term and comparative analysis, however, clearly shows that the main factors of inadequacy are not only *regime* but also *region specific*, thus revealing deeper layers of historical-peripheral determinants.

The naive belief that sweeping away state socialist economic and political structures, getting rid of harmful ideological constraints, and adopting the successful Western core's free-market philosophy and policies would automatically lead to similar results of adjustment for these regions that had experienced the deepest structural crisis of modern economic history was a serious miscalculation.

When discussing some of the most important determinants of East-Central European transformation, a third factor should be considered: The dramatic *transitory economic decline* that is accompanying the transition from a planned to a market economy. Although almost everyone forecasted a one- to two-year moderate decline, nobody anticipated the severity and scope of the economic turmoil that ensued.

Although statistics are rather inaccurate, the first three to four years of transformation were accompanied by an unprecedented decline in the entire region. Countries both adopting shock therapy or overgradualist policies in their transition toward a market economy suffered approximately a 20- to 30-percent decrease in their GNP and a 30- to 50-percent decrease in industrial and agricultural output. Unemployment reached a level of between 13 and 20 percent of the workforce. The decline is comparable to the destruction caused by World War II and forced Stalinist collectivization.

The steep decline did not halt until the summer of 1992 in Poland but continued in most of the other countries throughout 1993 and, according to the forecasts, will continue in several countries in 1994.

"The most dramatic output losses—measured output has fallen by more than half—have been in Albania," concluded two World Bank experts in 1992. "These extreme ... [collapses are] attributable to special circumstances ... [including] the disruptive disintegration of an unusually closed regime. " Describing the severe deterioration in the region in general, two World Bank experts noted: "The prospects for a rapid resurgence in production do not seem favorable across the region. In some countries, such as Czechoslovakia and Hungary, it has been estimated that real output per capita might return to pre-reform levels by 1996; in Bulgaria and Romania it may take until the next decade."[12]

There are several factors contributing to this decline, and I will differentiate among three sets of them at least. One group of factors is accidental and transitory by nature; examples include the collapse of the previously decisive Soviet and Comecon market, the turmoil in the world economy (such as a short-lived oil crisis during the Gulf war), and most of all the Western recession of the early 1990s.

Another group of factors related to the decline is connected to the economic transition "from non-market to market systems ... [whose] leap is both acrobatic and hazardous."[13] Halted subsidies, liberalized imports, and the attendant and immediate emergence of world-market competition all created an extreme change of condition that is similar to opening all the windows of a previously well-heated hothouse in the middle of winter. Sacrificing short-term losses for long-term gains is unavoidable.

These two sets of factors are generally mentioned as responsible for the decline. If this is the case, then János Kornai is right to speak about a "transformation recession": "There are cyclical and market factors contributing to the decline, but their role[s] were secondary. The primary explanation is the following: [T]he severe decline of output is a painful side effect of a healthy process of the change of the system ... [I]t is caused by the transition from socialism to capitalism."[14]

There is, however, a third set of reasons for the decline, though it is connected to the second one: East-Central Europe is opening its economy and competing in the world market without being able to adjust to it by restructuring its production and exports. "The fall in output," according to the two World Bank experts quoted earlier, "does not seem to have been accompanied by the radical economic restructuring that many expected as part of the reform process."[15] The most frightening aspect of the economic decline in East-Central Europe is not its harshness and scale, but the lack of a convincing beginning of structural changes. This is also the main reason for the decrease of output. The demise of technologically obsolete, noncompetitive firms and branches because of the lack of subsidies and preserved, isolated markets is indeed a "painful side effect of a healthy process" (to use Kornai's words). The deficiency of newly emerging, competitive leading sectors that could counterbalance the decline of the old ones, which is one of the main factors of the severe, "unexpected" economic decline, is, however, not connected to any kind of healthy process but is a sign of the painful fact of a weak, inadequate peripheral reaction to the structural crisis. To overlook this determination might lead to further naive predictions and miscalculations.

The forecasts and calculated decrease of output and gross domestic product (GDP) proved to be over-optimistic, since the experts predicted a rapid, flexible adjustment and restructuring. One of the main reasons for this optimism was the belief of massive Western participation in investing in, privatizing, and restructuring the East-Central European economies. Hungarian governmental circles, expressing the general expectations in the region, counted on approximately a 30-percent participation of foreign capital in rebuilding the Hungarian economy. In reality, the participation is only about 3 percent, and Hungary gained by far the greatest part (more than half) of total foreign investments reaching East-Central Europe.

The possibility and role of *capital inflow* and *integration into the European Community*—the external factor of transition—is the fourth distinctive determinant that deserves special attention. All the three previously discussed main determinants of transformation are connected to it. The legacy of the past and the traditional role of foreign capital in modernization along with capital's special importance in coping with a structural crisis all emphasize the significance of this fourth factor.

In November 1989, during the crucial month of the collapse of state socialism, Western enthusiastic readiness to assist was clearly expressed: The European Community's Executive Commission hosted a meeting of representatives of 24 leading industrial nations and pledged $6.5 billion in economic aid for Poland and Hungary, the pioneering countries of the process. In three days, the foreign ministers of the European Community offered temporary trade concessions, including an end of restrictions on certain imports. On the next day, President Bush signed a bill authorizing nearly $1 billion in aid for Poland and Hungary. The impressive rush to help concluded with a pledge by the G–24 bloc of $45 billion to East-Central Europe for three years between 1989 and 1991. The doors—at least apparently—opened toward Europe and major Western assistance.

One should be reminded that this happened at the beginning of the process when the new Western reaction still followed the old reflexes of the cold war, and it seemed to be a vital interest to contribute to the disintegration of the Soviet bloc and to provide incentives for the destruction of state socialism throughout East-Central Europe. In other words, as in the beginning of the cold war in 1947, the same "Marshall strategy" re-appeared at the end of it in 1989.

When state socialism collapsed and the cold war ended, Western enthusiasm (although its rhetoric continued) was replaced with doubts and then revulsion. In the summer of 1991, almost at the end of the three-year period, the European Commission announced that only 11 percent of the commitments (for Poland, Hungary, Czechoslovakia, Romania, and Bulgaria) was disbursed.

The amount of private investments, which according to several governmental statements would be responsible for financing a greater part of the transition and privatization, was about another $5 billion until the middle of 1992, as calculated by the European Bank for Reconstruction and Development (EBRD). According to the New York-based *East European Investment Magazine*, the number of American deals in the region more than doubled and their value increased sixfold in 1993. The total value of the deals (if plans will be realized) was $28 billion, and one-third of this total was to be invested in the 12 East-Central European countries. Ironically, it is exactly the same amount of investment that was to go to Kazakhstan, the new "oil sheikdom."

Although foreign investments certainly will be continued, the 1993 deals suggest that the main attraction is oil and mining, a characteristically "peripheral-type" investments that represent roughly 60 percent of planned or prepared investments. Moreover, growing political uncertainty and civil wars at the two ends of the region made a new infusion of foreign investments unpredictable.

Western assistance that was actually disbursed and private investments to the countries of transformation thus totaled approximately $10 billion between 1989 and 1991, which increased to $15 billion and then to $18 billion by the end of 1993. Counting the huge capital outflow from the region in the form of payment of interests and principles (one of the main receivers of foreign capital, Hungary, has had a repayment burden of $3.5 billion annually, which the country has fulfilled in an orderly way), and the outflow of profits and capital withdrawals, one certainly cannot speak about an impressive net capital inflow to the region in the first three to four years of transition. Moreover, there are several calculations that reflect a net capital outflow from the region. One of the Hungarian experts, Gyözö Pongrácz, calculated a $6 billion net capital outflow from Hungary, a country which gained the most investments from the West.

One cannot exclude the possibility that the credits that were granted mostly ensured the repayment of old accumulated debts but could not generate a new prosperity. If one accepts the calculations of Jeffrey Sachs, who maintained that financial aid should amount to 3 to 5 percent of GDP of the recipient countries (as in the case of the Marshall Plan), then the region did not receive more than 10 to 20 percent of its minimal requirements. Foreign assistance thus was not sufficient to sustain the desired result and could not play a determinant role in helping a smooth transition.

Regarding the other pillar of Western contribution—integration with the European Community—actual progress is very small. After certain initial steps and agreements, the acceptance was delayed without any exact deadline. Agricultural, steel, chemical, and textile products, the only important potential export items of the East-Central European countries to the West, remained highly protected in the West. The November 1992 episode of a recent "tariff war" and restrictions against the expansion of Eastern steel products to the European markets is rather telling: four countries of the region—Czechoslovakia, Hungary, Poland, and Croatia (the first three of which signed an agreement with the Community on decreasing trade barriers)—more than doubled their share in the European steel-pipes market in the last five years (from 7.8 percent to 18 percent). The Community immediately introduced a special dumping tariff of 30 percent, 22 percent, 17 percent and 11 percent respectively in the case of the Czech, Hungarian, Croat and Polish products. The incident well proved the truth of the statement by Jacques Attali, the (now former) president of the EBRD, in the fall of 1992: "The limited measures of the European Community did not lead to results until now. Western Europe, in reality, is building up a new kind of Maginot-line."[16]

The opening of the doors of the Community for the three most advanced and rapidly transforming countries of the region will take, in the best of circumstances, at least more than a decade; however, the other East-Central European countries cannot even foresee such a thing happening. The opportunity of joining Europe—the prerequisite par excellence for transformation—is being deliberately delayed until the next century and thus will come too late to be of any help during the most difficult years of transformation for many in the region.

From an early, although never manifested "Marshall strategy," the Western world has turned to, as I call it, "Münchhausen strategy." Freiherr Münchhausen, the eighteenth-century soldier and liar, claimed to have pulled himself out from a trap with his own hair. This is now the task of the East-Central European countries. They must do the next-to-impossible and save themselves for they cannot count on organized and massive Western assistance.

Conclusion

Economic and political realities are shifting in the countries and governments of the region, which hesitated among several different strategies in the beginning but then followed a more similar road toward laissez-faire capitalism. The "Third Road" strategy of the Balkans was harshly attacked by the militant political opposition, which gradually emerged after 1989 and was able to convince large numbers of people that the overcautious policy of the reformed communists who had gained power during the first free elections was responsible for the severe decline and deterioration of economic conditions. They did not want to remain "second-rate" competitors in the race toward parity with Europe and sought to follow the seemingly successful and highly praised model of shock therapy.

While the reform-oriented Petre Roman government in Romania was removed as a result of a violent miners' revolt, and an emerging extreme populist Right denounced a "Cosmopolitan-Jewish-Hungarian conspiracy against Romania," which strengthened a sort of populist-nationalist and nationalist-reformist communist coalition and "Third Road" strategy, just the opposite happened in other countries such as Bulgaria and Albania: The opposition criticized "Third Road" gradualism and cried out for shock therapy. There are very few parties and governments in the area that could win re-election and continue their initial policies. A most-telling example, Bulgaria turned from an overgradual Balkan "Third Road" to a drastic strategy of shock therapy. President Sali Berisha's Albania similarly turned toward free-market ideology.

However, the countries and governments that applied shock therapy also had to pay a tremendous political price for it. Their opposition argued that the harsh decay, rocketing unemployment, and strongly decreasing output and living standards were the consequence of an exaggerated and rushed free-market strategy. In Poland, for example, the unquestioned position of the highly celebrated Solidarity and its first government was soon undermined. Solidarity rapidly disintegrated, and those who remained in charge of the militant trade union and political party not only attacked its former leaders and organizations but sought to use the same fighting methods of strikes and occupation of mines and managerial buildings to achieve a radical policy change in the summer and autumn of 1992. In Czechoslovakia, a badly hit Slovak economy (that suffered much more than its Czech counterpart) served as a basis for resurrecting Slovak nationalism and anti-Czech sentiment and strongly contributed to the division of the country into two independent states in January 1993. Consequently, Slovakia is going to change its transition strategy.

In Hungary, right-wing populist radicalism, criticizing Westernizing "cosmopolitans," has emerged inside the government party itself. It seeks to save the "Hungarian land" from foreigners and proclaims itself as the defender of the "Hinterland of the Magyar Society," which has allegedly been victimized during the transition by a vast former reform-communist–American–Jewish conspiracy.

The unexpected difficulties of transformation, the disappointing, exclusive attitude of the European Community, and the reluctance of the Western governments to assist, together with the extremely limited interest of Western capital to invest in the region, all intensify the pain of transition and postpone the possibility of consolidating the economies.

After exaggerated expectations ("Albania wants to be like America!" cried picketers in the crowd at Tirana Airport when Secretary of State Baker visited the country a few weeks after the first free election), there is an emerging disappointment and spreading humiliation in the region. Nationalist fundamentalism, xenophobia, and right-wing extremism have appeared. Despite such developments, the Polish election of the fall of 1993 and the polls forecasting the Hungarian elections in the spring of 1994 clearly showed a turn toward social-democratic trends and former reform-communist parties.

In some of the countries, such as the successor states of Yugoslavia, Romania, and in many successor states of the former Soviet Union, nationalism has already become a leading political trend. Right-wing extremism, although exceedingly visible and often violent, is on the periphery of East-Central European politics. However, a Funar and Munteanu in Romania, a Csurka and Zacsek in Hungary, and a Republican party in the Czech Republic are already present in politics with their semi-fascist, authoritarian, anti-Semitic, and anti-minority views. Their followers, according to their electoral percentage and figures presented by recent polls, make up only 5 to 10 percent of the population of their countries. Their emergence and loud presence, which was partly connected with a deteriorating economic situation, has already caused a lot of harm to the reputation and credibility of their countries and is clearly counterproductive for their countries' economic recovery (and foreign participation).

The world is witnessing a rapidly developing vicious circle: Economic difficulties and loss of hope generate political extremism as well as the frightening, though still marginal, appearance of extremist political trends, which themselves are contributing to the curbing of the economic recovery … (and so the chain of events continues).

The recently often-heard pessimistic prognoses are forecasting a region with endangered, fragile political systems, multiparty pseudo democracies, and a Latin-Americanization with its clientalist, authoritarian dirigisme. The emergence of right-wing, nationalist-populist governments in neighboring, confrontational countries in an over-Balkanized East-Central Europe might represent an unpredictable danger of local conflicts and small civil wars, a permanent challenging of borders, and the rivalries between majority and minority interests. This view is widely shared. Jan Urban, the former Czech dissident and Charta 77 spokesman, forecasted a defeat of the democratic parties and the victory of the right-wing, nationalist forces in the next Hungarian elections because of the disintegration of Czechoslovakia and an emerging Slovak-Magyar conflict over the Hungarian minority's autonomy in, and probably even border questions with, Slovakia. Jim Brown, the well-known American expert, warned of the danger of an escalation of local conflicts, especially through the revisiting of old unresolved and unsolvable national issues by rising nationalists. His list of potential "danger spots" includes the Macedonian, Bessarabian, and Transylvanian questions, and a potential demand by extreme nationalist forces (governments) in Hungary, Romania, and Bulgaria to revise post–World War I border dictates, including the Trianon treaty. The most pessimistic analysts are signaling the possibility of a third Balkan war if the Western world is reluctant to intervene in the Balkans. They are certainly overpessimistic but express dangers that are nonetheless relevant.

As the prospect of a rapidly emerging and prosperous East-Central European market democracy, integrated as an equal partner in the European Community, is disappearing, the exclusiveness of the European Community is strengthening. The harsh reality of this situation for the region still involves integration with Europe—however, *not* as an equal partner that is gradually catching up to the West but as its periphery. This means that the countries' only comparative advantage may remain its cheap labor, and the region might find its place as a "backyard" of the European Community (or of a strengthened Germany). This is a rather familiar pattern relative to past European policy and also one that conforms to present American policy concerning Latin America and Japanese policy concerning other Asian countries. Such "backyard" status also can ensure economic development, more employment, and improved standards of living, and most of all the rise and enrichment of a new elite. Peripheral development, however, also might be characterized by a continuous lack of restructuring and lack of development of competitive modern sectors of the economy that are based on the new technology of the age. A missed adjustment to the new technological regime, in spite of increasing income and employment (related to non-science-based sectors), will preserve and might even increase East-Central Europe's relative backwardness and its growing competitiveness gap compared to the advanced core. Such "development" means a fragile prosperity and causes further humiliation and political instability.

If this will be the leading trend in most of the countries of the region, then the determination and need for economic dirigisme and state interventionism might re-emerge. If populist demagoguery will prevail, some sort of state redistribution might continue. A mixed economy, in which certain dirigiste state positions and ownership would be retained and in which foreign investments, ownership, and competition would be open to limitation, is a likely development under such conditions.

Just as an emerging new elite rapidly and rationally adjusted to Western values, models, and requirements at the initial stage of transition, the new disappointment and humiliation may generate an entirely different sort of shift. The economic and political pressure of reality may push the countries in a direction that was, in most cases, initially rejected because it went against the will and determination of the parties and governments during the first years of transition; but such ironic twists are deeply rooted in East-Central European societies and history.

The real dilemma of transition for the region is thus not the choice between shock therapy and gradualism. The question is whether laissez-faire free marketism is applicable. Economic and political austerities may undermine the possibility of going along the road from "primitive accumulation" to a welfare society in a few years or even in a few *decades.* Kowalik strongly questioned the mere possibility of a primitive accumulation in East-Central Europe at the turn of the twenty-first century in the face of a prosperous West.[17] Indeed, historical processes are not reproducible in an entirely changed environment centuries later. Severe doubts have risen about the potential of the free-market mechanism in the midst of a challenging structural crisis in the peripheral economies.

There are thus economic, social, and political constraints that may push the countries toward a search for other solutions to their problems. A new state interventionism and selective protectionism might emerge. Others may turn to an Austrian or Swedish path to build the recovery into a "Sozialpartnerschaft." *Dirigist, populist regimes* and *social-democratic roads* and their combinations were practically excluded in the first years of transformation in East-Central Europe. Now all these alternatives may come to the surface and be part of the political reality.

Which policy will victoriously emerge in the region? One certainly cannot predict a single, uniform road. Differing historical factors may play a determinant role in rising dissimilarities.

Challenges and responses, and the region's common problems are, of course, not simply a consequence of the previous half-century. Major differences and dissimilarities always existed. East-Central Europe as a whole, although it entails certain general similarities, is still divided into different subregions that have distinctive characteristics of their own. As generations of Polish and Hungarian historians have documented, the western rim of the region, after long periods of belonging to the East, "shifted" toward the West and became a part of it as a result of favorable internal and international circumstances from the Middle Ages on.[18]

The western rim of East-Central Europe, nowadays the Czech Republic, Slovenia, probably Hungary, and later Poland and Croatia, are in a better position to depart from the periphery and also to "arrive" in Europe than several other countries in the region. A successful transition for the rest may remain a dream. Russian, Romanian, and Albanian answers to the historical challenge might and certainly will be rather different than the Czech, Croatian, and Hungarian ones. The answers are formulated by both long-term historical determinants and short-term policy decisions.

Notes

1. Vaclav Havel's essay was published in John Keane, ed., *The Power of the Powerless: Citizens Against the State in Central and Eastern Europe* (London: Hutchinson, 1985).

2. *Radio Free Europe Research,* Vol. 14, No. 48, December 1, 1989 (Part IV of 4 parts), pp. 23–24.

3. D. Ionescu, "Quest of a Model: Development Strategies Under Discussion." *Radio Free Europe Research,* Vol. 1, No. 39, September 28, 1990, p. 28.

4. L. Walesa and J. Merkel, "International Assistance Program for Poland," in T. Kowalik, "The 'Big Bang' as Political Phenomenon: A Case Study on Poland." In I. T. Berend, ed., *Global Transition to Market Economy at the End of the 20th Century* (Munich: Suedosteuropa-Gesellschaft, forthcoming—August 1994).

5. B. Geremek, "Rok 1989," *Warsaw,* 1992, p. 365; A. Olechovski, "Integracji," *Warsaw,* 1993. Both in T. Kowalik, "The 'Big Bang' as Political Phenomenon" pp. 10, 15.

6. I. T. Berend (head of the Committee and editor of the published program), *A Gazdasági Reformbizottság Programjavaslat, 1990–1992* (The Program of the Reform Committee, 1990–92). Budapest: Közgazdasági és Jogi Könyvkiadó, 1989, pp. 11, 160.

7. A. K. Kozminski, "Transition from Planned to Market Economy: Hungary and Poland Compared." *Studies in Comparative Communism,* Vol. XXV, No. 4, December 1992, p. 320.

8. The World Bank. *Transition: The Newsletter About Reforming Economies,* Vol. 3, No. 5, May 1992, p. 3.

9. G. Szekfü, *Három Nemzedék* (Budapest: Meacenas, 1989).

10. G. Sartori, "Rethinking Democracy." *International Social Science Journal* (Blackwell Journals, UNESCO) No. 129, (August 1991), p. 447.

11. A. Maddison, "Measuring European Growth: The Core and the Periphery." Paper presented at the Xth International Congress of Economic History, Leuven, Belgium, 1990.

12. M. I. Blejer and A. Gelb, "Persistent Economic Decline in Central and Eastern Europe: What Are the Lessons?" In the World Bank's *Transition: The Newsletter About Reforming Economies,* Vol. 3, No. 7, July-August 1992, pp. 2–3.

13. G. Sartori, "Rethinking Democracy," p. 438.

14. J. Kornai, article in *Magyar Hírlap,* Budapest, Hungary, December 24, 1992.

15. Blejer and Gelb, "Persistent Economic Decline," p. 2.

16. J. Attali, "Towards a Continental Common Market." *Népszabadság.* Budapest: September 26, 1992.

17. T. Kowalik, "Creating the Economic Foundation for Democracy" (manuscript presented at the University of California–Los Angeles, 1992).

18. See I. T. Berend, "Ungarns Stellung in Europa. Politisches Denken und Historiographie in 20. Jahrhundert." In W. Mommsen (Hrsg.), *Der Lange Weg nach Europa: Historische Betrachtungen aus Gegenäwrtiges Sicht.* "The Long Way to Europe: Historical Analyses from the Present"). Berlin: Edition Q, 1992.

7

Continuity and Change in Eastern Europe: Strategies of Post-Communist Politics

ANDREW JANOS

A few years ago when the communist governments of East Europe fell, the mood about the prospects of the region tended toward optimism. Although a few voices of caution, or even of doom, made themselves heard, studies of "transition" from authoritarianism to democracy and from socialism to capitalism proliferated, and at least one author gained temporary fame by predicting the advent of a liberal millennium and a "Hegelian end of history."[1]

Such optimistic forecasts were largely the products of the understandable euphoria of the historical moment. But in good measure they also reflected on a nostalgic, perhaps propagandized, but in any case overly romanticized view of an "old Europe" that had never really existed yet that was now fondly recalled by many on both sides of the Iron Curtain. Winston Churchill, whose forceful rhetoric bequeathed the very term to posterity, was an early and effective propagator of this view, depicting Europe in his famous Fulton speech as a closely integrated cultural and historical entity, now torn asunder by brute force and the sheer vagaries of power politics. In this view, adopted by many after Churchill, the eastern, "captive" part of Europe was cast in the role of Dornröschen from the German fairy tale, a flawlessly beautiful creature immobilized by trickery yet always ready to resume normal life, should the sleeping beauty be delivered from the curse by some miraculous occurrence. In 1989, the moment appeared to have arrived, with some willing to cast the West in the role of the prince of the fairy tale, with whom the sleeping beauty would enter into union and live happily ever after in marital bliss.

Attractive as this metaphor may have been to some practitioners of the new art of post-communist studies, it had serious limitations as a potential analogy and organizing paradigm for the discipline. First and foremost, the metaphor ignores the all-too-obvious fact that, unlike the sleeping beauty of the tale, Eastern Europe was far from flawless: Its face had been marred by many wrinkles even before the advent of communism, and some of these wrinkles became only more deeply etched during the long years of sleep and separation under Soviet-style socialism. To put it more simply, throughout much of its pre-1989 history, Eastern Europe was a deeply troubled corner of the world, with numerous ethnic, economic, and political problems that put its countries on a developmental track completely different from the ones followed by the nation-states of the West. Furthermore, while the princess in the tale of the Grimm brothers, once awakened, found herself in her familiar environment and could resume her life without missing a beat, the countries of Eastern Europe, when liberated from their satellite status in the Soviet Bloc, reentered an international environment that in the previous forty-five years had been developing in new directions at a fast and furious pace. In this respect, a more appropriate metaphor would be Washington Irving's tale of Rip van Winkle, who in American folklore returned from the wilderness after a long lapse of time to encounter a new reality that he could barely comprehend and could not easily adjust to. Much like him, the nations of Eastern Europe face the problem of adaptation. They are, to use the words of A. E. Housman, "strangers and afraid in a world they never made."

My general thesis in this chapter is that much that goes under the rubric of politics in contemporary Eastern Europe must be approached from the perspective of this process of adaptation to a new, dynamic, and dominant international environment by a number of troubled societies with their own historical consciousness and memories. In pursuit of this theme, I will address three interrelated topics in this chapter: (1) the continuities between past and present; (2) continuity and change in the international environment; and (3) patterns of adaptations and political strategies by East European actors. By following these topics, we can accomplish at least two purposes: We can direct attention from the formal-institutional to the substantive aspects of politics that have been frequently lost amid the preoccupation of scholars with processes of "democratic transition" and liberalization, and we can introduce a comparative perspective in post-communist studies by focusing on typical adaptations of political actors to their internal and external environments.

The Wrinkles: Continuities in East European History

Perhaps the most striking of the historical continuities is the fact that, at least from the sixteenth century onward, Eastern Europe has been and remains an economically underdeveloped, marginalized part of the European continent. (See Berend's discussion of this in Chapter 6.) Worse still, throughout the past centu-

TABLE 7.1 Per-Capita Income of East European Countries as Percentage of Advanced European Countries and Each Other

	1926–1934		1980			
			Calculation I		Calculation II	
	Europe = 100	E. Germany = 100	Europe = 100	E. Germany = 100	Europe = 100	E. Germany = 100
E. Germany	81.8	100.0	44.9	100.0	65.0	100.0
Czechoslovakia	56.9	69.5	36.4	80.1	54.7	84.1
Hungary	44.8	54.8	33.4	74.2	40.8	62.7
Poland	35.1	42.9	28.4	63.1	39.1	60.1
Yugoslavia	40.8	49.8	19.8	44.0	31.1	47.8
Bulgaria	32.3	39.4	27.0	60.0	39.9	61.3
Romania	29.7	36.3	20.4	45.3	24.1	37.1
Average of six	36.9		27.6		38.3	

NOTE: East German (future GDR) per-capita income: 103 percent of total German income per capita. Figures (100) in columns, 1, 3, 5 represents averages of six advanced industrial countries: Germany, France, Sweden, Belgium, Holland, and Switzerland.

SOURCES: Cols. 1–2: Colin Clark, *The Conditions of Economic Progress* (London, 1940); cols. 3–4: Paul Marer, *Dollar GNPs of USSR and Eastern Europe* (Baltimore, 1985); Cols. 5–6: *U.N. Yearbook of National Accounts* (New York, 1980).

ries and decades, the degree of this marginalization has tended to increase rather than to decrease. Thus, if we take the ratio of the aggregate national product per capita in the East and the West around 1800 (perhaps the earliest period of time at which we can make halfway meaningful estimates), we will find the figures to be about 80:100.[2] Whatever the accuracy of this estimate is, comparing aggregate per-capita income figures between six East and six West European nations in 1910 will yield a much more unfavorable ratio of 48:100.[3] In the next two decades, as Table 7.1 shows, the income gap further increased to a ratio of approximately 37:100. The Communist period complicates the tasks of calculation and comparison. However, if we take two different sources using different methods of calculation (ranging from purchasing power parities to physical indicators and the dollar equivalents of reported gross domestic product) and average their results, we will arrive at an East-West ratio of 32.9:100 (Table 7.1) for 1980.[4] This is to say that whatever methodological assumptions we make, Communist economies were drifting downward from the relative position that their countries had held in the world economy prior to World War II. It should be noted here that the above figures relate to per-capita *product* and not consumption, and if we had reliable sources to calculate consumption we would, in view of high investment rates and military spending, likely find even greater economic disparities between the two halves of the Continent. At any rate, the figures we have for the years 1975 to 1980 represent a peak, from which the East European countries began their long descent, culminating in the abrupt decline in per-capita incomes that followed the collapse of communist governments. No reliable figures yet exist for the true scope of economic deterioration in the post-1989 period. But available figures for the years 1990 to 1992 show a 14.2-percent decline in the Hungarian gross domestic product (GDP), and declines of 17.5 percent in the Czechoslovak, 17.6 percent in the Polish, 25.2 percent in the Romanian, and 34.8 percent in the Bulgarian national product.[5] Another source estimates the decline of GDP in the former Yugoslav economy at 50 percent.[6] Again, nobody can vouch for the accuracy of these calculations made in a period of extreme economic turmoil and statistical darkness. But on the average, these figures amount to a 26.5-percent decline in East European GDPs, which, given the rate of growth in Western economies, permits us to estimate the current ratio of Eastern to Western GDP/GNPs at a historical low of 25:100. The sad fact is that Eastern Europe has never been more economically backward or underdeveloped compared to the West than it is today. As before, and indeed with greater intensity, the symptoms of this backwardness are the emigration of talent, and a deep sense of relative deprivation that impels governments to respond either by designing comprehensive economic reform programs or by finding alternative strategies to divert attention from increasing economic marginalization and malaise.

Hardly less significant than this pattern of regional income inequality is the persistence of income disparities among the individual countries of Eastern Europe. Throughout history, these disparities followed a geographically regressive slope running from the northwest to the southeast and dividing the semiperipheral "borderlands" of the advanced capitalist countries (Poland, Hungary, Slovenia, and the Czech Republic) from the peripheral southeast. As Table 7.1 shows, during the years of communism, these intraregional disparities narrowed somewhat, only to reopen again in 1989, permitting us to differentiate further among the more developed northwest region with its presumed potential for "fast adjustment," and the "catastrophe economies" of the southeast region (Romania, rump Yugoslavia, and Albania), with a few semideveloped countries (Bulgaria, Slovakia, and Croatia) occupying an intermediate position. The same formula applies to the formerly multiregional countries of Yugoslavia and Czechoslovakia. In Yugoslavia, the historical income gap between Slovenia and the rest of the republics opened up dramatically during the years of state socialism in spite of the fact that the government had made a concerted effort to reduce income disparities between "developed" and "underdeveloped" regions.[7] In Czechoslovakia, policies of regional developments were more successful, reducing an earlier 66:100 ratio between Slovak and Czech per-capita incomes to a ratio of 96:100.[8] But the closing of the income gap was mainly attained by massive transfers of Czech capital into Slovak armament industries, a policy that would have disastrous consequences for the Slovak economy after the fall of communism.

The third link between past and present arises out of the ethnic fragmentation of the area. The complex ethnic picture of individual countries need not be redrawn here. Suffice it to say that significant incongruities between ethnic and political boundaries remain in spite of the genocidal ravages of World War II, ethnic purification authorized by the Potsdam conference, emigration, and some of the practices of communist governments.[9] Accordingly, and much as in the past, almost all of the societies of Eastern Europe can be described as multinational because, even though during the Communist period at least some countries of the area (West Germany, the Czech lands, Poland, and Hungary) could, for all practical purposes, be regarded as ethnically homogeneous, today all of them show the presence of minorities in their recent census figures. In Poland, the German and Ukrainian minorities re-emerged in 1990, each counting several hundreds of thousands of persons who had previously found it more expedient to identify themselves as members of the "titular" nations (the ethnic majorities). In Hungary and the Czech Republic, a substantial percentage of the population identify themselves as Gypsies, and in Hungary the largely assimilated German, Croat, and Slovak ethnic communities have been resurrected by the prospect of preferential treatment granted by recent parliamentary legislation. The other East European countries, of course, have their "historical" minorities: Romania and Slovakia their Hungarians and Gypsies, Albania its Greeks, Bulgaria its Turks, and the republics of the former Yugoslavia their own peculiar mosaic of nationalities. Conversely, a number of East European countries have their "nationalities" problem in reverse; that is, they have conationals—Hungarians in Romania, Serbia, and Slovakia; Albanians in Kosovo and Macedonia; and Serbs in Croatia and Bosnia-Herzegovina—in adjacent countries. The tensions that arise out of these configurations are twofold: Titular nations (ethnic majorities) perceive threats to their culture or demographic superiority; alternatively, these majorities express solidarity with conationals living in an adjacent country often in an economically inferior position. Thus, ethnic fragmentation has both internal and international consequences. Internally, the "higher purpose" of ethnic survival may be used to subvert political systems based on pluralistic principles; externally, the sentiment of ethnic solidarity may foster conflict among states. The most egregious example of this is the war that currently engulfs the republics of the former Yugoslavia.

These ethnic tensions remain salient and acute because, to return to our initial metaphor, Eastern Europe went to sleep at mid-century and awoke nearly fifty years later with deeply entrenched conventional attitudes concerning the nation-state. For one thing, the idea of national sovereignty remained sacred and supreme, unwillingly fostered by the communist regimes, partly because Soviet-imposed limitations on independence became the most obvious common focus of opposition to the status quo, and partly because, in a seeming contradiction to communist internationalism, Marxist dialectics glorified national struggles for independence and treated them as part of the progressive heritage of humanity. In addition, thinking about minorities also remained stuck in a prewar mold. While few communist regimes actually resorted to brutal measures of open persecution or forced expulsion, many encouraged the emigration of minorities or resorted to aggressive measures of cultural assimilation through the educational system, and some simply practiced a policy of "benign neglect" of the national question, trusting that the forces of social mobility would have the same integrative effect. In this respect, the policies of ethnic autonomy and multiculturalism practiced in Yugoslavia were more of an exception than a rule, because even in Czechoslovakia the principle of federalism in practice meant a special license to Slovakia to pursue an aggressively assimilationist policy toward its own minorities.

We should remind ourselves here that the communist states on the whole not only fostered traditional forms of ethnic consciousness but a whole host of traditional attitudes as well, especially with respect to relationships of authority in the family, school, politics, and the workplace.[10] This communist neotraditionalism goes back to the first years of Stalinism and reflects certain functional needs of a political system engaged in wholesale mobilization of its energies. But communist neotraditionalism survived Stalin, and on through the Brezhnev period and even thereafter it was amply evident in the public symbolism of communist states, in their insistence on the dignity of rank, in their Victorian adherence to conventional proprieties, as well as in their negative attitudes toward social and artistic experimentation. On all these counts, communist states were profoundly conservative. This fact was most disconcerting to Western fellow travelers who cherished the other side of communism, its anti-imperialist rebellion against the global status quo, but appealed to at least some Western conservatives who felt a touch of nostalgia for the more simple, more robust, and more straightforward values of the common man and woman in these otherwise menacing societies.[11] This traditionalism is now hard to ignore by the rising new political elites, whatever their own attitudes may be.

Last but not least, there is the matter of collective memories that East Europeans preserved during their long years of political hibernation under Soviet communism. It is one of the timeless clichés of East European studies that these peoples tend to live in their history, and there is a grain of truth in this. While Americans live in the present and think about the future almost compulsively, East Europeans are inclined to seek solace in the past, for their recent experiences have been full of adversity. It is perhaps not too outlandish to say that had Darwin or Spencer been born in Poland or Hungary, they would never have gotten the idea that history was tantamount to evolution and progress, and would today be remembered as great theorists of decline and decay. In this historical context, it is not surprising—indeed, it is quite logical—for people to invoke the memories of great medieval kings or to daydream about the world before such setbacks as Kosovo Polje in Serbia, Mohács in Hungary, or the partitions in Poland.

Of all the memories of the past, none are more vivid than those of World War II, the event that has been so significant in shaping the character of our century. These memories are not confined to Eastern Europe. They are vivid in many other countries, including the United States, where they provide a common bond, perhaps the only one that today spans the entire political spectrum between Left and Right and thus can serve as one of the few bases of social consensus. In Eastern Europe, however, these memories tend to divide because some nations—Poles,

Czechs, and Serbs—fought with the Allies, while others—Hungarians, Romanians, Slovaks, Croats, Bulgarians, and perhaps more ambiguously, the Albanians—were more closely identified with the Axis side.

For the countries in the first group, the image of the war is that of a crusade in which the nation was associated with a noble and victorious cause. However much or little blood was shed, the memories of struggle, suffering, and sacrifice became deeply etched into collective consciousness and contribute to the positive self-image of the community. Despite the fact that in this way the memories of the war have long represented an integrative force, this force has become a burden in the post-communist period. In this new age, integration with Western Europe has emerged as a desirable political option but the key to Europe seems to be held by Germany. Thus, patriots who identify Germany with oppression and injustice, and see themselves as victims, must now compromise, indeed curry favor, with the past victimizer on their way to supranational harmony and prosperity. In the words of a German journalist, "the renewed relationship is harder ... there is a complex linkage of mutually caused pain and fear, and the knowledge that while they fear Germany, they also need her as an interlocutor and as a helper with economic reform."[12] Those who seek the European option thus carry political baggage and may become the targets of righteous indignation on the part of their opponents in the rough-and-tumble of politics.

In the former Axis countries, the memories of the war raise still more complex problems, for in subtle ways they intrude upon their relations with the United States, where significant segments of the body politic expect these former German allies to confront their own past and to make amends for it by showing forbearance toward their neighbors as well as solicitousness toward once-persecuted minorities. These expectations and the scrutiny of present political behavior are widely resented and create outcries against political "supervision" by the "gendarme of the universe."[13] The fact that the war was fought in this part of the world mainly against the Soviet Union, the "evil empire" of the next fifty years, only complicates matters further, by encouraging shows of self-righteousness and the rejection of the notion of collective guilt. Seen from this perspective, the war acquires historical justification. Atrocities against neighbors and minorities turn into unavoidable, if unfortunate, incidents committed in the heat of combat with shared responsibility between victims and victimizers. It has been in this spirit that the new political Right in the former Axis countries has spearheaded efforts to rehabilitate political figures convicted and executed as war criminals and, on occasion, has treated matters of rehabilitation as acts of defiance, if not as declarations of independence from foreign tutelage.

The International Environment

When speaking of Eastern, and more recently East-Central, Europe, I am referring to a number of small states that, ever since their birth in the nineteenth and early twentieth centuries, lived under some form of international regime. This is to say that, given their size and military potential, these were countries that had low capabilities to change their external environment. Rather, they had to adapt their own behavior to the expectations and exigencies of the world around them. At certain times, this world was chaotic. At others, however, it was relatively orderly with predictable rules of the game laid down by major actors in continental affairs. It is in terms of these rules that, between 1878 and today, we can distinguish among at least six different types of international regimes that had a role in shaping the politics of East European states.

The first of these different types of regimes may be located chronologically between the years 1878 and 1914. It may be described best as consensual-pluralist in character in that it rested on a "concert" of the major powers—or more simply and tellingly, of "the powers"—of the European continent. The main declared purposes of the regime were to prevent conflagrations among these powers, and, as a corollary, the encouragement of "civilized" forms of government in territories in the newly independent states that emerged from the gradual process of Ottoman decline. The main instruments of this international regime were ad hoc congresses that would assign special peacekeeping and civilizing missions to one or more participants. One of these was the long-forgotten assignment given to Austria-Hungary to pacify Bosnia-Herzegovina, two Ottoman provinces that were thought to be ungovernable troublespots by the participants of the Congress of Berlin in 1878. While the congresses were quite adept at containing international conflagrations, they were less successful in their "civilizing missions" to set up constitutional governments. Lacking both the will and the resources adequate to address the problem of economic backwardness in these peripheral areas, liberal institutions in Southeast Europe were quickly reduced to mere political facades to cover up the political reality of authoritarian, bureaucratic governments. Still, while liberalism was simulated rather than practiced in this part of the world, such simulation in and by itself put some restraint on the behavior of governments that made them different from the openly arbitrary, totalitarian regimes of a later day.

This concert of the powers began to falter around the turn of the twentieth century, and ultimately foundered on German hegemonical ambitions that brought about the conflagration of World War I. After the war, however, the previous regime was restored with some modifications. The old system of ad hoc conferences was replaced by the institutionalization of collective security arrangements embodied in the League of Nations. While in principle this body was responsible for enforcing the standards of the new international regime, in reality this function was performed by the victors of World War I, Britain and France. In the 1920s the system worked, because both of these powers were ready and able to assume this responsibility and because no other power was able or ready to challenge the order enshrined in the peace treaties of 1919 to 1920. In 1919, the two powers sponsored military intervention against the Hungarian Soviet Republic, both to compel it to comply with the territorial provisions of the armistice and to replace it with a more liberal form of government. Shortly thereafter, France enforced the new order against its own allies, Serbia and Romania, by compelling them to evacuate Hungarian territories *not* awarded to them by the Armistice Agreement and subsequent peace treaty. In 1921, France and Britain took joint action to arrest former Emperor Karl von Habsburg on Hungarian territory to forestall any attempt at imperial restoration in the Danube Valley. Then, in 1923, France occupied the German Rhineland to enforce the reparation clauses of the Treaty of Versailles.

Like its predecessor, this Franco-British–dominated international regime showed preference for liberal-democratic forms of government and pressured the lesser nations of East-Central Europe to extend the suffrage, to modify constitutions, and for the first time in history, to extend citizens' rights to ethnic and religious minorities. But again like its predecessor, this was more of a political than an economic regime, and in an age of ever-increasing economic nationalism, neither France nor England would provide resources or grant preferential treatment to alleviate the plight of these depressed East European economies. Not surprisingly, therefore, just as in the nineteenth century, these liberal-democratic experiments quickly deteriorated into simulated democracy serving as a facade for military-bureaucratic regimes.

This consensual-pluralist and liberally inspired international regime itself disintegrated in the 1930s with the rise of the Soviet Union, Germany, and Italy as challengers to the League of Nation's philosophy and to Franco-British hegemony on the Continent. This development ushered in a period of conflictual pluralism that divided the countries of Eastern Europe, as well as their domestic political spectrum, between the supporters and the opponents of the international status quo. Both Left and Right radicalism were advancing among the electorates, and under pressure from these movements, liberal (or quasi-liberal) governments gave way to open dictatorships.[14] These instances of political decay were, of course, preliminaries to World War II, an event that first ushered in a brief (1938–44) German hegemonic regime and then the much longer, and constantly evolving, hegemonic regime of the Soviet state. Under the latter, East European countries were forced to adopt the very institutions of the Soviet authority, though as time passed some of these "satellites" slipped out from the rigid Soviet mold and embarked on social and political experiments of their own. If in the 1890s and 1930s we could speak of simulated democracy in the region, now we encountered and had to recognize the phenomenon of simulated state socialism.

In different ways and to a different extent, all of these international regimes had domestic political implications for the smaller nations of Eastern Europe in that they provided a structure of opportunities for elites while at the same time also constraining their range of choice in building institutions and making public policy. It would therefore be hard to explain the rise of liberal constitutionalism in Eastern Europe in the nineteenth century or the extension of suffrage in the 1920s, without taking into consideration the larger international milieu. Moreover, when it comes to the Soviet period, political sociology—the art of divining political outcomes from domestic social, economic, and cultural configurations—is far less helpful than the study of the twists and turns of politics in the imperial center. Stalin's death in 1953, Khrushchev's overthrow in 1964, or Gorbachev's succession to power in 1985 were certainly more important milestones of political change than any particular stage of economic or social progress on a linear developmental scheme.

The new international regime that emerged in the wake of the upheavals of 1989–90 must be examined against this historical background. In some significant ways, this regime represents a return to the liberally oriented consensual pluralism of earlier times, though with certain pluses and minuses on a comparative balance sheet of capabilities. On the plus side, the leading powers of the contemporary period have both the resources and experience needed for international economic cooperation and aid. They certainly have the capability to offer a series of positive inducement in the form of loans, investment capital, direct aid, and, most significantly, of the prospect of admission to one of the large and prosperous trading blocs of the West (the European Community, or EC). All this, however, is being offered in exchange for East European willingness to play the liberal economic and political game by introducing market economies and democratic government, showing respect for minority rights, and accepting some limitations on the traditional prerogatives of the sovereign state.[15] At the same time, this regime, led by the United States and Germany, and institutionalized by the United Nations, has weaknesses: Hamstrung by domestic political considerations, it is less able than the "powers" of yesteryear to mobilize itself militarily and therefore less able to enforce by threats or action the high standards it sets for international behavior. The reasons for this are complex, but they seem to boil down to the changing social character of the great powers of the West. Though their predecessors fifty or a hundred years ago were semiagrarian, semimobilized political communities, today's great powers are modern industrial states with highly mobilized middle-class constituencies that are conscious of the social costs of foreign policy and highly protective of their own physical and material well-being. Some of the great statesmen of the nineteenth and early twentieth centuries could advocate the primacy of foreign policy (*Primat der Aussenpolitik*).[16] Their successors today live by the canon of the primacy of domestic policy.[17] To quote one of the popular mottos of American public life: "All politics is local." The net result of this is a glaring discrepancy between high-minded ends and limited means, which makes the new order a frequent target of skeptical critics and accounts for the diversity of East European responses to the international regime. Whereas some governments of the region are willing and able to play the political game by Western rules, others merely simulate playing by these rules, while still others openly defy the norms set down by the leading liberal powers of the Continent.

Patterns of Adaptation

The first of these political responses has historical antecedents that date back to the nineteenth and early twentieth centuries. It may be designated as "liberal" or "civic"—as the majority of the parties in this "response category" refer to themselves. These are the Czech Liberal Social Union, the "Liberal Forum" (faction) with the Hungarian Democratic Forum, the Croat Social Liberal Party, the Slovenian Liberal Democrats (earlier, Liberal party), the National Liberal Party of Romania (a former member of the broader Democratic Convention that challenged the ruling National Salvation Front in the 1992 elections), and the Czech Civic Democratic Party. Others, however, prefer the more inclusive "democratic" label, though they frequently describe themselves as liberal in spirit and legacy, as does the Hungarian Alliance of Free Democrats and Young Democrats, the Polish Democratic Union and Center Alliance, and at least certain elements of the Serbian Democratic Opposition, the Bulgarian Union of Democratic Forces, and the Albanian Democratic Party. Again others, or factions of others, like the Hungarian Smallholders' Party, or the Romanian Peasant Party, do not use any of these labels, but may qualify as members of the civic-liberal camp.[18] Irrespective of label, the common denominator among these parties, and the link to their historical forerunners, is the view that the main problem their countries face is the backwardness of their economies and that this condition may be best overcome by adjusting their economic, political, and legal institutions to square with models presented by the more advanced West. In the nineteenth century, this developmental model was closely and unambiguously associated with the desire to establish and assert distinctive national identities. Today, however, such desires are tempered by the ideals of universalism and supranationalism embodied in the ideal of the European Community. Indeed, the liberal parties of the area now actively solicit closer association with Western Europe and, in exchange, try to offer clean human-rights records, meticulous adherence to Western economic and political norms, and tolerance toward both neighboring countries and national minorities. It was in this same vein that the liberals of Czechoslovakia and Poland hastened to sign treaties of accommodation with Germany and, likewise, that Hungarian liberals led the way in legislating collective rights for the country's national minorities, pledging to honor the inviolability of existing international boundaries, and resisting attempts by the Right to rehabilitate political figures associated with past political regimes. Such resistance and the pursuit of accommodationist policies does not always come easily because domestic detractors are apt to denounce liberals for having no historical memories, or worse, for selling out the patrimony of the nation-state.[19] Some East European liberals, most notably Czech President Vaclav Havel, Jiri Dienstbier, the Polish Tadeusz Mazowiecki, or the Hungarian Free Democrats, refused to bow to nationalist agitation and sentiment, but all of them paid some political price for their reluctance, if only the price of being labeled cosmopolitans without roots in the nation.[20]

Others, and perhaps a majority of Eastern Europe's liberals, however, tried to diffuse the issue by rhetorical devices and symbolic action. It is in this spirit that Hungary's József Antall has made a habit of referring to himself as the prime minister of fifteen million Hungarians (rather than of the ten million living inside the boundaries of the country);[21] that Vaclav Havel has found it expedient to combine his pro-European policies with thinly veiled appeals to ethnic solidarity;[22] and that Walesa of Poland combines his pro-Western policies with occasionally vitriolic speeches, for example, either on Western greed and selfishness or on the sacredness of Polish sovereignty, "to get a handle on the nationalist and xenophobic drift of Polish politics."[23]

As defined above, of course, liberalism becomes a very large tent that shelters parties and factions of considerable ideological diversity. As Figure 7.1 shows, we are dealing with what American common parlance refers to as "liberalism with a small l," as in, say, the "liberal heritage of the West." Within this general category, we can draw distinctions along two major faultlines. The first of these has to do with relations between the states and markets in terms of which we can distinguish between the classical, or radical, free marketeers (associated with the practices and theories of Margaret Thatcher, Ronald Reagan, and Milton Friedman) who put their faith in the capacity of markets to distribute goods justly and efficiently, and the "social liberals" who are ready to use the state to redistribute the profits of enterprise either to obtain greater equality or to promote some social goal, such as the cohesion of the family. As for radical free marketeers in contemporary Eastern Europe, representatives include Klaus (the Czech Republic's prime minister), Balcerowicz (Poland's former minister of finance), and Mazowiecki (Poland's prime minister), together with some of the leaders of the Hungarian liberal opposition to Parliament.

The second split within the larger liberal family of parties arises with respect to attitudes toward traditionalism between cultural radicals and cultural conservatives. The former, much as do the "life-style liberals" of the United States, define the essence of freedom as freedom from traditional normative restraints. The latter, while recognizing the rights of the individual in the political community, are more sympathetic toward traditional social norms and are quite comfortable with the nineteenth-century liberal principle that sees state and society as two sharply divided realms in which two different sets of norms may well prevail. Thus, while the cultural radical is ready to apply the egalitarian norms of the democratic state to the family, school, and workplace, the cultural conservative is quite comfortable with contract and democracy in the public realm, while maintaining paternalism and traditional relationships in the private sphere.

To make this scheme of classification more descriptive, a centrist position has been inserted into both of the figure's coordinates, to separate pragmatic redistributionists from ideologues, and culturally neutral liberals from those leaning either toward or away from traditional cultural norms. By doing so, a three-by-three matrix of nine categories in which we can attempt to place the lib-

FIGURE 7.1 Liberal Forces in East Europe (incomplete)

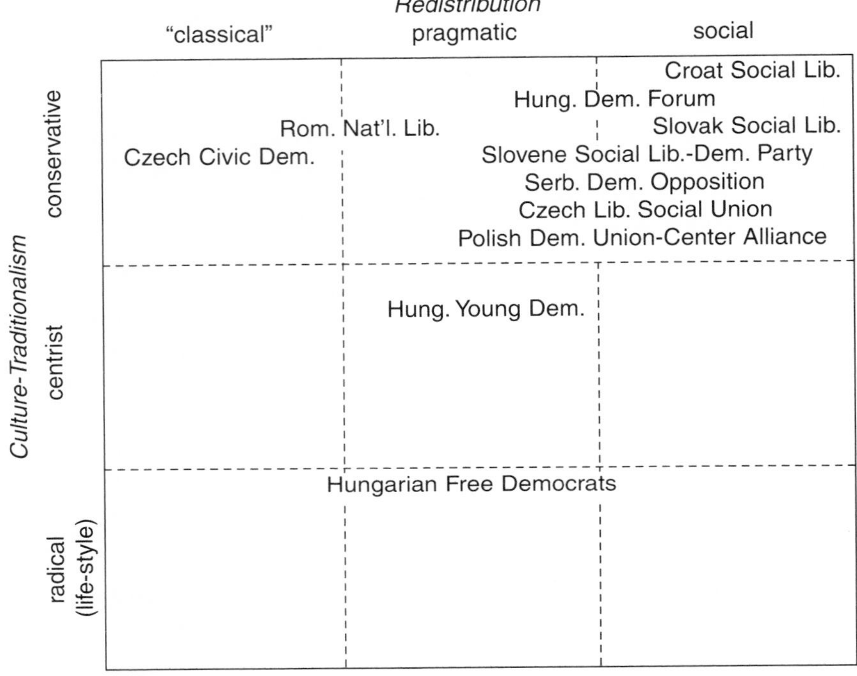

eral forces of the area according to their etatist and cultural proclivities. Although the current situation is too fluid for accurate classification, and though many parties are divided into several factions, a cursory examination of current distributions of preference will put the majority of East European liberals in the upper righthand corner of Figure 7.1 where social liberals and cultural conservatives congregate. As of now, "Western-style" cultural liberalism and an aggressive renunciation of traditional values (including the values of ethnic nationalism) have proven to be less of a political asset than an electoral liability.[24]

The second strategy of adjustment in contemporary Eastern Europe may be described as technocracy. Whereas it is frequently used in common political parlance, this term is full of ambiguities, but overall, and for the present purposes, it refers to a political formula in which the rational calculation of economic ends and means takes precedence over the idea of popular sovereignty, because people are seen either as being incapable of grasping the complexities of economics or as being too weak by nature to adjust to temporary austerity on the long road of economic development. Technocracy may also be seen as an alternative to reliance on an unrestrained market mechanism, and its practitioners, therefore, may be seen as sympathetic to the idea of economic planning and regulation. In politics as well as in economics, technocracy is leaning toward some form of etatism, though it is capable of coexisting uneasily with parliamentary institutions and regimes.

In Eastern Europe, the contemporary revival of technocratic thinking in politics stems from two different historical roots. One of these goes back to the 1930s, when it appeared in most of the countries of the region as a political alternative to the then prevailing liberal policies of development with their positive orientation toward markets, legalism, and to a corrupted form of parliamentary government. This alternative had vocal proponents in nearly all East European states, perhaps the best known of them being the Romanian Mihail Manoilescu, the author of numerous treatises in which he advocated policies of import-substitution industrialization, a model of social corporatism, and a strong, centralized state designed to mobilize the resources of economically backward countries for development.[25] Manoilescu's ideas gained widespread popularity in his own time and were put into practice in part or as a whole by most East European governments, including those of premiers Stoyadinovic of Yugoslavia, Gömbös of Hungary, the royal dictatorships of Romania and Bulgaria, and several governments of Poland under Marshal Pilsudski and the so-called "colonel's regime."[26] All of these governments introduced some form of central planning and regulation of the market mechanism and either abolished or severely curtailed the functions of already flawed parliamentary institutions that had provided the region's liberal government with a thin veneer of legitimacy. But what was most distinctive about this form of technocracy was that its own legitimacy derived from nationalism, often invoked in a highly opportunistic fashion either to neutralize nationalist and populist extremists or to deflect attention from the economic austerity to such convenient targets as the neighboring states or the national minorities residing in their own country.

The other source of this revival of technocracy is more recent. It goes back to the reform, or "liberal," communism of the 1960s and 1970s. The term "liberal" is somewhat misleading here, for while these communist reformers were rational planners who believed that the logic of economic efficiency required freedom from the stifling political restraints of Leninism and Stalinism, they had little use for political democracy. Indeed, much like their predecessors in the 1930s, they believed that popular government might frustrate their rational economic design to increase the standard of living and levels of economic efficiency.

In the 1960s and 1970s, this line of thinking was most evident in Tito's Yugoslavia, Gierek's Poland, and Kádár's Hungary, where the idea of economic development and national redistribution gradually replaced the grandiose social designs of earlier years and where the parties systematically diminished state intervention in the economic process and in the private lives of citizens. In the rest of Eastern Europe, however, these principles were either regarded as a dangerous form of deviationism, as was the case in Albania and Romania, or were subordinated to the political goals of maintaining and expanding the international power position of the Soviet bloc. The fact is, however, that even where "liberal communism" was regnant, it failed to fulfill popular (and Western) expectations of economic efficiency.

Thus, it is somewhat ironic that when the great crisis of 1989–90 came, the ideas of liberal communism were used as a kind of political life raft on which some of the less compromised and prominent members of the old establishment navigated from one-party monopoly to the multiparty system. On the way to pluralist politics, these "moderates" jettisoned some of their more embarrassing colleagues as well as the names of their old parties. Thus in Albania, Bulgaria, Serbia, and Hungary, former communists adopted the socialist label. In Romania, the post-Ceaușescu leadership assumed the name of National Salvation Front (now split into two factions); in the former Czechoslovakia, communists became the Democratic Bloc; in Poland, the Democratic Left Alliance. In Croatia and Slovakia, the metamorphosis was more complex because it involved a process of uniting the lower echelons of the administrative, political, and economic apparatus with some elements of the nationalist intelligentsia, and it was from this alliance that the Croat National community and the Movement for a Democratic Slovakia eventually emerged. Some of the most conspicuous leaders of these parties—the Slovak Vladimir Meciar, the Romanian Ion Iliescu, the Croat Franjo Tudjman, the Bulgarian Velko Vukanov, the Serbian Slobodan Milosević—were former high functionaries, but the hard core of the new parties' supporters came from the social segment that had lost some emolument or office in the process of transition.

These politicians and their followers do profess the desire to create genuine market economies. But in practice, their rhetorical commitment to the market economy is weakened by their not altogether irrational fears that unleashing the market mechanism would have catastrophic results for their weak economies and eventually result in massive unemployment. Thus, their real commitment is to "gradualism," controlled prices, a semiplanned economy, and, in Meciar's own words, "temporary *dirigisme*."[27] In politics, likewise, these ex-communist technocrats profess to be democrats. But the process of democratization is sometimes condemned as an "enforced" and "inorganic" process imposed from the outside.[28] Moreover, in a number of states under their control, a quasi-authoritarian state lurks behind the democratic facade, justified by the need to hold society together, to redistribute the burdens of transition, and to mobilize savings for rapid economic development. Far less likely to be hosts to foreign investment or recipients of Western largesse, these technocratic regimes are less constrained than the liberals in their political behavior. Thus, elections in their countries have been less than fully fair and have occasionally been marred by violence, and once elected, technocratic governments reached out for the monopolistic control of the media, and, in the case of Iliescu's National Salvation Front, for the support of raucous mobs and even former security policemen.[29]

To some degree, all of the successor parties are burdened by their past association with the failures of communism and have had to struggle for popular support in order to widen their electoral base. This struggle has not been easy and has required a critical choice between the political idiom of universalism and particularism. A few of the parties—the Czech, the Polish, the Slovenian, and, perhaps more ambiguously, the Hungarian—chose the universalist route and have made their case to their potential voters by promises of social redistribution and continued industrial subsidies. But the majority of the successor parties have thrown themselves headlong into the murky waters of ethnic politics, either by embracing national issues or by allying themselves with populist and radical nationalist parties. In this respect, the history of the 1930s seems to be repeating itself. To be sure, in public and for the benefit of Western audiences, even these parties like to parade as paragons of tolerance, national equality, and even multiculturalism. Thus, both President Iliescu of Romania and Premier Meciar of Slovakia have recently assured their Western audiences and negotiating partners that their countries were genuine multinational states in which each and every group enjoys the same rights.[30] This rhetoric, however, only thinly veils constitutional documents that declare the legal primacy of the titular nations—this being the case in Croatia and Slovakia as well as in Romania—or that contain provisions that ban political parties promoting the interests of ethnic groups—as in the case of Bulgaria.[31] These constitutional principles have then been given a ring of authenticity by petty repressive measures such as changing the language of street signs in minority districts, insistence on particular orthographies and first names (in the language of the majority), the defacing of public monuments, or curtailing the activities of the educational system of national minorities.

The third strategic alternative that presented itself after the fall of state socialism is most frequently referred to as neopopulism. The designation seems to be appropriate, because of obvious similarities between this contemporary brand of populism and its forerunners in the nineteenth and early twentieth century. Like the Russian *narodniki* and their numerous East European counterparts of the past—the Polish Wyzvolenie, the Bulgarian Agrarians, the Croat and Romanian Peasant parties, the Serbian radical socialists, the Hungarian *népiesek*, the Slovak People's Party, associated with the names of Stambulisky, Radić, Stere, and Mihalahe, Svetozar Marković, Erde, Szabó, and Hlinka, to mention just a few leaders—today's populists are egalitarians and socialists yet represent antipodes of both liberalism and Marxism, for they reject both the liberal idea of the market and the Marxist infatuation with industrialism. Further, though both liberals and Marxists believe in sacrificing at least some aspects of the traditional value system in exchange for material welfare, populism rejects this kind of materialism in favor of the integrity of culture and community. In this respect, the classical populism of Europe anticipated the ideologies of Chinese Maoism, Islamic fundamentalism, the Sendero Luminoso ("Shining Path") of Peru, or the Khmer Rouge of Cambodia, all of them preoccupied with the fight against the corrupting influences of "cultural imperialism," and its locus in the society's urban centers. In some sense, this populism also anticipates Green preoccupations with the impact of technology on the "life-world." While the slogan "small is beautiful" was not invented by populists, it is embodied in their practices, especially in their attempts to satisfy society's needs by the product of small enterprise and of the peasant smallholding.

Originally focusing on the commune and the extended family, the *obshchina, mir,* and the Balkan *zadruga,* in the 1920s, East European populism began to flirt with the idea of the peasantry as a universal class to be united in a Green International. Far more fatefully, in the same decade some populist movements also embraced the idea of nationalism, exchanging the earlier ideas of the folk, or the *narod,* for those of the ethnic community organized in the form of states. It is on this issue that the movement split and that many an East European populist crossed the borderline between Left and Right, for even though they remained "Left" in their emphasis on equality within the national community, they now became "Right" in accepting hierarchy in interstate relations and in the relations among ethnic groups. At the same time, and as part of this conversion, many right-wing populists began to accept, indeed to glorify, violence, not only as an instrument of national power but as a functional substitute for sophisticated economic strategies. Although most of these movements in small countries felt inadequate by themselves to manipulate their external environment, they felt strong enough to persecute national and religious minorities—not only to create a homogeneous and pure community but to redistribute wealth and income from the "aliens" to the native element. The most striking example of this new populism—now remembered as a variety of fascism—was the Romanian All for the Fatherland Party, better known as the Iron Guard, whose program mixed egalitarian slogans—"each man his acre"—with religious mysticism, the idea of otherworldly reward, and with the advocacy of the expropriation and expulsion of ethnic minorities.

Much of what has been said here about the past may be repeated about East European populism today.[32] While anti-developmentalism or anti-industrialism are not clearly articulated centerpieces of the doctrine, the populists of today bluntly reject the implicit quid pro quo offered by the West and show open contempt for "liberty supervised" by America and Germany.[33] Thus, Hungary's populists reject the lure of consumer society and the advance of foreign capital to forestall the moral pollution of traditional culture,[34] and Serbia's Milosević is prepared to eat "grass" or the "barks and roots of trees" rather than surrender Serbian sovereignty over Kosovo in exchange for foreign aid.[35] It is in these quarters that World War II lives on as a symbol of national unity and as a definer of national identity. While Serbian populists justify their genocidal war as revenge for atrocities inflicted on them by Croat and Muslim allies of Germany, the Czech and the Polish Right have fought resolutely against their countries' treaties with their former enemy. Conversely, Romanian and Slovak populists in their formerly pro-Axis countries became strong and successful advocates of rehabilitating General Antonescu and Monsignor Tiso, their countries' executed wartime leaders, and members of the Hungarian and Croatian Right were no less vigorous, though less successful, in doing the same for once condemned major political figures.[36]

As in the past, today populists are not just different from liberals but aggressively antiliberal as a matter of personal and political identity. In the past this meant, above all, rejection of the *city* as the locus of foreignness and as a mediator of corruptive cultural influence. Just as Bulgaria's Stambulisky or Hungary's Dezsö Szabó of yesteryear, the populists of today rail against the city with its ethnically and spiritually alien residents.[37] Milosević obviously dislikes Belgrade with its westernized intellectuals, and his allies wantonly shell Dubrovnik and Sarajevo, the arch-symbols of cosmopolitan tourism and multiculturalism. For Hungarian neo-populists, the term "urbanism" has become synonymous with all that they themselves stand against, and Romanian neopopulists once again celebrate the peasantry and the village as the symbol of national identity.[38]

What we have to remember, though, is that in the interim the character of liberalism itself has undergone significant changes. If beforehand, "antiliberal" meant opposition to the freedom of markets and "selfish" individualism, today to some it means resistance to an activist movement ready to change the cultural makeup of society by changing its sexual constitution, by rejecting traditional proprieties, and by cultivating the symbols of the victim and the weak. These ideas of cultural liberalism are controversial even in the West and provide convenient targets for conservatives who rise to the defense of traditionalism. Thus the contemporary populists, be they in Serbia, Romania, or Hungary, not only lash out against the selfishness of markets and of the individualist creed but target the very groups that liberals cultivate and wish to emancipate. While this new anti-antitraditionalism has not yet been crafted into coherent doctrine, the sentiment is alive. It provides plausible explanation for bizarre rituals of brutality as well as meaning to seemingly senseless acts of violence in the Balkans and in other parts of the former communist world. If this assumption is valid, the mass rape of women and the subsequent use of force to ensure that they carry children to term are not only the depraved acts of men who have lost their moorings in society but an intuitively choreographed response to the cultural liberal agenda of "choice" and "empowerment." Similarly, repeated attacks on the disabled, the beating of the wheelchair-bound, or setting fire to amputees in other post-communist societies are not just chapters from the fantasy of a new Marquis de Sade[39]—they are part of the political ritual of a Nietzschean counterrevolution of the "strong" against what they see as power masquerading as the morality of the victim and of the weak.[40] It certainly is symbolic politics that is better elucidated in Nietzsche's *The Genealogy of Morals* than in Marx's *Manifesto* or *German Ideology.*

Parties and Regimes: Thinking About the Future

Surveying the political scene in Eastern Europe, we will find advocates of these political strategies in each and every country of the region, though such advocacy often hides behind Aesopian political language or a neutral "democratic" label. Thus, at first sight, the region provides us with a bewildering mosaic of political persuasions, parties, and groupings. But upon closer examination, we will be able to discern certain patterns that will allow us to make, however tentatively, generalizations about the dynamics of post-communist politics.

After the first round of recent elections, these patterns seemed to be reasonably clear in that they showed strong correlations with levels of economic development measured by per-capita income and productivity. In terms of these, one could make neat distinctions between the countries of the more developed European Northwest—Poland, the Czech Republic, Hungary, and Slovenia—bordering on the industrial democracies of the West, and the European Southeast, including the countries of the Balkans and the new Republic of Slovakia, with their far less developed economies. While even the "borderlands" of the northwest are underdeveloped in comparison to their neighbors in the West, these countries possess sufficient infrastructure, trained personnel, and productive potential to offer at least some hope of success for democratic and market-oriented reform strategies. It is for this reason that in these elections the electorates returned liberal majorities to their new parliamentary institutions, thereby opting for a strategy of "fast adjustment" to the economics and politics of the West.

In contrast to this experience, the elections in the southeast have produced a political spectrum that tilted heavily toward technocracy allied, sometimes uncomfortably, with nationalist and populist elites. As Table 7.2 shows, the successor parties to state socialism have had no difficulty in winning comfortable majorities in Albania, Bulgaria, and rump Yugoslavia, together with the Democratic Community and Democratic Movement of Croatia and Slovakia respectively. In all these countries, right-wing, or nationalistic, populism is a significant political factor. This radicalism is perhaps most powerful in Serbia (see Tables 7.2 and 7.3), but Romania is not far behind in this respect, for even though only 11.6 percent of the voters chose one of the parties of the neopopulist Right, their weekly newspaper *Romania Mare* (with a circulation of 600,000) sells more copies than any other print medium in the region, and a recent poll gave the parties a 57-percent favorable rating.[41]

The second round of elections, held in a number of countries in 1992–93, made this picture more complex, though perhaps without bringing about substantive changes in the public policies of individual countries. In the northern tier, the Polish elections of September 1993 returned to power parties associated in the public mind with the communist past, though it is questionable whether, in view of the material expectations of the population and the structure of the international economy, the new government will be able to deviate significantly from the reform policies of their liberal predecessors. In the southeast, a year before the Polish events, liberals defeated ex-communist technocrats in Bulgaria and Albania. But these victories, too, seemed somewhat hollow. In Bulgaria, the liberals, holding but a plurality of the seats in the Assembly, could not hold on to power

TABLE 7.2 Popular Vote for Selected Parties (see Table 7.3)

Country	*Year*	*Party*	*Percentage of Vote*
Albania	1991	Workers' (communist)	56.2
		Dem.	38.7
	1992	Socialist	25.8
		Dem. Coalition	69.6
	1992	Dem. Coalition	43.1
	Local	Socialist	41.3
Bulgaria	1990	Socialist	47.1
		Union of Dem. Forces	37.8
	1991	Socialist	33.1
		Union of Dem. Forces	34.4
Czech Republic	1992	Civic Dem./Christian Dem.	33.9
		Liberal Social	5.8
		Republican	6.5
		Left Bloc	14.3
Slovak Republic	1992	Social Dem.	6.1
		National	9.4
		Movement for Dem. Slovakia	33.5
		Dem. Left	14.5
Hungary	1990	Dem. Forum	24.7
		Free Dem	21.4
		Young Dem.	8.9
		Socialist	10.9
Poland	1991	Dem. Union	12.3
		Center Alliance	8.7
		Solidarity	5.1
		Dem. Left	12.0
		Confed. for Indep. Poland	7.5
	1993	Dem. Union	10.6
		Peasant	15.4
		Solidarity	4.9
		Dem. Left	20.4
Romania	1990	National Salvation Front	66.3
		Liberal	6.4
		Peasant	1.6
	1992	Nat'l. and Dem. Salvation	47.7
		Dem. Convention	20.1
		National Unity	7.7
		Greater Romania	3.9
Serbia	1992	Socialist	40.2
		Dem. Opposition	20.4
		Radicals	30.4
Croatia	1990	Dem. Community	56.7
	(presidential)	Social Liberal	21.9
		Socialist and Soc. Dem.	4.7
Slovenia	1992	Liberal Dem.	23.3
		Christian Dem.	14.5
		Left Unity	13.6

TABLE 7.3 Ideological Affiliation of Major Political Parties in Eastern Europe

<table>
<tr><th>Country</th><th>Civic Liberal</th><th>Neo-Populist</th><th>Technocratic Right</th><th>Technocratic Left</th></tr>
<tr><td>Albania</td><td colspan="2">Democratic</td><td>Workers'</td><td></td></tr>
<tr><td></td><td></td><td></td><td>Labor</td><td></td></tr>
<tr><td>Bulgaria</td><td>Union of Dem. Forces</td><td></td><td>Socialist</td><td></td></tr>
<tr><td>Czech Republic</td><td>Civic Dem.</td><td>Republican</td><td></td><td>Left Bloc</td></tr>
<tr><td></td><td>Liberal Social Union</td><td></td><td></td><td></td></tr>
<tr><td>Slovak Republic</td><td>Social Dem.</td><td>Slovak National</td><td>Movement for Dem. Slovakia</td><td>Dem. Left</td></tr>
<tr><td>Hungary</td><td>Free Dem.</td><td></td><td></td><td>Socialist</td></tr>
<tr><td></td><td colspan="2">Dem. Forum</td><td></td><td></td></tr>
<tr><td></td><td>Young Dem.</td><td></td><td></td><td></td></tr>
<tr><td>Poland</td><td>Dem. Union</td><td>Confederation for Indep. Poland</td><td></td><td>Dem. Left Alliance</td></tr>
<tr><td></td><td>Center Alliance</td><td></td><td></td><td></td></tr>
<tr><td></td><td>Solidarity</td><td></td><td></td><td></td></tr>
<tr><td>Romania</td><td>Nat'l. Liberal (1990)</td><td>National Unity</td><td>National Salvation Front</td><td></td></tr>
<tr><td></td><td>Nat'l. Peasant (1990)</td><td>Greater Romania</td><td></td><td></td></tr>
<tr><td></td><td>Dem. Convention</td><td></td><td></td><td></td></tr>
<tr><td>Serbia</td><td>Dem. Opposition</td><td>Radical (Arkan)</td><td></td><td></td></tr>
<tr><td></td><td></td><td colspan="2">Socialist</td><td></td></tr>
<tr><td></td><td></td><td>Radical (Seselj)</td><td></td><td></td></tr>
<tr><td>Croatia</td><td>Social Liberal</td><td colspan="2">Croatian Democratic Community</td><td></td></tr>
<tr><td></td><td>Social Dem.</td><td></td><td></td><td></td></tr>
<tr><td>Slovenia</td><td>Liberal Dem.</td><td>National</td><td></td><td>Left Unity</td></tr>
<tr><td></td><td>Christian Dem.</td><td></td><td></td><td></td></tr>
</table>

and abandoned the government to a group of technical experts. In Albania, politics remains chaotic, and close observers have doubted whether the election results have lifted the country out of its "neo-monist" mold.[42]

In the short run, such fluctuations and swings in majorities will be inevitable, given the vast gap between the material expectations of the populations and the economic and political means available to satisfy them. In the long run, of course, the political fate of these countries will be closely related to their ability to generate economic growth—and to do so by maintaining a tolerable balance between the numbers of winners and losers in the new economies. In the absence of such a balance and of tangible improvements in the general standard of living, liberal strategies will increasingly lose their appeal, and democratic multiparty systems will operate in a vacuum, though the current balance of power in Europe might at least temper the drift into open and blatant authoritarianism. Political development, as I suggested at the beginning of this chapter, is shaped by responses to both internal and external exigencies. So neofascist and neobolshevik regimes are not likely to appear without the rise of an aggressive restorationist regime in the former Soviet Union or without some other major challenge to the current continental hegemony of the Western powers and their liberal democratic principles.

Notes

An earlier version of this chapter appeared as "The Domestic and International Contexts of East European Politics" in the journal *East European Politics and Societies* 1, Spring 1987. Permission to reprint it here, with modifications, is gratefully acknowledged.

1. Francis Fukuyama, "Are We at the End of History?" *Fortune*, January 15, 1990, pp. 75–77. In book form, *The End of History and the Last Man* (New York: Maxwell MacMillan International, 1992).

2. Extrapolated from figures for "earliest industrialized West Europe" (minus Great Britain), given as $211 per capita in 1960 dollars, and from figures for "Eastern Europe" (excluding Hungary) reported as $170, in Ivan T. Berend and György Rankí, *The European Periphery and Industrialization, 1780–1914* (Cambridge and New York: Cambridge University Press; Paris: Editions de la Maison des Sciences de l'Homme, 1982), p. 15.

3. Calculation based on the purchasing parities of wages in Colin Clark, *The Conditions of Economic Progress* (London: MacMillan and Co. limited, 1940). The six Western countries are Belgium, Holland, France, Switzerland, Sweden, and Germany; the six Eastern countries are Hungary, (Russian) Poland, Bulgaria, Serbia, Romania, and Bohemia.

4. A slightly better ratio for the period 1975–82, 36:100, can be derived by averaging the results of *six* contemporary research projects using different methods of calculation: U.S. Department of State, *The Planetary Product, 1977–78* (Special Report No. 58) (Washington, D.C., 1979); Thad Alton, *Research Project on National Income in East-Central Europe* (New York: L. W. International Financial Research, 1983); Peter Havlik, *Comparison of Real Products Between East and West, 1970–83* (Vienna: Wiener Institut für Internationale Wirtschaftsvergleiche, 1985); *World Development Report, 1978* (Washington, D.C.: World Bank, 1978); *Yearbook of National Accounts* (New York: United Nations, 1980); and Paul

Marer, *Dollar GNPs of USSR and Eastern Europe* (Baltimore: Published for the World Bank by Johns Hopkins University Press, 1985).

5. Ben Slay, "The Polish Economy Between Recession and Recovery," Radio Free Europe/ Radio Liberty (RFE/RL) *Research Report*, September 11, 1992, p. 17.

6. The *Economist*, August 31, 1991, p. 24. See also Blaire Harden and Mary Battieta, "Eastern Europeans Discover that Freedom Comes at a Price," *Washington Post* (weekly edition), January 7–13, 1991, p. 9. This latter source speaks of a 20-percent decline in industrial production, 21 percent unemployment, and a 30-percent drop in real consumption.

7. Apparently, the historical ratio between most-developed Slovenia and least-developed Kosovo increased from an earlier (1945) 3:1 to a ratio of 6:1, or even 8:1 by the 1980s.

8. Sharon L. Wolchik, *Czechoslovakia in Transition: Politics, Economics and Society* (London and New York: Pinter, 1991), pp. 187–191.

9. See Richard V. Burks, *The Dynamics of Communism in Eastern Europe* (Princeton: Princeton University Press, 1961), esp. pp. 131–149.

10. For this point, and on the larger issue of "neotraditionalism" in communist and post-communist societies, Ilja Srubar, "War der reale Sozialismus modern?" ("Was Real Socialism Modern?" Quoted *in extenso* from *Pritmost* 11:2, by Jirina Siklova, in "Nationalismus in Ost und Mitteleuropa," ("Nationalism in East and Central Europe"), *Frankfurter Allgemeine Zeitung* (hereafter *FAZ*), September 4, 1991, p. 10.

11. See George Kennan's comparison between the "hippies, drugs, pornography, drunkenness" in a Danish port and a "company of robust Soviet infantry," in Paul Hollander, "From Containment to Understanding," in Hollander's *The Survival of the Adversary Culture* (New Brunswick, N.J.: Transaction Books, 1988), pp. 39–40.

12. Berthold Kohler, "Der Vertrag ist kein Wundermittel," *FAZ*, September 4, 1991, p. 14.

13. See, for instance, Eugen Barbu, "Romania in libertatea supravegheata," *Romania Mare*, October 23, 1992, p. 4.

14. Burks, *Dynamics*, pp. 40, 66–67, 77–78, and 151.

15. See Tibor Varady, "Collective Minority Rights and Problems in Their Protection," *East European Politics and Society* 6:3 (Fall 1992), pp. 260–282.

16. For an excellent introduction to these principles, see Ernst-Otto Czempiel, "Der Primat der Auswartigen Politik: Kritische Wurdigung einer Staasmaxime," *Politische Vierteljahrschrift* 4:3 (September 1963), pp. 266–287.

17. For a critique of the new international regime, see Gunther Nonnenmacher, "Prinzipiell internationalistisch," *FAZ*, October 22, 1992, p. 12.

18. For some of the relevant literature on these liberal parties, see Luisa Vinton, "The Polish Government in Search of a Program," RFE/RL *Research Report*, October 18, 1991, p. 13; David McQuaid, "The Political Landscape Before the Elections," RFE/RL *Research Report*, October 18, 1991, p. 14; Jan Oberman, "The Czechoslovak Elections: A Guide to the Parties," RFE/RL *Research Report*, June 29, 1992, pp. 17–21; Imre Furmann, ed., *Liberalis Forum, October 12–13, 1991* (Budapest, 1991); Michael Shafir, "Romania's Election Campaign: The Main Issues," RFE/RL *Research Report*, September 11, 1992, p. 36; and by the same writer, "National Liberal Party Quits Democratic Convention," RFE/RL *Research Report*, June 12, 1992, p. 24.

19. See, for instance, "Az Antall kormany arulasa," *Nemzeti Ujsag* 1:9 (September 1991), p. 11.

20. On Havel, see "Havel: Vertreibung der Deutschen immoralisch," *FAZ*, March 31, 1993, p. 8. Also, Jan Obrman, "Czechoslovak Assembly Affirms German Friendship Treaty,"

RFE/RL *Research Report,* May 22, 1992, pp. 18–23. For Hungary and the Free Democrats, "Kiut vagy zsakutca?" *Magyar Nemzet,* October 30, 1991, p. 6.

21. For this by now well-worn phrase, see, for instance, *FAZ,* May 5, 1992, p. 14.

22. Berthold Kohler, "Nur Hame gibt es umsonst," *FAZ,* March 18, 1993, p. 6.

23. See "Walesa Blames the West for Poland's Economic Woes: Angry Speech in Strasbourg Reflects Mood in Poland," *San Francisco Chronicle* (from here on referred to as *SFC*) (reprinted from the *Washington Post*), February 5, 1992, p. 14.

24. For an illuminating debate on the Hungarian Free Democrats and their reluctance to formulate a national program, see Toth, "Kiut," 6, and response to his article "Megvedem az SzDSz-t" in *Magyar Nemzet,* November 13, 1991, p. 6.

25. See his *Fortele productive si comertul exterior,* 2d ed. (Bucuresti: Manoilescu, 1986); in English, *The Theory of Protectionism and International Trade* (London: P. S. King & Son, 1931); also *Die einzelne Partei als politische Institution der neuen Regime* (Berlin: O. Stollberg, 1941); for a critical appraisal of his work, see Philippe Schmitter, "Reflections on Mihail Manoilescu and the Political Consequences of Delayed-Dependent Development on the Periphery of Western Europe," in Kenneth Jowitt, ed., *Social Change in Romania, 1860–1940* (Berkeley, 1977), pp. 72–117.

26. See Andrew C. Janos, "The One Party State and Social Mobilization: Eastern Europe Between the Wars," in Samuel P. Huntington and Clement H. Moore, *Authoritarian Politics in Modern Society* (New York: Basic Books, 1971), pp. 204–239, and Joseph Rothschild, *Pilsudski's Coup d'Etat* (New York: Columbia University Press, 1966), esp. p. 263.

27. Meciar quoted in *FAZ,* March 19, 1993, p. 12.

28. See Attila Agh, "A kenyszerdemokracia paradoxonjai," *Tarsadalmi Szemle* 47:4 (December 1992), pp. 3–15.

29. For these parties in power, see Leslie Chang, "Foes Tumble as Meciar Tightens Grip on Slovakia," the *Prague Post,* March 24–30, 1993. On Iliescu, see Michael Shafir, "Government Encourages Vigilante Violence," RFE/RL *Research Report,* July 6, 1990, pp. 32–38; Mihai Sturdza, "The Politics of Ambiguity: Romania's Foreign Relations," RFE/RL, *Research Report,* April 5, 1991, pp. 13–19; and Crisula Stefanescu, "The New Press Law," RFE/RL, *Research Report,* September 21, 1990, pp. 26–28. Equally suggestive observations may be found in David Ottaway, "Romania Leader's New Image," *SFC,* March 19, 1993, p. A22. On Tudjman, Ivo Bicanic, "Tudjman Dominant," RFE/RL *Research Report,* September 18, 1992, pp. 20–22; Ivo Bicanic and Iva Danilus, "Tudjman Remains Dominant," RFE/RL *Research Report,* September 18, 1992; or "Croatia Clamps Down on Opposition," *SFC* (reprinted from the Washington Post), April 26, 1993, p. A8. Still more recently, Patrick Moore, "Paraga Criticizes Croatian Democratic Community as Authoritarian," RFE/RL *Daily Reports* (via LISTSERVE, Buffalo, N.Y.), June 8, 1993.

30. See Ottaway in *SFC,* March 19, 1993, p. A22, or Meciar's interview in the German press. See *FAZ,* January 5, 1993, p. 7.

31. This provision, however, has so far remained ineffective, in that, for example, the Turkish party has renamed itself as the Movement for Freedom and Rights and with token Bulgarian membership managed to win the votes of the Turkish minority. In Romania, a bill with similar language and intent was before the National Assembly, but, perhaps discouraged by the failure of the Bulgarian experiment, the assembly did not vote the bill into an act of parliament.

32. For a good summary, see Jiri Pehe, "The Emergence of Right-Wing Extremism," RFE/RL *Research Report,* June 28, 1991, pp. 2–5.

33. Barbu, "Romania in libertatea supravegheata."

34. "Szemelvenyek a Csurka tezisekbol," *Népszabadság,* August 27, 1992, p. 6.

35. For this by now famous Kosovo statement, see Victor Meyer, "Unter Intervention in Bosnien versteht jede Partei etwas anderes," *FAZ,* January 5, 1993, p. 7.

36. In Hungary, the government rejected demands for the reestablishment of the good name of former Prime Minister Bardossy, executed for declaring war on the Soviet Union, together with the rehabilitation of a number of generals whose main crime was that they had led troops on the Eastern Front. Meanwhile the government of Croatia, or at least some authorities in Zagreb, rehabilitated Mile Budak, a writer and minister of culture in the Ustasha government, by naming one of the main avenues of Zagreb after him. Yet the decision was reversed in a few days, presumably under American and German pressure. For this matter, see "Croatians Honor Author of Anti-Semitic Laws," *SFC,* February 3, 1993, p. A12.

37. For Stambulisky, see Joseph Rothschild, *The Communist Party of Bulgaria* (New York: Columbia University Press, 1959), esp. pp. 85–116. Szabó, Hungary's first and perhaps most authentic "Right populist" writer (who nevertheless condemned the fascist Arrow Cross), was a dominant literary figure of the interwar period and died in 1945. For a brief survey of Szabó's work and public career, see Andrew C. Janos, *The Politics of Backwardness in Hungary* (Princeton: Princeton University Press, 1982), pp. 237, 253.

38. Perhaps nowhere more evident than in the press of the Romanian populist Right, *Romania Mare* thus carries a peasant theme on the front pages of each of its issues. See also Michael Shafir, "The Greater Romania Party," RFE/RL *Research Report,* November 15, 1991, pp. 26–28; also, Shafir, "The Movement for Romania: A Party of Radical Return," RFE/RL *Research Report,* July 17, 1992, pp. 18–19.

39. Tamara Jones, "For Germany's Disabled the Horror Is Back," *San Francisco Examiner,* May 16, 1993, p. 4.

40. For the famous dichotomy between master morality and slave morality, and power masquerading as morality, see Friedrich Nietzsche, *The Birth of Tragedy and the Genealogy of Morals* (New York: Doubleday, 1956), esp. pp. 158–188.

41. Don Ionescu, "Party of National Unity and Greater Romania Party Pledge Cooperation with National Salvation Front," RFE/RL *Daily Reports* (LISTSERVE, Buffalo, N.Y.), June 28, 1993. See also Michael Shafir, "The Greater Romania Party," RFE/RL *Research Report,* November 15, 1991, pp. 26–28.

42. Louis Zange, "Albanian Turmoil," RFE/RL *Research Report,* July 31, 1992, p. 16.

PART FOUR

Economic Policy Choices

8

Labor, Class, and Democracy: Shaping Political Antagonisms in Post-Communist Society

DAVID OST

One of the key questions in this volume, and in discussions of post-communist transition in general, concerns the timing and sequencing of political and economic reform in post-communist society. As usually put, the question is: How quickly and in what sequence should reforms be introduced in order to end up with a liberal market economy?

I should say that I do not particularly like this dependent variable. In this chapter, I am more concerned with the consolidation of a liberal polity, in which full citizenship rights are guaranteed for all, than with a liberal economy. I focus this way not only because it reflects my personal predilections, but because I see good theoretical grounds for believing (even before Vladimir Zhirinovsky began demonstrating it in practice) that the pursuit of a liberal economy may jeopardize the consolidation of a liberal polity. This does not, of course, mean that I think market reforms are unnecessary. But I do question the kinds of market reforms that are needed, and my concern for the integration of labor also means that I oppose what is commonly referred to as "shock therapy" (see Berend's discussion in Chapter 6).

In her introduction, therefore, Beverly Crawford presents me as a gradualist. Insofar as the kind of inclusiveness I urge is anathema to those who desire a liberal market economy precisely *because* it undermines the influence of labor, my differences with the "radicals" concern more than just timing. Nevertheless, timing divides us too. I argue that the focus on rapid marketization is a sure way to destroy the broad political consensus supporting reform that constitutes the liberalizers' most valuable asset. The radicals say "push full-steam ahead and don't look aside"—or, more to the point, don't look to the *wayside,* where increasing numbers of working people are ending up. 'Don't look *that* way," we are told, because we may not like what we see and may be persuaded, for irrational emotional reasons, to do something about it, which the radicals say will only make things worse. "Labor's going to suffer anyway," they say. Better to let them get on with it and get over it, so as to build the prosperity that we are assured comes next.

The problem with this line of reasoning, of course, is its assumption that people will simply wait patiently, accepting the new rules until they're told it's "OK" to demand more. But while the neoliberal radicals do have a rather long honeymoon period in which to introduce their policies, thanks to labor's peculiar promarket predilections that I will discuss later in this chapter, goodwill does not last forever. In order for the resulting conflicts to be managed within a politically liberal framework, labor must be integrated into the reform process, through state-sponsored measures such as employee share-ownership schemes, active employment policies, and guaranteed influence for enterprise councils and trade unions. This proposal, however, can work only if workers identify themselves as part of the working class. In other words, the political problem can be resolved through class-based solutions only if conflicts are structured in a class-based way.

Let us go back and begin with the essential political question. How can political democracy be made secure in Eastern Europe? Four years after the fall of the Berlin Wall, few look at the political future of post-communist countries with the same dewey-eyed optimism of 1989. At scholarly panels, meetings, conferences, and journals, one of the most popular topics of discussion is whether democracy can be fully consolidated in Eastern Europe. Threats to democracy seem to lurk everywhere, from explosive nationalism to implosive religious fundamentalism and political authoritarianism. Nationalism has already produced civil war and dictatorships in the former Yugoslavia and much of the old Soviet Union, while fundamentalist and authoritarian temptations can be seen in the numerous efforts to establish religious values as state policy or to exclude from public life those with an allegedly "suspect" past. With party identities still tenuous, and vast numbers of people voicing disdain for allegedly ineffective democratic institutions, consolidating democracy is proving a much tougher challenge than one might have expected while watching the dancing at the Brandenburg Gate.

Probably the best explanation is that illiberal nationalism and fundamentalism feed on people's economic frustrations. As working people lose the social guarantees of the past and come to feel marginalized and excluded from the new system, they become receptive to appeals that blame liberal democracy for their woes and that offer simple, easy-to-understand solutions that promise to make things better. In this view, the danger to political liberalism comes from the reliance on economic liberalism.[1]

The obvious problem with this explanation, however, is its implication that people are opposed to economic liberalism, that they do not like the values of capitalism and market reform. Yet virtually every opinion poll taken in every post-communist country, from 1989 to the present, clearly shows that this is not the case. Surveys in fact demonstrate the opposite: Working people approve of the economic values behind the policies making their lives worse. Indeed, at every critical election when the future of neoliberal reform seemed to be up for grabs, from the first semifree election in Poland in June 1989 to the referendum in Russia in April 1993, the population voted overwhelmingly for the reformers. Some observers pounced on these results as refutation of the view that economic liberalism jeopardizes political liberalism. When Yeltsin easily won the 1993 referendum despite numerous predictions of defeat, one neoliberal proponent wrote that maybe the answer was simply that people actually like painful neoliberal reform programs. It's only leftist intellectuals who protest, wrote Jeffrey Sachs, while the common people understand that all the upheaval is good for them in the long run.[2] Of course, in late 1993 prominent neoliberals finally began losing elections—first in Poland in September and then in Russia in December. Even then, however, most people still said that they supported the idea of economic reform and even the ideals of the market. They were opposed only to the ways these were being implemented.

Quarreling over whether people support or oppose neoliberal reform programs misses the point that they do both at the same time. The reality is that people support neoliberal economic reform *and* that they don't like what neoliberal reform is bringing about. But whereas the common view is that the continued belief in market reform is a good thing for democratic stabilization, since it shows that people are not nostalgic for communism and that they recognize the need for painful reform, I argue in this chapter that this state of affairs is quite dangerous to democracy, because it describes a situation in which people are *unable to express their economic grievances in economic ways.* Belief in the market combined with opposition to its effects, in conditions of a discrediting of the concepts of socialism, leaves people without an economic language to articulate their economic grievances. Labor in particular suffers as a class but does not protest as a class: This only means that its grievances are more likely to be expressed in *non-economic, non-class* ways—in other words, by gravitating to the policies of the political illiberals who offer substitute satisfactions for people's dashed hopes.

Class as the Cleavage of Democracy

Politics is about the organization of antagonisms. Parties organize people not so much by giving them something to support but by giving them something to oppose. They offer targets for villification, or an "other." A party or political organization, in a democratic as well as nondemocratic system, tries to attract supporters by claiming that the subordination of its proposed "other" will bring good to great numbers of people. The targeted "other" can be anything: typically an ethnic group, a racial group, a religion, a government, a region, an ideology, a gender, an industry, a life-style, or a class. The party that will succeed in politically dominating post-communist society is the party that can organize sufficient numbers of people behind its claim of what is wrong with things at present and who or what is responsible for those wrongs.

In the first years of post-communism, liberal parties were able to win easily by identifying the communist system as the reprehensible "other" and offering a vision of a prosperous market-oriented future. As communism has receded to the past, however, liberal parties have lost their enemy—precisely at a time when neoliberal policies have created new inequalities and entirely new kinds of social conflicts. Fearful of new conflicts, the liberals tend to argue that people should just tighten their belts, try to make good for themselves, and not let their angers lead them into the arms of demagogues. Fearing that any conflicts will lead to the triumph of the demagogic masters of hatred—the ethnic cleansers, religious purifiers, or nationalist fanatics like Zhirinovsky—the liberals propose that people refrain from all kinds of conflicts, even economic ones, and wait patiently for the correct, "tried and tested" liberal market program to succeed. Everyone will make out fine, they say, if people keep their passions and angers under control.

This is a laudable sentiment. But it also is a doomed one. The conflicts natural to a liberal market economy can never be suppressed. A stable democracy requires that conflicts be minimal. But it also requires that they be expressed and not lie latent waiting to blow up. In the modern Western experience, conflicts have been kept minimal and manageable, allowing democracy to become secure, only when the large, politically organized working class was able to win real economic gains, as in the post-war period. Post-communist society is in no position to guarantee economic gains for all, even though this is what people were led to believe. Instead, it has a large working class facing declining prospects. In these conditions, conflicts cannot be avoided. Consolidating democracy in post-communist society, therefore, depends not on avoiding conflicts, which is impossible, but on structuring conflicts in the most democratic (constructive) way.

The question, then, is how antagonisms should be organized. How must conflicts be structured so that they are most compatible with democratic politics? It is the responsibility of *democratic* political cleavages to structure political antagonisms in an *inclusive* way. What democratic politics is about, then, is not the elimination of anger and the suppression of conflicts, but the structuring of social anger in a way that does not treat particular groups or individuals as enemies because of what they think or believe or because they happen to be members of a different ethnic or racial group. Only cleavages that accept the fact and the permanence of difference will ultimately respect the principle of tolerance central to political liberalism.

The experience of Western democracies shows that class is the political cleavage of liberalism—not just of socialism. Class cleavages are most compatible with liberal politics. Class cleavages are democratic because the proferred enemy is an impersonal economic system, not an ethnic, political, or religious "other" slated for expulsion from the community. Class conflicts lead to democratic outcomes because they seek to resolve conflicts through bargaining among different groups of people, all of whom are accepted as citizens of the same state. Unlike the enemy of nationalist and fundamentalist politics, the class enemy is represented by a citizen just like you.

Practitioners of illiberal politics try to exploit economic discontent. They speak to problems of class inequalities but propose non-class solutions to the problems. They claim that things will improve for people if only the right enemy is defeated. Illiberal politics in post-communist society appeals chiefly to those who are dissatisfied with the new market system. That means it appeals chiefly to labor. Labor represents the potential base of support for illiberalism because it constitutes the majority of the population and is full of anger. The political future will be shaped in large part by the way labor's anger is mobilized.

Those tendencies are considered dangers to democracy because of how they seek to structure antagonisms. What they have in common is that they identify ethnic groups, individuals, or political and religious tendencies—and not economic classes—as the enemy responsible for the problems of the day. Nationalism, for example, vilifies the ethnic "other." Hungarians in Romania, Muslims in Bosnia, Russians in Estonia, or imagined Jews everywhere are depicted as the group monopolizing the good jobs and good land and thus causing the impoverishment of the ethnic majority. Those calling so stridently for "de-communization," meanwhile, attribute problems of the nascent market economy to the evil ones who had power before and must therefore be deprived of rights today. Proponents of religious fundamentalism seek to recruit the disadvantaged by arguing that today's problems are the result of moral conflicts, not economic or class conflicts. Things will get better, they say, when the Church obtains more power in the world, counteracting the corrupt values (and, by the way, the rights) of the liberals and heathens.

We might also mention here the pervasive attacks on women's rights and the ongoing "masculinization" of the economy and public sphere.[3] Here it is women who constitute the vilified "other." Working men threatened by unemployment are told that their woes are due not to the actions of or policies favoring a different class, but to the presence of too many women in the workplace. Moreover (and unsurprisingly), the newest enemies in the illiberal pantheon are the foreigners, from the East, coming to take "our" jobs and livelihood away. All of these tendencies seek to tap economic discontent, though they express that discontent in non-economic ways. Religious fundamentalism attributes corrupt economic practices to the absence of a codified religious ethos, while de-communization proponents attribute economic problems to bad individuals and their secretive networks. Nationalism seeks to direct antagonisms toward the ethnic "other," while "masculinism" suggests that economic woes will be eased with the restoration of "proper" family and gender roles. Their long-term impact is the shaping of a citizenry accustomed to seeking scapegoats for underlying economic, class-based problems.

Different economies generate different kinds of conflicts. By monopolizing all industry, communism generated a unified opposition. All antagonisms could legitimately be directed toward the state. Market economies create class-based conflicts in which the interests of labor run contrary to the interests of capital. A democratic system in a market economy requires that conflicts be expressed in a way that taps the underlying causes of the conflict, because only then can the conflict be resolved. Cleavages based on non-class criteria, such as religion, gender, or ethnicity, are incommensurable with democratic systems not only because they entail the persecution of a minority but because their proposed substitute satisfactions are incapable of solving the problems that led to the social anger in the first place.[4] Class conflicts in market societies mitigate antagonisms by being able to challenge and ameliorate the sources of anger. Building a liberal political system requires the organization of antagonisms along class lines because only in this way can the majority of people win a stake in the economy, and thus become defenders of the liberal system that maintains that economy.

The Centrality of Labor

The problem is not just that liberal parties are not seeking to organize along class lines. The problem is also that in post-communist society, labor itself does not yet think in class terms. Class sensibility remains weak because of the structure of communism (which turned all social antagonisms into conflicts only with the state), the historical legacy of anticommunism (with its liberal universalist ideology), and the policies of post-communist governments (which aim to weaken the class-based institutions of labor).

A crucial fact about post-communist societies, so important for understanding the political conflicts ahead, is that the sociological landscape is dominated by an old-fashioned working class. Communism may have collapsed only in the late-twentieth century, but it certainly had not yet produced an equivalent of the West's post-industrial society. The characteristic signs of post-industrialism—a dying manufacturing sector, huge service economy, and overpowering consumerist ideology that wreaks havoc on sociological surveys by persuading everyone that they're part of the middle class—still had not yet come to the East when communism fell. Communism created a gritty industrial society and stopped there. As Daniel Chirot so nicely put it, communist governments succeeded in building "the world's most advanced late-nineteenth-century economy."[5] Furthermore, such economies create large working classes. As anyone actually traveling around any of the former communist countries soon finds out, these places are filled with people who looked like they've stepped out of the pages of fading *Life* magazines from a half century ago. Here we find "labor" like it no longer exists elsewhere in the world.

Since labor constitutes the majority of the population, democracy can succeed only if it has the support of labor. The political problem today (and this is what presents opportunities for the political illiberals) is that liberalizing post-communist governments do not take the demands of labor very seriously. They do not do so for two main reasons: because most reformers believe that capitalism cannot be constructed except by excluding labor, and because labor, currently sharing this reigning antisocialist ideology, is not demanding inclusion. As a result, social systems are being constructed that do not have the majority support of the population. Polls throughout the post-communist countries show that a plurality of people (sometimes a majority) believe that they were in many ways better off under the old system. But because of the belief—and the desire to believe—that the new system cannot possibly be worse than the old, there is little working-class organization or collective action to oppose the new governments and policies. In the first years of post-communism, people are still willing to wait a bit. The result is that the depth of discontent is usually overlooked, as politicians become convinced that if they only stay the market-oriented path, the discontent will continue to subside. The problem, however, is that since this path excludes labor, it is only likely to generate more opposition, not less, as time goes on.

The question, then, is which way will labor move? For perhaps the most important point about the post-communist political world today is that labor remains thoroughly unorganized in the political sphere. There are no labor parties and no parties to which workers have any deep allegiance. The post-communist political future will in large part be shaped by the party or tendency that is able to win labor's allegiance. Which party mobilizes labor, and for what political ends, is the crucial political question of the day. A recent major study of democratization in the United States, Western Europe, and Latin America argues that the working class historically has been the "most consistently democratic force," due to its long struggle for political inclusion. "Exceptions" to this pro-democratic position, however, have taken place "where the class was initially mobilized by a charismatic but authoritarian leader or a hegemonic party linked to the state apparatus."[6] There is no shortage of pretenders to charismatic leadership, and in Russia and Poland, where individually popular presidents rule without a party of their own, the temptation to create "hegemonic parties linked to the state" is quite great. (President Walesa, in fact, has recently tried to do just that.)[7] The illiberal politics practitioners currently prominent in post-communist society are also trying to "initially mobilize" the working class according to their own non-class agendas. So far, as we shall see, it is only the politically liberal parties—feeling that since they are pursuing rapid market reform they have nothing to offer the working class—that lag far behind in trying to organize labor. It is a remarkably naive shortcoming that could have quite unfortunate consequences for the future of political democracy in Eastern Europe and the former Soviet Union. Labor will be mobilized by some political tendency, and its angers organized in some political direction. The still unresolved question is which one.

Recent opinion surveys among Polish workers give us an opportunity to assess labor's own proclivity to thinking in class-based terms. By class consciousness or class sensibility, I mean labor's sense of itself as having interests contrary to those of other social groups and a commitment on the part of labor to build up its own independent organizations willing and able to articulate and fight for the interests of working people.

The surveys show a labor movement mistrustful of its own class institutions and confused over where its real interests lie. The surveys also show strong support for liberal economic values, as well as a desire to believe that these values will yield outcomes beneficial to all. The surveys make clear how it was that the effort to construct a new market system, in the interests of a class that did not exist, came into being with the strong support of the class slated to be at the bottom. Of course, different workers faced different prospects. Those in efficient firms, with good technology, producing goods not only for the Soviet market, saw nascent capitalism as an opportunity for social advancement. The overwhelming majority of workers, however, at the state firms where most of these surveys were conducted, worked in firms with more dubious prospects, made even more dubious by the state-sponsored recession of 1990, when a virtual abolition of tariffs resulted in a flood of Western goods with which domestic firms could not compete. As the surveys show, even the destructive effects of such policies did not dampen support for the ideas behind such policies.

Let us turn to the data. In 1991, Dr. Juliusz Gardawski of the Warsaw School of Economics conducted a major survey of 2,817 employees, about 80 percent blue collar, from 383 medium and large state enterprises. Only 16 percent of the sample, according to Gardawski, expressed loyalty to the values or perceived security of the state socialist past. Nearly 75 percent of the sample responded that they were strong supporters of neoliberal economic reform. This includes 52 percent whom Gardawski characterizes as "moderate modernizers," or supporters of neoliberalism except for misgivings about unemployment and the prospect of foreign capital controlling Polish industry, and 21 percent who responded that they were ready to accept the entire neoliberal package.[8]

The results are quite clear on attitudes toward some of the key features of market transition, including bankruptcy, competition, and layoffs. Asked whether companies that do not make a profit should be forced into bankruptcy, 72 percent of the sample answered yes, with only 12 percent saying no and 15.6 percent saying they were unsure. Moreover, only slight disparity was recorded between the views of rank-and-file workers and management, with 70.9 percent of the former and 79.1 percent of the latter supporting the idea of firm bankruptcy. Other questions showed similar support, with similar disparities, for other neoliberal economic features (see Table 8.1).

The numbers vary predictably according to education and skill, but even the lowest numbers (in the affirmative case) are still quite high. While 93.8 percent of those with higher education answered yes to this question, so did 70.9 percent of those with only primary education. While 96.4 percent of engineers and 83.6 percent of skilled workers answered yes, so did 72.7 percent of unskilled workers.

TABLE 8.1 Survey of Polish Workers and Management

	Support for the introduction of full enterprise autonomy, with tough (*ostra*) competition between firms (percentages):		
	Yes	*No*	*Hard to say*
Workers	82.0	6.9	10.8
Management	93.0	3.2	3.9
Total	83.6	6.2	9.8
	Support for dismissal of superfluous workers (percentages):		
	Yes	*No*	*Hard to say*
Workers	70.2	13.6	16.0
Management	81.1	7.0	11.9
Total	71.5	12.8	15.5

SOURCE: Gardawski 1992, pp. 215, 60.

These figures, like many others, suggest strong support for market reform. When we look closer, however, we see that while Poles approve of capitalist values, they tend to have idealized notions of the kinds of things capitalism provides. For example, even with such strong support for the dismissal of employees, only 23.7 percent of the workers and 36.2 percent of managerial personnel thought that there should be unemployment in the country. The 59.4 percent of workers and 46.1 percent of management who said there should *not* be unemployment apparently felt quite sure that workers laid off in one firm would and should find little difficulty getting a new job. An honest worker, they believe, is rewarded in a proper system like capitalism, unlike in the communist system of the past. This belief in capitalism's basic goodness comes out in the assessment of the value of competition, too. Polish workers simply do not associate enterprise competition with unemployment, wage pressure, forced overtime, slackening of safety standards, or any of the other things competition often leads to, particularly in poor capitalist economies. Instead, competition is identified with the absence of lines in front of stores and with an arrangement that efficiently, productively, and honestly utilizes all available labor.

The trust that workers in 1991 expressed in the values of elite-dominated capitalism is reflected in a remarkable willingness to see their own role in the workplace disappear. Polish workers desire enterprise autonomy and competition under conditions where workers themselves have little say on how the firm is run. One of the most remarkable developments in recent years has been the decline in workplace support for employee participation in firm governance. Perhaps better than any other indicator, this testifies to the new prestige of pro-capitalist values in post-communist society. The numbers from comparable nationwide surveys of workers in state enterprises in 1983 and 1991 are quite instructive: Asked whether they agreed with the view that worker participation is good for the firm, 64.3 percent of the 1983 national sample said that they did. In 1991 that figure dropped to

21 percent.[9] When asked whether they agreed that worker involvement in management affairs is detrimental to the firm, only 5.1 percent of the 1983 workforce said they agreed. In 1991, 29.3 percent agreed.[10] These results are corroborated by other enterprise surveys from 1992, which also show widespread support, among all categories of workers, for the statement that managing is the responsibility of the management alone and that workers should not get involved in such things.[11]

As Gardawski puts it, Polish workers of 1991 expected that a fully competitive economy, with full enterprise autonomy and minimal employee involvement in management, would lead to an arrangement where "the good worker always succeeds," "the honest firm always survives," and no one needs to fear unemployment. As a commonly expressed view has it, "How can there be unemployment where there is so much that needs to be done?" Gardawski concludes that "workers tend to have a very idealized belief that competition will lead to exactly the kind of just order that they sought in vain from the old system: Everybody will get paid according to how much work they do, all privileges will be eradicated, [and] dishonesty will be eliminated."[12]

Who then is to protect workers' interests? The answer, rather astonishingly, is that Polish workers in 1991 tended to feel that their interests would be represented through the workings of the new market economy alone. They certainly are not looking to trade unions to protect them. Although 57.7 percent of Gardawski's sample belonged to trade unions (34 percent to Solidarity and 23 percent to OPZZ, the former pro-party trade union), only 20.5 percent said that either of these unions best represented workers' interests in the firm. Nearly 7 percent said that management best represented workers' interests, slightly less than half of the 15.1 percent who thought Solidarity best looked out for workers' interests. As these low numbers indicate, the most common response—one that has been reproduced in every firm-level survey I have seen from the past few years—is that "*no one*" represents the interest of workers in the workplace. That response was chosen by 56.2 percent in Gardawski's sample.[13] A mid-1993 national survey of workers saw 57 percent responding that "no one defends the interests of people like me."[14] What is perhaps most revealing about attitudes toward trade unions is that although absolute majorities consistently reply that no one defends workers' interests on the job, there is no widespread effort on the part of these apparently disenfranchised workers to take over the unions in order to *make* them serve rank-and-file interests. In fact, 35.7 percent of blue-collar workers thought that trade unions should be completely deprived of influence in economic affairs.[15]

Workers, in other words, are expecting their interests to be protected through the workings of the market economy itself. They do not see a need, in this initial post-communist period, to organize to defend their interests. They are politically unorganized and thus politically available.

Specific firm-level surveys from 1992 show even greater rejection of trade unions. In an electronics firm with 2,000 employees, only about 35 percent belonged to any trade union, and only 10.5 percent said that they thought the unions represented their interests. Even fewer, 8.1 percent, said that they trusted the trade unions—meaning that about 75 percent of union members themselves did not trust the unions! Moreover, a full 87.4 percent responded that they did not trust *any* firm-level institution.

Of 1,100 brewery employees who also were surveyed in 1992, about 75 percent of them belonged to the unions, but only 25 percent said that the unions represented their interests. At this particular enterprise, workers actually trusted management more than they trusted the trade unions![16]

In a national survey of some 1,700 workers in September 1992, 54 percent answered "no one" when asked who best represented them. Among Solidarity's own membership, itself making up a bit more than one-fourth of the sample, nearly 41 percent answered "no one." In fact, slightly more than one-third of Solidarity's members believed that the union represented their interests. When asked what firm-level institution they trusted most, 71 percent of the total—and 56 percent of Solidarity members—responded that they trusted no one. Younger workers were somewhat more likely than older workers to trust no one, but age did not affect response concerning representation.[17]

This lack of trust for trade unions is perhaps not very surprising given the attitudes of many trade union leaders. Ever since victory, or the end of communist government in 1989, Solidarity has been stuck in a profound, to put it mildly, identity crisis. Having previously identified communist rule as the enemy, Solidarity had to deal with the new situation in which there was no more communist rule and in which scores of union officials and advisers were in power. Solidarity's first response—still under the leadership of Lech Walesa, who did not become president until December 1990—was to support the neoliberal reform that the new government introduced. Even the second generation of Solidarity officials, taking over after the first had gone off to positions in government (and in business), remained loyal to the position of their predecessors. For the first year after the formation of a Solidarity-sponsored government in August 1989, the Solidarity trade union actually argued that it was in the interests of workers, and of the union, to have a weak and inobtrusive union. The union had accepted the ahistorical but pervasive neoliberal claim that the road to prosperity required a weak labor movement. Workers and unions only needed to step aside and let the market do its magic. Later on, someday, they would secure their fair share. The whole process, they were assured, would not take long. (When Lech Walesa sought to sell the neoliberal Balcerowicz Plan in late 1989, which effectively cut unions out of the policy-making process, he said that there would be three months of pain, before month four brought relief and real economic growth.)

The extent to which even union activists adhered to this line is evident from a survey of the delegates to the Third National Convention of Solidarity in February 1991. Their responses show that Solidarity leaders themselves favored a weakening of union influence in the workplace. Asked whether they thought employees should elect directors in state-owned firms, 50 percent of the white-collar delegates and 44 percent of the blue-collar delegates answered "never" or "rarely."[18] When asked the same question about the private sector, 85 percent of both groups answered "never" or "rarely." It can of course be argued that choosing management is not usually part of the workforce's charge and that opposing employee involvement in this area does not signify abandoning the trade union's mission. The point, however, is that at the time of this poll, employees of state firms already had this right (to choose management), having won it during the first Solidarity period. Nearly half of Solidarity's leaders were saying that workers should be deprived of this way of influencing enterprise governance, even as all the other traditional firm-level social welfare programs were rapidly eroding.

Having a say in layoff decisions is surely a crucial function for trade unions at a time of recession. When asked whether employees should have any such say in state firms, about 25 percent of Solidarity delegates answered "never" or "rarely," a surprising number for the leaders of the main trade union. As far as layoffs in the private sector are concerned, the number of Solidarity national representatives who said that employees should never or rarely have any input jumped to nearly 45 percent. Indeed, Solidarity has been so generously disposed toward the private sector, so convinced that honest work and honest pay will prevail, that they have scarcely tried to recruit there. Except for state firms that have been privatized, unions hardly exist at all in Poland's growing private sector, leading to precisely the kind of contract violations, poor safety record, and uncompensated forced overtime that one could predict would arise. A July 1993 report by Poland's Labor Inspection Bureau documented a steady rise in the number of job-related accidents in the private sector, with private firms regularly neglecting to install basic safety equipment, and pressuring jobseekers to work "off the books" so they will not be in a position to complain.[19]

The attitude of Solidarity officials in the first stage of post-communism was perhaps best summed up in an early 1991 encounter I had with a vice-chairman of Warsaw Solidarity, who was visiting the United States to take part in a training program for trade unionists. Asked what he saw as his main task today, he responded, without hesitation, that the chief task was to restrain rank-and-filers who were upset with the pace of change. His emphasis was on restraint, not on pushing or even testing the limits of possibility. He was not interested in securing institutionalized influence for the union and made no mention at all about trying to win material concessions for its members. Rather, like most Solidarity leaders, he preferred to trust the government's goodwill and to use his position primarily to keep his troops in line.

All this evidence demonstrates little class sensibility on the part of Polish labor. There is no sense that labor has a program of its own, little sense that there is any need to organize as a class, and profound distrust of the class-specific institutions that already exist. The surveys show that Polish workers, despite experiencing the crisis in class-specific ways, tend not to think, and are highly reluctant to organize, along class lines. They seem to believe that they can improve their lot only by having weak class organizations of their own and by going along with neoliberal reform. The surveys show workers to be rather strong believers in economic liberalism, persuaded by the view that the construction of a capitalist system is the best way for workers to improve their situation.

Paradoxically, as argued before, it is this very *belief* in the new system that is one of the great problems for consolidating political democracy. Where labor is opposed to government, it forms its own organizations that seek to challenge government and in that way obtains satisfaction for its members that translates into acceptance of the system. Labor is well integrated into Western polyarchies[20] precisely because it maintained its distance from government and had a clear sense of its own interests. When labor accepts the ideological claims of a rival class yet has a negative experience of the policies such claims uphold, the resulting cognitive dissonance can easily drive them into the arms of the illiberals, who also profess to be believers in the superiority of the market but who try to channel class antagonisms in non-class directions. Of course, if the new economic system met the expectations of labor, there would be no problem. But the economy cannot meet the expectations of labor, because those expectations include a just economic distribution that market economies do not and cannot provide on their own. Fair economic distribution can be won only where labor fights for fair economic distribution. It can only be won where labor is organized, and where its anger (which it still hardly knows how to express) is structured along class lines. Those conditions are still lacking.

The Successes of Illiberalism

How have these beliefs affected the political realm so far? We can begin by looking at the electoral record in post-communist society. Electorally, the most common and effective approach so far, in the short history of post-communism, has been the combination of economic liberalism with political illiberalism.

One thinks of Lech Walesa's 1990 presidential campaign, in which the former Solidarity leader argued that the problem with the first post-communist government led by Tadeusz Mazowiecki was that that government was carrying out a reform program against the interests of workers. This was a very class-based appeal. But the problem, said Walesa, was not capitalism but the *absence* of capitalism. The way workers can avoid suffering, he suggested, was not by organizing against market-based inequalities, but by supporting a policy and an individual (himself) who would hasten the onset of "real" capitalism—that is, the good kind. Moreover, the absence of capitalism, he contended, was caused by the presence of political enemies within, such as former communists, errant intellectuals ("eggheads"), and even Jews. Class-based inequalities, his campaign suggested, could best be resolved by non-class policies of exclusion.

Walesa's chief opponent, Tadeusz Mazowiecki, waged a liberal campaign saying that now that communism had been defeated, there should be no more antagonisms at all: Let's draw a "thick line" with the past and move on together toward the market-oriented future. Things will be hard on some people, but we should just tighten our belts and wait for better times, which are coming, rather than organize in any way against the bad times now. This proved to be such an inadequate approach that Mazowiecki got drubbed in the polls, winning only the support of intellectuals and professionals[21]—that is, those who knew that times were improving for them—and coming in third behind the unknown Stan Tyminski, who rode a wave of "wannabe" capitalist sentiment by campaigning as someone who had wisely abandoned communist Poland to make it in the West and who would now bring that magic back home. Walesa won the runoff and promptly abandoned the illiberal themes he had utilized in the campaign. He has been searching for a new political grounding ever since.

The same political line also proved popular in Poland's 1991 parliamentary elections. Several new parties emerged that spoke of the problems facing workers but promised to address these problems not by defending labor in the marketplace or empowering them in the workplace but by punishing some deserving minority, such as "communists" or "atheists." Though these parties did not win outright, they joined together and had enough votes to form the first post-election cabinet under Jan Olszewski.

Political events in 1992 in the former Czechoslovakia show similar processes at work, as the old Charter 77/Civic Forum liberals who came to power in November 1989 were swept away by Vaclav Klaus's new Civic Democratic Party. Klaus, like Walesa, promised a more rapid transition to capitalism as well as a decisive effort to root out the "communists" said to be obstructing the people's efforts. In Slovakia, meanwhile, Vladimir Meciar mobilized Slovak anger about economic decline into political antagonism directed at the Czechs, an approach to which Klaus soon responded in kind. The result of all these political manipulations of popular dissatisfaction was the passing of a wide-ranging "lustration" law, ostensibly directed at former communists but frequently jeopardizing liberal democratic rights and due process as well,[22] followed soon thereafter by Czechoslovakia's breakup into two states, despite opinion polls showing continued support for union.

We can conclude this section with some observations from recent developments within Solidarity. Rank-and-file disillusionment with the unions has grown in tandem with disillusionment in the outcomes of the new market economy. Labor can increasingly see that the new system has brought with it not the hoped-for magic for everyone but the more prosaic realities of greater inequalities, together with an absolute decline in living standards for many. Economic decline is particularly pronounced for the least educated and least skilled, as well as for those working in nonproductive sectors such as schools and hospitals. In the summer of 1992, workers in dozens of state-owned firms, including some soon scheduled for privatization, staged a series of strikes throughout the country.[23] Solidarity, as a rule, refused to join these strikes, sharing the government's view that they were part of a demagogic campaign by Solidarity's rivals and other political forces hostile to reform. Solidarity's approach, however, was leaving it increasingly out of touch. In 1993, the union began to change its tune. Its National Commission became more militant, leading a major strike among school and hospital workers and even threatening a general strike.

However, even this increased militancy does not yet indicate a shift to class-based antagonisms. For labor disillusionment with the *outcomes* of the market economy has not led to rejection of the *values* of the market economy. Workers still believe in the market, want private capital to succeed, and distrust the state. They still lack a vision of an alternative. They still lack a sense of an economic program that can be said to be in workers' interests. As their distrust of unions makes clear, they are still wary of class-based institutions.

The labor movement is thus still a long way from having found a new identity for itself. It remains confused. It still essentially believes in the economic program even though it dislikes the results of that program. It is this cognitive dissonance, this confusion stemming from the absence of a program or ideology that knows how to speak in class-specific terms, that leads many in Solidarity to turn to new political programs for the way out.

Here we get to the union's flirtation with the nationalist and fundamentalist parties. It began with Lech Walesa's presidential campaign but took on new strength during the "lustration" crisis of June 1992, when Antoni Macierewicz, the Christian nationalist minister of the interior, released the names of several dozen parliamentarians said to be listed in communist documents as collaborators with the secret police. In the ensuing outcry over violation of due process of the accused and the illiberal besmirching of political opponents, the government was forced to resign. Solidarity was one of the few prominent organizations to come to the government's defense.

Uncertain as to what positions to take in the critical economic issues facing its members, Solidarity seemed to relish this opportunity to appear militant in a situation in which it did not really matter. At its 1992 National Congress, angry union delegates even mercilessly mocked Lech Walesa. The president, who had also been named in the Macierewicz files, was reduced to pleading with the delegates just to let him speak, his stammering presentation sounding like Richard Nixon's ill-fated "I am not a crook" speech of 1973. The union seemed to find a new role here, certain at last about something. If it didn't know what to do about the economy, where it had no program and no ideology, at least it could do something quickly in the political world. The union's proclivities in 1992 seem to confirm the view that support for illiberal political fundamentalism increases in the absence of class-specific programs concerning the economy.

Explaining the Lack of Class Consciousness

How can we explain this weakness of class sensibility in post-communist Eastern Europe? There seem to be several reasons, due both to the legacy of the past and the policies of the present. Let us look at each of them in turn.

The Communist Past. Communist rule represses class differentiation through its monopoly control of the economy. This turns every complaint on the part of every social group into a complaint against the state, not against each other. Communism thus organizes antagonisms by directing them against itself, eliciting a liberal universalist opposition of society against the state. Class consciousness requires a class against which to direct one's angers, but in communist society no particular class can be presented as the enemy of any other class since all are equally subordinated to the state. All this was apparent in the kind of opposition movement that communism generated. In contrast, say, to Spain or Brazil, where workers, students, business people, and intellectuals each had their own organizations fighting against dictatorship as well as being protective of their own particular interests and wary of each other, East European opposition movements tended to embrace all social groups at once. Skilled workers, unskilled workers, farmers, professionals, intellectuals, and even enterprise managers all joined with Solidarity in Poland. Independent organization according to class interest made no sense because communism stifled any sense of autonomous classes. Labor had no time to prepare politically for the class society that prevails today. It does not think of itself in class terms today because it did not think of itself in class terms yesterday.[24]

The Ideology of Anticommunism. The struggle against communism was organized successfully around an essentially liberal paradigm.[25] Opposition was mobilized around the slogans of freedom and human rights; class was the language of the enemy. Even when the original civil society theorists such as Michnik, Kuron, Havel, Konrad, and Kis embraced left-wing ideas of citizenship and full participation, theirs was always the leftism of the New Left with its cult of autonomy and individuality, not of the Old Left with its theory of class struggle. Even Solidarity, with its focus on autonomy and self-determination *(podmiotowosc),* embraced a liberal discourse early on. Despite its working-class foundations, it lacked a specifically working-class program. Far from focusing on bread-and-butter issues, Solidarity in 1980–1981 continually offered to bargain away economic gains to further its fundamentally liberal goal of free association. The union repeatedly emphasized procedural over substantive outcomes, and as a result, when the procedural problems were finally resolved with the coming of political democracy in 1989, Solidarity had no working-class program to fall back on. Instead it became increasingly mired in a liberal pro-market ideology, following its former intellectual advisers who, while maintaining their focus on individual rights, actually revised their theoretical views quite dramatically. Whereas in the early 1980s these theorists believed that the citizenship rights underpinning civil society were based in political participation, by the late 1980s most of them came to believe that citizenship was best grounded not in participation but in private property. The very language that yesterday justified widespread civic activism, providing the theoretical foundation for Solidarity and the struggle against communism, is used today to legitimate policies aimed at creating and empowering a new bourgeoisie. Now that there is a class-based economy, labor is stuck in a discourse embracing the ideology of the wrong class.[26]

The Ideology of the Cold War. For all of their differences, both sides in the cold war agreed that the working class occupied a subordinate role under capitalism. Communist ideology claimed that capitalism oppressed workers, while capitalist ideology claimed that workers gained enormous benefits in return for allowing business to shape the economy and dominate public life. As it became obvious to all that workers in the West (more precisely, the North-West) had indeed attained standards of living unimaginable in the East, the capitalist claim seemed to be more persuasive. It was, however, constructed on myths: Western labor made its gains not by passively allowing business to shape the economy but by forming strong class organizations and, in Western Europe, large socialist parties that challenged the rights of business and insisted on labor's economic inclusion. *That* history, however, is largely unknown in Eastern Europe, since the strong role of labor in shaping modern Western capitalism ran counter to the official ideologies of both sides. East European labor thus tends to read the Western experience as confirmation of the myth that it is the domination of capital and the passivity of labor that brings wealth to labor. And it is this myth, unfortunately, that sets the path that Eastern European labor wants to follow today.

Personal Experience. It is wrong to say that East European workers have experienced capitalism only since 1989. Hundreds of thousands have already had that experience—as temporary (and usually illegal) workers in the West. But what does such an experience entail? It means that one has no possibility of government protection, is part of no trade union, has no say in the business, and frequently works in dangerous conditions with forced overtime. It is a life of no rights and low wages—but not completely. For the wages were low only in the country where they were earned. Back home in Eastern Europe, those same wages became transformed into valuable hard currency, worth far more than anything that could be earned at home. For the millions of East Europeans who either worked illegally in the West or knew of others who had done so, capitalism appeared as a system in which labor has no rights yet gets good pay for a hard day's work. Little surprise that this is what workers seem to have expected from the new market economy at home.

The Collapse of Socialism. The collapse of socialism has had two important implications: It leaves no available ideology encouraging independent working-class organization, and it deprives the political sphere of the ideology that sought to organize labor's anger in a democratic direction. The discrediting of socialism, by the practice of communism and the abandonment of socialism by intellectuals, has meant that even trade unions are frequently seen as unnecessary or harmful institutions. And when workers turn against organization according to class, they become more available for mobilization along ethnic or religious lines.

Socialism has too rarely been recognized for what it is: *The ideology that facilitated the consolidation of liberal democracy in the West.* It did so by facilitating the integration of labor into the system. By mobilizing labor's antagonisms into class conflicts and standing at the head of the movement, socialism gave labor a political voice it never had before. By winning real concessions, socialism served to reconcile labor with the market, precisely the feat that conservatives like Gasset, with their apocalyptic fear of "the masses," doubted anyone could accomplish.

Socialist parties thus made it possible for marginalized working classes to believe that civic involvement could bring vast social transformation. These parties also encouraged pro-democratic beliefs by pointing out that workers could resolve their economic grievances through voting, but only if they organized along class lines rather than ethnic lines, since only as a class did workers constitute a majority of the population.[27] Generations of Western workers were won to democracy because of this deep-seated belief. Even when it did not work out that way—that is, when democratic victory did not bring the new world that workers were hoping for—the civic involvement itself served to integrate working people into a democratic public sphere. It also forced other parties to speak to labor's interests, if only to obviate this new threat from below. The upshot of both outcomes was that labor developed a stake in democracy.

In Eastern Europe, however, labor is suspicious of socialism, is wary of class-based organization, and tends to believe that the market itself will take care of its interests. But since the market alone cannot do so, the danger is that labor will be left with something called democracy alone, in which it is not a key player. Democracy may thus become equated with privation rather than opportunity, leaving labor open to mobilization by political illiberals. Whereas socialism helped consolidate democracy in the West, its absence helps discredit democracy in the East.

State Policy

Of course, the lack of class-based organization and the paucity of class-based political alternatives is not due solely to objective legacies and labor's own ideological tendencies. It is due in large part to the energetic activity of post-communist states. For conflicts and cleavages do not simply develop on their own. They are shaped by state economic policy as much as they are by historical legacies and hegemonic ideologies. And in post-communist Eastern Europe, the state has consciously tried to eliminate class-based cleavages. It has done this by seeking to increase the prerogatives of management, to empower new owners, and to limit the scope and weaken the influence of class organizations of labor. The state has succeeded both in antagonizing labor and restricting labor's ability to express its antagonisms in class-based ways.

The first priority of the market reformers has been to create a new class of entrepreneurs committed to generating as much wealth as it can and to do so quickly. The economic reform strategy of post-communist Eastern Europe can be characterized as a "wager on the elite." The reformers do not particularly care who the elite is as long as it is based on property ownership. As the state seeks to demonstrate a new hands-off policy, labor rights are systematically eroded. Hoping to attract private capital, the state relaxes job-safety standards, ignores violations of health and safety codes, sanctions forced overtime, and cuts off numerous former benefits such as housing subsidies, education benefits, and day-care and summer-camp contributions, while eliminating, of course, job security. It would be erroneous to view this simply as an attempt to "cut back the state." The neoliberals are great proponents of the state. They use the state to construct property rights favorable to private business.[28] They sever subsidies to state-owned firms but offer large subsidies to private firms in the form of generous tax breaks.

The neoliberal attack on labor can be seen most clearly in Poland. As Poland entered the post-communist era, labor was in a very strong position. This was due not so much to the status of Solidarity—in many ways that status actually helped to weaken the labor movement, since the authority of the union was bound up with the success of market reform. Rather, the strong position of labor resulted from the institutional position of employee councils in the workplace. When communism collapsed, Poland found itself with a system of enterprise governance that put employees, via the enterprise council that they elected, in charge of state firms. Self-management laws that had been gutted by the old regime went into effect with the new one. As a result, state enterprises became independent units that competed in a market environment but were under the control of the employee council, which elected the director and had final say over all major economic decisions for the firm. Poland had inherited de facto, without really knowing it or wanting it, a classic market socialist arrangement.

Many of the people who had been responsible for the 1981 self-management law that, in 1989, gave the employee councils such power, spent their time after 1989 trying to undo what they now considered to be the damage. Economists like Leszek Balcerowicz and Stefan Kawalec, theorists of the pro-self-management *Siec* (Network) movement of 1981, became, respectively, minister and vice-minister of finance in 1989 and turned their efforts to excluding those they had earlier sought to empower.

Their efforts began to bear fruit with the privatization law of July 1990, which explicitly favored elite ("capital") privatization strategies over employee-sponsored buyouts,[29] and, even more significantly, led to the evisceration of the employee councils. At the insistence of the Finance Ministry, and with no opposition from the unions, a provision was written into the law stipulating that employee councils would be eliminated in all firms as soon as the privatization process was under way.

The so-called "capital privatization" process in Poland consists of three steps. First, firms ask (or are asked to ask) to be privatized. Then the state, in the form of the Ministry of Property Transformation, takes them over, appointing a new board of directors and *abolishing the employee councils.* The Ministry then tries to sell the firm to the highest bidder. To detract opposition, the state reluctantly agrees to allow employees to purchase 20 percent of the shares of newly privatized firms. (In practice, the workforce usually cannot afford all these shares, even at the special prices at which they are offered.) The state stayed firm, however, on the point that the employee councils had to go.

There was little labor resistance to this in the early stages, when so many employees were readily charmed by the prospects of capitalism. Over time some resistance has emerged, due chiefly to a fear of unemployment in the private sphere. Insofar as the privatization process depends on the initial approval of the employee council, employee resistance poses a potential danger to the entire privatization strategy. The state, therefore, has devised ways of pressuring state-firm employees to make the "correct" choice. First, there is the "excess-wage tax" *(popiwek),* applied to state firms alone. Supposedly designed to stop inflation, the *popiwek* is based on the assumption that workers are irrational and that employee councils will inevitably forego modernization and seek only to "eat" profits in the form of wages. Second, there are "dividends," rooted in a rather absurd legal interpretation. The argument is that while the state may not have management rights in state-owned firms, employee councils do not have ownership rights. Strictly speaking, they are only managing assets that belong to no one. The state, however, has decided to reclaim formal rights of ownership, and thereafter to charge state firms "dividends" on the "capital" they are said to be "borrowing." Together, these taxes can take up to 90 percent of a firm's revenue. The result has been to pull the rug out from under state-sector firms, even those doing quite well in the new market environment. The tax burden makes it difficult for state sector firms to raise wages even in accordance with productivity gains or in order to lure quality personnel. It thus blocks creative restructuring programs. The widespread view that Polish "shock therapists" seek to rely on the market alone to determine economic winners is clearly mistaken. The state has done its best to weaken the state firms, in large part because that is where labor is strongest.

Trade unions have also been weakened in post-communist Poland, though in this matter Solidarity bears as much responsibility as does the state. When the Solidarity-sponsored government of 1989 drafted its program of "shock therapy," the union did not even try to negotiate a pact institutionalizing a role for labor. Until 1993 Solidarity barely took any action against government economic policy. These were costly mistakes, leading workers to the belief that nobody was defending their class-specific interests and leaving workers open to illiberal political appeals. (It has also contributed to widespread defection from Solidarity, whose national membership has declined from 9.5 million in 1981 to 1.2 million in 1993.) When the summer 1992 strike wave laid bare the extent to which Solidarity had lost control of labor activism, the government itself proposed comprehensive negotiations with Solidarity and other trade unions in order to carve out an agreement governing rules and responsibilities in the large state sector. The ensuing "Enterprise Pact"[30] marked the first time that union rights were officially recognized. But the unions won so little that some activists decried this first foray into corporatism as a betrayal.

If Solidarity has lost influence in the state sector, the union has been almost completely absent in the private sector. Although not many workers have tried to organize unions there, reports speak of the routine dismissal of those who do. There is little data on this because Solidarity does not care much about organizing this sector, and the state does not want to promote it either. One angry union supporter complained to the *Solidarity Weekly* in July 1990 that "a wild 19th-century capitalism" ran rampant in the new private sector, with employers refusing to sign regular contracts, ignoring health and safety codes, demanding 12-hour days without overtime pay, dismissing employees before they become eligible for their first paid vacation, and hiding income so they can cheat the treasury. Further, Solidarity, he charged, was not doing or even writing a thing about this.[31]

Meanwhile, in the privat*ized* sector (consisting of firms that were once state owned, as opposed to those that begin as private firms), data show a pattern of decline of union membership and influence. A 1992 study of 100 privatized firms, each with more than 100 employees, shows that Solidarity survived the change in ownership status only in 85 firms. Moreover, in 44 of those firms, its membership soon declined; only in 12 did membership rise.[32]

All in all, the post-communist state has tried to empower a new market elite and weaken the labor movement. Helped along by labor's own attitudes and the support of the dominant political parties, the state has had great success in doing so. With the class institutions of labor, such as trade unions and employee councils, being systematically eroded, and in the absence of a labor party anywhere in the post-communist world, labor is increasingly being deprived of class-specific ways to articulate its many economic grievances.

Many East European neoliberals proudly see the weakening of the labor movement as their historic contribution to the building of democracy. Ignoring the long record of labor opposition (and intellectual complicity) and forgetting that it was labor's uprising in Poland that triggered the collapse of communism, liberal intellectuals now frequently say that they agree with the communists on one point alone: Communism favored workers. Through an odd logic, they take this to mean that democracy means weakening labor. The only way to ensure that communism cannot return, they argue, is to weaken the labor movement and stifle class-based conflicts.

The neoliberals thus demonstrate only that they remain mired in the ideological blinders of the cold-war past. For it is not class conflicts—the political cleavage of modernity—that endanger democracy in the post-communist world, but the premodern phenomena of integral nationalism and religious and political fundamentalism that do—precisely the sort of cleavages that capitalists and socialists alike used to think were extinct. Class conflicts, of course, can threaten democracy too, as they have done when communist parties have taken state power for themselves. But in Eastern Europe, where not only communism but even socialism has been discredited and where class allegiances are felt economically without being articulated politically, class conflicts are far from posing any kind of danger. Instead, insofar as they run counter to appeals of nationalism and fundamentalism, class conflicts are a *condition* of democracy.

Neoliberals may be right that weakening the labor movement is a historic contribution. It is not, however, one that augurs well for political democracy.

Conclusion—And a Note of Hope

I have shown in this chapter how and why a radical neoliberal economic transformation, when carried out with a labor movement that is unorganized along class lines and with a government committed to holding back class conflicts, ends up helping the possibilities of illiberal parties committed to undermining democracy. The best way to integrate labor as a pro-democratic force into the new political system is on the basis of an appeal that argues that capitalism is the enemy. In that way, worker antagonisms that might otherwise be directed at other citizens, thus potentially violating their democratic rights (and therefore weakening political liberalization), are directed instead at the impersonal economic system.

Building a democratic consensus requires integrating labor in such a way that it accepts the democratic rules of the game. Integrating labor does not mean granting all its wishes. But neither does it mean denying its wishes under the guise that market logic alone will improve things. The new capitalist system is creating huge economic conflicts that are not fully expressed as economic conflicts, because the state does not promote the organization of labor (and the healthy systemic antagonisms that that would create) and labor does not recognize its own role as a separate class nor the "real" enemy of capital. And this arrangement simply does not facilitate the political integration of labor, which is crucial for the consolidation of democracy.

The fears of post-communist governments that labor conflicts can too easily get out of hand and threaten the new democracies are therefore misplaced. Constructing a market economy *must* create serious class conflicts; that, after all, is what capitalism is all about. The task for political democrats is to see that the antagonisms generated by the new system are structured in a way that includes and integrates citizens rather than excludes and alienates them. By recognizing all protagonists, even the enemies, as legitimate members of the community, class antagonisms are the most inclusive. Rather than try to eliminate class-based institutions, therefore, post-communist governments should promote them, in the interests of a stable liberal democracy. Similarly, liberal political parties *ought* to articulate their claims in class-based terms, rather than seeking to stifle them. The chief problem with liberal political parties in Eastern Europe is their assumption that all conflicts potentially undermine the new democracy. They have worked to stifle class-based antagonisms and then are horrified by the nationalistic, fundamentalist, and exclusionary antagonisms that rise up in their place. Liberals commonly plead helplessness: "We have nothing to propose, just freedom."[33] Or else they blame the lower classes for spoiling democracy by expressing dissatisfaction when they should, according to the liberals, be grateful that the hated communism has been abolished.[34] Yet why should non-elites not be angry at the current distribution of wealth into the hands of a new (and old) elite? The liberals do not understand that some conflicts undermine democracy whereas others consolidate it and that the liberals' responsibility is to promote the ones that consolidate democracy so as to undercut the ones that undermine it.

I sum this up as follows. Organization according to class is not only important but inevitable in a class-divided system, which Eastern Europe has become. But labor in Eastern Europe does not think politically in terms of class, having emerged from a system in which class conflicts were secondary and having struggled against communism armed with an ideology that originally downplayed class and that then transformed itself into a defense of the class interests of an emerging bourgeoisie alone. Labor is not now attracted to democratic class-based appeals, as can be seen in the weak showing of liberal social democrats.[35] This leaves labor open to illiberal political parties that address class concerns but offer irrelevant scapegoats as being responsible for the problems. The task facing post-communist governments and parties is to push labor toward expressing their class interests in a democratic way.

My final conclusion depends on which perspective I am looking at things from. As an analyst, I would conclude by noting that democracy is far from being consolidated because of the nonintegration of labor yet add the hopeful comment that recent events have shown greater class conflict over economic issues, as labor appears to be getting over its initial confusion about its role and is trying to develop its own autonomous program.

If I look at the situation as an adviser, I would conclude that post-communist liberal parties, if they want to maintain the public's commitment to liberal democratic norms, should try to organize labor along class lines. The parties must seek to empower labor, to get labor involved in defending its *own* interests—not just defending reform in general.

I also am able to conclude with one optimistic note. There are signs that at least some political liberals understand the need to get involved in class issues. I am referring to the Wroclaw section of the Democratic Union (DU) party in Poland. From a study of the activity of various local organizations of the DU,[36] I found that only in Wroclaw has the DU consistently organized activities seeking to defend workers as workers. It has helped run local employment bureaus and retraining programs and has actively intervened to help displaced workers find jobs. The Wroclaw DU goes to those who are in need and, without making grandiose promises, simply gets involved in trying to make things better. The results became apparent in the 1991 parliamentary elections, when Wroclaw gave DU its highest vote total in the whole country: more than 20 percent, or about 50 percent more than its national average. This demonstrates that class-based programs—or programs addressing economic inequalities and seeking benefits for workers as workers and not just as free individuals—can succeed. With such programs, labor can feel included in the new democratic system. Eastern Europe may well be too poor for a redistributive corporatist arrangement today. But the democratic integration of labor does not require buying people off. It requires liberal democratic parties actively demonstrating that they are interested not just in empowering a new class but in protecting labor too, just as the DU has demonstrated in Wroclaw.

As Maoists might put it, the lesson is "Learn from Wroclaw!"

Notes

I would like to thank the following people for comments on various drafts and presentations of this paper: George Breslauer, Valerie Bunce, Albert Fishlow, Antoni Kaminski, Pearl-Alice Marsh, Dijana Plestina, Kazimierz Poznanski, Philippe Schmitter, and David Stark. A special thanks to Beverly Crawford for inviting me to the conferences that made me work on this contribution in the first place.

1. A distinction between political and economic liberalism is crucial in this paper. I use the concept of liberal politics, or political liberalism, to refer to universal tolerance, the systemic guarantee of individual rights such as suffrage and freedom of speech and association, and the maintenance of democratic political representation. Economic liberalism, however, refers to policies and rules establishing individual property rights, promoting market-based inequalities, encouraging the growth and consolidation of a strong bourgeoisie, and limiting government intervention in the economy except as is needed to solidify entrepreneurial rights. On the theoretical origins and connections between each kind of liberalism, see Russell Hardin, "Liberalism: Political and Economic," in *Social Philosophy and Policy* 10:2, Summer 1993.

2. Jeffrey Sachs, "Hey, Pundits, What About Yeltsin?" Op-ed in *New York Times*, April 30, 1993.

3. Peggy Watson, "The Rise of Masculinism in Eastern Europe," in *New Left Review* No. 198, March/April 1993. Also, see Nanette Funk and Magda Mueller, *Gender and Post-Communism* (New York: Routledge, 1993).

4. This statement is particularly true for Eastern Europe, though it is not fully generalizable. Cecil Rhodes, after all, openly saw the exploitation of Africa as a way to ease class conflicts at home. But such conflicts, within a single racial group, have also been eased by expropriating enemies closer to home. In South Africa, for example, policies based on the subordination of Blacks and the erosion of power for English-speaking peoples clearly contributed to resolving problems of gross inequality for white Afrikaners. In other words, racist policies helped the class interests of working-class Afrikaners, since wealth was stolen from those who were excluded to benefit the previously excluded working-class whites. In

the United States, similarly, nineteenth-century policies that persecuted Blacks and Chinese helped improve the lives of working-class whites, thus turning them into supporters of democracy. It was, of course, a "democracy" that still excluded most of the population, but the principles then accepted by white workers would, much later, be used to empower those still left on the outside. These examples, therefore, suggest that racist policies can facilitate the improvement of working-class conditions, and the inclusions of workers into a formally democratic system, if there are numerous enough and politically powerless enough minorities that can be plundered. Obviously, it is no longer so acceptable, in the late-twentieth century, to disenfranchise and openly exploit internal minorities. But Eastern Europe could not resolve class animosities this way even if some political leaders were brazen enough to withstand international condemnation and try it anyway. For there is simply no minority in Eastern Europe whose oppression or expropriation could improve the conditions of anyone else. There is no minority—ethnic, religious, or political (e.g., "communists")—either large enough or rich enough to subsidize the larger society. That is why the various schemes of Eastern Europe's would-be authoritarians could not work even if their proponents did come to power. Class inequalities will have to be worked out the way they were worked out in post-war Western Europe: through the political inclusion of labor and economic redistribution.

Readings on these points include Alistair Sparks, *The Mind of South Africa* (New York: Ballantine Books, 1991), esp. chapter 7; and Michael Shafter, "Trade Unions and Political Machines: The Organization and Disorganization of the American Working Class in the Late 19th Century," in Ira Katznelson and Aristede Zolberg, *Working-Class Formation* (Princeton: Princeton University Press, 1986); also Katznelson's Introduction in the same.

5. "What Happened in Eastern Europe in 1989?" In Daniel Chirot, ed., *The Crisis of Leninism and the Decline of the Left* (Seattle: University of Washington Press, 1991), p. 5.

6. Dietrich Rueschemeyer, Evelyne Huber Stephens, and John D. Stephens, *Capitalist Development and Democracy* (Chicago: University of Chicago Press, 1992), p. 8.

7. In June 1993, Walesa announced the creation of a presidential party for the September 1993 parliamentary elections, using the same acronym, BBWR, that Marshal Pilsudski used for his presidential party in the 1930s.

8. Juliusz Gardawski, *Robotnicy 1991* (Warsaw: Friedrich Ebert Foundation, 1992), pp. 43–45 and 58.

9. Gardawski, *Robotnicy*, p. 28. The exact wording differs slightly in each survey. In 1991 workers were asked whether they agreed that "employee participation in firm governance will definitely improve the situation of the firm." In 1983 the statement read, "the more employee participation in firm governance, the better."

10. *Ibid.* Again, there was some difference in the exact wording of the statements. In 1991: "Regular workers should not in general get involved in management, since that can only make the situation worse." In 1983: "Enterprise management is the business of the managers, and workers should not interfere in such matters."

11. Workplace surveys conducted by Artur Czynczyk and Andrzej Chelminski, and summarized by Marc Weinstein, untitled manuscript, November 1992.

12. Gardawski, *Robotnicy*, p. 51.

13. *Ibid.*, p. 218.

14. "Jak krzyk dziecka," interview with Lena Kolarska-Bobinska, head of the Center for Public Opinion Research, in *Zycie Gospodarcze*, June 27, 1993, p. 3.

15. Gardawski, *Robotnicy,* p. 215.

16. Data from both firms based on workplace surveys conducted by Artur Czynczyk and Andrzej Chelminski, as summarized by Marc Weinstein, untitled manuscript, November 1992.

17. These figures come from Marc Weinstein's analysis of the data collected by Czynczyk and Chelminski.

18. From a survey conducted by Marc Weinstein. Weinstein wrote up some of the results, including data cited in this section, in "Competing Notions of Stakeholders Rights in Poland" (paper presented to Eighth International Conference of Europeanists, Chicago, March 1992).

19. Zaneta Semprich, "Niedostateczna ochrona pracownikow" ("Inadequate Protection for Employees"), in *Rzeczpospolita,* July 13, 1993.

20. I prefer the use of Dahl's term "polyarchy" instead of "democracy" to describe the liberal parliamentary systems of the West. Virtually all recent theorists of democratization define democracy as polyarchy but are unwilling to use the term because it has little popular currency. While it is probably impossible to use "polyarchy" consistently, we ought to at least use it occasionally in order to indicate that even when polyarchy is achieved, struggles for greater democracy are far from over.

21. Statistical analysis of the presidential voting by Ireneusz Bialecki, "Pracownicze interesy i orientacje polityczne," in Wladyslaw Adamski et al., *Polacy '90* (Warsaw: Instytut Filozofiji Socjologii-PAN, 1991).

22. See Lawrence Weschler, "The Velvet Purge: The Trials of Jan Kavan," in *The New Yorker,* October 19, 1992.

23. The best work on strikes and other forms of employee protest in Poland in the post-communist period has been done by Kazimierz Kloc. See his "Polish Labor in Transition, 1990–1992," in *Telos* No. 92, Summer 1992, and "Konflikt przemyslowy doby transformacji," in *Przeglad Spoleczny* (Warsaw) No. 10, 1993.

24. For a longer discussion of the concept of interests, see my article, "The Politics of Interest in Post-Communist Society," in *Theory and Society* 22:4, August 1993.

25. This brief discussion on East European anticommunist ideology is based on several of my earlier writings, particularly *Solidarity and the Politics of Anti-Politics* (Philadelphia: Temple University Press, 1990), chaps. 1–3; "The Crisis of Liberalism in Poland," in *Telos* No. 89, Fall 1991; and my "Introduction" to Adam Michnik's *The Church and the Left* (Chicago: University of Chicago Press, 1993).

26. On the effect of changing democratic discourses on working-class politics, see Ronald Aminzade, "Class Analysis, Politics, and French Labor History," in Lenard Berlanstein, ed., *Rethinking Labor History* (Urbana: University of Illinois, 1993), esp. the section on "republican discourses of representation," pp. 105–108.

27. In Eastern Europe, for example, socialist parties helped minimize fascist success by consistent efforts aimed at transforming anti-Semitic sentiment into anticapitalist sentiment. Early Russian socialists, meanwhile, helped reduce pogroms by urging class antagonisms upon labor instead of ethnic and religious ones. See Charters Wynn, *Workers, Strikes, and Pogroms: The Donbass Dnepr Bend in Imperial Russia, 1870–1905* (Princeton: Princeton University Press, 1992).

28. Even the most consistent liberals must use the state to shape property rights. See John Campbell and Leon Lindberg, "Property Rights and the Organization of Economic Activity by the State," in *American Sociological Review* 55, October 1990.

29. Interestingly, despite this underemphasis on employee-buyouts, that has been by far the most successful privatization strategy to date. As Anthony Levitas writes, "most privatizations have been nursed into the world by the employee councils, precisely the instititution that the state has regarded as being most opposed to property reform." See Levitas, "Rethinking Reform: Lesson of Privatization," in *World Policy Journal* IX:4, Fall/Winter 1992, p. 790.

30. Its various provisions had been ratified only in part when Congress was dissolved, pending new elections, in June 1993.

31. Wojciech Olpinski, letter to the editor, in *Tygodnik Solidarnosc*, July 27, 1990, p. 5. In a letter printed alongside, another reader asks why the union paper never even printed basic information about workers' rights to combat layoffs.

32. Marek Kozak, Piotr Kozarzewski, and Marek Marczewski, "Przedsiebiorstwa sprywatyzowane," in Maria Jarosz, ed., *Prywatyzacja: Szanse i Zagrozenia* (Warsaw: Instytut Studiow Politycznych PAN, 1993), p. 70. The authors do not actually state that Solidarity disappeared in 15 firms as a result of privatization, but since the union was present in almost all firms with more than 100 employees, that seems the likely explanation for the union being active only in 85 of the 100 firms.

33. Here is Professor Zoran Pajic from Sarajevo: "After the Communist system collapsed, all that liberals like me could offer was the free market and free institutions. People were terrified. They were not ready for these insecurities. And this was a gap that had to be filled by nature. So the nationalists arose. ..." What is revealing, and so common among post-communist liberals, is the resignation in the voice and the sense that liberalism is doomed if and when too many people are "terrified." (See Hall's discussion on Tocqueville in Chapter 4.) We see here a familiar inability to recognize that liberalism must try to address insecurities too, not by letting the nationalists structure antagonisms but by trying to structure antagonisms the way they are successfully structured in already existing liberal democracies—along class lines. (Quoted in *The New Yorker*, "Quiet Voices from the Balkans," March 15, 1993, p. 6.)

34. This attitude was manifested in abundance at the conference on "Intellectuals and Social Change in Central and Eastern Europe," at which numerous leading liberal politicians and intellectuals from Eastern Europe appeared. The conference was held at Rutgers University from April 9–11, 1992; proceedings published in *Partisan Review*, October 1992.

35. Such groups as this are not to be confused with the ex-communists. I am referring here to groups such as the Union of Labor Party in Poland, remnants of the old Civic Forum in Czechoslovakia, or the short-lived Social Democratic Party in Hungary. None of them have yet received even 5 percent of the vote in elections.

36. Based on a study of the Democratic Union's internal newsletter, *Biuletyn Informacyjny*.

9

Political Economy of Privatization in Eastern Europe

KAZIMIERZ Z. POZNANSKI

The most critical decisions to be made in the economic transition from state planning to market capitalism in Eastern Europe are in the content and timing of institutional changes, including privatization. These choices can be said to be of an economic nature in that they involve optimization of resource allocation within a certain time frame. As such, they should be subject to cost-benefit calculus. Building new institutions as well as scrapping existing ones (to make room for the new institutions) consumes economic inputs—hopefully to be recovered through related efficiency gains. This is so because, by determining the incentive structure—the payoff matrix—for individual agents, institutions affect the efficiency of resource utilization as well.

The question of selecting the optimal path for reintroducing private property and voluntary contracting is typically framed as a choice between a radical (shock therapy) and a gradual approach. A number of economists trained in neoclassical theory have developed arguments in support of radical privatization, such as the elaborations offered by Sachs (1992), Blanchard (1991), and Brada (1993) (for further discussion of this point, see the Appendix. Theoretical support of the gradual privatization program has been developed by Kornai (1990), Murrell (1992), and Poznanski (1992a), all of whom make frequent references to the broader body of evolutionary economics (as outlined by Hayek, 1988, and Mises, 1920).

Given the long-term consequences of privatization methods for economic structure, I posit in this chapter that the optimal approach is one that contains sufficient flexibility in terms of multiple choices and reversibility. Following this postulate, I argue that a gradual approach to privatization—measured in pace and proceeding largely from the bottom up—is the most appropriate as it allows for greater adaptation to change. The initial choice of many post-communist reformers in Eastern Europe was, however, to endorse radical-type reform, that is, state controlled and assuming a short timetable. Similar preference can be found in the former Soviet Union, particularly in Russia and some of the Baltic states.

Certain political factors have played a significant role in the early choice of a radical, rather than gradual, approach to privatization. In part, preference for the radical version has reflected the newly emerged political elites' desire to distance themselves from the communist party, which for decades resisted any thought of relaxing their grip on public capital. The radical approach was also favored in the hope that relatively weak, recently formed state bureaucracies might be able to escape the demands of workers (demands that the communist parties were unable to manage by the end of their rule). A fast-paced transfer of assets was also seen by some of the newly established political forces as an agenda capable of establishing strong constituencies for themselves.

However, the choice of radical methods of privatization has not come without a certain economic cost to the transition economies. Whatever the long-range positive outcome of radical privatization, in the short term it seems to have contributed—in combination with other factors—to the post-1989 recessions in the region. The announcement of radical reforms in itself dramatically weakened the incentive (principal-agent) structure of state-owned industry. Not knowing what the future legal status of their enterprises would be, managers and workers decided, quite rationally, to slacken their efforts. Moreover, with relaxed (and sometimes non-existent) state supervision, outright decapitalization—including waste and theft—by collectives was more widely tolerated.

Actual patterns of privatization (at least in industry) have, in turn, been shaped by the realities of the post-1989 recession. Given the sharp deterioration of economic conditions, foreign buyers look more desirable to the state bureaucracy (since it lacks domestic buyers). Workers, too, have become more agreeable, when faced with their enterprises' imminent insolvency. For domestic agents, whose financial resources have been greatly reduced, it has not always been privatization, as intended by the post-communist reformers, that has driven the expansion of the private sector—most often, it has been small-scale "entries" (as in the case of Polish and Hungarian industry).

Theoretical Framework

To meaningfully debate the choice between a radical and a gradual approach to privatization—as well as to transition in general—one must first carefully define these terms. Much of the discussion to date has taken place in the absence of any clear understanding of the exact meaning of these two phrases. Effort has been focused mostly on normative analysis, that is, advocacy of specific practical solutions, some labeled "radical" and others "gradual." In most cases, "radical" is associated with "fast" and "gradual" with "slow," and some specific techniques—or "models"—are given one of these labels. But such efforts fail to clearly identify what exactly—in terms of specific actions—constitutes a radical or gradual approach.

Principal Features

In fact, the real difference between the two approaches to privatization is often not in the schedule at which change actually occurs but rather in the underlying intention or rhetoric of reform. Thus, the radical approach to divestment of assets is one that emphasizes speed and offers quick payoffs, even though it may actually result in unexpected reversals, so that change ends up coming about slowly. The gradual approach advocates a slower pace and promises less, but this does not mean that in fact it always takes more time than the radical program—an observation well developed by Murrell (1992), who aptly points out the generally inverse relationship between reform rhetoric and accomplishment.

The radical approach, on the one hand, stresses speed in the belief that anything less than a "shock" treatment administered by the state will not have the credibility necessary to alter economic agents' behavior. The gradual view, on the other hand, holds that taking smaller but frequent steps can be equally credible. Radical reformers assume that the broader and more fast-paced the program, the more credible it will be because it will seem harder to reverse, whereas gradualists argue that agents may find bolder moves by the state less realistic and therefore ignore them. While radical programs view even a weak state as gaining strength in its dealing with economic agents by launching a crash program, gradualists stress that weak states are rather more believable when they try limited measures that they can back with authority.

Another substantive difference is that the radical approach assumes a strategic role for the state, whereas the gradual approach does not. This focus of radical reform on the state seems consistent with its premium on speed, since the state may not only be helpful in neutralizing opponents but also in focusing social energy on a single reform program. In contrast, gradual reform calls for only low-level state involvement, or so-called piecemeal engineering (Popper, 1971). Among other reasons, this is called for out of fear that the involvement of a strong political agency, having a vested interest in defending a once-selected variant, may unnecessarily constrain potentially valuable searches for the optimal path of reform.

Next, the radical reform approaches are derived from certain end-state models or untested blueprints, which define the type of property structure to be achieved. This approach puts trust in theoretically conceived "projects," or ideas extrapolated from the experience of other economies. The gradualist type of reform rejects such a method as unable to address the real complexity of change in a given—and always unique—economy. Measures favored in the gradual type of reform are therefore reactive, that is, driven mostly by the needs that emerge at each step of the process. Radical reform thus, by and large, takes the form of the execution of a "project," whereas gradual reform proceeds in a trial-and-error fashion.

The radical privatization reform approach is based on the assumption, consistent with neoclassical thinking, that economic agents—firms and households—can be rather easily reshaped, and if they fail, then the resources at their disposal can, with only a little delay, be reused by others. Gradual-type reform, in contrast, stresses that existing agents, due to their long-established routines (or firm-specific knowledge), can change only very slowly and that their resources cannot be recycled at low cost, if at all. Thus, whereas the radical approach to reform expects the "exit" of old agents to drive transition, gradual-type reform depends more heavily on "entries" of new agents.

Another difference of opinion concerns the cost of each approach were it to succeed. The radical theory claims that harsh measures carry high front-load costs—such as recession—but that the total price of change is less than that of piecemeal reform. This is because slow-paced reforms permit extended misallocation of resources, as some less-than-perfect measures—as well as enterprises—remain in place. In contrast, the gradualist theory presents reforms as low-cost, or even cost-free, that is, as involving no immediate deterioration in overall performance (since under normal, stable circumstances, only short-term measures offering net gain would be pursued and retained by enterprises).

Underlying Assumptions

There is another useful way of looking at the above two reform (transition) approaches, namely, examining their alternative definitions of "natural" or acceptable institutional arrangement. The essential difference is between the radical view's assumption that uniformity—singularity of game rules and economic agents—is a virtue, and the gradual reform's belief that duality, or certain differentiation of rules and agents, is permissible or even desirable. These assumptions are consistent with the radical call for quick execution of an end-state model and the gradualist insistence on a more balanced procedure, in which some sort of temporary dualism—mixed-type economy—becomes inevitable.

According to the radical approach, if rules are not uniform (e.g., fixed and free prices operating side by side), then waste of productive resources results, and if such differentiation is allowed during the reform process, then its success may be undermined by the waste. The gradual-type approach assumes that a certain amount of waste is unavoidable in any economy, whether it undergoes reform or not (a point made in particular by Hirschman, 1970, and by Kornai, 1981). The goal of reform is not the elimination of all waste, but, rather, marginal improvement in resource utilization through creation of an expanding enclave based on superior rules and agents—where the amount of waste is less.

The radical-type reform perceives disuniformity of rules as leading to undeserved rewards, that is, monopolistic rents, shifting gains to dominant actors (as, for instance, under a dual-price system wherein products supplied at lower fixed prices to state-owned firms are resold at higher free-market prices). Within the gradual approach, monopolistic rents are viewed as acceptable, or even desirable, if put to the proper economic applications. Such rents may, for instance, be quite helpful in bringing about change in property structure if income from speculation (as in the illegal resales mentioned above) is used to finance "entries" by private agents.

The radical approach looks at the duality of agents—coexistence of state along with private firms—as inefficient or unworkable, since relations between them are generally adverse (e.g., the private sector corrupts the state sector with the help of money, whereas the state sector restricts the private sector by exercising its political influence). The gradual approach to institution-formation assumes that such inter-sectoral relations are, or can be, positive. For example, the state sector, by allowing overmanning, can help to stabilize the labor market for the whole economy. The private sector, in turn, may exert additional competitive pressure on less cost-sensitive state enterprises—but only if the two are not formally separated (as generally practiced under the communist system).

Radical reformers, on the one hand, not only stress the negative nature of intersectoral relations, but also argue that, given the initial size advantage, the state sector may cause more damage to the private sector than the other way around, so that the private sector would only gain ground after it was too late for economic recovery, if at all. On the other hand, the gradualists argue that it is not size but efficiency that matters, and with the natural cost advantage of individual agents, the private sector will eventually take over the economy. While radical reformers view competition between sectors—state and private—as based on "market shares," gradualists characterize this competition as centered on unit costs of production.

Models of Privatization

When the post-communist governments, first in Eastern Europe and then in the former Soviet Union, began designing their privatization programs, the idea of property reform was not new. Even during the final years of communism, as in Hungary and Poland, a lively debate on property structure reforms was under way, though no serious attention was given to possible means to implement the large-scale transfer of state assets. A full-blown debate on this practical issue erupted when the first post-communist governments began preparing for deliberate programs of transition to competitive capitalism. A plethora of methods have been outlined, though not in a very systematic way, given the differences in background and preference of their designers.

Radical Methods

One of the radical methods that has been suggested, or at least implied, is to simplify the transfer process by abandoning most public assets. This would be done on the assumption that only a fraction of state enterprises are recoverable through restructuring at an acceptable total cost. Given the negative "routines" learned by managers and workers as well as obsolete or ill-chosen capital (or both), a large portion of the state sector is doomed to generate negative value. Once introduced, competition should weed out all such value-detracting enterprises, automatically changing the industrial structure in favor of the private sector. However, there is some question as to whether the imperfect market that would initially emerge during transition could properly select masses of enterprises for this kind of quick closure.

Even if many state assets were simply phased out, the question remains as to how to dispose of the rest rapidly. One key radical (blueprint) model offered is that of "popular capitalism," which calls for the state to distribute public capital through free-of-charge vouchers. Such a method would, of course, help bypass the financial barrier to quick privatization—lack of personal savings. While everybody would receive the same number of vouchers, only the fittest would stay in the game, so that active shareholders will ultimately dominate. However, for such a natural selection to work, voucher distribution would have to be supported by the proper institution—the stock market, which is lacking in Eastern Europe. As long as stock markets are being formed, even if these shares were put in proper hands, allocation of capital is going to be greatly hindered.

Yet another radical proposal is for the state to adopt wholesale transfers in return for some compensation, or at a price—another measure not tried before. Recognizing the enormous scope of work involved, this proposal assumes the utilization of simplified procedures of valuation and limited competition, including direct sales to strategic buyers. However, selected buyers, even if offered assets for free, may need considerable time to assess a given enterprise just to determine the possible liabilities. For the state, in turn, to release the potential buyer from liabilities without knowing their exact "weight" would be fiscally rather irresponsible (especially under conditions of already sizable budgetary deficits).

Another relatively untested method outlined is for the state to transfer control over a majority of state assets to foreign agents, without selling equity. Under one plan, foreigners are offered long-term contracts to manage state enterprises after they have been converted into joint-stock companies (with incentives including bonuses—such as share acquisitions—linked to stock-value enhancement). An alternative scheme is for the state to put foreigners in charge of investment funds, giving them the power to allocate shares as well as to make direct decisions on production in converted state companies (supervision over these managers is to be left in the hands of stockholders or the state bureaucracy or both).

Into this broad category of radical ownership reforms also falls the concept of a "simulated market," wherein assets of state-owned enterprises are primarily entrusted to state-owned—or already privatized—financial institutions such as insurance companies, commercial banks, pension funds, and so forth (for early work on the subject, see Tardos, 1989; also Schaffer, 1992). This model is said to resemble the practice of advanced capitalist economies, where such investors, often representing the public sector, are a major source of financing. It is also true, however, that institutional investors—relatively passive—operate in the public sector through the securities market, which is driven mostly by other, more active, players—that is, corporate investors (Kornai, 1994).

Gradual Approaches

One gradual-type approach to privatization is to simply leave the state sector under direct control, even allow it to grow, and at the same time to liberalize the private sector. Under such a "dual-track" approach (for more details, see: Poznanski, 1992c), of course, the state has to develop a heterogeneous system of instruments—pricing, financing, and taxation—aimed at still-public and private enterprises, respectively. (For a conceptual analysis of such a hybrid financial system, see McKinnon, 1992.) The formation of capitalist markets is left primarily to the private sector, so that as long as this sector grows at a higher rate than the state sector, a capitalist structure will emerge.

Another gradual-type approach is one that combines a permissive policy toward private "entries" with reform of corporate structure within the state sector. Here, the state—say, to broaden its tax base—introduces incentives to turn managers from mere executors of orders into revenue-maximizers. Long-term contracts, stable tax schemes, and higher prices for above-quota output are a few examples of such measures, designed to alter the motivation of managers. By shifting attention away from bureaucratic bargaining for resources to revenue maximization, such reform prepares state-owned enterprises for possible, though not unavoidable, privatization.

Gradual privatization may also be conducted through market-driven "public offerings," that is, sales of state-targeted assets closely following the supply-and-demand principle. Under this approach—fully consistent with the experience of advanced capitalist economies—sales are only concluded when fully qualified buyers are available from the private sector. To ensure that assets are transferred to the proper private hands, sales have to be competitive—based on open bidding—and conducted at full price. This kind of procedure thus assumes that public enterprises targeted for transfer will have first been restructured by the state to reach the fullest profit potential possible.

The state may become even more active by adopting what I will call "enhanced privatization," where, unlike in the previous model, demand for public assets is stimulated through financial incentives. Offering low-interest credits to be fully or partially repaid to the state is one such option; offering various tax preferences to buyers is another. Leases with the option to buy or payments for assets that are stretched over a longer period also fall into this category of models (Poznanski, 1992b). With increased state involvement comes, however, an additional risk—that with so many incentives, private choices will be driven more by the desire to take advantage of state preferences than by the profit potential of the assets offered.

Finally, there is the so-called "spontaneous privatization" model, partly resembling the previously discussed technique of "enhanced privatization." This particular method gives priority to in-house asset acquisitions, involving collectives acting on their own, rather than on state, initiative. "Spontaneous privatization" allows insiders—possibly in tandem with outside parties—to partition state enterprises and price their assets with limited supervision. There is, here, at least a loose legal framework in place, which allows the state to persecute cases of gross corruption. Since under this model, acquisitors can be kept in reasonable check by the state, a runaway transfer of assets is not very likely here.

Political Preferences

The privatization methods that offer the best economic payoffs—reduction in transaction costs for economic agents—should be the ones selected for implementation; however, selection is not always based on purely economic considerations—politics may interfere. Whereas it well might be that gradual methods can proceed very much on their own, or without much political stimulation, radical techniques cannot, for they are largely the product of unusual political circumstances. Thus, in trying to understand the initial preference by post-communist reformers for radical methods of privatization, it is useful to examine the peculiarities of the political context within which such choices were made.

State-Society Balance

What made the political conditions under which asset-transfer programs had to be formulated unusual was, among other things, the imbalance between unrealistically high societal expectations and the state's inhibited ability to deliver "welfare" goods. While inviting excessive demands on the state—as exclusive employer—for secure jobs, constant wage increases, and fixed prices, the communist property system—where the state was the only owner—offered few incentives for efficiency. Caught in this impossible situation, the communist leaders eventually began considering property reforms, that is, privatization, and a similar motivation was present when the the newly formed post-communist elites began deliberating on the property-rights issue.

This particular concern was evident, for instance, in Poland, where the freely elected government of Mazowiecki, in mid-1989, quickly endorsed a fast-paced divestment of state assets, in great part for the sake of redirecting worker demands. For much the same reason, the government stopped giving orders to state-owned enterprises, except for wage-fund setting, or indexation. For rapid privatization to improve the state's power, it has been imperative that such a transfer of assets not flow overwhelmingly into the hands of worker collectives. Accordingly, Mazowiecki rejected the labor-managed option, long favored by the "free" unions, the government's main political supporter at the time. Instead, mass direct sales and less-favored, voucher privatization were endorsed with provisions that would exclude collectives from having major say in the procedures.

Using privatization to affect the state-society balance has not gone unresisted, as there have been pressures on the cabinet of Mazowiecki to assume a slower pace and to allow collectives to decide on the merits—and the exact type—of privatization in their enterprises. These conflicting interests clashed in early 1990, when the government presented its radical program—placing almost complete discretion in the hands of the central bureaucracy—to the Parliament, only to see it defeated. Other governments—those of Bielecki and Suchocka—seeking fast-paced transfer from above have not been much more successful than Mazowiecki. As a consequence, the state-society balance has not dramatically changed on that account—with the political situation characterized by cabinet instability and labor unrest, including general strikes.

Poland's case fundamentally differs from the pattern that has emerged in Russia, where a weak government also sought fast-paced privatization. The original program in Russia, announced in 1992, was heavily influenced by Polish "shock therapy," as reflected in its endorsement of the distribution of vouchers that would allow citizens to directly acquire shares in enterprises of their choice. Unlike in Poland, this radical program quickly gained broad support, though not in the exact version that the government of Yeltsin outlined. Conceived as being geared mostly to outsiders, with the almost complete exclusion of foreigners, the program was reshaped into an "insider" type, where the majority—or entirety—of capital assets released by the state has been directed to enterprise collectives.

Although the state—within the "path" that has evolved in Russia—has succeeded in releasing its property rights faster than the government in Poland, this does not mean that demands on the state have been reduced; it could well be that the state-society balance has actually worsened. Once centered mostly around the central state, the paternalistic structure has been refocused on a local level, where most of the shares have been acquired. (This follows the logic of a general decentralization—or fragmentation—of political power since the departure of Gorbachev.) As the majority of assets have been transferred to enterprise collectives, their expectations might have increased (with legal titles used as additional protection against job losses or wage cuts or both).

Political Payoffs

One could productively conceptualize political conflicts over the post-communist privatization within the framework of state-society theory, but "real life" struggles involve smaller aggregates—parties, factions, groups, and so on. The category of the "state" is very much a holistic fiction, because political power is always contested, and the category of "society" is another such fiction, since "collective action" is relatively rare. It is not, of course, entirely accurate to suggest that the "state" changes its economic course only when effectively pressed by a "society" that changes its mind and acts with sufficient resolve (Migdal, 1988). Thus, as a first approximation, or a selective inquiry, working with a state-society model is sufficient but if a fuller picture is being sought, it fails to provide a full explanation.

At this disaggregate level, choice of privatization paths has also been affected by political factors, one of them being the struggle between the departing communists and their contenders for office. Once permitted into political space, these anticommunist forces found themselves at a disadvantage, both in terms of organizational resources and intraparty discipline. Whenever anticommunist forces took political control away from communists, the anticommunist leaders feared that, given this imbalance, the communists might launch a comeback. The perception was that there was only a narrow window of opportunity for newly emerged leaders, so that if there was anything to gain politically from reforms—including privatization—it had to be done immediately, which encouraged radical measures.

This has been the case in post-communist Poland, whose (quasi) freely elected government of Mazowiecki was the first to opt for radical privatization, even though, with the backing of long-time anticommunist groups, it enjoyed relative strength. There is a great irony in this choice, since the radicalism of reforms might have actually weakened support for the government. For example, ownership reforms met with popular resentment, which to some extent helped bring back parties with communist roots in mid-1993. The government of Pawlak, formed then by these "coalition" parties, though supportive of privatization, took immediate steps to slow it down (with the dominant Peasant Party—the former communist partner in the coalition—providing the most fuel for such a policy shift).

A similar pattern can be detected in the Czech Republic, but in its case one other concern seemed to play a particularly important role—the search for political identity. Unlike in Poland, the anticommunist forces were marginal in the Rupublic, and when new parties began to form, they had to define themselves to the public (particularly given the presence of communist elements legitimized by their 1968 efforts to humanize socialism). One of these parties, led by Klaus, recognized the benefits of promising quick fixes, such as the immediate giveaway of vouchers (despite verbal disapproval of "social engineering"). This promise of "popular capitalism" helped Klaus to win the mid-1992 elections and then proceed with mass voucher distribution implementation, without causing any visible damage to his party.

Radical privatization has also been adopted by the major challenger to the communist party in Russia, namely, the so-called "democrats" under Yeltsin—even though this case is not fully comparable to the previous two. The difference is that in Russia, the "democrats" saw fast-paced privatization also as a way for quickly dissolving the Soviet Union. They hoped that by releasing strong property interests, Russia would emancipate itself faster, thus denying Gorbachev the federal structure he needed to survive. After winning this battle, Yeltsin continued with rapid privatization, this time hoping that it would produce strong political support for him from within the regions. It did, but only initially, since in their relentless drive to "parcel" national resources, many regions eventually began seeking independence for themselves.

Property Patterns

In addition to preferring fast-paced privatization, many post-communist governments have leaned toward a "recipient-specific" type of asset distribution. As indicated earlier, avoiding a heavy concentration of property in the hands of worker collectives has frequently been a goal; the desire to involve as many citizens as possible has been another. When the East European economies were embarking on transition, the common official view was that assets would have to be transferred mostly to domestic agents. Another early assumption was that massive privatization—rather than independent "entries"—should become the main mechanism for the rapid creation of a private-type economy.

Asset Acquisitions

The initial intention of the majority of post-communist governments with respect to foreigners was to lure capital into their long underinvested economies through joint-ventures or green-field projects, rather than equity acquisitions. In reaction to this, the Hungarian government of József Antall applied strong antiforeign rhetoric in its early privatization program, partly to distance itself from the former communists, traveling westward with lists of state enterprises for sale. In Poland, Mazowiecki's government put a 10-percent ceiling on foreign acquisition through "public offerings," and Czechoslovakia excluded foreigners from the first round of bidding for shares in its voucher distribution program (though foreigners were allowed to establish investment funds to participate in the second, and final, round in 1994).

However, this desire to privatize rapidly without foreigners was eventually tempered, or reversed, in favor of large-scale transfers to capital-rich foreigners (an important exception being Russia, for reasons explained earlier). The most important reason behind the eventual decision to turn to foreign agents was the post-1990 stagflation, since it drained the savings of domestic agents and aroused so much uncertainty that few dared invest in generally risky capital acquisitions. The same stagflation has made states less inclined to freely distribute public assets or to offer them at fire-sale prices, since falling production has badly hurt their tax base (for more details, see Poznanski, 1993).

The dominant role of foreign actors in privatization is reflected in the structure of revenues from sales of state assets. In Hungary, for instance, dollar payments by foreigners accounted for about three-quarters of the total revenue from privatization in 1991, and the same proportion held for 1992. Equity acquisitions represented, in 1992, more than two-thirds of the total value of foreign capital invested in Hungary. An identical trend has evolved in Poland, where most of the sales of large- and medium-scale state enterprises went to foreign buyers (with most of these acquisitions providing foreigners with majority ownership rights).

The critical role of foreign agents in privatization is also reflected in their dominant role in the emerging securities markets. The majority of capital pumped into these markets has come from foreign investors—for example, in Poland, where foreign-investment share was estimated at between 30 and 40 percent. It is this injection of capital that has greatly contributed to the surge in average share prices, as in Poland from mid-1993 through early 1994. Foreigners have also been most active in acquiring large blocks of shares through the stock exchange, as in Poland, where controlling packages were purchased in two beer companies in 1994. Even more active have been share acquisitions in the Czech Republic (on the top of some large-scale early—pre-voucher—direct sales of assets to foreigners, e.g., car manufacturer Skoda).

By way of digression, this early pattern may suggest that Eastern Europe is returning to its historical—that is, prewar—pattern, marked by a strong foreign presence in key manufacturing sectors (see: Berend and Ranki, 1974, and the more recent account by Berend, 1994). Importantly, so far, many of the same factors seem to have been responsible for shaping this kind of ownership structure before the war and at the initial stage of transition. As in the past, the economic conditions of Eastern Europe are much worse than in the capital-exporting countries (that is, Western Europe). Again, states appear to be critical in bringing foreign capital into the region, and it is this function that seems to distinguish Eastern European "etatism" from that of the Western European countries.

Private Entries

Another unintended development has been the critical role played in the ongoing formation of the private economy by independent "entries," that is, the internally financed creation of enterprises (rather than acquisition of existing entities). Statistics on newly funded enterprises indicate that they have been increasing at a phenomenal rate throughout Eastern Europe, particularly those that deal in services (somewhat less in manufacturing). For example, in Hungary, the total number of private enterprises increased from about 150,000 in 1989 to 670,000 in 1993. These statistics must be approached with caution since, on the one hand, many "entries" are fictitious and, on the other hand, a substantial fraction of private activities are conducted undetected (that is, illegally).

While the expectation of the post-communist reformers was that relaxation of regulations on private business would bring illegal activities aboveground, the scope of such activities has often increased. In Poland, for instance, there has been large-scale smuggling of cars (often stolen), and imported alcohol and cigarettes enter mostly through illegal channels. This, combined with pervasive tax evasion, more widespread than in the communist past, has resulted in a doubling of the volume of the so-called second economy (estimated at from 25 to 30 percent of the value of the national product in 1994). Even more pervasive is illegal activity in Russia, where in addition, large-scale illegal imports of raw materials have been taking place.

The strong interest of individuals in operating new businesses—often motivated by loss of job or unsatisfactory wages—has been tempered not only by "soft" domestic demand related to generally recessionary conditions but also by the shortage of financing. Credit, when made available, is typically very costly (even if the rates charged are negative, since the behavior of inflation in the long run is not easily predictable) and high, often cost-prohibitive, collateral is frequently required. Large banks have been unprepared—as well as unwilling—to lend to individual clients with little or no credit record to examine (though so-called "curb banks" have been emerging within the private sector to target smaller businesses).

Another obstacle to private "entries" has been the lack of effective legal protection for individual property. Law and order has almost universally deteriorated and the number of "economic crimes" has increased tremendously. The legal system has been totally inadequate for the rapidly multiplying number of private contracts and commercial entities. Most striking has been the case of Russia, where state protection has been largely replaced with mafias that apparently control about 70 percent of recently established private enterprises (and collect between 15 and 20 percent of the proceeds of the enterprises in exchange for "protection").

This critical role of private "entries" seems to suggest that the gradualist theory of privatization might be quite correct at least on one point, namely, that competitive capitalism can best be conceived of as a bottom-up process, as McKinnon (1992) puts it. This process of individual "entries" has probably been such a powerful force behind market-building because it assures the most careful scrutiny (natural selection) of would-be capitalist actors. In addition, private agents progress in this system from smaller to larger units of capital so that they can learn simpler tasks before embarking on more complicated ones. Only such a bottom-up process, McKinnon argues, can fully release the "animal spirit" that best drives the capitalist economy.

Process of Implementation

While political processes in some cases permitted radical ownership reforms, such fast-paced divestment has only rarely produced substantive positive changes in property rights in the short run. The only post-communist economy where rapid transfer of titles has quickly produced well-defined ownership structure with viable private agents put in place is East Germany—there, in two years, almost two-thirds of state assets were dispersed, primarily through direct sales at heavily discounted prices. This is, by general admission, a rather special case; elsewhere, rapid transfer of titles has produced a rather confusing property structure, with no prospect for immediate significant improvement through secondary allocations—by means of stock operations or otherwise.

Mass Privatization

Besides East Germany, the other case of radical privatization that produced a massive transfer of legal titles is the program of "popular capitalism" adopted by Czechoslovakia in 1991. Initially, the program stumbled because of a temporary shortage of voucher booklets, but it also faultered due to confusing legislation (e.g., there were no rules as yet to regulate investment funds allowed to manage vouchers obtained from recipients). When Czechoslovakia split apart on January 1, 1993, a serious delay in registration resulted from efforts to revoke shares acquired by Slovaks in Czech enterprises, as well as Czech claims on Slovak property. But, overall, the whole process of allocating shares—with a complicated, stepwise procedure of evolving at actual share prices—was executed in a remarkably short period of about two years.

While very rapid, this divestment has produced results quite different from those expected, as a majority of shares did not end up in the hands of individual shareholders. More than 70 percent of vouchers were entrusted to investment funds, with two-thirds of these funds capturing 40 percent of vouchers (and presumably a similar share in the actual value of privatized assets). This significant ownership concentration should allow for more effective control over the managers of privatized enterprises (though no individual fund has been allowed under the existing law to capture a majority equity position in any single enterprise). But such a structure also permits, or even invites, collusion by funds to artificially raise the value of their portfolios rather than to maximize these portfolios through prudent investment.

It is also questionable whether investment funds—even those with a majority of holdings—have the potential to effectively allocate capital. The funds have been established, as mentioned, only very recently and their ability to process necessary information is very limited. There has been neither sufficient personnel nor experience to professionally evaluate the viability of individual enterprises. With existing accounting practices falling short of accepted standards, critical information needed for such evaluation has not been readily available. Nor have regulations to prevent enterprises from feeding investment funds with distorted data yet been formulated. In addition, funds have lacked the political clout needed to force personnel changes in poorly managed enterprises.

The other (and last) recent case of rapid transfer of ownership titles is Russia, though it did not proceed in such a well-controlled manner as in the Czech Republic. In both countries, to facilitate strong corporate management, vouchers for shares were issued to all citizens, but in Russia, very few investment funds have been set up to pull shares together. Simultaneously, however, managers and workers were allowed to acquire—using cash and vouchers—up to 51 percent of their assets at 170 percent of the book value not adjusted for inflation (Frydman and

Rapaczynski, 1992, p. 112). Rather than outsiders, insiders—collectives—managed, with practically no state supervision, to quickly take control over their assets, so that transfer of legal titles was almost completed by the end of 1994.

Similar to the Czech Republic, the fast-paced privatization in Russia initially produced a weak property structure. In many ways, the ownership conditions created in Russia are even more blurred than in the Czech Republic and offer less prospect for a positive re-adjustment. In the absence of larger investment funds, or any other major "outsider" equity holders, there is little pressure on collectives to maximize the value of their capital stock. For such control to develop, outsiders would have to be given substantial stakes, but in the climate of uncertainty—due to unenforceable contracts—attracting outsiders may not be easy. Managers could protect the value of capital, if not for the fact that a majority of shares is held by workers and that changing the initial distribution might lead to labor disputes.

Slow Privatization

While those countries that quickly divested state capital have seen their ownership structure change dramatically, it is not the case that economies that tempered such efforts have not also experienced major changes in property rights. If measured in terms of their contribution to private-sector expansion, the "failed" radical reforms have not produced much. However, if their impact on the remaining—dominant—state sector is taken as a measure, then these reforms turn out to have substantial effects. While the completed radical privatization programs have produced suprisingly weak ownership structures, those radical programs that have "failed" to materialize have caused deterioration of property rights in respective state sectors.

One such case of "failed" radical reform is Hungary, where the initial program called for divesting a majority—70 percent—of state assets within three years through mass-scale direct sales. A more radical (blueprint) technique, "popular capitalism," was rejected without lengthy deliberation or political turmoil. Direct sales proved very difficult, so that the transfers proceeded slowly, and with the dispersion of the most promising enterprises, the pace of this process declined. In late 1992, when faced with this apparent slowdown, the government of Antall turned its attention again to the idea of free distribution. The idea of "popular capitalism" was also revived in 1994, this time largely in response to growing public resentment against the privatization practices (Nuti, 1994).

The majority of Hungarian enterprises have not been privatized but have been undergoing important changes in their ownership structure anyway. Left very much to themselves, state-owned enterprises have continued a process of the breaking up of existing entities into clusters formally owned by holding companies (themselves having few assets and burdened with outstanding debts accumulated by their split-enterprises). These elusive structures are further complicated by the fact that individual enterprises widely engage in cross-ownership, mostly with their suppliers/customers (see comments on so-called "recombination," in Stark, 1990). The essence of this institutional "recombination" has been decentralization of control rather than clarification of property rights.

In the process, it has become clear not only that privatization must be carried out at a slow pace but that large segments of the state sector are not viable for privatization and are hurt by inconclusive attempts at divestment. The advantage of the wholesale attempt to divest all state entities is that it makes it possible to identify enterprises that should remain under state control. With this knowledge, in 1993, the Hungarian government decided to set aside "nonrecoverable" state enterprises and to put them under joint management by state holding. Czechoslovakia, before the 1993 decision to split into two nations, identified state-owned enterprises that were not marked for privatization (accounting for about one-third of the total asset value). In Poland, discussion has been conducted on offering management contracts for enterprises that seem unlikely to privatize soon.

Recession Anatomy

Since the initial phase of the post-1990 transition has been accompanied by a drastic decline in industrial production and regionwide high inflation (sometimes even hyper-inflation, as in Romania in 1991–1992), one wonders whether the privatization process has added to the decline. This hypothesis is worth testing, since the severe nature of the recent recession suggests that some fundamental, structural factors—such as property rights—are the most likely source of it. The fact that recession has been universal in the region also points to ownership reforms as a possible contributing factor, since they have been implemented widely throughout Eastern Europe.

Effects on Production

In the state-planned economy, capital interests are weak unless the state can coerce workers to stay out of the allocation process (Poznanski, 1992c). If workers gain leverage to affect the distribution of surplus, then wages tend to consume profits, thus hurting the reproduction of state capital. This type of power balance became very common in the final stages of the communist-type economy—one assuming the form of the labor-managed model (see Milanovic, 1989; Svejnar, 1992). Transfer of assets away from the nominal owner, the state—and effective owners, the workers—thus generally promises stronger representation of capital and better prospects for economic growth.

However, transfer of property title to private parties and assumption of ownership functions can never be instantaneous, and the longer the procedures take, the more interest in maximizing the capital value deteriorates. This can be expected to be the case whenever agents for the state—managers—are left with little insight into the future status of their enterprises or of their personal fortunes. Under such uncertainty, hardly any incentives can prevent the intensification of "opportunistic behavior" ("moral hazard") on the part of managers. The risk of dysfunctional behavior increases if lengthy divestment is combined with less-diligent supervision of agents (managers) by the state (either due to doctrinal concerns or weakened state capacity to execute its controlling rights).

It could be argued—following my earlier determinations—that privatization in Eastern Europe initially produced exactly this kind of condition of suspended property rights in the state sector. While almost all state enterprises have been slated for privatization, very few of them have been able to follow it through in an orderly fashion. Programs have been loosely formulated and subject to frequent modifications, with unclear division of authority regarding particular aspects of privatization. Unable to quickly form the "rational expectations" needed to develop growth plans for their enterprises, managers have reacted in a rational way by reducing their effort, that is, by letting much of the capital idle and tolerating some decline in production (for more on this point, see Charemza, 1992; Poznanski, 1993).

This negative reaction was initially almost uniform,[1] but eventually, even without clarification of property status, the "natural selection" process was initiated. This diversification of state enterprises into expanding "winners" and stagnating "losers" has intensified whenever managers or workers (or both) became more certain over their future status. Such solidification of property status—and interest in capital maximization—has either been related to increasing prospects for concluding ownership transfer or been in response to growing certainty that collectives will have decisive control over property transfers (including their prevention). With such change, greater interest in increasing production might be expected (through mobilization of idle capital rather than through fresh investment).

While the initial dilution of property rights during transition could legitimately be viewed as a factor behind the recent regionwide recession, it could well be that the signs of recovery present in some of the economies might reflect a solidification of ownership in the still dominant state sectors (as well as in the privatized enterprises). This interpretation could apply to Poland, where a sharp decline in production since 1990 has been followed by a mid-1992 recovery. Since the recovery—quite robust—has occurred with only a fraction of state industry privatized and since this sector has experienced expansion, it would follow that property conditions might have improved in this case (this without negating the principal role of the private sector in leading the recovery).

Implications for Inflation

Besides creating capital-based groups, privatization could be expected to help keep wages in check and reduce potential for cost-push inflation. Labor "redundance"—or overmanning—was a pervasive phenomenon under the state-planned system, though not chiefly because of the Communist party's commitment to full employment (see Granick, 1978). Rather, the reality of such a system was that planners were less masters than hostages and that the state was in no position to refuse the financing of wage overruns (Kornai, 1981; Hinds, 1991). With wage pressures hard to control, the party had to permit severe shortages (that is, hidden inflation) or even high open inflation (as in Poland during 1982–1989).

While private agents may be more eager to remove excess workforce than are state managers, the actual result depends on the political strength of the respective actors. Political resilience is crucial, since any substantial reductions of the workforce invariably leads to tensions—that is, lower discipline, disputes, and strikes. It could be that confronting "new" private owners—whose resources are limited and whose "legitimacy" has yet to be established—may be an easier task for workers threatened with unemployment than dealing with the "strong" state (which is needed as a backup for private actors under almost all circumstances anyway).

Recent experience suggests that firms created through divestment have typically executed deep reductions in employment; those employees who have retained their jobs have been offered more attractive wages. Most often, such labor contraction followed sizable layoffs under state management when the firms in question were faced with liquidity problems or demand barriers or both. All these reductions have been particularly helpful in driving down inflation, since resultant unemployment has drawn wages down. Since, however, very high levels of unemployment were already reached early during privatization, as in Poland, such a method of checking inflation has become increasingly controversial.

While privatization has been helpful in reducing wage-push inflation, it has also contributed to price increases through erosion of the tax base for the state budgets. In many cases, privatization of state assets has been combined with tax incentives (e.g., in Poland, where converted enterprises are released from a highly progressive tax on above-limit wages). After privatization, enterprises typically have opportunities to evade taxes due to the fluidity of their legal status and to the weakness of the state collection apparatus. With a reduced tax base, state budgets have run into large deficits, which after monetization, have added to inflation (as in Hungary or Poland—see Kolodko, 1993).

If revenues from asset sales (or lease fees) are generated, then, of course, the state budget is provided with additional revenue to help balance it. In fact, privatization has been generating income for state budgets, most notably in Hungary and Poland. In Hungary, revenues have been utilized mostly for foreign debt repayment (serviced by the state budget). In Poland, proceeds have been used to supplement the budget without specification. However, in both cases, this help has been limited and not sufficient to repair greatly imbalanced state budgets (e.g., respective revenues reached $500 million in Hungary and less than half this sum in Poland, both in 1991).

Preliminary Recapitulation

It appears that with continuous efforts to accelerate asset transfers, the actual pace and extent of these transfers has been relatively slow and much less than expected. While radical efforts to privatize quickly have most often not materialized, the question is whether what has been transferred so far has helped much in improving general economic conditions. It takes more than just turning property titles over to private agents to ensure that privatization will be effective. To avoid "narrow" or purely formal privatization (Charemza, 1992), the state has to provide numerous supports, including some elements of industrial policy (e.g., anti-monopoly actions, selective subsidies, and information support).

The initial fear of the reformers was that state assets might be turned over to interest groups that would push the transition process off the optimal track and produce an inferior "final model" of capitalism. There were, for example, great reservations in many post-communist countries about allowing assets to be captured mainly by worker collectives, because the earlier experiments with labor's management of the assets appeared to be negative. Measures were also taken to prevent assets from being captured mostly by the former nomenklatura and to ensure that domestic agents were given priority over foreigners.

It is too early to establish with any confidence who the main beneficiaries of the current privatization will be, but some early patterns can be detected. Judging by the experience of Hungary and Poland, foreigners—mostly through direct sales—have captured a majority of the privatized public assets in industry. Another significant avenue for divestment has been the insider acquisitions by enterprise managers and workers, with the chief difference between Hungary and Poland being that in the former, workers have not benefited as much as in the latter. In Czechoslovakia, foreigners have also made critical acquisitions of shares, though the voucher program at least initially shifted transfer in favor of domestic agents, that is, the broad public.

These early patterns of asset distribution seem to confirm that radical reform programs are difficult to implement. Although many programs designed by reformers have failed to materialize or have proceeded very slowly, a number of unplanned changes have gained ground quickly. That so many of the outcomes were unintended does not mean that the post-communist economies have not benefited from at least some of them. The fact that they were retained, even though inconsistent with reform "blueprints," would suggest that they were beneficial. When "blueprint" designs are not met, it is often precisely because they are not fit for survival in a "real life" situation.

The emerging pattern of privatization, which started with radical rhetoric, seems to increasingly display features of the gradual approach. That foreigners have been most successful in asset acquisitions is consistent with the gradualist theory's claim that transfers are mainly a function of the supply of well-rounded private agents (offering the best promise of increasing capital efficiency). The slow pace of privatization, combined with a strong contribution to market formation by independent "entries," in turn, resembles the dual-track model, which the gradual theory considers to be one of the most viable—less disturbing and less costly—options for transition.

It could be that as long as state-owned enterprises are not fully privatized, it is rational to improve their performance by redesigning some elements of agency structure. Introduction of long-term management contracts, stabilization of tax burdens and subsidies, or allowing for job contestation are among the measures that may help to make state enterprises more effective (for the Chinese experience, see Naughton, 1993). If successful, such an improved incentive structure would help state managers to acquire skills needed in the non-state sector, as well as prepare their enterprises for acquisition by private parties at some point.

To understand the early outcomes of privatization, one might benefit from examining the power structure at the end of the communist period. At that point, great political influence, at least in the indebted countries, was enjoyed by foreigners. The state managers were also quite powerful, whenever, as in Hungary, they liberated themselves from strict party control. In countries such as Poland, industrial workers managed to increase their political standing. It seems that in recent years, this power has been employed by particular interest groups to influence the distribution of state assets, which by themselves can shape the future power structure in these countries.

The politics of privatization is usually touched upon by economists in the context of trying to determine the general prerequisites for strong supportive coalitions (Olson, 1992). An even more important aspect, which receives little attention from economists, is the impact of privatization on the political system itself (i.e., the structure). The issue of replacing a party-based system with a rule-based system is being widely discussed by political scientists today—but mostly within paradigms that ignore economics. The prevailing formulas are those of comparative politics (Przeworski, 1991), "process" politics (Schmitter and Karl, 1992), and path-dependence (Jowitt, 1992).

While politics has intervened extensively in economic choices, economic processes have been sufficiently powerful to lead post-communist countries toward a capitalist system of sorts. Even ill-advised reform attempts cannot prevent the spontaneous formation of market-based organization of production, the best proof being the eventual collapse of the communist system. Communism's total assault on the market system, through nationalism and price fixing, gave up under the pressure of ever-growing self-interest and desire for privacy—or exclusive property rights. It is, thus, politics that mainly determines the price society pays for creating this kind of order.

Appendix

While the gradual-type reform is derived from evolutionary economics (as developed by Hayek, Mises, and Schumpeter), the radical approach does not seem to be based on any broader school. The latter approach is often linked to neoclassical economics, but, in fact, there is no such clear connection. The simplest explanation for this is that the neoclassical theory does not offer any coherent view of institution-formation—it, rather, analyzes how institutions function (e.g., theories of asymmetric information, of transaction costs, or of public goods) and not how they emerge or "exit."

Since the neoclassical theory stresses the importance—and feasibility—of uniform prices across the economy, be it national or worldwide, one may consider it as providing support for radical reform, with its call to quickly equalize prices. However, the notion of institutional duality, stressed by the gradual theory, is not entirely foreign to the neoclassical framework—an example being the developmental model of a two-sector economy with excess labor supply. This model describes a transition process in which labor is shifted from agriculture—operating under one type of wage-setting rules—to industry—using another set of rules.

The neoclassical economy with its tendency to perceive economic agents as highly adaptable (that is, rational) may suggest that shock-type reform is acceptable, since the more drastic the measures, the greater the adjustment of behavior of individual actors. However, the same theory stresses the benefits of equilibrium, including the preference for balanced change—through incremental adjustments to relative prices—in the economy. While the foregoing neoclassical assumption that "natural" means balance is usually only applied to production, if extended to institution-formation, it suggests that gradual-type reform is more appropriate.

If we consider institution-building as involving production of public goods, then the neoclassical theory suggests that the state needs to get involved in the process of privatization—an argument in favor of radical reform. But the general predicament of the neoclassical school is in the competitive (i.e., pursued according to a supply-and-demand interplay) allocation of assets, one case being the transfer of capital between agents. The latter assumption will have to be read as a call for only low-level state involvement, as suggested in the gradual approach to the privatization process.

Notes

1. That privatization may have been a factor behind the recent recession seems to be reflected in empirical data, including statistics on sectoral patterns of output decline. One would expect deflation, as applied by Poland in 1990 and Czechoslovakia in 1991, to have a differential impact on the output of various sectors, but it appears that it did not. Apparently, there has been little difference in cross-industry decline in production in post-1990 Czechoslovakia (Svejnar, 1992). A similar pattern can be found for Poland during 1990–1992 (though initially the deepest decline took place in light industry, which reported the most severe output losses).

Further evidence that supply factors such as property dilution (or credit shortage—see Calvo and Coricelli, 1992) could have been involved seems to come from export data. Poland's industry (but also that of Hungary and Czechoslovakia) responded to the deflation with a rapid expansion of exports to convertible currency markets. Since foreign demand substituted, to a degree, for domestic, this would suggest that the aggregate demand was probably less critical in causing a recession than the depth of deflation might suggest. As there was very little change in the export product structure (for evidence, see Rosati, 1993), this could further point to the critical role of supply factors.

References

Berend, I. 1994. Comments made at the workshop "Circulation of Elites in Eastern Europe." Department of Sociology, University of California—Los Angeles, June 3–4.

Berend, I., and G. Ranki. 1974. *Economic Development of East-Central Europe in the 19th and 20th Century,* New York: Columbia University Press.

Blanchard, O., et al. 1991. *Reform in Eastern Europe.* Cambridge: Massachussetts Institute of Technology (MIT) Press.

Brada, J. 1993. "The Transformation from Communism to Capitalism: How Far? How Fast?" Arizona State University (mimeo).

Calvo, G., and F. Coricelli. 1992. "Stabilizing a Presumably Centrally Planned Economy: Poland 1990." *Economic Policy,* no. 19 (April).

Charemza, W. 1992. "Market Failure and Stagnation: Some Aspects of Privatization in Poland." *Economics of Planning,* vol. 25, no. 1.

Frydman, R., and A. Rapaczynski. 1992. "Privatization and Corporate Governance in Eastern Europe: Can Market Be Designed?" In G. Winckler, ed., *Central and Eastern Europe: Roads to Growth,* Washington: International Monetary Fund.

Granick, D. 1978. *Job Rights in the Soviet Union: Their Consequences.* New York: Cambridge University Press.

Hayek, F. 1988. *The Fatal Conceit: The Errors of Socialism.* Chicago: University of Chicago Press.

Hinds, M. 1991. "Issues in the Introduction of Market Forces in Eastern European Socialist Economies." In S. Commander, ed., *Managing Inflation in Socialist Economies in Transition* Washington: The World Bank.

Hirschman, A. 1970. *Exit, Voice, and Loyalty: Response to Decline in Firms, Organizations and States.* Cambridge: Harvard University Press.

Jowitt, K. 1992. "The Leninist Legacy." In I. Banac, ed., *Eastern Europe in Revolution.* Ithaca: Cornell University Press.

Kolodko, G. 1993. "From Output Collapse to Sustainable Growth in Transition Economies: The Fiscal Implications." Warsaw: Institute of Finance (working paper no. 35—mimeo).

Kornai, J. 1981. *Economics of Shortage.* Amsterdam: North Holland.

Kornai, J. 1990. *The Road to a Free Economy: Shifting from a Socialist System.* New York: Norton.

Kornai, J. 1994. "The Principles of Revolution in Eastern Europe." In K. Poznanski, ed., *The Evolutionary Transition to Capitalism.* Boulder: Westview Press.

McKinnon, R. 1992. *The Order of Economic Liberalization: Financial Control in the Transition to a Market Economy.* Baltimore: Johns Hopkins University Press.

Migdal, J. S. 1988. *Strong Societies and Weak States: State-Society Relations and State Capabilities in the Third World.* Princeton: Princeton University Press.

Milanovic, B. 1989. *Liberalization and Entrepreneurship: Dynamics of Reforms in Socialism and Capitalism.* Armonk, N.Y.: Sharpe.

Mises, L. 1920. "Economic Calculation in the Socialist Commonwealth." In F. Hayek, ed., *Collectivist Economic Planning.* London: Routledge and Kegan, 1935.

Murrell, P. 1992. "Evolutionary and Radical Approaches to Economic Reform." *Economics of Planning,* vol. 25, no. 1.

Naughton, B. 1994. "China's Economic Success: Effective Reform Policies or Unique Conditions?" In K. Poznanaski, ed., (forthcoming).

Nuti, M. 1994. "Costs and Benefits of Instant Privatization." London School of Business (mimeo).

Olson, M. 1992. "The Hidden Path to a Successful Economy." In C. Clange and G. Rauser, eds., *The Emergence of Market Economies in Eastern Europe.* Oxford: Blackwell Publishers.

Popper, K. 1971. *The Open Society and Its Enemies.* Princeton: Princeton University Press.

Poznanski, K. 1992a. "Market Alternative to State Activism in Restoring the Capitalist Economy." *Economics of Planning,* vol. 25, no. 1.

Poznanski, K. 1992b. "Privatization Process in Poland: Problems of Transition." *Soviet Studies,* vol. 44, no. 4.

Poznanski, K. 1992c. "Property Rights Perspective on the Evolution of Communist-Type Economies." In K. Poznanski, ed., *Constructing Capitalism: Reemergence of Civil Society and Liberal Economy in the Post-Communist World.* Boulder: Westview Press.

Poznanski, K. 1993. "Poland's Transition to Capitalism: Shock and Therapy." In K. Poznanski, ed., *Stabilization and Privatization in Poland: An Economic Evaluation of Shock Therapy.* Boston: Kluver Academy Publishers.

Przeworski, A. 1991. *Democracy and the Market: Political and Economic Reforms in Eastern Europe and Latin America.* Cambridge: Cambridge University Press.

Rosati, D. 1993. "The CMEA Demise, Trade Restructuring, and Trade Destruction in Eastern Europe: Initial Assessment." In K. Poznanski, ed., *Stabilization and Privatization in Poland: An Economic Evaluation of Shock Therapy.* Boston: Kluver Academy Publishers.

Sachs, J. 1992. "The Economic Transformation of Eastern Europe: The Case of Poland," In K. Poznanski, ed., *Stabilization and Privatization in Poland.* Boston: Kluver, 1993.

Schaffer, M. 1992. *The Enterprise Sector and Emergence of the Polish Fiscal Crisis, 1990–1991.* Centre for Economic Performance, London School of Economics, August (mimeo).

Schmitter, P., and T. Karl. 1992. "What Democracy Is and Is Not." *Journal of Democracy,* vol. 2, no. 3.

Schmitter, P., and T. Karl. 1991. "Modes of Transition in Latin America and Southern and Eastern Europe (Democratic Transition in the East and the South)." *International Social Science Journal,* vol. 43, no. 2 (May): 269 (16 pages).

Stark, D. 1990. "Privatization in Hungary: From Plan to Market or from Plan to Clan." *East European Politics and Society,* vol. 4, no. 3.

Svejnar, J. 1992. "Labor Market Adjustment in Transitional Economies." CERGE Working Paper Series, no. 22 (November).

Tardos, J. 1989. "The Property Rights in Hungary." Budapest (mimeo).

10

Economics of Transition: Some Gaps and Illusions

ALEC NOVE

The formerly communist-ruled countries of Eastern Europe differ widely among themselves in resources, in population, in level of development, in the degree to which market-type reforms had already been introduced before 1989, and in the political and economic measures taken after that date. In this chapter I explore those differences and their consequences for policy outcomes. I adopt what Beverly Crawford has referred to as the "gradualist" approach, arguing that those countries that have been overly hasty in pursuing reform have found that markets cannot be created overnight. I will leave out of account here those ex-Soviet republics that devote most of their energies to fighting—for example, Armenia, Azerbaijan, Georgia, and Moldova. The others, despite the differences already mentioned, have in common the high priority that they all give to the creation of a market economy—to a transition from what was called socialism to some variety of capitalism. They also share in common a steep decline, in 1990–1992, in gross national product (GNP), in industrial production, in real wages, in investment, and the use of a "shock therapy" to make the transition from socialism to a market-based economy.

It is true that the scale of the decline may be incorrectly measured or wrongly interpreted. Thus Wienecki has pointed out[1] that (1) there is considerable private activity that is unrecorded; (2) that citizens do now have a wider choice and do not have to stand in line; and (3) useless, unsalable production ought to have ceased to be produced anyway. There is evidence for each of these propositions. However, the fact of decline is surely not in dispute. I will now list its causes, while bearing in mind that the relative weight of the causes varies between countries. I will then consider to what extent the decline was unavoidable (or even desirable), given the chosen "transition" strategy, and also the relevance (or otherwise) of mainstream economic theory. Finally, I will categorize Western aid and investment as a factor, bearing in mind the role of the Marshall Plan's aid in the postwar recovery of Western Europe, and I also will note the very different strategy being adopted in China.

Why the Decline?

The following generalizations apply (in varying measure) to all countries.

1. *The consequences of political disruption.* This includes the collapse of Comecon, which deprived some industries of markets and others of supplies. Thus, for example, Poland, Hungary, Czechoslovakia, and Bulgaria depended greatly on the Soviet market. The former Soviet Union depended on these countries for various industrial components, medical drugs, and consumer goods. The disruption (dissolution) of the Soviet Union had similar deleterious effects, in that national republics and even regions obstructed trade and payments, a process stimulated by the progressive devaluation (and nonconvertibility, even into goods) of the ruble and by the role of barter deals.

2. *The consequences of institutional disruption.* Again in varying degrees, management (and bureaucrats) found themselves in a situation with which they were unfamiliar—the disappearance of the system to which they had been accustomed. Market-type institutions were still in the process of formation. Management had not developed marketing skills, the necessary information flows were missing or inadequate, the legal structure all too often ambiguous or confused, and "market culture" was lacking (albeit less lacking in Budapest, say, than in Kiev or Rostov). Commercial banks were inevitably run by men or women inexperienced in commercial banking. Management from countries that had retained the state monopoly of foreign trade lacked the skills of marketing their products abroad. In some countries, underpaid bureaucrats turned to corruption on a large scale. All in all, the moral, institutional, and legal infrastructure of markets was still in the process of formation. To these problems must be added the uncertainty engendered by change in ownership, or what one Czech economist (Mertlik) has called "privatization agony": Management, no longer subject to control from above, had no long-term prospect of job security, in that the enterprise could be privatized at any time, on terms not yet clear. There will be much more to say later about the forms and effects of privatization. But it is only natural that this circumstance affects managerial behavior.

3. *The consequences of inherited structural distortions.* Some economies were heavily "slanted" toward the military-industrial complex, and the end of the arms race led to an immediate reduction in the output of military end-products and of inputs for these products, while "conversion" required time and scarce resources. Nearly all these countries had an overdeveloped heavy-industry sector, sometimes based on artificially low-priced energy and materials that were transported long distances (e.g., steelworks in Hungary and Poland). There were serious deficien-

cies in infrastructure as well as some of the world's worst cases of atmospheric pollution. This called for a major redistribution of resources to previously neglected sectors, but meanwhile output fell in those sectors that were plainly uneconomic in the new circumstances (there were cases where, if evaluated in world prices, the net product was negative—i.e., the value of inputs exceeded the value of output).

4. *The effect of deflation on consumer demand.* Again in varying degrees, all countries have seen a decline in real incomes. This has had the effect of increasing the share of income devoted to food (Engel's law in reverse) and a corresponding fall in demand for manufactured consumer goods and durables. In Russia and Ukraine—and even Poland—there was also a fall in demand for the dearer foodstuffs, such as sausage. Therefore, the fall in consumption was due partly to the drop in output and in imports, and partly to the fall in purchasing power, which was also a cause of the drop in output. Price relativities have been greatly affected by the elimination of most subsidies. Thus in Russia, the (official) prices of bread and meat have multiplied a hundredfold between 1980 and the end of 1982, while average incomes rose roughly twentyfold in the same period.

5. *The consequences of (premature?) currency convertibility and import liberalization.* Consumer goods production is seriously affected by the citizens' preference for goods imported from the West. This is noticeable in Poland and Czechoslovakia, but in Russia it has even affected vodka. (Some prefer to buy Smirnoff!) The effect has been most shattering in former East Germany—its citizens have real German money to spend, but they buy West German produce.

6. *The consequences of the collapse of investment.* As we shall see, investment has fallen very sharply in all these countries, despite the urgent need for restructuring and conversion, and this naturally is associated with a fall in demand for machinery, building materials, and other investment goods. For reasons to be examined later in this chapter, foreign investment can only very partially fill the gap.

7. *The consequences of "marketization" of the formerly social.* For example, medical services, education, culture, creches, holiday homes, scientific research, and so on, have all been cut back or put on a commercial basis or both. Thus, the steep decline in many of the "services" components in GNP, especially in Russia.

All this must be seen in the context of the triumph of neoclassical economics in its "Chicago" form, as represented in the attitude toward the role of the state of such economists as Milton Friedman and Gary Becker, though the influences of the International Monetary Fund (IMF) and the World Bank are responsible too. Extremist neoconservative think-tanks send missionaries to expound the gospel: Roll back the state, do not copy Western Europe or even the United States, where government remains on the people's backs. Laissez-faire is seen as the answer, along with shock therapy to get the pain over more quickly.

The neoconservatives invoke Hayek's authority. However, they may have overlooked Hayek's warning in his *The Road to Serfdom.* In 1944, looking forward to the desired postwar economic freedom, he wrote: "This is perhaps the place to emphasize that, however much one may wish for a speedy return to a free economy, this cannot mean the removal at one stroke of the wartime restrictions. Nothing would discredit the system of free enterprise more than the acute, though probably short-lived, dislocation and instability such an attempt would produce."[2] Not quite the spirit of Jeffrey Sachs, one would have thought! Here Hayek emphasizes the political and social cost of transition. But, as we shall see, there is an economic cost too, and all the greater because, unlike Western Europe in 1945, Eastern Europe still has to create many of the institutional and social-psychological preconditions that would be re-created or mobilized with relative ease in the West.

A Theoretical Detour: Investment and Neoclassical Economics

The neoclassical paradigm is based on general equilibrium as an ideal—based on perfect competition, perfect markets, and perfect knowledge, in which a large number of producers of homogeneous products are price takers and can sell all they produce at the market-determined price, which either emerges spontaneously or is announced by the Walrasian Auctioneer. Of course, it is well known not only to the critics but also to the authors of such models that the real world is not like that. Axel Leijonhofhud divided economists into two categories: those who believe that, left to itself, the economy is self-balancing, and those who, on the contrary, envisage the possibility of cumulative disequilibrium. Then there are critiques from those known as "Austrians," who stress the importance of the function of the entrepreneur under conditions of uncertainty, and who are surely closer to the problems of the real world, whether in Moscow or in Chicago itself. This is not the place to discuss the merits and demerits of neoclassical models or of those who question their relevance, except in one respect: their irrelevance to investment.

The believers in the neoclassical paradigm will foster the view that the closer we get to perfect competition, the more likely is the desired optimum. But this is clearly wrong if we are concerned with investment. Moreover, this is not only because *time* is involved, and with it the inescapable uncertainty as to future prices of both output and inputs. (Neoclassical mainstream has problems with both time and uncertainty, as many critics have pointed out.) There is also the uncertainty as to how competitors might react to future prices, even if they are in some sense known. Real investment commits resources irreversibly. The assumptions on which perfect competition rests include that of perfect knowledge, that is, your competitors know what you know. But one thing the model lacks is information about what the competition will do. As G. B. Richardson pointed out over thirty years ago,[3] a profitable opportunity seen by all may prove available to none. If we know that a horse will win the race at odds of 10 to 1, the odds would not be 10 to 1.

Even in theory, equilibrium and profits from investing are uneasy bedfellows; in fact, they cannot coexist. In equilibrium, profits tend to equal the rate of interest. Profits from investment arise out of existing or anticipated *dis*equilibrium. Thus, the concept of an "equilibrium growth path" is theoretically dubious: Why should economic agents cause growth to occur by actions which, in equilibrium, would yield them no profit? Here the "Austrians" are much closer to real life, and many years ago Ludwig Lachman wrote: "There can be no such thing as dynamic macroeconomic equilibrium."[4]

Investment occurs, to repeat, because of disequilibrium, and also, as Richardson points out, because of so-called market *imperfections*, such as imperfect knowledge (the competitors have not yet caught on); temporary monopoly or market dominance; long-term tie-up with banks; customers, and suppliers; collusion with competitors; protection from foreign competition; and coordination through government (as in Japan, South Korea, Taiwan, and even France). All this would surely be understood by economists brought up in the Schumpeter tradition. One recalls, too, a recent article by Baumol pointing to circumstances in which expensive investment in "high-tech" research can be undertaken jointly by several firms, spreading the cost and the risk, under conditions (frequently met with in real life but disliked by neoclassical model-builders) of increasing returns to scale.

All the above considerations apply in real capitalist economies. One other point, of a more institutional kind, should be added to these considerations. The process of investment requires a financial system that supplies the venture capital needed for long-term commitments. In both Germany and Japan, the banks and finance houses have traditionally invested in industry, and many sources, including a recent National Bureau of Economic Research (NBER) report, deplore the absence of such banks in the United States and Great Britain. So that when the "eastern" countries speak of the need to create a modern and efficient capital market, they should be aware of the differences in this respect between capitalist countries.

The theoretical gap leads to gaps in thinking. Recent British experience provides a few examples. When electricity generation and supply were privatized and fragmented, the effect of this on investment was ignored. Yet there is plainly a major difference between having *one* (monopolist) institution responsible for estimating total future demand of this universally used and totally homogeneous product, and a large number of enterprises, none of which carry this responsibility. It is true that the monopolist could (and sometimes did) get its sums wrong, but it at least tried to do the sums. With many generators and distributors, with no knowledge of each other's intentions, and with electricity demand uneven through the year, one could have either insufficient investment to provide for periods of peak demand, or overinvestment, as each generator or distributor tried to cash in on what it thought was a profitable opportunity. I took the view that the first of these possibilities was most likely, but I was proved wrong. What we have had is overinvestment and overcapacity.

This has been paralleled by overinvestment in office building, in London, Tokyo, and New York, which has contributed to the recession and has led to a surfeit of empty offices and to bankruptcies of property companies and finance houses.

Alternatively, I present a different example: The British government, guided by ideologists, has privatized and fragmented public transport. This has disrupted ties between the big public transport undertakings and the suppliers (of vehicles, railroad equipment, and so on)—ties that exist in other countries of Western Europe—thereby contributing to a decline in British transport equipment production and to a large increase in imports. These consequences would simply not have occurred to the authors of the policies, as their kind of economics does not stress systemic interrelationships. The effect of increasing uncertainty on the investment intentions of input-providers is not a question to which their training would draw their attention. (For one thing such matters fall into the gap that separates macro- from microeconomics.)

It is also worth stressing, as theory seldom does, the link between investment (or lack of it) and unemployment. If it is the case that, in 1995, tens of millions are out of work (and do *not* "prefer leisure"), it is surely naive and unrealistic to imagine that the competitive lowering of wage rates would result in a full-employment equilibrium, if only because of the "deflationary" effect on demand. Of course, the converse does not hold either: A rise in money wages is no cure for unemployment. In practice, though substitutable at the margin, labor and capital are most often complementary: Employment and investment are linked. That is why, both in the West and in the East, there are good reasons for being troubled when a rise in unemployment and a fall in investment coincide, as they have done in 1990–1992 in both Britain and Russia.

The Investment Problem in the "East"

As already stressed, the ex-communist countries face a very large task of restructuring their economies, which calls for substantial investments. In the past, the state had played the predominant role in planning and financing investment, and all too often this reflected not only the often arbitrary priorities of the leadership but also the influence (or decibels) of sectional interests, represented in and through the ruling party. A sizable literature on investment criteria was largely ignored in practice, the more so because the irrational price system failed to indicate in any objective fashion either the urgency of need or the most economical way of meeting it.

It was therefore an understandable reaction for reformers to abandon investment planning and to believe the Western mainstream textbooks: Investment (like most other things) will be determined and directed by market forces, which will also create spontaneously the needed capital-market institutions. Hence the ideas that are best represented by Marek Dabrowski: He is all for resisting "interventionist pressures," he is against "the demand for a kind of government investment policy," or budgeting sums allocated for restructuring, or "state influence on the branch structure of the economy," or any "priority in government (economic) policy," or "interventionism as a substitute for the market mechanism."[5] Similar views have been expressed by Vaclav Klaus. Similar problems were (at first) followed by Egor Gaidar and, of course, by Margaret Thatcher in the United Kingdom. This view has no industrial policy, no energy policy, no transport policy, and no investment strategy. It holds that all will come about by itself if and when macroeconomic stabilization is achieved (or in Thatcher's case, the ideals of zero inflation—as inspired by Milton Friedman).

Yet it is a feature of all "eastern" countries, in varying degrees, that there is as yet only a rudimentary capital market, and little privately owned capital. True, state enterprises have in some instances accumulated financial reserves and could reinvest their profits. However, for reasons to be expounded, they have little incentive to do so and are also subject to heavy taxation. In some countries more than in others, there is also the uncertainty generated by inflationary expectations and political turmoil, with the result that would-be investors, domestic and foreign, are deterred. With the state increasingly withdrawing from investment financing, it is not surprising to find very steep declines in investment: by 49.3 percent in Bulgaria, by 36 percent in the former Czechoslovakia, by 50 percent and more in Russia and Ukraine, and by 35 percent in Romania, in a single year (1991 or 1992).[6]

Yet "restructuring actually understates the scope of the task in hand, because what is needed is nothing short of the orderly closing of the existing production structure and the creation of a whole new economy."[7] We can see the scale of the task when observing the huge level of West German expenditure in East Germany (estimated at roughly $200 billion in three years), though only part of this sum represents investment expenditures. This is roughly ten times the total sum of Western aid that might be allocated to all the republics of the former Soviet Union, which have seventeen times the population of East Germany. Foreign capital is, needless to say, a valuable and desired source of investment financing. However, it can meet only a small part of total need. Internal sources of accumulation are vital, and yet one has the strong impression that this problem of investment has not figured high on the list of concerns of reformers and their Western advisers. Yet the matter is surely of vital importance. The voucher schemes, of which I will say more in a moment, are not investment in real terms; they are a means of privatizing existing capital assets, not new capital designed to create or modernize productive capacity.

Relevant Experience in Southeast Asia and Western Europe

Restructuring on a large scale, after the disasters of war, was successfully carried out in Western Europe in the ten or so years after 1945 and also in Japan and South Korea. This involved large-scale investments to reconstruct war damaged areas and to create a competitive (all *too* competitive) and modern industry and infrastructure. Despite legend, this was *not*—repeat, *not*—achieved by immediate laissez-faire measures, nor by introducing full currency convertibility. The role of the state varied in different countries and in fact still does. The NBER report on South Korea had much to say about the coherence and predictability of government investment policy. The focus on investing in export-oriented business was critical to the success of this model.

The active role of Japan's Ministry of International Trade and Industry (MITI), including selective protectionism as well as investment coordination, is surely well known, if not notorious. Taiwan shows similar features. This was not anything resembling Soviet-type centralized planning, for at least two reasons. First, the plans were not compulsory (outside of the state sector itself, which did provide essential infrastructure); private business reacted to profitable opportunities—its investments were facilitated, not prescribed. Second, alongside whatever the state was planning or encouraging, private investors were actively investing, and in some instances (notably in Japan) made a major independent contribution, unhampered by plan bureaucracy. But this was emphatically not just the spontaneous free market or laissez-faire.

To restate what should be obvious, large-scale, long-term investment in productive capacity is encouraged by a reduction in uncertainty and risk. I heard a South Korean economist tell a conference (it was in Hanoi) how the president held regular meetings with senior officials and top businessmen to discuss proposals for structurally significant investment and whether coordination or assistance was required.

Postwar Western Europe had a big backlog of investment after many years of uncreative destruction. Different countries handled the problem in different ways. But laissez-faire was not seen as the answer. Priority was naturally given to reconstruction (e.g., of houses, transport facilities, and energy). In Great Britain, for several years a Capital Issue Committee deliberately "rationed" private-sector investments. Interest rates were kept artificially low, and to receive permission to invest it was necessary to show that such investment was to meet priority internal needs or that it was a contribution to the export drive (the balance of payments was a major bottleneck item in those years, dollar shortage being particularly severe.)

Internal priorities were closely linked with foreign assistance. Marshall Plan aid provided resources that had to be used for specified purposes and approved by donor as well as recipient, even though it meant that exports of American consumer goods suffered as a result of the rationing of the available dollars. The aid was intended primarily for reconstruction, to enable these countries, enfeebled by years of war, to stand on their own feet. So the reequipment of industry was more important than imports of American cars, for instance.

It is worth dwelling for a moment on this issue of priorities. It can be most vividly seen in a war economy. In theory, no doubt, the needs of war (e.g., guns, ammunition, planes) could compete for resources in the market with automakers, television sets, and tractors. In fact this is not allowed to happen: The needs of war were, so to speak, incommensurate. Or take a famine, howsoever caused: Food for the starving becomes a priority task, even if there is more profit in importing Mercedes cars and Scotch whiskey, and just as (one hopes) the sight of a child fallen into a canal will cause a would-be rescuer to act without first examining the financial reward that might be involved. (Economic orthodoxy in the 1840s prevented relief measures for the Irish famine in those years.)

So the extent to which one supersedes or modifies market forces depends in some degree on the presence or absence of emergency situations, as well as on the presence or absence of adequate market institutions, plus political uncertainty and inflationary expectations. To provide one last example, suppose that power cuts are inevitable unless special measures are taken to supply the required fuel for electricity generation. It may well be that producing or importing many kinds of consumer goods would yield higher short-term profits. But if power is cut off, everything comes to a halt. One can readily envisage emergency situations in which reliance on the price mechanism alone would not have the desired result.

This brings us to the important and related issue of *currency convertibility* and liberalization of foreign trade. As a Russian report has noted: "Let us recall how many years after World War II it took West Germany, France, Japan, to move to convertibility. It took them not one or two years, but fifteen to twenty years, in the course of which they created a competitive economy."[8] France and Italy finally freed capital movements as recently as 1990. Several countries (including Great Britain and France) limited the amounts that their citizens could use for vacations abroad, decades and more after the end of the war.

Several reasons can be advanced for delaying convertibility. One is closely linked with the point already made about priorities: Thus in Great Britain the need to pay for imports of food, and raw materials for industry, seemed more vital than to allow the pent-up demand (pent-up as a result of wartime shortages) to use up scarce dollars on what were regarded as non-essentials. Similarly, domestic capital, and private-enterprise earnings of foreign currency, were as far as possible prevented from freely moving or staying abroad. (Thus in the 1950s and 1960s it was illegal for British or French residents to keep accounts outside the sterling or franc areas.) A second factor of importance concerned exchange rates: This was a time when fixed exchange rates were the rule, though subject to occasional devaluations. To prevent or minimize the growth of currency black markets and to avoid too great a devaluation, it was necessary to limit legitimate forms of convertibility, thereby reducing demand for dollars. By "too great" a devaluation, I mean an exchange rate that, fully reflecting the immediate scarcities of both dollars and potentially importable goods, would lower the domestic currency exchange rate far below purchasing-power parity, and by increasing sharply the cost of essential imports, contribute to inflationary pressures. Of course there were some "leaks" and some evasions, but in fact there was only a very limited black market in dollars in Western Europe in those years. There can be no doubt that if currency convertibility had been introduced as early as (say) 1947–1949, the rate for the dollar would have been far more unfavorable. There would also have been what I might call premature import competition. Dollar shortage provided temporary protection for infant (or convalescing) industries, some of which (especially in Japan and Germany) were later able to compete very effectively indeed, including in the United States itself.

A feature of those years was the creation of the European Payments Union to facilitate trade and clearing between the countries of Western Europe at a time of dollar shortage. In effect, this provided a form of "soft-currency preference." Had the countries of Western Europe demanded settlement in dollars, this would have obstructed trade—in just the way that trade between former members of Comecon has plummeted since 1989. This has done evident harm to the economies of all these countries. No doubt past memories, plus the inadequacies of the so-called transferable ruble, help to explain what occurred. Again, the contrast of today's "East" with the postwar "West" is striking.

Ideology and the IMF's pressures have combined to produce a belief in the swiftest possible liberalization of both trade and payments. Thus, for, example Konstantin Kagolovsky spoke of a "rate for the rouble that will be the same for all, licenses and quotas will be liquidated. All foreign loans will be realized in the market at the market rate. ... Any administrative ways of supporting critically essential imports are shown to be totally pointless."[9] Other and different views have already been quoted. Here is another, from a group of Polish economists: "Import liberalization in Poland was introduced prematurely and on too wide a scale. ... We consider it necessary to protect the domestic market temporarily. ... Most in need of protection is the domestic market for consumer products."[10] Moreover, at a conference in Washington, D.C., in June 1992 sponsored by the IMF and the World Bank, the "recessionary" consequences of "premature free trade" were recognized.

The Russian report cited earlier also noted the effect on costs of the highly unfavorable exchange rate. Materials and components that need to be imported become extremely expensive at this rate, and "it is impossible at such prices to sell final products on the home market. Meanwhile we are told that an open economy is preferable to a closed one. Sure it is. But to transit from one state of affairs to another one needs time and clearly defined stages. ... Otherwise one can proceed through revolutionary rush from crisis to deeper crisis and then to chaos."[11] The situation in some countries (e.g., Hungary and the Czech Republic) is different, but the above remarks seem quite apt if applied to Russia, Ukraine, and Bulgaria.

World Prices?

Should world prices, measured at a free exchange rate, be applied as quickly as possible throughout the "East"? Again, some countries (Hungary, for instance) had been edging toward world prices for many years before the collapse of communism, and so the needed adjustment was not too severe—the advantages clearly outweighing any disadvantages. But Russia is quite different in this regard, as is Ukraine. At the time of this writing, the exchange rate equals 415 (Russian) rubles to the dollar, or more than 600 Ukrainian karbovantsi. At this exchange rate, the average wage was below 20 dollars *a month*. Bread then cost about 100 times more than in 1989—about 20 rubles for a kilo loaf. It is surely a fantasy to regard 20 rubles (i.e., 5 cents) as "too cheap." A ride in the Moscow or St. Petersburg metro has just risen to 6 rubles. At the free exchange rate, the (heavily subsidized) San Francisco "muni" charges the equivalent of 330 rubles, that is, much more than a day's wages. (All the above figures have changed greatly by January 1994, when the exchange rate was 1,250 rubles, and 40,000 Ukrainian karbovantsi to the dollar. The Moscow metro charges 50 rubles a ride, but average wages exceed 100,000 rubles a month.) Since Sachs and similar advisers recommend that controls over wages be tightened as part of the anti-inflationary package, it hardly needs to be proven that prices of necessities cannot rise to "world" levels. (Imported consumer goods, however, do sell at high prices, as can be seen in the privately operated stalls. But citizens with normal ruble incomes cannot afford to buy them.)

However, a wide difference between internal and world prices creates a number of problems. One relates to the effect on internal costs of imports of materials and components and also of such items as grain and medical drugs. The Russian government inherited the practice of a special exchange rate, well below the free one, used for so-called "centralized" imports, that is, of those items deemed essential. This, while understandable, creates opportunities for corrupt deals. Yet it would be difficult to avoid some sort of subsidy, so long as personal incomes are so low. For example, imported medical drugs would be beyond the pocket of at least four-fifths of the population, while domestically produced supplies have long been known to be seriously deficient.

More acute still is the problem in reverse: Any good or service that is exportable yields a far higher sum than its sale for rubles in the internal market. Thus, a taxi in Moscow will take you to the suburbs for 4 dollars (in London a ride for the same distance would cost four times as much), but this represents about twenty times the authorized ruble fare, so taxi drivers naturally sell their services to foreigners by preference. Far more important is the effect on the oil and gas industries. With a world price of oil at around $120 per ton, the equivalent price in Russia would be more than 50,000 rubles. This would also be the price charged to Ukraine and other ex-Soviet republics as and when trade with them ceases to be on a preferential basis. The internal wholesale price of oil was far too low for far too long. But even during December 1992, though nominally "freed," producers and wholesalers were subject to a steeply rising tax or levy in respect of any sales at a price that exceeded 8,000 rubles. (Here again, prices and exchange rates have greatly altered. The domestic price for crude oil in January 1994 exceeds 50,000 rubles, and the rise in energy prices has contributed significantly to cost inflation.) To multiply this sixfold would have catastrophic effects on agricultural and industrial costs and, indeed, also on real incomes of citizens. (What would then be the cost of a gallon of petrol or of electricity for lighting or heating, relative to existing wage levels?) In practice, the regions and oil-producing enterprises are allowed to sell a portion of their output at genuinely free prices. There have been a variety of quotas, export licenses, and export taxes; however, there also has been corruption, since the money to be made by transferring oil (and other exportable commodities) between categories is a standing temptation to the dishonest.

The *reductio ad absurdum* of the free exchange rate for the ruble may be seen in the fact that GNP in 1992, 15 trillion rubles, if converted into dollars at the exchange rate operating in December 1992, is actually less than Russia's exports in that year ($38 billion).

Everyone agrees that a single exchange rate, world prices, liberalized trade, and convertibility are desirable. But can such things be introduced in the present stage in Russia, given the distorted exchange rate and inflationary expectations? Already there is a substantial capital flight *from* Russia, far exceeding foreign aid and foreign investment, even though most of this flight is illegal.

A paper by the German banker, Axel Lebahn, after reminding his readers that convertibility was not achieved by West Germany until the 1960s or by France until the 1970s, stated: "It is for me totally astonishing that, given the lack of trust among the people and the managers, who mostly think only of transferring a quick profit abroad, that anyone should propose convertibility within two months. I beg Western reform-advisers to take into account the specific conditions of Russia."[12]

Privatization, Investment Finance, and the Budget Deficit

A full discussion of the pros and cons of various forms of privatization would require another (and quite lengthy) chapter. Different countries tackle the question in different ways. Several (first Czechoslovakia, and later Russia) provide investment *vouchers* to all citizens. In practice, privatization has proceeded more slowly than had been envisaged by the radical reformers: Valuation problems, in some cases restitution to former owners, lack of private capital with which to purchase, fears of so-called "nomenklatura privatization," or acquisition at low prices by "the mafia," or by foreigners, and also in some cases bureaucratic delays, all played their part. Anyhow, at the time of this writing a high proportion of productive enterprises remains in the public sector, while most private firms operate in the area of trade and distribution.

Vouchers do provide the means to purchase shares in privatized enterprises. However, they do not represent investment in any real sense, unless the proceeds of the sale of shares are invested. The vouchers are, after all, pieces of paper issued by the government, which, being salable, increase the money supply. True, some voucher-owners will "invest" them in mutual funds now being created. However, as is pointed out by V. Kantorovich (son of the Nobel laureate) in a major article, given lack of experience, of knowledge, or of even the beginnings of a normal stock market, conditions will be most favorable for fraud and various machinations, of which he cites examples.

Both Kantorovich and the Czech economist Mertlik[13] point to what Mertlik called "privatization agony." The term relates to the ambiguous situation of management of state enterprises. In Kantorovich's words: "State enterprises before privatization were, so to speak, suspended in mid-air, waiting, with no incentive for normal work." There is also no incentive to pay bills or debts: In Russia, Czechoslovakia, and Poland, unpaid debts hugely increased. In the former Czechoslovakia, most bank credits were used to finance privatization purchases, and hardly any credits were available for investment, according to Mertlik. Further, if the object of management is to acquire the enterprise during the privatization process (e.g., by buying out vouchers or through closed or open auctions), the lower the valuation, the better. This actually provides a motive for inefficiency, as the valuation is inevitably affected by performance. Certainly there is no incentive for management to invest profits, and in Poland for example, these are subject to almost confiscatory tax rates.

The mass distribution of vouchers—as a means of privatization—conflicts with the aim of encouraging a new class of entrepreneur-proprietors. Anatoli Chubais, trying to square the circle, publicly welcomed the purchase of vouchers from the poor by the rich: The poor might then be able to "afford meat," that is, they would use the proceeds of the sale of vouchers for current consumption.[14] The point, well put by Caselli and Pastrello,[15] is: "Too many people who invoke Schumpeterian entrepreneurship forget that Schumpeter clearly had Weberian entrepreneurs in mind. Even if such entrepreneurs do emerge during a process of "learning by doing," such a process necessarily takes a long time to accomplish, and meanwhile it is the "trade-orientated entrepreneur who emerges." A similar point was made by Laszlo Csaba concerning Hungary: referring to what he called "private entrepreneur of the irregular or 'Mafia' economy," he duly noted that "productive investment is the last thing they would think of."[16]

Privatization is too easily seen as a cure for the inefficiency associated with state monopoly-enterprises. However, privatization does not of itself guarantee competence in management, and private monopoly can have the same effects as public monopoly. In fact, as the British experience shows, public monopoly (at least before Thatcher) can be associated with a sense of duty to the public. It is worth noting one other consequence of privatization policies, most visible in Poland. The new private dealers avoid taxes, and most of the budget revenue in fact accrues from the public sector, which (in Poland) "still accounts for the larger part of national income and provides the budget with 84 percent of its revenue." Yet "far from protecting the state sector, the economic programme of the government ... applied various discriminatory and restrictive measures against it," including a heavy tax (the so-called *popiwek)* on excessive wage increases, which nonetheless had to be paid." Privatization "was unprepared, hasty and chaotic. It was carried out for ideological rather than rational reasons" and contributed to a fall in output and especially of investment.[17]

Proposals to Revive Production and Investment: Foreign Participation

The "investment gap" has, of course, not passed unnoticed. The Hausner-Owsiak pamphlet just quoted speaks of the need for "active state intervention, above all an industrial policy of the kind pursued by modern states with market economies. ... For example, the restructuring of the steel industry, heavy industry, environmental protection, support for research, etc." The private sector "has grown mainly in the sphere of services and trade, particularly the import of consumer goods." So the state has clear structural responsibilities—one that cannot be left to market forces.[18] Another Polish pamphlet—critical of laissez-faire policies—speaks of "identification of medium and long-term objectives of structural change and economic development, including an industrial policy."[19] Similar Russian criticisms of the "Gaidar" (or Sachs, or IMF) policies were numerous. I will only quote again the Economic Research Institute of the Russian Ministry of Economics: After deploring the lack of any long-term foreign-trade policy, the report goes on to advocate "state sectoral (production) and regional programmes, worked out together by state institutions, domestic entrepreneurs, foreign partners and investors, [and] international organizations. ... Today, when such programmes do not exist and the economy is drifting rudderless, foreign investors grant us loans unwillingly, imposing harsh conditions. This is quite understandable, since they do not know where their money will go and whether it will be properly used. The presence of clearly defined programmes, of carefully selected projects, drafted with the help of foreign experts, will change the situation. The programmes will act as magnets for our creditors." Special priority would be given to develop exports. It is, the authors point out, absurd for a vast Russia to export only half of the exports of Taiwan or South Korea.[20]

One can foresee the objections: Discrimination between sectors, a state role in financing investment, or subsidized interest rates open up possibilities of abuse, distortions through political pressures by lobbyists, and corruption. It is true, as Dabrowski pointed out, that in order to administer one needs "a good civil service," and some "eastern" countries do not have competent administrators (I heard Ukrainian ministers speak of "cadre hunger," and Russia too has yet to replace the political mechanism provided by party functionaries.) But the fact remains that an *investment strategy* is needed; one cannot expect the capital market to function when it does not yet exist, or entrepreneurs to borrow for investment at market rates of interest when these can be 50 percent (Poland) or 150 percent and more (Russia—and even this is, astonishingly, very far below the rate of inflation). And Western aid-givers, including the IMF, will surely be less than enthusiastic if their credits are disposed of by auction to the highest bidder, which would most likely be to importers of Mercedes, panty-hose, and Nintendo, for instant profitable resale, while livestock is slaughtered for lack of food, and the (dollar-earning) oil industry continues its decline for lack of equipment. After all, credits are supposed to be repaid one day. Donors should expect them to be used for constructive purposes. There is a contradiction between this requirement and the IMF's own laissez-faire ideology—and the IMF itself is beginning to be aware of this.

I can only echo Caselli and Pastrello: We cannot "simply postulate that the shrinking state sector's place will be automatically taken by the private sector." This is "sidestepping the real problems: what to do with state enterprises, which are crumbling under the brunt of the recessionary environment. This is precisely the task of an explicitly-designed economic policy: such a policy has yet to be found."[21] It had better be, and soon! One can also agree with a Russian research team: "The underdevelopment of private financial institutions does not make possible the required investment activity," so that it is desirable to create a "state investment bank," linked with "a conscious policy of structural development."[22]

I would stress that the above argument applies much more strongly to countries in the grip of acute crisis (e.g., Russia, Ukraine, and Romania) and much less to Hungary, the Czech Republic, and Poland.

Agriculture: A Brief Diversion

A full discussion of this topic, like privatization, would require a separate chapter. However, I will only briefly address the topic—but this brevity should not belie its importance.

Question one is linked with privatization (or in some cases restoration to former owners). Should existing collective (coöperative) and state farms be dissolved? How many of the present members (employees) wish to take up independent farming? Should their views decide the issue? How can the existing farm-management network function if it has no confidence that the farms it manages will still exist in a year's time? What equipment (and other kinds of investment) would be needed by a new breed of small farmers? What size of farm would be economic? Are credits to be made available and, if so, on what terms? Should land be bought and sold freely and should nonagricultural interests and foreigners be allowed to participate?

Question two: prices. In most of the "East," terms of trade have turned very strongly against agriculture. Thus in Poland (where smallholders predominate), peasant incomes have fallen sharply, and purchases by peasants of inputs (fertilizer, machines, and so on) have fallen too. In Russia and Ukraine, too, the prices of farm inputs have risen about twice as fast as the prices of agricultural products. In the former Czechoslovakia, "average producer prices in industry in 1991, as against 1989, grew by three-quarters … [75 percent], only prices of agricultural products stagnated; their average level in 1991 was only 3.8 percent higher than in 1989."[23] Agricultural output is depressed by the fall in urban consumer purchasing power. In addition, exports to the "natural" markets of Western Europe are largely blocked by the West Europeans.

So, what policy should be adopted? Should there be price support, which exists in most of the world? Subsidies? Low-interest credits? Priority in fuel supplies where these are scarce? Can laissez-faire be the answer? And, most important, what policy should be adopted for the surviving state and collective farms (and, in Poland, for private farms too small for an efficient agriculture)? China's agriculture, mostly based on small fields and hand cultivation, by methods which appear to hardly have changed in a thousand years, does not provide a model for the Russian and Ukrainian prairies.

"The Chinese Model": An Alternative Strategy?

Several Russian critics, including the influential Arkadi Volsky, have spoken of the Chinese model. The November (1992) issue of *Voprosy ekonomiki* contains two articles on the subject, one by an Englishman (J. Ross) and one by a Chinese (Shan Weiyan). What do such critics have in mind? Some think above all of political order, the continued dominant role of the Communist party in China, and of order as a precondition for marketization. All recognize that in China there have been big moves toward a market economy. However, these authors stress another and surely more important element in the Chinese road, which does give ground for serious thought. For unlike the countries of Eastern Europe, China's road has involved no fall in output, investment, or living standards. On the contrary, GNP in China in the last few years has risen by impressive percentages—as has consumption.

China has advanced not by privatizing large state enterprises, but by allowing or encouraging a wide variety of activities alongside them, apparently owing much to provincial initiatives: The enterprises are cooperative, collective, municipal, rural, and private; some with foreign capital and some in special enterprise zones. Their growth has been most rapid. In many cases, to cite Martin Weitzman and Chenggang Xu, ownership is far from clear ("vaguely-defined cooperatives" is their label).[24] Weitzman questions the validity, at least for China, of the widely accepted dogma associated with the "property rights" school—that only private ownership (i.e., the appropriation of profit by the owner) is consistent with efficiency in resource utilization and the avoidance of shirking. His point is reinforced (in my view) when one adds the element of *scale.* Most Chinese enterprises in the non-state sector are small. Suppose twenty individuals (of any nationality!) jointly undertake any activity. It is by no means clear either that it is always preferable for one to employ the other nineteen or that they would shirk more if they worked in an enterprise jointly owned by them all. Likewise, it also is uncertain that ownership vested in a municipality or a rural council must be less effective than ownership by one man.

As for larger enterprises, employing (say) a thousand workers, although it is much more difficult to envisage smoothly functioning cooperative ownership, it is equally unlikely that such an enterprise would have an identifiable *owner.* More likely (East and West), the larger enterprise is a joint stock company with diffused, probably institutional, ownership, with a largely autonomous management.

Interestingly, several Russian critics of the privatization program have argued for the desirability of a positive attitude toward employee buyouts and against replacing one anonymous owner (the state) by another (what the French call *société anonyme,* the impersonal corporation). Yet this is viewed with suspicion even by such moderate critics as Janos Kornai, and most of the reform proposals give cooperative or joint ownership a cold shoulder.

The essential feature of the Chinese model for our present purposes, however, is its gradualism. It does not disrupt the work of existing state enterprises and retains a degree of control over them, subjecting them to market pressures, including competition from the non-state sector, while the latter expands greatly, so that, by 1992, almost half of all labor outside agriculture was "non-state" (but only a minority of "non-state" labor was privately engaged or employed). To cite another conference paper: "The non-state sector's share of industrial output increased from 22 percent in 1978 to 47 percent in 1991, and the private sector's share increased from zero in 1978 to over 12 percent in the same period, both being achieved without destroying or radically changing the existing system."[25]

Time will tell whether this is a slower road toward a "capitalist" destination or whether the aim is a mixed economy that would be characterized as "market socialism," on lines envisaged in my book on *Feasible Socialism* (which it so happens was translated into Chinese).

Conclusion

Most of the ex-communist world must rely on internally generated resources for the reconstruction and modernization of their economies. They require accumulation for investment and also require an investment strategy, involving some conscious choices of priorities, into which foreign capital can and should make a contribution. The idea that this can happen in some automatic way, once macroeconomic stabilization is achieved, is surely a fantasy. A process of privatization is under way and requires encouragement, but time is needed before market institutions and market culture are in place. They cannot just be decreed into existence.

Meanwhile the role of the state is bound to be substantial, as it was also in the years of postwar reconstruction in Western Europe, Japan, and Korea as well as in social services—but that is not the subject of this chapter. Existing state enterprises are operating under highly unfavorable conditions.

Free-market dogma has become an obstacle, the more so as ex-Marxists find "Chicago" neoclassical economics a congenial alternative to their former beliefs. Devotees of this doctrine must face up to the theoretical and practical gap: There can be *no progress* without investment (indeed, *regress* without investment). How are investment choices to be made, by whom, and how financed? If these questions are not adequately addressed, all will not be well. And furthermore we must look at the example of China's success to see what can be learned from it.

Notes

1. J. Wienecki, "The Inevitability of a Fall in Output ...," in *Soviet Studies*, vol. 43, no. 4) (1990) pp. 669–684, and "The Polish Transition Programme," *Soviet Studies*, vol. 44, no. 5, (1992).

2. F.A. Hayek, *The Road to Serfdom* (Chicago: University of Chicago Press, 1944), p. 209. I owe the quotation to B. Milvanovic.

3. G. B. Richardson, *Information and Investment* (Oxford: Oxford University Press, 1960).

4. Ludwig Lachman, *Capital, Expectations and Market Process* (Kansas City, 1977), p. 117.

5. Marek Dabrowski, "Reforming Communist Economies" (London, 1992).

6. See Economic Commission of Europe (ECE) *Economic Survey of Europe, 1991–1992*, Geneva, 1992, and a variety of Russian and Ukrainian sources.

7. O. Blanchen and R. Dornbusch et al., *Reform in Eastern Europe* (Massachusetts Institute of Technology Press, 1991).

8. Report of the research institute attached to the Russian Ministry of Economics, *Ekonomika i zhizn*, no. 49 (December 1992), p. 5.

9. Konstantin Kagolovsky, quoted in *Izvestiya*, May 6, 1982.

10. "How to Get Out of the Present Economic Crisis in Poland," pamphlet circulated by the Polish Economic Society, Warsaw, 1992, pp. 15, 31, 32.

11. See Note 8.

12. Axel Lebahn, "Stand und Perskeptive neuer Deutsch-Russischer Wirtschaftskooperation," Berlin, 1992 p. 11. (My translation–A.N.)

13. V. Kantorovich in *Nezavisimeya gazeta*, April 20, 1992, and P. Mertlik: "Macro-economic Development and Privatization in Czech-Slovakia." Conference paper, Prague, September 1992.

14. A. Chubais, interview in *Literaturnaya gazeta*, November 18, 1992, p. 10.

15. G. P. Caselli and G. Pastrello, "The Transition from Hell to Bliss," a model. *Most*, no. 3, 1992, p. 51.

16. Laszlo Csaba, in *Acta Oeconomica*, vol. 43 (1991), nos. 3–4, p. 283.

17. J. Hausner and S. Owsiak, *Financial Crisis of a State in Transformation–the Polish Case* (Ebert Foundation, Warsaw, October 1992), pp. 39, 40.

18. Ibid., pp. 40, 42.

19. "How to Get Out of the Present Economic Crisis," p. 33.

20. *Ekonomika i zhizn*, no. 49 (December 1992), p. 5. See also D. Kuzminov et al., "Rossiyskie reformy i mezhdunarodnyi opyt," *Voprosy ekonomiki*, no. 11, 1992, where the authors recommend, among other things, a "bank of economic recovery."

21. Caselli and Pastrello, "The Transition from Hell to Bliss," p. 51.

22. Report of the research institute attached to the Russian Ministry of Economics, *Ekonomika i zhizn*, no. 40 (October 1992).

23. K. Janacek et al., "Macro-economic and Social Analysis, Spring 1992," Institute of Economics, Prague, 1992, p. 9.

24. M. Weitzman and Chenggang Xu, "Vaguely Defined Cooperatives" (unpublished conference paper), September 1992.

25. Yingyi Qian and Chenggang Xu, "Why Chinese Economic Reforms Differ: Changing the Existing System" (unpublised conference paper, n.d.).

11

Political Economy of Introducing New Currencies in the Former Soviet Union

LINDA GOLDBERG, BARRY W. ICKES, AND RANDI RYTERMAN

Many countries of the former Soviet Union (FSU) have strong incentives to introduce independent currencies. At the most basic level, an independent currency is an important symbol of national sovereignty. Moreover, an independent currency may enable a country to pursue an independent monetary policy. Already, new currencies have been introduced by Estonia, Ukraine, Kyrgyzstan, Latvia, and Lithuania. Sovereign currencies or some form of coupon systems are at least under consideration in Azerbaijan, Belarus, Georgia, and Uzbekistan.

Beyond the symbolic and initial political importance of introducing a national currency, this action also can have very important economic implications. In Section I of this chapter, we argue that the likely consequences of adopting independent currencies in the FSU depend upon, (1) the pattern of implicit inter-republican transfers from trade, payments, and monetary systems, and (2) the likely role of seignorage rents in financing the fiscal expenditures of independent republics.[1]

Earlier drafts of this chapter were presented at "Markets, States, and Democracy: The Transformation of Communist Regimes in Eastern Europe and the former Soviet Union" conference at the University of California at Berkeley, and at the International Institute for Applied Systems Analysis (IIASA) conference on the Commonwealth of Independent States (CIS) payments, Laxenburg, Austria. Parts of this chapter are excerpted from or closely follow our larger work on this topic, entitled "Departures from the Ruble Zone: The Implications of Adopting Independent Currencies." (See Goldberg, Ickes, and Ryterman, 1993, in the References.)

The economic implications of a largely political decision of whether to introduce an independent currency are based on whether a country will have, on balance, larger fiscal/output gains upon departure from the ruble zone (and thereafter) as compared with the country's situation within the ruble zone.

In the medium and long term, adoption of a national currency is intricately linked to a country's reform agenda. A country may adopt an independent currency in order to have the latitude of following a different schedule of reform initiatives than those adopted by Russia. Thus, in addition to the two aforementioned categories for analysis of the economic implications of currency independence, we also add (3) the reform agenda of a country and the extent to which economic reforms already had been introduced within the country and by a country's trading partners. The timing of these economic implications is crucial for the political support of a reform trajectory. While some countries may have to absorb short-term economic and distributional costs that outweigh the pure currency sovereignty benefits of the new currency, if properly timed, the introduction of an independent currency can reinforce the reform path upon which a country has embarked. Adopting an independent currency can be an important device for signaling and reinforcing radical economic reform.

In Section II, we consolidate our conclusions about the effects of the introduction of national currencies by concentrating on the short- and medium-term political implications for reformers in different countries of the FSU, including Russia. If there are to be short-term negative economic effects from introducing the new currency, the political impetus for the continuation along the initial reform trajectory (i.e., the trajectory advocated by those initiating the withdrawal from the ruble zone) depends in part on the assignment of blame or responsibility for those negative consequences. Conditional on the timing of introducing the sovereign currency, blame for the short-term negative consequences could potentially be levied on the reformers in the former (non-Russian) republics or, potentially, on Russia. The timing of respective reformers and the strength of leadership during these reforms have important effects on the outcomes. In addition, we argue that Russia's incentives are in favor of allowing the ruble zone to deteriorate while distancing itself from responsibility for this disintegration.

Our line of argument regarding the implications of independent currencies in the FSU is quite distinct from the "optimal currency area" arguments traditionally expounded for such issues.[2] The "optimal currency area" literature provides the conditions under which independent currencies and flexible exchange rates can effectively contribute to short-run output stabilization. However, we reject the relevance of this approach for the countries of the FSU in the near term. There are strong reasons to expect that the output of enterprises in the FSU would not be very responsive to movements in these bilateral exchange rates. Within these countries there are likely to be high rates of "pass through" of exchange-rate changes into price changes rather than into output adjustment. Low output responsiveness to exchange-rate changes would arise because of the types of soft-budget constraints facing many firms and the relatively high (local) monopoly power of industrial enterprises.[3] In addition, in the short term, exchange rates will be ineffective tools because problems in the payments system continue to hamper inter-republican trade. The pervasiveness of barter trade also limits the effectiveness of the exchange-rate instrument by reducing the sensitivity of the decision to export to fluctuations in the nominal exchange rate.

In the present context, we also dismiss another important argument for participating in a common currency area, an argument that frequently has been raised in the context of the European Monetary System. A currency union may be desirable if it imposes a degree of monetary discipline on a country—a discipline that its government seeks but cannot independently attain. If a country subordinates its monetary policy to a "strong" center, the currency union acts as an enabling mechanism: "Weak" central bankers unable to credibly commit to low inflation are able to borrow credibility from the independent central banking authority associated with the authorities in charge of the policies of the union.

In the case of the former Soviet Union, Russia is likely to remain the center of any ruble zone configuration. Yet, it is difficult to argue unequivocally that Russia would pursue an agenda of tight, low-inflation monetary policies. At the current stages of institution-building and economic reform, it is difficult to predict the relative inflationary tendencies of the emerging central banks of different republics or the future inflationary tendencies of Russia. The temptation to inflate may be very high in some countries, especially for the non-oil-producing nations. Moreover, Russia's tendencies to inflate may be reduced with its cessation of transfers to those countries that leave the ruble zone. This uncertainty over the balance of these inflationary tendencies, as well as the politics of the independence movements, does not provide any compelling arguments that the non-Russian republics will want to submit to the authority of a strong Russian Central Bank.

From our aforementioned arguments, we conclude that the optimal currency area approach and the monetary discipline argument are not the appropriate frameworks for analyzing the near-term appropriateness or implications of independent currencies. Thus, in this chapter we confine our attentions to: (1) public-finance issues, and more specifically the linkage between currency independence and inter-republican transfers; and (2) the political implications of these transfers for the reform objectives of those countries departing from the ruble zone and the implications for Russia.

I. Public-Finance Implications of Introducing National Currencies

In the economics literature, recent arguments for maintaining independent currencies versus participation in a common currency area have emphasized the importance of national money as an important tool for budgetary finance. One source of finance is seignorage, often called the inflation tax because it taxes existing holders of money balances. When a government prints money to pay for its expenditures, it generates inflation, lowering the real value of the payments. Any country within a common currency area will attempt to secure a (disproportionately) large share of the money balances and seignorage rents as well as political influence in a currency union. These efforts, if successful, can provide the compelling logic behind a country's decision to forego an independent currency and instead submit itself to centralized monetary discipline. Without attainment of some threshold level of political influence or transfers from the rest of the currency area, a country may choose to stay outside of a common currency area.[4]

In the context of the former Soviet Union, we discuss the issue of seignorage division but also go beyond this narrow form of inter-republican transfers to cover a broader range of transfers associated with remaining in the ruble zone. Due to the extensive interdependence of these economies and the Soviet policies of maintaining a sphere of influence through transfers, a wide range of explicit and implicit vehicles operate to provide cross-country fiscal transfers and subsidies. Many of these transfers are contingent upon a country's participation within the common currency area. Depending on public awareness and political maneuvering, the population may attribute the short-term losses of income from the fiscal transfers to the new currency and to its supporters, rather than to the unavoidable costs of restructuring and of independence from Russia.

In this section, we analyze the functioning and quantitative importance of some of the mechanisms for transfers that have been in place in the FSU. These mechanisms include the regimes of monetary control and emissions, the system of inter-republican payments, and the pricing of inter-republican trade. The monetary system is quite important since it reveals whether the former republics had been able to recover a beneficial or even a "fair" allocation of seignorage rents and other credits under the unified ruble zone. The system for inter-republican payments and settlements also is key, since it highlights both the degree of autonomy that countries already had achieved in monetary control and the direct access of the countries to credits from Russia. However, one of the most important determinants of inter-republican transfers is the distorted pricing system on inter-republican trade. The loss of transfers upon departure from the zone largely depends on whether reforms in pricing of inter-republican and extra-republican trade has occurred prior to a country's departure. This timing issue, that is, whether the independent currencies are introduced before or after substantial movements toward world-market pricing, also is critical for the political ramifications of the departures to be discussed in Section II.

IA. Monetary Control and Emissions Within and Across Republics

The importance of seignorage and the role of independent currencies in the FSU can be understood only in the context of the system of control over monetary (cash and credit) emissions across the central banks remaining in the ruble zone.

This system affects the ability of the former republics to capture the benefits and export the costs of inflation.

The conduct of monetary policy in the FSU is greatly complicated by the coexistence of two types of rubles that circulate in the area, a legacy of the Soviet period. A strict separation between cash and noncash rubles has been enforced within the ruble zone. Enterprises have been required to use noncash rubles to make payments to other enterprises. Cash rubles have been used for paying wages and for other incidental expenses.[5] This system separated payments between enterprises, where credit was lax, from payments to and from households, where hard-budget constraints applied. To some extent, this characterization still applies today: Many central banks have pursued a policy of easy credit to enterprises to maintain production.

This dual monetary structure complicated monetary control in the ruble zone, since each of the countries in the zone had its own central bank, each of which could issue noncash ruble credits. However, the Central Bank of Russia (CBR) retained the exclusive authority to issue cash rubles.[6]

Control Over Cash Emissions and the Division of Seignorage. In its capacity as the single source of ruble banknotes within the FSU, the CBR also controls division of seignorage revenues across members of the ruble zone. Each member of the zone seeks an allocation rule that would maximize its share of the total revenues: In principle, receipt of a "fair" allocation would play an important role in decisions about whether or not to stay in the zone. This view of fair allocation and the costs of surrendering control of the money supply to Russia are linked to a country's size and its reform objectives.

Under the old regime, cash rubles were distributed territorially, based on the aggregate wage bill of a region and allocated according to the needs of the plan. This history suggests that one natural criterion for dividing seignorage revenue across countries is the level of a region's economic activity, which can be used as a rough proxy for aggregate wage bills. Such a scheme seems a natural successor to the old regime's plan and has the advantage of being easy to negotiate. The bulk of seignorage revenue would remain in Russia, as under the old system.

In 1992 and early 1993, Russia apparently retained a much higher share of cash issuance than was suggested by rules based on country shares in net material product, population, or wage bills. Not surprisingly, attempts to formalize the division of benefits, such as the negotiations that occurred in Tashkent in June 1992, have met with failure: Russia always demands a higher proportion of implied proceeds and control than other republics are willing to voluntarily accept. There is evidence that Russia retained a significantly higher proportion of total seignorage revenue—close to 80 percent—during the first half of 1992, than it did in 1990 and 1991, when the Russian share was closer to 65 percent.[7]

The adequacy of these cash receipts can be interpreted in light of the historical experiences of market-based economies and in terms of the interaction between cash issuance and reform objectives. Based on worldwide experiences, between the 1960s and the 1980s the ratio of seignorage to total government revenues was substantial for some countries, sometimes in excess of 10 percent.[8] Moreover, there are likely to be sharp differences in seignorage reliance across countries of the FSU. Based on research on the seignorage use by market-based economies,[9] reliance on seignorage significantly increases with the share of agricultural output in an economy, with the degree of urbanization, and with observed political polarization and instability. Reliance on seignorage declines with the extent of industrialization and the dependence of an economy on foreign trade. Reliance on seignorage may be less important for those countries with strong extra-republican trade relations because these countries can rely on external tariffs as a revenue source. Since inflation and seignorage reliance are strongly inversely related to the efficiency of tax-collection systems and positively correlated with political instability, seignorage reliance is expected to be high in the FSU.

Low receipts of seignorage and ruble banknotes pose problems beyond the obvious revenue issues. This division of cash also can pose restraints on reform objectives, especially for more radical reformers. If deliveries of cash are inadequate, enterprises are unable to fully pay wages.[10] Indeed, during the period of cash shortage—in the first half of 1992—delays in wage payments were a common occurrence, not only in parts of Russia, but in other parts of the zone as well. These cash shortages were differentially experienced across countries, in part due to the presence of non-uniform rates of reform of countries during the transition era.

Countries that pursue different rates of reform differ in their needs for cash balances. The reason is that the demand for cash rubles depends on nominal income; therefore, it is related to the price level. Although inflationary pressures are strong throughout the ruble zone, those parts of the zone that liberalize prices and wages first have, other things being equal, a higher demand for cash. This last consideration is not a minor issue. Since Russia liberalized prices on January 2, 1992, prices have risen dramatically. Throughout the first half of 1992, there was a cash shortage in Russia, and the CBR was reluctant to distribute scarce cash outside Russia. The other countries of the FSU found themselves importing Russian inflation and having the real value of their cash holdings eroded. For both slow and more rapid reformers, the reluctance of the CBR to distribute cash posed a serious threat to their own economies. However, those countries that implemented radical price reform and received inadequate cash shipments from the CBR experienced the greatest immediate erosion in the purchasing power of their populace. The inability of those governments to pay wages threatened to erode popular support for reform programs and potentially threatened the continued existence of the more radical reforms.

Therefore, for reforming countries of the FSU, the introduction of independent currencies undertakes a function distinct from those discussed in the context of experiences of pure market-based economies: Independent currencies can be used to prevent cash withholdings by Russia from undermining political momen-

tum for more radical reform programs. At the same time, the decision to introduce an independent currency would free a country to obtain its own seignorage.

Based on country characteristics, it is clear that those countries most likely to rely heavily on seignorage and those countries with the more radical reform programs would find it most costly to remain in the ruble zone. However, an important exception to this rule arises if the potentially seignorage-dependent economy is sufficiently compensated via other forms of transfers and subsidies by the other countries participating in the ruble zone—particularly if compensated by Russia. *The significance of the public-finance or seignorage arguments for independent currencies cannot be discussed in isolation from the other transfers associated with participation in the ruble zone.* Below, we elaborate on two main classes of transfers: direct transfers via the monetary and payments regimes, and indirect transfers via the distorted system of inter-republican trade pricing.

Control over Credit and Noncash Ruble Emissions. Although the CBR controls cash emissions, each republic's central bank maintains the selective, quantitative control over credit (or noncash) ruble emissions as its main instrument for conducting monetary policy. The fungibility of the credit emissions of the central banks located in different countries, and the contributions of these emissions to aggregate inflation, are closely related to the type of inter-republican payments regime in place. We consider two payments scenarios: one in which the CBR automatically recognizes and finances negative balances in inter-republican trade, and a second scenario in which a strict credit limit is specified. The payments regimes are discussed at greater length in Section IB.

When the CBR automatically finances significant negative balances in inter-republican trade, clear free-rider problems arise in the issue of noncash credits. The political-economic benefits of credit expansion, including the effects on domestic output and the sustenance of ailing industries, in addition to the use of these credits for financing import purchases, are primarily internal to the country in question. But the costs of credit expansion are distributed throughout the FSU in the form of higher inflation. Therefore, each central bank has an incentive to extend credit. The resulting equilibrium is one of excessive domestic credit issuance and high inflation. This lax regime was in place in the FSU in the first half of 1992.

The alternative payments regime, introduced on July 1, 1992, provided a clear mechanism for reducing the inflationary tendencies of the republican central banks. The automatic financing of inter-republican trade deficits was constrained to fixed limits. The effect of this reform was to restrict the degree to which credit expansion in one country, say Ukraine, could spill over into the rest of the FSU. Once Ukraine had reached the ceiling in its correspondent account with the CBR, further credit expansion would not expand aggregate FSU credit. Rather, Ukrainian credit expansions would result in a depreciation of Ukraine credit rubles relative to the credit rubles issued by other parts of the FSU. Although these reforms worked to increase monetary discipline and to limit this channel for transfers from Russia, the payments system was once again modified to restore leniency into the noncash credit-emissions mechanism by August 1992.

Inter-Republican Transfers Through the Payments Regime

As noted, each of the series of inter-republican payments regimes in place since the breakup of the FSU provided for a different set of inter-republican transfers via credit extension. The first regime—implemented in January 1992—set up a system of bilateral "correspondent accounts" between each of the republican central banks and the Central Bank of Russia. All deficits in trade between the non-Russian republics and Russia were to be accommodated only up to the level of bilateral credit provided to the republics by the CBR. But, despite setting up these correspondent accounts, the CBR did not establish an adequate mechanism for dealing with overdrawn balances on these accounts. Accordingly, the central banks of the non-Russian republics issued credit to enterprises that were then used to finance imports from Russia. This system basically was exploited as an open line of credit from Russia.

This system was supposed to be partially reformed in February 1992 when the Commonwealth of Independent States (CIS) agreed that states had the right to impose payments restrictions if imbalances in trade were to occur.[11] However, this system also was poorly implemented and led to extensive delays in payments and clearing. The settlement delays lasted 2 months or even longer, and the parties originating the transactions ultimately were compensated for their sales at uncertain ruble values. These delays caused enterprises to avoid market-based transactions, settled using the monetary mechanisms, and thereby promoted barter transactions and trade via inter-republican agreements. The flawed payments regime interfered with institution-building and economic reforms, led to an accumulation of inter-enterprise and intercountry payments arrears, and was costly to all participants.

The payments regime was reformed again on July 1, 1992, with balances previously accumulated in the correspondent accounts frozen and unresolved inter-republican claims to be bilaterally settled. Payments channeled through the CBR, including inter-republican cash transfers, thereafter were to be honored by the CBR only to the extent that there were sufficient funds in the relevant correspondent accounts. Inter-republican payments were only to be processed subject to formal agreements and negotiated credit lines. This reform meant that the CBR effectively placed a cap on access to bilateral direct cash transfers from Russia. Once a country reached the ceiling of the credit line in its correspondent account, further trade payments to Russia (and purchases of cash rubles from Russia for wage payments) typically required the use of noncash credits issued by the central bank of the deficit country. In contrast to the previous regime, the CBR now required prepayment on inter-republican trade—that is, payment prior to the delivery of goods. The purpose of this policy shift was to eliminate inter-enterprise arrears.[12] But, by limiting inter-republican transfers through trade and by restricting trade finance, the spillover effects of this policy posed contracted demand for Russian products and severely constrained traditional Russian enterprises. These constraints were most binding on countries running deficit positions in inter-republican trade, since their primary source of trade credit was eliminated.

In effect, the tight payments system made each republic issue its own "money" used in enterprise-level transactions, and the values of the respective moneys were determined flexibly in informal markets. The individual countries were restricted in their ability to export inflation, gain discretionary access to additional cash, and collect seignorage within the ruble zone. Thus, this payments regime provided countries with a taste of the implications of pursuing monetary independence. However, the regime did not last.

While the reformed regime intended to limit transfers out of Russia, it also contracted the market for some of Russia's traditional exports. Under pressure from the adversely affected industries, by the end of August 1992 the CBR backtracked on the previous settlements-system reforms and began to selectively issue transfers, (that is flows of cash and credits) to former republics and to choice industries that supported Russia's traditional exporters. These actions muddied market-based mechanisms for executing transactions, further biased conditions against the restructuring of industry, and propagated a preexisting system of inter-republican trade subsidies.

IC. Implicit Inter-Republican Transfers via Trade Activity

To understand the scale of inter-republican trade subsidies as a form of transfers, first recall that significant bilateral concentration of trade and economic activity remains between Russia and the other former republics. Except for Russia, most countries of the former Soviet Union have conducted close to 85 percent of their trade intraregionally. This trade is extremely important relative to the size of their economies, often directly accounting for more than 40 percent of gross domestic product (GDP). An important share of Russia's trade with the former republics continues to be transacted through the vehicle of negotiated bilateral agreements, rather than through enterprise-to-enterprise negotiations. The persistence of such agreements is important because it limits the impact of market forces on pricing and production decisions. Much of this inter-republican trade continues to be conducted at prices that differ dramatically from those observed on world markets.

Inter-Republican Trade in the Ruble Zone and Implied Transfers. Russian officials have stated that world-market prices on petroleum will be charged to any country that leaves the ruble zone. The movements to world-market prices with hard-currency settlements on inter-republican trade will lead to significant changes in the pattern of bilateral inter-republican subsidies and implicit transfers associated with the current price structure. As we develop further in Section

II, the effects of this pricing shift in the short term and in the longer term are important for assessing the implications of adopting independent currencies. The timing of price reforms and new currency introductions are critical since these will influence whether the decision to introduce a new currency is fully distinguishable from the choice of price structure, income shocks, and—implicitly—a reform strategy.

Tarr (1992) has shown that the only countries expected to experience large improvements in their terms of trade[13] (TOT) from moving to world prices on inter-republican transactions are Russia (with a 39.3-percent improvement), Kazakhstan (a 13.5-percent improvement) and Turkmenistan (a 43.3-percent improvement).[14] According to the bilateral agreements for the 1992 trade between Russia and the other countries, Turkmenistan and Kazakhstan have been creditors in bilateral trade with Russia. These countries are not net recipients of subsidies from Russia through the trade channel. By severing bilaterally imposed prices and moving to national currencies, Turkmenistan and Kazakhstan would (1) improve their returns to exporting relative to the cost of importing and (2) reduce net outward transfers through the trade channel.

The change in the rules governing the prices of goods traded by countries of the ruble zone would have two effects. First, countries that are net recipients of subsidies (e.g., all countries except for Russia, Turkmenistan, and Kazakhstan) could no longer expect to have these subsidies partially insulate them from negative economic shocks. In the short term, the movement to world-market pricing on inter-republican transactions implies a worsening of the TOT by at least 25 percent for eight of the remaining twelve republics.[15] From the TOT shock alone, these countries will experience significant short-run income contractions. The countries that would experience the largest short-run income declines are Moldova, Lithuania, Estonia, Latvia, Belarus, and Armenia, with the pure TOT effects implying that each of these countries will lose in excess of 10 percent of their GDP.

Further short-term losses also will be caused by the negative effects of these large price shocks on economic coordination within each country. Rapid changes in the production environment, such as those caused by these TOT shocks, cause the old rules of enterprise interactions to become inadequate. Within affected firms, factors of production need to be reallocated. Without experience in marketing or information regarding alternative suppliers and customers, enterprises in the FSU remain bound to current patterns of distribution, leading to even more severe contractions. Therefore, even Russia, with its expected large TOT gains, may experience short-term contractions due to the large TOT disruptions. The high level of interdependence of all the countries of the ruble zone[16] suggests that these negative effects from a pricing shift can be widely distributed. The net short-run impact of changes in the terms of trade on the national economies may be sharply contractionary, even for countries that have been net creditors to the ruble zone.

While sharp short-term income losses associated with TOT adjustments are likely for most countries, recall that the fundamental theme of this chapter is the relationship between these income effects and participation in the ruble zone. To relate these, the timing of these pricing shifts in relationship to the timing of new currency introduction must be specified. This timing issue is critical, since a country's populace may misconstrue the implications of adopting national currencies as the "inevitable" implications of adoption of world-market prices on inter-republican trade. If introduction of national currencies does not influence the system of trade pricing, that is, if trade continues at distorted internal prices, national currency introduction will not be viewed as synonymous with TOT shocks and will not have the same "immediate" political consequences. Under this scenario, there would be a continuation of implicit subsidies from Russia, despite the fact that these countries have left the ruble zone. Russia would gradually align prices according to negotiated timetables, but this would be a distinct policy decision.

Alternatively, if the introduction of national currencies entails a sharp realignment of inter-republican trade pricing, the full extent of this realignment's implications will depend on the scale of output contractions or expansions that ensue. Beyond the short-run income effects, the continued implications depend, in part, on the extent to which the economy had previously moved toward world-market pricing on inter-republican and extra-republican trade. If energy prices had been adjusted prior to departure from the ruble zone, some of the *incremental* contractionary income effects otherwise associated with departure from the zone would have been mitigated.

By the end of 1992, a limited amount of adjustments in the relative prices on inter-republican transactions already had occurred. First, Russia attempted some bilateral adjustments in relative values of traded goods by negotiating the terms of bilateral agreements with the other former republics. The progress in this particular sphere was limited, especially when one considers the widespread failure of enterprises to participate in the largely voluntary bilateral trade agreements. Second, there was gradual movement by Russia to price its inter-republican energy exports closer to world-market levels. Currently, part of Russia's oil is delivered at world prices, part is delivered at subsidized prices, and part is delivered according to barter arrangements. If substantial reforms in energy pricing occur, the incremental TOT effects of moving to world prices and of introducing national currencies would be considerably less significant than those previously noted.

II. The Political Economy of Introducing National Currencies

A variety of forces interact in a country's decision to adopt a new currency. In some cases, the importance of an independent currency overrides other factors—such as the loss of transfers from Russia—that might otherwise have played a decisive role. In other cases, the shortages of cash that developed in the first half of 1992 pushed some countries in the direction of monetary independence even though they previously may have been reluctant to pursue this path.[17]

The decision to adopt an independent currency may be used to signal that comprehensive economic reform will be undertaken. This decision begins to address a key problem in the transition: Governments have difficulty making their reform programs credible. Adopting a new currency signifies a break with former policy. If combined with a comprehensive reform package, the independent currency can improve the country's situation, even when the country is a net loser of explicit and implicit transfers from Russia. Overall gains can arise if the new currency is successful in enhancing the credibility of the reform package. We will return to this issue later.

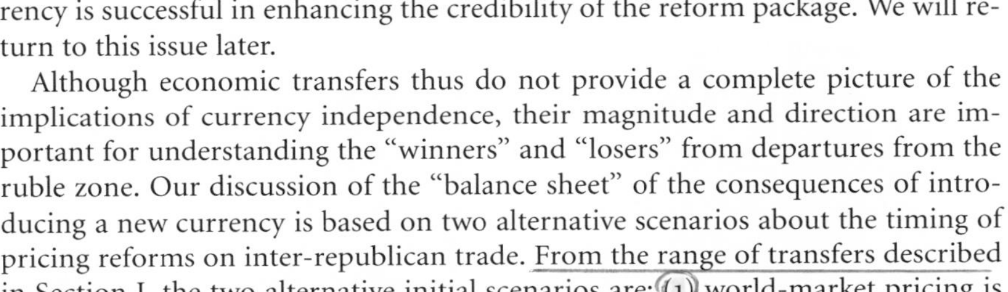

Although economic transfers thus do not provide a complete picture of the implications of currency independence, their magnitude and direction are important for understanding the "winners" and "losers" from departures from the ruble zone. Our discussion of the "balance sheet" of the consequences of introducing a new currency is based on two alternative scenarios about the timing of pricing reforms on inter-republican trade. From the range of transfers described in Section I, the two alternative initial scenarios are: (1) world-market pricing is not yet introduced on inter-republican trade, and (2) world-market pricing is already introduced on inter-republican trade.

IIA. The Incentives Facing Non-Russian Republics

Suppose world-market pricing is not yet introduced on inter-republican trade. If Russia carries out its threat to immediately move to world-market pricing on trade with countries departing from the ruble zone, the non-oil-producing nations will immediately experience sharp income losses and large TOT shocks. A country (or governing group) that does not want to implement rapid reforms in order to mitigate the effects of these shocks in the medium run, or those countries that do not want to accept a radical shift in prices, will view departure from the ruble zone as leading to an unacceptable outcome. This suggests that countries engaged in more gradualist programs of economic reform would seek to remain within the ruble zone. In addition, slow reformers also would be under relatively less pressure to accumulate large cash allocations needed to pay nominal wages, since their nominal wages would not increase as rapidly as those of rapid price liberalizers. For reluctant reformers, it is difficult to imagine that the "undesirable" economic effects would outweigh the relative symbolic importance of having a national currency.

The oil-producing nations of Kazakhstan and Turkmenistan are possible exceptions to this rule. These countries may seek independence to discontinue their subsidies to the rest of the union, since they may experience income gains from the movement to world-market pricing on inter-republican trade.[18] For Kazakhstan and Turkmenistan, participation in the ruble zone makes sense mainly if

Russia had been providing transfers and shares of seignorage that were larger than both the allocations possible with independent national currencies and the amount of their implicit transfers to Russia.

For more rapid reformers, the choice of currency area participation is more likely to weigh in favor of independent currency introduction. We have noted that the TOT changes and disruption of trade will have strong short-run sectoral and distributional effects. In principle, these could be dispersed in the medium run via a redistribution program, or, more practically, would be limited if a reformist regime allows productive inputs to reallocate rapidly in response to the new relative prices. With an independent currency, the reforming countries would be able to capture a higher proportion of seignorage revenues and of cash allotments than they captured within the system dominated by Russia. With control of the money supply in the hands of a reform-minded government, it is less likely that reform efforts that led to relatively high inflation would be undermined by the inability of a government to make adequate wage payments to the population.[19] Even without resorting to arguments based on symbols of sovereignty, a government undertaking radical reforms may be politically strengthened and more credible if its country departs from the ruble zone.

The important outlying nations, that is, those nations that would experience very large and immediate income losses (in excess of 10 percent of GDP) following the TOT shock, are Estonia, Latvia, Lithuania, and Moldova. The losses of implicit subsidies from Russia are unlikely to be compensated by the net gains from the seignorage revenues that these countries are able to extract with independent national currencies. These countries require an extremely rapid adjustment—*more rapid than regional and global history suggest*—to limit prolonged losses from departure from the ruble zone prior to movements toward world-market pricing on inter-republican trade. Unless the costs of independence from Russia and the sources of these costs are well understood by the populace, and unless dramatic ancillary reform policies are enforced, the sharp contractions following currency independence bode poorly for the tenure of the political parties that initiated monetary independence. This conclusion is based on the assumption that the consequences of TOT adjustments will be attributed to the introduction of a national currency, and the blame therefore assigned to those individuals responsible for its introduction.

Suppose, alternatively, that independent currency initiatives are implemented after the bulk of price reforms on inter-republican trade already have occurred. In this case, the negative income shocks from inter-republican TOT adjustment already have buffeted the former republics and may even be viewed as having been imposed by Russia. The negative income shocks experienced by countries cannot be reversed if a country alters its position vis-à-vis the ruble zone. Unless the non-Russian republics receive a new allocation of direct subsidies from Russia, which is quite unlikely, both slow reformers and more rapid reformers are likely to capture larger shares of seignorage revenue under independent currencies than within the monetary union. At the same time, these countries, after attributing the TOT shocks to Russia, can make an affirmative statement of political sovereignty by introducing their own currencies. Since recovery will be stoked by policies facilitating resource reallocation, such policies—along with the introduction of an independent currency—act to signal and affirm a country's commitment to rapid reform.

IIB. Russia's Role and Incentives Within the Ruble Zone

The departure of countries from the ruble zone also has important implications for the center of the ruble zone—Russia. As already discussed, Russia implicitly subsidizes the other former republics through the price and payments structure on inter-republican trade and, in turn, extracts rents from these countries in the form of seignorage. In terms of income and net-transfer effects, Russia is a net loser from this strategy. However, this regime also permits Russia to maintain a degree of influence over the activities of the other nations of the FSU. This influence promotes demand for some Russian products and indirectly props up traditional Russian industries. Although the assertion of influence and control is not expressed publicly as a goal of Russian economic policy, historic precedent suggests that this factor probably retains considerable force among some circles in Moscow.

In Russia, the primary supporters of the ruble zone are those who have the most to lose from a disruption in the status quo. Large enterprises that rely heavily on inter-republican trade would object to the (perceived) increases in the cost of inter-republican trade as well as object to anticipated reductions in markets for their products. Maintenance of the ruble zone is one way to preserve the "large economic space" of the former Soviet Union and to minimize the short-term disruptions faced by these industrialists.

However, despite these objectives of supporters of traditional industries, throughout the second half of 1992 and early 1993, the magnitude of Russian transfers to other members of the ruble zone became increasingly transparent. Continuation of the status quo was more problematic, as the government struggled to stabilize and reduce the budget deficit. Moreover, attempts to limit the size of the Russian trade surplus with the rest of the ruble zone, estimated to be between 6 and 8 percent of Russian GDP, already provided some impetus to enterprise adjustment, despite their continued reluctance to do so. Consequently, the forces within Russia that sought to hold the ruble zone intact were seriously weakened.

The paradox of 1992 was that the attempts to maintain the ruble zone increased the costs of trade between the former republics. This made an alternative currency control and allocation regime imperative. One of the alternative regimes, wherein Russia itself would leave the ruble zone, was not a serious alternative. Russia's abandonment of the ruble is not an idea well motivated by any sovereignty or nationalist motives: The ruble already is controlled by Russia and already is a national symbol (even if a weak one). Moreover, Russia's withdrawal from the ruble zone would lead to a collapse of the entire monetary system in place in the zone.[20] If combined with the cessation of oil and raw materials sales at subsidized prices, Russia would be freed from its transfers problem but at the expense of essentially declaring "economic war" on its neighbors. This would impact poorly on Russia's designs to maintain some influence in the region.

In the absence of Russian withdrawal from the ruble zone, three more plausible alternatives were available to Russia in this economic and political environment:

1. A Ruble Area arrangement: Russia maintains the ruble, other former republics introduce new currencies, and a common payments system is established to reduce the costs of trade.
2. Russia maintains the ruble as its sovereign currency and forces other countries to depart from the ruble zone.
3. Russia maintains the ruble as its sovereign currency and leaves other countries to decide unilaterally whether to depart from the zone.

The first option—setting up a payments system that uses the ruble as a means of settlement—has been widely discussed, and a proposal to set up an Interstate Bank for smoothing trade was approved. The basic idea of this scheme is to use the ruble as a reserve currency for settling payments imbalances that are incurred in the course of normal trade activity. The advantage of this system is that it would facilitate trade within the area. Though countries would have their own currencies, they would settle imbalances with their ruble reserves. This mechanism would require a continuation of Russia's status as a structural creditor to the system. A major hurdle to the success or feasibility of this payments system is the absence of a prior agreement on how to deal with Russia's structural creditor status. Suppose there is an agreement that other members of the area will have a fixed-credit or inter-republican deficit ceiling in the Ruble Area. As long as Russian inflation remains high, the other members have incentives to front-load their import purchases from Russia and move quickly to these deficit ceilings. Payments thereafter would be disrupted.[21] Despite the fundamental flaws in this system, there still was a point in time when the Ruble Area was politically feasible. But, this point has passed. Now that there is increased transparency and more widespread knowledge of the extent to which Russia transferred resources to other members of the zone, any windows of opportunity that may have existed for the Ruble Area are now closed.

Absent a workable agreement on a Ruble Area, Russia is left with the option either of forcing other countries out of the ruble zone or simply raising the costs of letting them remain in the zone. The former option, maintaining the ruble but explicitly forcing other countries to abandon it, is a possibility, but as such must be assessed in light of Russia's other objectives and its inter-republican relations.

In part, if Russia forces countries to depart from the ruble zone, Russia assumes blame for the consequent internal and inter-republican effects from the change in the relative price structure and from the costs of collapsing the preexisting monetary regime.

If Russia can avoid responsibility for imposing a large TOT adjustment, Russia also may avoid direct responsibility for important issues of inter-enterprise income redistribution that would follow a large shift in relative prices on inter-republican transactions. Moreover, by initiating the breakup of the existing system in such a heavy-handed way, Russia risks reducing both its influence in the area and any chance of gaining the cooperation of the other republics in settling the debt of the former Soviet Union.

This leads to the last option. Russia maintains the ruble as its sovereign currency but creates a set of circumstances within which the other members of the zone initiate their departures. As we have observed, Russia can create these conditions by limiting seignorage allocations and reducing various transfers to zone members. This strategy partially isolates Russia from the wrath of lobbying groups from Russia's large enterprises and also reduces some of the immediate fiscal burdens associated with outward transfers from Russia. This approach does have distributional impacts on Russia (and on its trading partners), but Russia still could receive the benefits from the improvements in its own terms of trade without receiving the full brunt of the blame for causing the contractions experienced by its trading partners.

Russia's decision to exercise the third option also reflects the increasing domestic importance of stabilizing the ruble. As domestic inflation has worsened, the costs of not eliminating the ruble-zone impediments to stabilization (including outward transfers to the other FSU republics) appear to outweigh any of the potential gains associated with keeping the zone intact. Moreover, a range of transfers from the West to Russia are associated with liberalizing energy prices on inter-republican trade. Both of these forces reduce the weight of the industrialists in blocking both the disintegration of the ruble zone and Russia's movement toward world-market pricing on inter-republican trade.

Finally, the importance of economic stabilization to Russia also should influence Russia's behavior toward the other FSU republics as they retire the ruble and introduce their own currencies. Some schemes for retiring the ruble may lead countries to dump their rubles on Russian markets, sharply contributing to inflationary stimuli in Russia. For example, when Ukraine left the zone at the end of 1992, a mechanism needed to be implemented to prevent the excess rubles from flowing back to Russia.[22] Russia's fear of "inflation spillover" from the "ruble return" gives some countries, in particular the larger countries of the FSU (Belarus and Ukraine) negotiating power in smoothing the movement toward independence from Russia.[23] The lack of a significant inflationary and retaliatory threat by small countries, such as the Baltic nations, underscored the weakness of their negotiating position in their attempts to ease the TOT and income effects from their departure from the ruble zone.[24]

III. Conclusion

This chapter has described the tradeoffs that countries of the FSU confront as the ruble zone disintegrates. This disintegration already is well under way. The Baltic nations have left the zone: Estonia has introduced the kroon, Latvia has introduced the Latvian ruble, and Lithuania has introduced the talonas coupons, soon to be replaced by the lit. As previously noted, the independence of these relatively small economies poses little economic threat to Russia. In turn, there was little Russian hesitation both in moving to world-market pricing on associated trade transactions and in cutting off transfers to these nations. Indeed, while a most-favored-nation trade (MFN) agreement with Latvia is in place, at the time of the writing of this chapter, Estonia and Lithuania have not yet signed agreements with Russia and taxes on imports from these countries are assessed at twice the MFN rates. All of the Baltic states have experienced sharp TOT losses and declines in real income, and each recently has gone into arrears to Russia in its payments on oil and gas imports. In June 1993, Kyrgyzstan began to introduce a new national currency. Azerbaijan, Moldova, and Belarus all have in place coupons traded in parallel to the ruble and have separate national currencies under consideration.

The ability of an independent currency to reinforce a reformist economic strategy is well exemplified by the experience of Estonia. When the kroon was introduced, its value was strictly pegged to the deutschemark. To enhance monetary stability, Estonia opted for a currency board,[25] the strictest type of monetary arrangement. Under this arrangement, the Central Bank cannot engage in an independent monetary policy and fiscal deficits cannot be monetized.[26] The currency board simply converts foreign exchange earnings into domestic currency at the fixed peg. Although this is an expensive way to remonetize the economy, Estonia's policies sent strong signals that reform intentions were serious and that a radical break with the past would be enforced. The reformers hoping to accelerate the process of economic adjustment harnessed the nationalistic fervor associated with the new currency to signal a willingness to work to end the painful reform policies that otherwise may have been unsustainable.

The signaling role of an independent currency also provides another more powerful explanation for why the calculus of costs and benefits does not predict the pattern of departures from the ruble zone. If the independent currency is a means of signaling a break with the other countries of the FSU, a government may hasten the process of economic reform. Indeed, to make the move to a new currency a success, a set of ancillary reforms are needed that may be painful to implement, such as price liberalization and control over fiscal deficits. It may be easier to undertake these reforms if they can be tied to the successful adoption of an independent currency.

While Ukraine also has introduced an independent currency, the karbovanets, its monetary break with Russia was much less dramatic than those of the Baltic nations. Ukraine still receives some (negotiated) credit from Russia via the correspondent accounts on trade transactions. Goods prices on inter-republican trade conducted via "indicative" and "obligatory" lists continues the process of TOT subsdidies from Russia. Although the country's volumes of recorded trade have contracted, Ukraine has been temporarily shielded from the sharp TOT blow that was received by the Baltic nations. In turn, Ukraine has proceeded with an orderly withdrawal of rubles from circulation and has refrained from dumping these in Russian markets, which whould have further aggravated Russian inflation.

Economic reforms in Russia have been slowed by political wrangling and have provided a prolonged voice to the large industries in Russia that resist restructuring and reform. This continued concentration of power had reduced the threat that Russia will impose rapid movements to world-market pricing on trade transactions at the time a country departs from the ruble zone. However, the increased urgency of economic stabilization pressures Russia to reduce the scale and scope of these transfers. For small countries departing from the ruble zone, Russia perceives few negative effects from rapid movements to world-market pricing.

For the larger trading partners of Russia and its prior recipients of implicit and explicit subsidies, there are incentives for movement toward world-market pricing—but at a slow enough pace that balances the concerns and political support of Russia's traditional exporters. This slow pace of pricing reform lessens the short-run costs of ruble-zone departure for other countries: The implicit TOT subsidies by Russia would continue, despite the fact that these countries have departed from the zone. The reduced costs associated with ruble-zone departure speed both the introduction of new currencies and the potential for countries to pursue more aggressive reform strategies. While this strategy delays some of the consequent output contractions and does not reinforce the need for adjustment, it also better situates countries to lay the foundations for the adjustment process when the TOT shocks are ultimately levied. This could reinforce more radical reform trajectories.

Our analysis has attempted to indicate the economic consequences of ruble-zone departures rather than to predict which countries will or should leave the zone. We have argued that the actual order of country departures from the ruble zone entails more than an economic decision. Politics matter. Given that the old basis for the ruble zone cannot be re-created, the best option for countries of the former Soviet Union is to facilitate a smooth transition to new currencies, where these new currencies reinforce rapid reform trajectories.

Notes

We are grateful to Andre Sapir, Wolfram Schrettl, and Kaz Stanczak for comments on an earlier draft of this chapter. Linda Goldberg is grateful for the research support provided by the C. V. Starr Center for Applied Economics, the National Science Foundation, and the Social Science Research Council. Barry Ickes and Randi Ryterman appreciate the financial support from the National Council for Soviet and East European Research, IRIS (Institutional Reform and the Informal Sector organization), and the World Bank.

1. Seignorage is the revenue that a government obtains by printing money.

2. For example, see Bayoumi and Eichengreen (1992) and Gros (1991). In addition, for an expanded discussion of this criticism, see Goldberg, Ickes, and Ryterman (1993).

3. See Goldberg and Karimov (1992).

4. For a more formal recent exposition of this theme, see Casella (1992).

5. In general, enterprises in the FSU must pay workers in either cash or commodities. Other instruments of payment, such as checks, are not widely recognized or used. During the cash shortage in 1992, some enterprises tried, with mixed success, to pay workers with vouchers that could be redeemed locally for commodities.

6. The other monetary instruments of the CBR include interest rates on CBR lending to commercial banks, restrictions on the interest rates paid by the Savings Bank (which deals with household transactions) and commercial banks (which deal with enterprise transactions), and reserve requirements. Reserve requirements are fairly ineffective since there exist excess reserves in the banking system, partially due to the inefficiencies in the payments mechanism. Lending rates, often used for manipulating demand for credit in developed financial markets, are not particularly useful in Russia since they are not a central factor in the availability or disbursement of loans.

7. See Spencer and Cheasty (1993): "Russia's share of rubles issued by the CBR rose from 64 percent in December 1991 to 77 percent in June 1992, while the shares of Belarus and Georgia dropped from more than 3 percent to about 1.5 percent, and the shares of Ukraine and the Baltic states fell even more sharply."

8. See Fischer (1982) and Cukierman, Edwards, and Tabellini (1992).

9. Cukierman, Edwards, and Tabellini (1992).

10. The domestic banking system has an alternative source of cash: the deposits of the retail enterprises that sell to the public.

11. "The introduction of correspondent accounts for inter-republican payments was the CBR's initial response to the problem of the spillover of ruble balances. The CBR announced its intention to treat the existing ruble stock in other republics of the former USSR, and a new ruble issue, as a liability of each republic's account. Thus, to increase its currency in circulation, a republic that maintains the ruble as its currency must either run a balance of payments surplus with Russia or must pay interest for any overdraft required to obtain additional rubles" (IMF, 1992, p. 20).

12. This is discussed further in Ickes and Ryterman (1993).

13. The terms-of-trade of a country is defined as the ratio between the prices of export goods and import goods.

14. The estimates of the terms-of-trade and output effects are from Tarr (1992). Given the usual caveats about the data problems encountered in using Soviet trade data, one can always debate the validity of the specific quantitative results. Tarr's estimates are, to our knowledge, the best available on this issue. We interpret these estimates as providing a rea-

sonable qualitative description of the implications of the relative pricing shifts. See also McAuley (1991) and Noren and Watson (1992).

15. Armenia, Belarus, Estonia, Georgia, Latvia, Lithuania, Moldova, and Ukraine.

16. In particular, consider the role played by Russia in the distribution of goods in the region.

17. This motive is independent from the seignorage motive. The shortage of cash allocations from the CBR interfered with economic activity and reform agendas in countries of the FSU.

18. Although it is possible that reductions in trade volumes could offset these gains.

19. However, the reform-minded government must resist some expenditures on popularist programs that would broaden fiscal deficits.

20. This is reminiscent of the asymmetry in the Bretton Woods system. Other countries could devalue their currencies against the dollar, but the United States could only devalue against gold. This was often referred to as the "*n*th country problem."

21. This defect of the payments union could be remedied by using an external currency, such as the dollar, as the reserve currency. But, this would require either a transfer of dollars to the Ruble Area by the international community or a purchase of dollars by the area participants. The former does not seem likely and the latter does not seem feasible.

22. If one country leaves the ruble zone, the remaining members, *with the exception of Russia,* can partially insulate themselves by stamping their currencies. Were Russia to attempt this, however, it would amount to the introduction of a new Russian ruble, and thus an end to the zone.

23. There also are third-party spillover effects. For example, when Kyrgyzstan introduced its own currency its relations with Uzbekistan worsened. Uzbekistan feared that it would suffer from "ruble dumping" in its markets.

24. This is discussed in greater detail in Noren and Watson (1992).

25. See, for example, Hansson (1992).

26. Thus, Estonia did not gain, in terms of seignorage revenue, from leaving the ruble zone. As long as the currency board is maintained, the government cannot obtain such revenue.

References

Bayoumi, Tamim, and Barry Eichengreen. 1992. "Monetary and Exchange Rate Arrangements for NAFTA" (manuscript).

Casella, Alessandra. 1992. "Participation in a Currency Union." *American Economic Review* 82, 4: (September) 847–863.

Cukierman, Alex; Sebastian Edwards; and Guido Tabellini. 1992. "Seignorage and Political Instability." *American Economic Review* 82, 3 (June): 537–555.

Fischer, Stanley. 1982. "Seignorage and the Case for a National Money." *Journal of Political Economy* 90 (April): 295–313.

Goldberg, Linda, and Il'dar Karimov. 1992. "Policy Initiatives, Internal Currency Markets, and Production Choices in the former Soviet Union." Revised National Bureau of Economic Research working paper no. 3614.

Goldberg, Linda; Barry Ickes; and Randi Ryterman. 1993. "Departures from the Ruble Zone: The Implications of Adopting Independent Currencies." C. V. Starr Center Working Paper (April).

Gros, Daniel. 1991. "Economic Costs and Benefits of Regional Disintegration in the Soviet Union." CEPS working document no. 55.

Hansson, Ardo. 1992. "Estonian Currency Reform: Overview, Progress Report and Future Policies." *Ostekonomiska Instituet,* Stockholm (August).

Ickes, Barry W., and Randi Ryterman. 1993. "Roadblock to Economic Reform: Inter-Enterprise Arrears and the Problems of Transition." *Post-Soviet Affairs* (formerly *Soviet Economy*) 9, 3: 231–252 (July-September).

International Monetary Fund (IMF). 1992. *Economic Review: Russian Federation* (IMF: Washington, D.C.).

McAuley, Alastair. 1991. "The Economic Consequences of Soviet Disintegration. *Soviet Economy* 7, 3: 189–214 (July-September).

Noren, James H., and Robin Watson. 1992. "Inter-Republican Economic Relations After Disintegration of the USSR." *Soviet Economy* 8, 2: 89–129 (April-June).

Spencer, Grant, and Adrienne Cheasty. 1993. "The Ruble Area: A Breaking of Old Ties?" *Finance and Development* (June): 2–5.

Tarr, David. 1992. "The Terms-of-Trade Effects of Countries of the former Soviet Union of Moving to World Prices" (manuscript; The World Bank), October.

About the Book and Editor

Much of the literature on the "sequencing" of economic and political liberalization suggests that new democracies cannot successfully implement market-oriented reforms. Yet, post-communist transformations have shown that under certain conditions, economic liberalizers *are* able to gain the upper hand in the political process. In this interdisciplinary volume, eminent scholars offer a cohesive framework for analyzing the factors that work either for or against liberalization.

Opening with a discussion of the liberal ideal, the book considers historical, international, and economic policy conditions that bolster or undermine the efforts of liberalizers. The contributions explain how these forces interact, pinpoint the political coalitions these forces support, and speculate on the potential outcomes of the liberalization process. The contributors develop four scenarios: (1) a liberal utopia; (2) a new global "periphery," open to the international economy, in which weak democracies persist because their political institutions are a precondition for international aid and because they provide benefits to rent-seeking domestic groups; (3) a successful state-led transition to economic development and political liberalization; or (4) failure of reform efforts and a return to despotism.

Beverly Crawford is director of research at the Center for German and European Studies at the University of California–Berkeley and lecturer in the program on the political economy of industrial societies.

About the Contributors

Ivan T. Berend is professor of history and director of the Center for European and Russian Studies at the University of California–Los Angeles.

Daniel Chirot is professor of international studies and sociology at the University of Washington's Henry M. Jackson School of International Studies.

Dieter Dettke is director of the Friedrich Ebert Foundation in Washington, D.C.

Linda Goldberg is assistant professor of economics at New York University.

Paolo Guerrieri is professor of economics at the University of Naples–Federico II.

John A. Hall is professor of sociology at McGill University, Montreal.

Stephen Holmes is professor of political science and law and director of the Center for the Study of Constitutionalism in Eastern Europe at the University of Chicago.

Barry W. Ickes is professor of economics at Pennsylvania State University.

Andrew Janos is professor of political science at the University of California–Berkeley.

Alec Nove was professor emeritus of economics at the University of Glasgow, Scotland.

David Ost is associate professor of political science at Hobart and William Smith Colleges in Geneva, New York.

Kazimierz Z. Poznanski is professor at the Henry M. Jackson School of International Studies at the University of Washington.

Randi Ryterman is an economist at the World Bank.

Index